THE GOLDEN TREASURY

THE
GOLDEN TREASURY

SELECTED FROM THE BEST SONGS AND LYRICAL
POEMS IN THE ENGLISH LANGUAGE
AND ARRANGED WITH NOTES BY

FRANCIS T. PALGRAVE

WITH A SUPPLEMENTARY FIFTH BOOK
SELECTED, ARRANGED, AND ANNOTATED BY

LAURENCE BINYON

MACMILLAN

SBN Boards: 0 333 06735 5

First Edition 1861
Second Edition 1891
Third Edition (with Book V chosen
  by L. Binyon) 1926
Reprinted 1927
Reset 1928
Reprinted 1929, 1930, 1932, 1933, 1935,
1936, 1938, 1939, 1944, 1946, 1947, 1950,
1952, 1954, 1955, 1959, 1962, 1971, 1973, 1977

Published by
MACMILLAN LONDON LIMITED
*4 Little Essex Street London WC2R 3LF
and Basingstoke
Associated Companies in Delhi, Dublin,
Hong Kong, Johannesburg, Lagos, Melbourne,
New York, Singapore and Tokyo*

Printed in Great Britain by
LOWE AND BRYDONE PRINTERS LIMITED
Thetford, Norfolk

CONTENTS

Εἰς τὸν λειμῶνα καθίσας,
ἔδρεπεν ἕτερον ἐφ᾿ ἑτέρῳ
αἰρόμενος ἄγρευμ᾿ ἀνθέων
ἁδομένᾳ ψυχᾷ———

THIS book in its progress has recalled often to my memory a man with whose friendship we were once honoured, to whom no region of English Literature was unfamiliar, and who, whilst rich in all the noble gifts of Nature, was most eminently distinguished by the noblest and the rarest,—just judgment and high-hearted patriotism. It would have been hence a peculiar pleasure and pride to dedicate what I have endeavoured to make a true national Anthology of three centuries to Henry Hallam. But he is beyond the reach of any human tokens of love and reverence; and I desire therefore to place before it a name united with his by associations which, while Poetry retains her hold on the minds of Englishmen, are not likely to be forgotten.

Your encouragement, given while traversing the wild scenery of Treryn Dinas, led me to begin the work; and it has been completed under your advice and assistance. For the favour now asked I have thus a second reason: and to this I may add, the homage which is your right as Poet, and the gratitude due to a Friend, whose regard I rate at no common value.

Permit me then to inscribe to yourself a book which, I hope, may be found by many a lifelong fountain of innocent and exalted pleasure; a source of animation to friends when they meet; and able to sweeten solitude itself with best society,—with the companionship of the wise and the good, with the beauty which the eye cannot see, and the music only heard in silence. If this Collection proves a store-house of delight to Labour and to Poverty,—if it teaches those indifferent to the Poets to love them, and those who love them to love them more, the aim and the desire entertained in framing it will be fully accomplished.

F.T.P.

MAY: 1861

PREFACE

THIS little Collection differs, it is believed, from others in the attempt made to include in it all the best original Lyrical pieces and Songs in our language (save a very few regretfully omitted on account of length), by writers not living,—and none beside the best. Many familiar verses will hence be met with; many also which should be familiar :—the Editor will regard as his fittest readers those who love Poetry so well, that he can offer them nothing not already known and valued.

The Editor is acquainted with no strict and exhaustive definition of Lyrical Poetry; but he has found the task of practical decision increase in clearness and in facility as he advanced with the work, whilst keeping in view a few simple principles. Lyrical has been here held essentially to imply that each Poem shall turn on some single thought, feeling, or situation. In accordance with this, narrative, descriptive, and didactic poems,—unless accompanied by rapidity of movement, brevity, and the colouring of human passion,—have been excluded. Humourous poetry, except in the very unfrequent instances where a truly poetical tone pervades the whole, with what is strictly personal, occasional, and religious, has been considered foreign to the idea of the book. Blank verse and the ten-syllable couplet, with all pieces markedly dramatic, have been rejected as alien from what is commonly understood by Song, and rarely conforming to Lyrical conditions in treatment. But it is not anticipated, nor is it possible, that all readers shall think the line accurately drawn. Some poems, as Gray's Elegy, the Allegro and Penseroso, Wordsworth's Ruth or Campbell's Lord Ullin, might be claimed with perhaps equal justice for a narrative or descriptive selection : whilst with reference especially to Ballads and Sonnets, the Editor can only state that he has taken his utmost pains to decide without caprice or partiality

A 2

This also is all he can plead in regard to a point even more liable to question ;—what degree of merit should give rank among the Best. That a poem shall be worthy of the writer's genius,—that it shall reach a perfection commensurate with its aim,—that we should require finish in proportion to brevity,—that passion, colour, and originality cannot atone for serious imperfections in clearness, unity or truth,—that a few good lines do not make a good poem, that popular estimate is serviceable as a guidepost more than as a compass,—above all, that excellence should be looked for rather in the whole than in the parts,—such and other such canons have been always steadily regarded. He may, however, add that the pieces chosen, and a far larger number rejected, have been carefully and repeatedly considered ; and that he has been aided throughout by two friends of independent and exercised judgment, besides the distinguished person addressed in the Dedication. It is hoped that by this procedure the volume has been freed from that one-sidedness which must beset individual decisions :—but for the final choice the Editor is alone responsible.

Chalmers' vast collection, with the whole works of all accessible poets not contained in it, and the best Anthologies of different periods, have been twice systematically read through : and it is hence improbable that any omissions which may be regretted are due to oversight. The poems are printed entire, except in a very few instances where a stanza or passage has been omitted. These omissions have been risked only when the piece could be thus brought to a closer lyrical unity : and, as essentially opposed to this unity, extracts, obviously such, are excluded. In regard to the text, the purpose of the book has appeared to justify the choice of the most poetical version, wherever more than one exists ; and much labour has been given to present each poem, in disposition, spelling, and punctuation, to the greatest advantage.

In the arrangement, the most poetically-effective order has been attempted. The English mind has passed through phases of thought and cultivation so various and so opposed during these three centuries of Poetry, that a rapid passage between old and new, like rapid alteration of the eye's focus in looking at the landscape, will always be wearisome and hurtful to the sense of Beauty. The poems have been therefore distributed into Books corresponding, I to the ninety years closing about 1616, II thence to 1700, III to 1800, IV to the half century just ended. Or, looking at the Poets who more or less give each portion its distinctive character, they might be called the Books of Shakespeare, Milton, Gray, and Wordsworth. The volume, in this respect, so far as the limitations of its range allow, accurately reflects the natural growth and evolution of our Poetry. A rigidly chronological sequence, however, rather fits a collection aiming at instruction than at pleasure, and the wisdom which comes through pleasure :—within each book the pieces have therefore been arranged in gradations of feeling or subject. And it is hoped that the contents of this Anthology will thus be found to present a certain unity, ' as episodes,' in the noble language of Shelley, ' to that great Poem which all poets, like the co-operating thoughts of one great mind, have built up since the beginning of the world.'

As he closes his long survey, the Editor trusts he may add without egotism, that he has found the vague general verdict of popular Fame more just than those have thought, who, with too severe a criticism, would confine judgments on Poetry to ' the selected few of many generations.' Not many appear to have gained reputation without some gift or performance that, in due degree, deserved it : and if no verses by certain writers who show less strength than sweetness, or more thought than mastery of expression, are printed in this volume, it should not be imagined that they have been excluded without much hesitation and regret,— far less that they have been slighted. Throughout this vast and pathetic array of Singers now silent, few have been honoured with the name Poet, and have not possessed a skill in words, a sympathy with beauty, a tenderness of feeling or seriousness in reflection, which render their works, although never perhaps attaining that loftier and finer excellence here required,—better worth reading than much of what fills the scanty hours that most men spare for self-improvement, or for pleasure in any of its more elevated and permanent forms.—And if this be true of even mediocre poetry, for how much more are we indebted to the best ! Like the fabled fountain of the Azores, but with a more various power, the magic of this Art can confer on each period of life its appropriate blessing : on early years Experience, on maturity Calm, on age Youthfulness. Poetry gives treasures 'more golden than gold,' leading us in higher and healthier ways than those of the world, and interpreting to us the lessons of Nature. But she speaks best for herself. Her true accents, if the plan has been executed with success, may be heard throughout the following pages:—wherever the Poets of England are honoured, wherever the dominant language of the world is spoken, it is hoped that they will find fit audience.

1861

Some poems, especially in Book I, have been added :—either on better acquaintance;—in deference to critical suggestions;—or unknown to the Editor when first gathering his harvest. For aid in these after-gleanings he is specially indebted to the excellent reprints of rare early verse given us by Dr. Hannah, Dr. Grosart, Mr. Arber, Mr. Bullen, and others,—and (in regard to the additions of 1883) to the advice of that distinguished Friend, by whom the final choice has been so largely guided. The text has also been carefully revised from authoritative sources. It has still seemed best, for many reasons, to retain the original limit by which the selection was confined to those then no longer living. But the editor hopes that, so far as in him lies, a complete and definitive collection of our best Lyrics, to the central year of this fast-closing century, is now offered.

1883–1890–1891

THE supplementary Fifth Book was planned to include, like the original Golden Treasury, selections from writers no longer living in the year of publication. It covers therefore the whole Victorian era, but contains also works by poets of the young generation cut off by the War. To bridge the gap between these and the older masters of the nineteenth century, a few living poets whose career began in the Victorian time are here partially represented. A fuller selection of these and other contemporaries is given in the Golden Treasury of Modern Lyrics.

During the period covered by this Book a great body of poetry has been produced in America, and in the Overseas Dominions, which should have been represented, had not considerations of space entirely forbidden.

CORDIAL acknowledgments are here tendered to the following authors and owners of copyrights who have given permission for poems to appear in these pages :—

Messrs. George Allen and Unwin, Ltd., for two poems from *Ionica*, by William Cory; Messrs. G. Bell and Sons, Ltd., and Mrs. Patmore, for the poems by Coventry Patmore; Mr. Edmund Blunden and Mr. R. Cobden-Sanderson, for the poems by John Clare; Dr. Robert Bridges and Sir John Murray; the Literary Executor and Messrs. Sidgwick and Jackson, Ltd., for the poems by Rupert Brooke; Messrs. Burns, Oates, and Washbourne, Ltd., for the poems by Alice Meynell and Francis Thompson; Messrs. Chatto and Windus, for the poems by Wilfred Owen and R. L. Stevenson; Messrs. Constable and Co., Ltd., for the poems by George Meredith; Mr. A. T. A. Dobson and the Oxford University Press for the poem by Austin Dobson; Messrs. Ellis, for the poems by D. G. Rossetti; Mr. Thomas Hardy; Messrs. William Heinemann, Ltd., for the poems by A. C. Swinburne; Miss Hopkins for the poem by Gerard Hopkins; Mr. A. L. Humphreys, for the poem by F. W. Bourdillon; Mr. Rudyard Kipling for " Sussex," from *The Five Nations*, and *A Dedication* (" My new-cut ashlar takes the light "), from *Songs from Books ;* Mr. John Lane, the Bodley Head, Ltd., for the poem by John Davidson; the Hon. Frederick Lawless for the poem by the Hon. Emily Lawless; Messrs. Longmans, Green and Co., for " Mother and Son," by William Morris; Mr. John Masefield, for " Cargoes," from *Collected Poems* (Heinemann); Messrs. Elkin Mathews, Ltd., for the poem by Lionel Johnson; Sir Henry Newbolt, for his own poems, from *Poems New and Old* (John Murray), and for those by Mary E. Coleridge from *Poems* (Elkin Mathews, Ltd.); Mr. Herbert Paul, for the poem by D. M. Dolben; Messrs. Martin Secker, Ltd., for the poems by James Elroy Flecker, from *Collected Poems ;* Messrs. Selwyn and Blount, Ltd., for the poem by Edward Thomas; Dr. W. R. Sorley, for the poem by Captain C. H. Sorley; Hallam Lord Tennyson, for the poems by his father; Mr. Harold Williams, for the poem by Herbert Trench; Mr. W. B. Yeats, for " The Stolen Child " and " The Lake Isle of Innisfree," from *Poems* (T. Fisher Unwin, Ltd.).

The Golden Treasury

Book First

SPRING

Spring, the sweet Spring, is the year's pleasant king;
Then blooms each thing, then maids dance in a ring,
Cold doth not sting, the pretty birds do sing,
    Cuckoo, jug-jug, pu-we, to-witta-woo!

The palm and may make country houses gay,
Lambs frisk and play, the shepherds pipe all day.
And we hear aye birds tune this merry lay,
    Cuckoo, jug-jug, pu-we, to-witta-woo.

The fields breathe sweet, the daisies kiss our feet,
Young lovers meet, old wives a-sunning sit,
In every street these tunes our ears do greet,
    Cuckoo, jug-jug, pu-we, to-witta-woo!
        Spring! the sweet Spring!
                T. Nash

II

THE FAIRY LIFE

1

Where the bee sucks, there suck I:
In a cowslip's bell I lie;
There I couch, when owls do cry:
On the bat's back I do fly
After summer merrily.
  Merrily, merrily, shall I live now,
   Under the blossom that hangs on the bough !

III

2

Come unto these yellow sands,
  And then take hands:
Courtsied when you have, and kiss'd
  The wild waves whist,
Foot it featly here and there;
And, sweet Sprites, the burthen bear.
   Hark, hark !
    Bow-bow.
   The watch-dogs bark:
    Bow-wow.
  Hark, hark ! I hear
The strain of strutting chanticleer
   Cry, Cock-a-diddle-dow !
        W. Shakespeare

IV

SUMMONS TO LOVE

Phoebus, arise !
And paint the sable skies
With azure, white, and red:
Rouse Memnon's mother from her Tithon's bed

That she may thy career with roses spread :
The nightingales thy coming each-where sing :
Make an eternal Spring !
Give life to this dark world which lieth dead ;
Spread forth thy golden hair
In larger locks than thou wast wont before,
And emperor-like decore
With diadem of pearl thy temples fair :
Chase hence the ugly night
Which serves but to make dear thy glorious light.

—This is that happy morn,
That day, long-wishéd day
Of all my life so dark,
(If cruel stars have not my ruin sworn
And fates my hopes betray),
Which, purely white, deserves
An everlasting diamond should it mark.
This is the morn should bring unto this grove
My Love, to hear and recompense my love.
Fair King, who all preserves,
But show thy blushing beams,
And thou two sweeter eyes
Shalt see than those which by Penéus' streams
Did once thy heart surprize.
Now, Flora, deck thyself in fairest guise :
If that ye winds would hear
A voice surpassing far Amphion's lyre,
Your furious chiding stay ;
Let Zephyr only breathe,
And with her tresses play.
—The winds all silent are,
And Phoebus in his chair
Ensaffroning sea and air
Makes vanish every star :
Night like a drunkard reels
Beyond the hills, to shun his flaming wheels :
The fields with flowers are deck'd in every hue,
The clouds with orient gold spangle their blue ;
Here is the pleasant place—
And nothing wanting is, save She, alas !

                    W. Drummond of Hawthornden

V

TIME AND LOVE

I

When I have seen by Time's fell hand defaced
The rich proud cost of out-worn buried age;
When sometime lofty towers I see down-razed,
And brass eternal slave to mortal rage;

When I have seen the hungry ocean gain
Advantage on the kingdom of the shore,
And the firm soil win of the watery main,
Increasing store with loss, and loss with store;

When I have seen such interchange of state,
Or state itself confounded to decay,
Ruin hath taught me thus to ruminate—
That Time will come and take my Love away:

—This thought is as a death, which cannot choose
But weep to have that which it fears to lose.

W. Shakespeare

VI

2

Since brass, nor stone, nor earth, nor boundless sea,
But sad mortality o'ersways their power,
How with this rage shall beauty hold a plea,
Whose action is no stronger than a flower?

O how shall summer's honey breath hold out
Against the wreckful siege of battering days,
When rocks impregnable are not so stout
Nor gates of steel so strong, but time decays?

O fearful meditation! where, alack!
Shall Time's best jewel from Time's chest lie hid?
Or what strong hand can hold his swift foot back,
Or who his spoil of beauty can forbid?

O! none, unless this miracle have might,
That in black ink my love may still shine bright.

W. Shakespeare

VII

THE PASSIONATE SHEPHERD TO HIS LOVE

Come live with me and be my Love,
And we will all the pleasures prove
That hills and valleys, dale and field,
And all the craggy mountains yield.

There will we sit upon the rocks
And see the shepherds feed their flocks
By shallow rivers, to whose falls
Melodious birds sing madrigals.

There will I make thee beds of roses
And a thousand fragrant posies,
A cap of flowers, and a kirtle
Embroider'd all with leaves of myrtle.

A gown made of the finest wool,
Which from our pretty lambs we pull,
Fair linéd slippers for the cold,
With buckles of the purest gold.

A belt of straw and ivy buds
With coral clasps and amber studs :
And if these pleasures may thee move,
Come live with me and be my Love.

Thy silver dishes for thy meat
As precious as the gods do eat,
Shall on an ivory table be
Prepared each day for thee and me.

The shepherd swains shall dance and sing
For thy delight each May-morning :
If these delights thy mind may move,
Then live with me and be my Love.

C. Marlowe

VIII

OMNIA VINCIT

Fain would I change that note
To which fond Love hath charm'd me
Long long to sing by rote,
Fancying that that harm'd me :
Yet when this thought doth come
' Love is the perfect sum
    Of all delight,'
I have no other choice
Either for pen or voice
    To sing or write.

O Love ! they wrong thee much
That say thy sweet is bitter,
When thy rich fruit is such
As nothing can be sweeter.
Fair house of joy and bliss,
Where truest pleasure is,
    I do adore thee :
I know thee what thou art,
I serve thee with my heart,
    And fall before thee !

Anon.

IX

A MADRIGAL

Crabbed Age and Youth
Cannot live together :
Youth is full of pleasance,
Age is full of care ;
Youth like summer morn,
Age like winter weather,
Youth like summer brave,
Age like winter bare :

Youth is full of sport,
Age's breath is short,
Youth is nimble, Age is lame :
Youth is hot and bold,
Age is weak and cold,
Youth is wild, and Age is tame :—
Age, I do abhor thee,
Youth, I do adore thee :
O ! my Love, my Love is young !
Age, I do defy thee—
O sweet shepherd, hie thee,
For methinks thou stay'st too long.

                 W. Shakespeare

x

Under the greenwood tree
Who loves to lie with me,
And turn his merry note
Unto the sweet bird's throat—
Come hither, come hither, come hither !
       Here shall he see
       No enemy
But winter and rough weather.

Who doth ambition shun
And loves to live i' the sun,
Seeking the food he eats
And pleased with what he gets—
Come hither, come hither, come hither
       Here shall he see
       No enemy
But winter and rough weather.

                 W. Shakespeare

XI

It was a lover and his lass
   With a hey and a ho, and a hey nonino !
That o'er the green corn-field did pass
In the spring time, the only pretty ring time,
When birds do sing hey ding a ding :
   Sweet lovers love the Spring.

Between the acres of the rye
These pretty country folks would lie :
This carol they began that hour,
How that life was but a flower :

And therefore take the present time
   With a hey and a ho and a hey nonino !
For love is crownéd with the prime
In spring time, the only pretty ring time,
When birds do sing hey ding a ding :
   Sweet lovers love the Spring.
                W. Shakespeare

XII

PRESENT IN ABSENCE

Absence, hear thou this protestation
    Against thy strength,
    Distance, and length;
Do what thou canst for alteration :
   For hearts of truest mettle
Absence doth join, and Time doth settle.

Who loves a mistress of such quality,
    His mind hath found
    Affection's ground
Beyond time, place, and mortality.
   To hearts that cannot vary
   Absence is present, Time doth tarry.

By absence this good means I gain,
    That I can catch her,
    Where none can match her,
In some close corner of my brain :
    There I embrace and kiss her :
And so I both enjoy and miss her.

J. Donne

XIII

VIA AMORIS

High-way, since you my chief Parnassus be,
And that my Muse, to some ears not unsweet,
Tempers her words to trampling horses' feet
More oft than to a chamber-melody,—

Now, blessèd you bear onward blessèd me
To her, where I my heart, safe-left, shall meet;
My Muse and I must you of duty greet
With thanks and wishes, wishing thankfully;

Be you still fair, honour'd by public heed;
By no encroachment wrong'd, nor time forgot;
Nor blamed for blood, nor shamed for sinful deed;
And that you know I envy you no lot

Of highest wish, I wish you so much bliss,—
Hundreds of years you Stella's feet may kiss !

Sir P. Sidney

XIV

ABSENCE

Being your slave, what should I do but tend
Upon the hours and times of your desire?
I have no precious time at all to spend
Nor services to do, till you require :

Nor dare I chide the world-without-end-hour
Whilst I, my sovereign, watch the clock for you,
Nor think the bitterness of absence sour
When you have bid your servant once adieu :

Nor dare I question with my jealous thought
Where you may be, or your affairs suppose,
But like a sad slave, stay and think of nought
Save, where you are, how happy you make those;—

So true a fool is love, that in your will
Though you do anything, he thinks no ill.

W. Shakespeare

XV

How like a winter hath my absence been
From Thee, the pleasure of the fleeting year !
What freezings have I felt, what dark days seen,
What old December's bareness every where !

And yet this time removed was summer's time :
The teeming autumn, big with rich increase,
Bearing the wanton burden of the prime
Like widow'd wombs after their lord's decease :

Yet this abundant issue seem'd to me
But hope of orphans, and unfather'd fruit;
For summer and his pleasures wait on thee,
And, thou away, the very birds are mute;

Or if they sing, 'tis with so dull a cheer,
That leaves look pale, dreading the winter's near.

W. Shakespeare

XVI

A CONSOLATION

When in disgrace with fortune and men's eyes
I all alone beweep my outcast state,
And trouble deaf heaven with my bootless cries,
And look upon myself, and curse my fate;

Wishing me like to one more rich in hope,
Featured like him, like him with friends possest,
Desiring this man's art, and that man's scope,
With what I most enjoy contented least;

Yet ın these thoughts myself almost despising,
Haply I think on Thee—and then my state,
Like to the lark at break of day arising
From sullen earth, sings hymns at heaven's gate;

For thy sweet love remember'd, such wealth brings
That then I scorn to change my state with kings.

W. Shakespeare

XVII

THE UNCHANGEABLE

O never say that I was false of heart,
Though absence seem'd my flame to qualify :
As easy might I from myself depart
As from my soul, which in thy breast doth lie;

That is my home of love; if I have ranged,
Like him that travels, I return again,
Just to the time, not with the time exchanged,
So that myself bring water for my stain.

Never believe, though in my nature reign'd
All frailties that besiege all kinds of blood,
That it could so preposterously be stain'd
To leave for nothing all thy sum of good :

For nothing this wide universe I call,
Save thou, my rose : in it thou art my all.

W. Shakespeare

XVIII

To me, fair Friend, you never can be old,
For as you were when first your eye I eyed
Such seems your beauty still.　Three winters cold
Have from the forests shook three summers' pride;

Three beauteous springs to yellow autumn turn'd
In process of the seasons have I seen,
Three April perfumes in three hot Junes burn'd,
Since first I saw you fresh, which yet are green.

Ah ! yet doth beauty, like a dial-hand,
Steal from his figure, and no pace perceived;

So your sweet nue, which methinks still doth stand,
Hath motion, and mine eye may be deceived :

For fear of which, hear this, thou age unbred,—
Ere you were born, was beauty's summer dead.

W. Shakespeare

XIX

ROSALINE

Like to the clear in highest sphere
Where all imperial glory shines,
Of selfsame colour is her hair
Whether unfolded, or in twines :
  Heigh ho, fair Rosaline !
Her eyes are sapphires set in snow,
Resembling heaven by every wink ;
The Gods do fear whenas they glow,
And I do tremble when I think
  Heigh ho, would she were mine !

Her cheeks are like the blushing cloud
That beautifies Aurora's face,
Or like the silver crimson shroud
That Phoebus' smiling looks doth grace ;
  Heigh ho, fair Rosaline !
Her lips are like two budded roses
Whom ranks of lilies neighbour nigh,
Within which bounds she balm encloses
Apt to entice a deity :
  Heigh ho, would she were mine !

Her neck is like a stately tower
Where Love himself imprison'd lies,
To watch for glances every hour
From her divine and sacred eyes :
  Heigh ho, for Rosaline !
Her paps are centres of delight,
Her breasts are orbs of heavenly frame,
Where Nature moulds the dew of light
To feed perfection with the same :
  Heigh ho, would she were mine !

With orient pearl, with ruby red,
With marble white, with sapphire blue
Her body every way is fed,
Yet soft in touch and sweet in view :
   Heigh ho, fair Rosaline !
Nature herself her shape admires ;
The Gods are wounded in her sight ;
And Love forsakes his heavenly fires
And at her eyes his brand doth light :
   Heigh ho, would she were mine !

Then muse not, Nymphs, though I bemoan
The absence of fair Rosaline,
Since for a fair there's fairer none,
Nor for her virtues so divine :
   Heigh ho, fair Rosaline ;
Heigh ho, my heart ! would God that she were mine !

T. Lodge

XX

COLIN

Beauty sat bathing by a spring
   Where fairest shades did hide her ;
The winds blew calm, the birds did sing,
   The cool streams ran beside her.
My wanton thoughts enticed mine eye
   To see what was forbidden :
But better memory said, fie !
   So vain desire was chidden :—
      Hey nonny nonny O !
      Hey nonny nonny !

Into a slumber then I fell,
   When fond imagination
Seeméd to see, but could not tell
   Her feature or her fashion.
But ev'n as babes in dreams do smile,
   And sometimes fall a-weeping,
So I awaked, as wise this while
   As when I fell a-sleeping :—
      Hey nonny nonny O !
      Hey nonny nonny !

The Shepherd Tonie

XXI

A PICTURE

Sweet Love, if thou wilt gain a monarch's glory,
Subdue her heart, who makes me glad and sorry :
    Out of thy golden quiver
    Take thou thy strongest arrow
    That will through bone and marrow,
And me and thee of grief and fear deliver :—
But come behind, for if she look upon thee,
Alas ! poor Love ! then thou art woe-begone thee
                          Anon.

XXII

A SONG FOR MUSIC

Weep you no more, sad fountains :—
    What need you flow so fast ?
Look how the snowy mountains
    Heaven's sun doth gently waste !
      But my Sun's heavenly eyes
      View not your weeping,
      That now lies sleeping
Softly, now softly lies,
      Sleeping.

Sleep is a reconciling,
    A rest that peace begets :—
Doth not the sun rise smiling,
    When fair at even he sets ?
      —Rest you, then, rest, sad eyes !
      Melt not in weeping !
      While She lies sleeping
Softly, now softly lies,
      Sleeping !
                        Anon.

XXIII

TO HIS LOVE

Shall I compare thee to a summer's day?
Thou art more lovely and more temperate:
Rough winds do shake the darling buds of May,
And summer's lease hath all too short a date:

Sometime too hot the eye of heaven shines,
And often is his gold complexion dimm'd:
And every fair from fair sometime declines,
By chance, or nature's changing course, untrimm'd.

But thy eternal summer shall not fade
Nor lose possession of that fair thou owest;
Nor shall Death brag thou wanderest in his shade,
When in eternal lines to time thou growest:—

So long as men can breathe, or eyes can see,
So long lives this, and this gives life to thee.
W. Shakespeare

XXIV

TO HIS LOVE

When in the chronicle of wasted time
I see descriptions of the fairest wights,
And beauty making beautiful old rhyme
In praise of ladies dead, and lovely knights;

Then in the blazon of sweet beauty's best
Of hand, of foot, of lip, of eye, of brow,
I see their antique pen would have exprest
Ev'n such a beauty as you master now.

So all their praises are but prophecies
Of this our time, all, you prefiguring;
And for they look'd but with divining eyes,
They had not skill enough your worth to sing:

For we, which now behold these present days,
Have eyes to wonder, but lack tongues to praise.
W. Shakespeare

XXV

BASIA

Turn back, you wanton flyer,
And answer my desire
     With mutual greeting.
Yet bend a little nearer,—
True beauty still shines clearer
     In closer meeting !
Hearts with hearts delighted
Should strive to be united,
Each other's arms with arms enchaining,—
     Hearts with a thought,
Rosy lips with a kiss still entertaining.

What harvest half so sweet is
As still to reap the kisses
     Grown ripe in sowing ?
And straight to be receiver
Of that which thou art giver,
     Rich in bestowing ?
There is no strict observing
Of times' or seasons' swerving,
There is ever one fresh spring abiding ;—
     Then what we sow with our lips
Let us reap, love's gains dividing.

T. Campion

XXVI

ADVICE TO A GIRL

Never love unless you can
Bear with all the faults of man !
Men sometimes will jealous be
Though but little cause they see,
And hang the head as discontent,
And speak what straight they will repent.

Men, that but one Saint adore,
Make a show of love to more;
Beauty must be scorn'd in none,
Though but truly served in one:
For what is courtship but disguise?
True hearts may have dissembling eyes.

Men, when their affairs require,
Must awhile themselves retire;
Sometimes hunt, and sometimes hawk,
And not ever sit and talk :—
If these and such-like you can bear,
Then like, and love, and never fear!

T. Campion

XXVII

LOVE'S PERJURIES

On a day, alack the day!
Love, whose month is ever May,
Spied a blossom passing fair
Playing in the wanton air:
Through the velvet leaves the wind,
All unseen, 'gan passage find;
That the lover, sick to death,
Wish'd himself the heaven's breath.
Air, quoth he, thy cheeks may blow;
Air, would I might triumph so!
But, alack, my hand is sworn
Ne'er to pluck thee from thy thorn:
Vow, alack, for youth unmeet;
Youth so apt to pluck a sweet.
Do not call it sin in me
That I am forsworn for thee:
Thou for whom Jove would swear
Juno but an Ethiope were,
And deny himself for Jove,
Turning mortal for thy love.

W. Shakespeare

XXVIII

A SUPPLICATION

Forget not yet the tried intent
Of such a truth as I have meant;
My great travail so gladly spent,
            Forget not yet!

Forget not yet when first began
The weary life ye know, since whan
The suit, the service none tell can;
            Forget not yet!

Forget not yet the great assays,
The cruel wrong, the scornful ways,
The painful patience in delays,
            Forget not yet!

Forget not! O, forget not this,
How long ago hath been, and is
The mind that never meant amiss—
            Forget not yet!

Forget not then thine own approved
The which so long hath thee so loved,
Whose steadfast faith yet never moved—
            Forget not this!

                              Sir T. Wyat

XXIX

TO AURORA

O if thou knew'st how thou thyself dost harm,
And dost prejudge thy bliss, and spoil my rest;
Then thou would'st melt the ice out of thy breast
And thy relenting heart would kindly warm.

O if thy pride did not our joys controul,
What world of loving wonders should'st thou see!
For if I saw thee once transform'd in me,
Then in thy bosom I would pour my soul;

Then all my thoughts should in thy visage shine,
And if that aught mischanced thou should'st not
   moan
Nor bear the burthen of thy griefs alone;
No, I would have my share in what were thine :

And whilst we thus should make our sorrows one,
This happy harmony would make them none.

W. Alexander, Earl of Sterline

XXX

IN LACRIMAS

     I saw my Lady weep,
And Sorrow proud to be advancéd so
In those fair eyes where all perfections keep.
     Her face was full of woe,
But such a woe (believe me) as wins more hearts
Than Mirth can do with her enticing parts.

     Sorrow was there made fair,
And Passion, wise; Tears, a delightful thing;
Silence, beyond all speech, a wisdom rare :
     She made her sighs to sing,
And all things with so sweet a sadness move
As made my heart at once both grieve and love.

     O fairer than aught else.
The world can show, leave off in time to grieve !
Enough, enough : your joyful look excels :
     Tears kill the heart, believe.
O strive not to be excellent in woe,
Which only breeds your beauty's overthrow.

Anon.

XXXI

TRUE LOVE

Let me not to the marriage of true minds
Admit impediments.   Love is not love
Which alters when it alteration finds,
Or bends with the remover to remove :—

O no ! it is an ever-fixéd mark
That looks on tempests, and is never shaken ;
It is the star to every wandering bark,
Whose worth's unknown, although his height be
        taken.

Love's not Time's fool, though rosy lips and cheeks
Within his bending sickle's compass come ;
Love alters not with his brief hours and weeks,
But bears it out ev'n to the edge of doom :—

If this be error, and upon me proved,
I never writ, nor no man ever loved.

                                    W. Shakespeare

XXXII

A DITTY

My true-love hath my heart, and I have his,
By just exchange one for another given :
I hold his dear, and mine he cannot miss,
There never was a better bargain driven :
    My true-love hath my heart, and I have his.

His heart in me keeps him and me in one,
My heart in him his thoughts and senses guides :
He loves my heart, for once it was his own,
I cherish his because in me it bides :
    My true-love hath my heart, and I have his.

                                    Sir P. Sidney

XXXIII

LOVE'S INSIGHT

Though others may Her brow adore
Yet more must I, that therein see far more
Than any other's eyes have power to see:
    She is to me
More than to any others she can be !
I can discern more secret notes
That in the margin of her cheeks Love quotes,
Than any else besides have art to read :
    No looks proceed
From those fair eyes but to me wonder breed.

                Anon.

XXXIV

LOVE'S OMNIPRESENCE

Were I as base as is the lowly plain,
And you, my Love, as high as heaven above,
Yet should the thoughts of me your humble swain
Ascend to heaven, in honour of my Love.

Were I as high as heaven above the plain,
And you, my Love, as humble and as low
As are the deepest bottoms of the main,
Whereso'er you were, with you my love should go.

Were you the earth, dear Love, and I the skies
My love should shine on you like to the sun,
And look upon you with ten thousand eyes
Till heaven wax'd blind, and till the world were done.

Whereso'er I am, below, or else above you,
Whereso'er you are, my heart shall truly love you.

                J. Sylvester

XXXV

CARPE DIEM

O Mistress mine, where are you roaming?
O stay and hear! your true-love's coming
    That can sing both high and low;
Trip no further, pretty sweeting,
Journeys end in lovers meeting—
    Every wise man's son doth know.

What is love? 'tis not hereafter;
Present mirth hath present laughter;
    What's to come is still unsure:
In delay there lies no plenty,—
Then come kiss me, Sweet-and-twenty,
    Youth's a stuff will not endure.

               W. Shakespeare

XXXVI

AN HONEST AUTOLYCUS

Fine knacks for ladies, cheap, choice, brave, and new,
    Good penny-worths,—but money cannot move:
I keep a fair but for the Fair to view;
    A beggar may be liberal of love.
Though all my wares be trash, the heart is true—
            The heart is true.

Great gifts are guiles and look for gifts again;
    My trifles come as treasures from my mind;
It is a precious jewel to be plain;
    Sometimes in shell the orient'st pearls we find:—
Of others take a sheaf, of me a grain!
            Of me a grain!
               Anon.

XXXVII

WINTER

When icicles hang by the wall
    And Dick the shepherd blows his nail,
And Tom bears logs into the hall,
    And milk comes frozen home in pail;
When blood is nipt, and ways be foul,
Then nightly sings the staring owl
          Tu-whit!
Tu-who! A merry note!
While greasy Joan doth keel the pot.

When all about the wind doth blow,
    And coughing drowns the parson's saw,
And birds sit brooding in the snow,
    And Marian's nose looks red and raw;
When roasted crabs hiss in the bowl—
Then nightly sings the staring owl
          Tu-whit!
Tu-who! A merry note!
While greasy Joan doth keel the pot.

                W. Shakespeare

XXXVIII

That time of year thou may'st in me behold
When yellow leaves, or none, or few, do hang
Upon those boughs which shake against the cold,
Bare ruin'd choirs, where late the sweet birds sang.

In me thou see'st the twilight of such day
As after sunset fadeth in the west,
Which by and by black night doth take away,
Death's second self, that seals up all in rest:

In me thou see'st the glowing of such fire,
That on the ashes of his youth doth lie
As the death-bed whereon it must expire,
Consumed with that which it was nourish'd by

—This thou perceiv'st, which makes thy love more
    strong,
To love that well which thou must leave ere long.

                  W. Shakespeare

XXXIX

MEMORY

When to the sessions of sweet silent thought
I summon up remembrance of things past,
I sigh the lack of many a thing I sought,
And with old woes new wail my dear time's waste·

Then can I drown an eye, unused to flow,
For precious friends hid in death's dateless night,
And weep afresh love's long-since-cancell'd woe,
And moan the expense of many a vanish'd sight.

Then can I grieve at grievances foregone,
And heavily from woe to woe tell o'er
The sad account of fore-bemoanéd moan,
Which I new pay as if not paid before :

—But if the while I think on thee, dear Friend,
All losses are restored, and sorrows end.

                  W. Shakespeare

XL

SLEEP

Come, Sleep : O Sleep ! the certain knot of peace,
The baiting-place of wit, the balm of woe,
The poor man's wealth, the prisoner's release,
Th' indifferent judge between the high and low ;

With shield of proof shield me from out the prease
Of those fierce darts Despair at me doth throw :
O make in me those civil wars to cease ;
I will good tribute pay, if thou do so.

Take thou of me smooth pillows, sweetest bed,
A chamber deaf of noise and blind of light,
A rosy garland and a weary head :
And if these things, as being thine in right,

Move not thy heavy grace, thou shalt in me,
Livelier than elsewhere, Stella's image see.

Sir P. Sidney

XLI

REVOLUTIONS

Like as the waves make towards the pebbled shore
So do our minutes hasten to their end ;
Each changing place with that which goes before,
In sequent toil all forwards do contend.

Nativity, once in the main of light,
Crawls to maturity, wherewith being crown'd,
Crooked eclipses 'gainst his glory fight,
And Time that gave, doth now his gift confound.

Time doth transfix the flourish set on youth,
And delves the parallels in beauty's brow;
Feeds on the rarities of nature's truth,
And nothing stands but for his scythe to mow :—

And yet, to times in hope, my verse shall stand
Praising Thy worth, despite his cruel hand.

W. Shakespeare

XLII

Farewell ! thou art too dear for my possessing,
And like enough thou know'st thy estimate :
The charter of thy worth gives thee releasing;
My bonds in thee are all determinate.

For how do I hold thee but by thy granting ?
And for that riches where is my deserving ?
The cause of this fair gift in me is wanting,
And so my patent back again is swerving.

Thyself thou gav'st, thy own worth then not knowing,
Or me, to whom thou gav'st it, else mistaking;
So thy great gift, upon misprision growing,
Comes home again, on better judgment making.

Thus have I had thee as a dream doth flatter;
In sleep, a king · but waking, no such matter.

W. Shakespeare

XLIII

THE LIFE WITHOUT PASSION

They that have power to hurt, and will do none,
That do not do the thing they most do show,
Who, moving others, are themselves as stone,
Unmovéd, cold, and to temptation slow,—

They rightly do inherit heaven's graces,
And husband nature's riches from expense;
They are the lords and owners of their faces,
Others, but stewards of their excellence.

The summer's flower is to the summer sweet,
Though to itself it only live and die;
But if that flower with base infection meet,
The basest weed outbraves his dignity:

For sweetest things turn sourest by their deeds;
Lilies that fester smell far worse than weeds.

W. Shakespeare

XLIV

THE LOVER'S APPEAL

And wilt thou leave me thus?
Say nay! say nay! for shame,
To save thee from the blame
Of all my grief and grame.
And wilt thou leave me thus?
Say nay! say nay!

And wilt thou leave me thus,
That hath loved thee so long
In wealth and woe among :
And is thy heart so strong
As for to leave me thus ?
Say nay ! say nay !

And wilt thou leave me thus,
That hath given thee my heart
Never for to depart
Neither for pain nor smart :
And wilt thou leave me thus ?
Say nay ! say nay !

And wilt thou leave me thus,
And have no more pity
Of him that loveth thee ?
Alas ! thy cruelty !
And wilt thou leave me thus ?
Say nay ! say nay !

Sir T. Wyat

XLV

THE NIGHTINGALE

As it fell upon a day
In the merry month of May,
Sitting in a pleasant shade
Which a grove of myrtles made,
Beasts did leap and birds did sing,
Trees did grow and plants did spring ;
Every thing did banish moan
Save the Nightingale alone.
She, poor bird, as all forlorn,
Lean'd her breast up-till a thorn,
And there sung the dolefull'st ditty
That to hear it was great pity.
Fie, fie, fie, now would she cry ;
Teru, teru, by and by :
That to hear her so complain
Scarce I could from tears refrain ;

For her griefs so lively shown
Make me think upon mine own.
—Ah, thought I, thou mourn'st in vain,
None takes pity on thy pain :
Senseless trees, they cannot hear thee,
Ruthless beasts, they will not cheer thee;
King Pandion, he is dead,
All thy friends are lapp'd in lead :
All thy fellow birds do sing
Careless of thy sorrowing :
Even so, poor bird, like thee
None alive will pity me.

R. Barnefield

XLVI

Care-charmer Sleep, son of the sable Night,
Brother to Death, in silent darkness born,
Relieve my languish, and restore the light;
With dark forgetting of my care return.

And let the day be time enough to mourn
The shipwreck of my ill-adventured youth :
Let waking eyes suffice to wail their scorn,
Without the torment of the night's untruth.

Cease, dreams, the images of day-desires,
To model forth the passions of the morrow;
Never let rising Sun approve you liars,
To add more grief to aggravate my sorrow :

Still let me sleep, embracing clouds in vain,
And never wake to feel the day's disdain.

S. Daniel

XLVII

The nightingale, as soon as April bringeth
  Unto her rested sense a perfect waking,
While late-bare earth, proud of new clothing,
    springeth,
  Sings out her woes, a thorn her song-book making;

And mournfully bewailing,
Her throat in tunes expresseth
What grief her breast oppresseth
For Tereus' force on her chaste will prevailing.

O Philomela fair, O take some gladness,
That here is juster cause of plaintful sadness :
    Thine earth now springs, mine fadeth ;
Thy thorn without, my thorn my heart invadeth.

Alas, she hath no other cause of anguish
  But Tereus' love, on her by strong hand wroken,
Wherein she suffering, all her spirits languish,
  Full womanlike complains her will was broken.
    But I, who, daily craving,
    Cannot have to content me,
    Have more cause to lament me,
Since wanting is more woe than too much having.

O Philomela fair, O take some gladness
That here is juster cause of plaintful sadness :
    Thine earth now springs, mine fadeth :
Thy thorn without, my thorn my heart invadeth.

Sir P. Sidney

XLVIII

FRUSTRA

Take, O take those lips away
That so sweetly were forsworn,
And those eyes, the break of day,
Lights that do mislead the morn :
But my kisses bring again,
    Bring again—
Seals of love, but seal'd in vain,
    Seal'd in vain !

W. Shakespeare

XLIX

LOVE'S FAREWELL

Since there's no help, come let us kiss and part,—
Nay I have done, you get no more of me;
And I am glad, yea, glad with all my heart,
That thus so cleanly I myself can free;

Shake hands for ever, cancel all our vows,
And when we meet at any time again,
Be it not seen in either of our brows
That we one jot of former love retain.

Now at the last gasp of love's latest breath,
When his pulse failing, passion speechless lies,
When faith is kneeling by his bed of death,
And innocence is closing up his eyes,

—Now if thou would'st, when all have given him
    over,
From death to life thou might'st him yet recover!
                                    M. Drayton

L

IN IMAGINE PERTRANSIT HOMO

Follow thy fair sun, unhappy shadow!
    Though thou be black as night
    And she made all of light,
Yet follow thy fair sun, unhappy shadow!

Follow her, whose light thy light depriveth!
    Though here thou liv'st disgraced,
    And she in heaven is placed,
Yet follow her whose light the world reviveth!

Follow those pure beams, whose beauty burneth,
    That so have scorchéd thee
    As thou still black must be
Till her kind beams thy black to brightness turneth.

Follow her, while yet her glory shineth !
   There comes a luckless night
   That will dim all her light;
—And this the black unhappy shade divineth.

Follow still, since so thy fates ordainéd !
   The sun must have his shade,
   Till both at once do fade,—
The sun still proved, the shadow still disdainéd.

T. Campion

LI

BLIND LOVE

O me ! what eyes hath Love put in my head
Which have no correspondence with true sight :
Or if they have, where is my judgment fled
That censures falsely what they see aright ?

If that be fair whereon my false eyes dote,
What means the world to say it is not so ?
If it be not, then love doth well denote
Love's eye is not so true as all men's : No,

How can it ? O how can love's eye be true,
That is so vex'd with watching and with tears ?
No marvel then though I mistake my view :
The sun itself sees not till heaven clears.

O cunning Love ! with tears thou keep'st me blind,
Lest eyes well-seeing thy foul faults should find !

W. Shakespeare

LII

Sleep, angry beauty, sleep and fear not me !
   For who a sleeping lion dares provoke ?
It shall suffice me here to sit and see
   Those lips shut up that never kindly spoke :
What sight can more content a lover's mind
Than beauty seeming harmless, if not kind ?

My words have charm'd her, for secure she sleeps,
  Though guilty much of wrong done to my love;
And in her slumber, see! she close-eyed weeps:
  Dreams often more than waking passions move.
Plead, Sleep, my cause, and make her soft like thee:
That she in peace may wake and pity me.

T. Campion

LIII

THE UNFAITHFUL SHEPHERDESS

While that the sun with his beams hot
Scorchéd the fruits in vale and mountain,
Philon the shepherd, late forgot,
Sitting beside a crystal fountain,
  In shadow of a green oak tree
  Upon his pipe this song play'd he:
Adieu, Love, adieu, Love, untrue Love,
Untrue Love, untrue Love, adieu, Love;
Your mind is light, soon lost for new love.

So long as I was in your sight
I was your heart, your soul, and treasure;
And evermore you sobb'd and sigh'd
Burning in flames beyond all measure:
  —Three days endured your love to me,
  And it was lost in other three!
Adieu, Love, adieu, Love, untrue Love,
Untrue Love, untrue Love, adieu, Love;
Your mind is light, soon lost for new love.

Another Shepherd you did see
To whom your heart was soon enchainéd;
Full soon your love was leapt from me,
Full soon my place he had obtainéd.
  Soon came a third, your love to win,
  And we were out and he was in.
Adieu, Love, adieu, Love, untrue Love,
Untrue Love, untrue Love, adieu, Love;
Your mind is light, soon lost for new love.

Sure you have made me passing glad
That you your mind so soon removéd,
Before that I the leisure had
To choose you for my best belovéd :
   For all your love was past and done
   Two days before it was begun :—
Adieu, Love, adieu, Love, untrue Love,
Untrue Love, untrue Love, adieu, Love;
Your mind is light, soon lost for new love.

                Anon.

LIV

ADVICE TO A LOVER

The sea hath many thousand sands,
The sun hath motes as many;
The sky is full of stars, and Love
As full of woes as any :
Believe me, that do know the elf,
And make no trial by thyself !

It is in truth a pretty toy
For babes to play withal :—
But O ! the honeys of our youth
Are oft our age's gall !
Self-proof in time will make thee know
He was a prophet told thee so ;

A prophet that, Cassandra-like,
Tells truth without belief ;
For headstrong Youth will run his race,
Although his goal be grief :—
Love's Martyr, when his heat is past,
Proves Care's Confessor at the last.

                Anon.

LV

A RENUNCIATION

Thou art not fair, for all thy red and white,
  For all those rosy ornaments in thee,—
Thou art not sweet, though made of mere delight,
  Nor fair, nor sweet—unless thou pity me !
I will not soothe thy fancies ; thou shalt prove
That beauty is no beauty without love.

—Yet love not me, nor seek not to allure
  My thoughts with beauty, were it more divine ı
Thy smiles and kisses I cannot endure,
  I'll not be wrapp'd up in those arms of thine :
—Now show it, if thou be a woman right—
Embrace and kiss and love me in despite !

T. Campion

LVI

Blow, blow, thou winter wind,
Thou art not so unkind
As man's ingratitude ;
Thy tooth is not so keen
Because thou art not seen,
Although thy breath be rude.
Heigh ho ! sing heigh ho ! unto the green holly :
Most friendship is feigning, most loving mere folly :
Then, heigh ho ! the holly !
This life is most jolly.

Freeze, freeze, thou bitter sky,
Thou dost not bite so nigh
As benefits forgot :
Though thou the waters warp,
Thy sting is not so sharp
As friend remember'd not.
Heigh ho ! sing heigh ho ! unto the green holly :
Most friendship is feigning, most loving mere folly :
Then, heigh ho ! the holly !
This life is most jolly.

W. Shakespeare

LVII

A SWEET LULLABY

Come little babe, come silly soul,
Thy father's shame, thy mother's grief,
Born as I doubt to all our dole,
And to thy self unhappy chief:
    Sing Lullaby and lap it warm,
    Poor soul that thinks no creature harm.

Thou little think'st and less dost know,
The cause of this thy mother's moan,
Thou want'st the wit to wail her woe,
And I myself am all alone:
    Why dost thou weep? why dost thou wail?
    And knowest not yet what thou dost ail.

Come little wretch, ah silly heart,
Mine only joy, what can I more?
If there be any wrong thy smart
That may the destinies implore:
    'Twas I, I say, against my will,
    I wail the time, but be thou still.

And dost thou smile, oh thy sweet face!
Would God Himself He might thee see,
No doubt thou would'st soon purchase grace,
I know right well, for thee and me:
    But come to mother, babe, and play,
    For father false is fled away.

Sweet boy, if it by fortune chance,
Thy father home again to send,
If death do strike me with his lance,
Yet mayst thou me to him commend:
    If any ask thy mother's name,
    Tell how by love she purchased blame.

Then will his gentle heart soon yield,
I know him of a noble mind,
Although a Lion in the field,

A Lamb in town thou shalt him find :
    Ask blessing, babe, be not afraid,
    His sugar'd words hath me betray'd.

Then mayst thou joy and be right glad,
Although in woe I seem to moan,
Thy father is no rascal lad,
A noble youth of blood and bone :
    His glancing looks, if he once smile,
    Right honest women may beguile.

Come, little boy, and rock asleep,
Sing lullaby and be thou still,
I that can do nought else but weep;
Will sit by thee and wail my fill :
    God bless my babe, and lullaby
    From this thy father's quality !

                    Anon.

LVIII

With how sad steps, O Moon, thou climb'st the skies !
How silently, and with how wan a face !
What, may it be that e'en in heavenly place
That busy archer his sharp arrows tries !

Sure, if that long-with-love-acquainted eyes
Can judge of love, thou feel'st a lover's case,
I read it in thy looks; thy languish'd grace,
To me, that feel the like, thy state descries.

Then, e'en of fellowship, O Moon, tell me,
Is constant love deem'd there but want of wit ?
Are beauties there as proud as here they be ?
Do they above love to be loved, and yet

Those lovers scorn whom that love doth possess ?
Do they call virtue, there, ungratefulness ?

               Sir P. Sidney

LIX

O CRUDELIS AMOR

When thou must home to shades of underground,
And there arrived, a new admired guest,
The beauteous spirits do engirt thee round,
White Iopé, blithe Helen, and the rest,
To hear the stories of thy finish'd love
From that smooth tongue whose music hell can move;

Then wilt thou speak of banqueting delights,
Of masques and revels which sweet youth did make,
Of tourneys and great challenges of Knights,
And all these triumphs for thy beauty's sake:
When thou hast told these honours done to thee,
Then tell, O tell, how thou didst murder me!

T. Campion

LX

SEPHESTIA'S SONG TO HER CHILD

Weep not, my wanton, smile upon my knee;
When thou art old there's grief enough for thee
    Mother's wag, pretty boy,
    Father's sorrow, father's joy;
    When thy father first did see
    Such a boy by him and me,
    He was glad, I was woe,
    Fortune changéd made him so,
    When he left his pretty boy
    Last his sorrow, first his joy.

Weep not, my wanton, smile upon my knee,
When thou art old there's grief enough for thee.
    Streaming tears that never stint,
    Like pearl drops from a flint,
    Fell by course from his eyes,
    That one another's place supplies;
    Thus he grieved in every part,
    Tears of blood fell from his heart,
    When he left his pretty boy,
    Father's sorrow, father's joy.

Weep not, my wanton, smile upon my knee,
When thou art old, there's grief enough for thee.
>   The wanton smiled, father wept,
>   Mother cried, baby leapt;
>   More he crow'd, more we cried,
>   Nature could not sorrow hide:
>   He must go, he must kiss
>   Child and mother, baby bless,
>   For he left his pretty boy,
>   Father's sorrow, father's joy.
Weep not, my wanton, smile upon my knee,
When thou art old, there's grief enough for thee.

R. Greene

LXI

A LAMENT

My thoughts hold mortal strife;
I do detest my life,
And with lamenting cries
Peace to my soul to bring
Oft call that prince which here doth monarchize:
—But he, grim grinning King,
Who caitiffs scorns, and doth the blest surprize,
Late having deck'd with beauty's rose his tomb,
Disdains to crop a weed, and will not come.

W. Drummond

LXII

DIRGE OF LOVE

Come away, come away, Death,
And in sad cypres let me be laid;
Fly away, fly away, breath;
I am slain by a fair cruel maid.

My shroud of white, stuck all with yew,
    O prepare it !
My part of death, no one so true
    Did share it.

  Not a flower, not a flower sweet
On my black coffin let there be strown;
  Not a friend, not a friend greet
My poor corpse, where my bones shall be thrown:
A thousand thousand sighs to save,
    Lay me, O where
Sad true lover never find my grave,
    To weep there.
          W. Shakespeare

LXIII

TO HIS LUTE

My lute, be as thou wert when thou didst grow
With thy green mother in some shady grove,
When immelodious winds but made thee move,
And birds their ramage did on thee bestow.

Since that dear Voice which did thy sounds approve,
Which wont in such harmonious strains to flow,
Is reft from Earth to tune those spheres above,
What art thou but a harbinger of woe?

Thy pleasing notes be pleasing notes no more,
But orphans' wailings to the fainting ear;
Each stroke a sigh, each sound draws forth a tear;
For which be silent as in woods before :

Or if that any hand to touch thee deign,
Like widow'd turtle, still her loss complain.
          W. Drummond

LXIV

FIDELE

Fear no more the heat o' the sun
    Nor the furious winter's rages;
Thou thy worldly task hast done,
    Home art gone and ta'en thy wages:
Golden lads and girls all must,
As chimney-sweepers, come to dust.

Fear no more the frown o' the great,
    Thou art past the tyrant's stroke;
Care no more to clothe and eat;
    To thee the reed is as the oak:
The sceptre, learning, physic, must
All follow this, and come to dust.

Fear no more the lightning-flash
    Nor the all-dreaded thunder-stone;
Fear not slander, censure rash;
    Thou hast finish'd joy and moan:
All lovers young, all lovers must
Consign to thee, and come to dust.

                 W. Shakespeare

LXV

A SEA DIRGE

Full fathom five thy father lies:
    Of his bones are coral made;
Those are pearls that were his eyes:
    Nothing of him that doth fade,
But doth suffer a sea-change
Into something rich and strange.
Sea-nymphs hourly ring his knell:
Hark! now I hear them,—
    Ding, dong, bell.

                 W. Shakespeare

LXVI

A LAND DIRGE

Call for the robin-redbreast and the wren,
Since o'er shady groves they hover
And with leaves and flowers do cover
The friendless bodies of unburied men.
Call unto his funeral dole
The ant, the field-mouse, and the mole
To rear him hillocks that shall keep him warm
And (when gay tombs are robb'd) sustain no harm;
But keep the wolf far thence, that's foe to men,
For with his nails he'll dig them up again.

J. Webster

LXVII

POST MORTEM

If Thou survive my well-contented day
When that churl Death my bones with dust shall
    cover,
And shalt by fortune once more re-survey
These poor rude lines of thy deceaséd lover;

Compare them with the bettering of the time,
And though they be outstripp'd by every pen,
Reserve them for my love, not for their rhyme
Exceeded by the height of happier men.

O then vouchsafe me but this loving thought—
' Had my friend's Muse grown with this growing age,
A dearer birth than this his love had brought,
To march in ranks of better equipage :

But since he died, and poets better prove,
Theirs for their style I'll read, his for his love.'

W. Shakespeare

LXVIII

THE TRIUMPH OF DEATH

No longer mourn for me when I am dead
Than you shall hear the surly sullen bell
Give warning to the world, that I am fled
From this vile world, with vilest worms to dwell;

Nay, if you read this line, remember not
The hand that writ it; for I love you so,
That I in your sweet thoughts would be forgot
If thinking on me then should make you woe.

O if, I say, you look upon this verse
When I perhaps compounded am with clay,
Do not so much as my poor name rehearse,
But let your love even with my life decay;

Lest the wise world should look into your moan,
And mock you with me after I am gone.

W. Shakespeare

LXIX

YOUNG LOVE

Tell me where is Fancy bred,
Or in the heart, or in the head?
How begot, how nourishéd?
    Reply, reply.

It is engender'd in the eyes;
With gazing fed; and Fancy dies
In the cradle where it lies:
Let us all ring Fancy's knell;
I'll begin it,—Ding, dong, bell.
    —Ding, dong, bell.

W. Shakespeare

LXX

A DILEMMA

Lady, when I behold the roses sprouting
   Which clad in damask mantles deck the arbours,
And then behold your lips where sweet love
    harbours,
My eyes present me with a double doubting :
For viewing both alike, hardly my mind supposes
Whether the roses be your lips, or your lips the roses.

Anon.

LXXI

ROSALYND'S MADRIGAL

Love in my bosom, like a bee,
      Doth suck his sweet ;
Now with his wings he plays with me,
      Now with his feet.
   Within mine eyes he makes his nest,
   His bed amidst my tender breast ;
   My kisses are his daily feast,
   And yet he robs me of my rest :
      Ah ! wanton, will ye ?

And if I sleep, then percheth he
      With pretty flight,
And makes his pillow of my knee
      The livelong night.
   Strike I my lute, he tunes the string ;
   He music plays if so I sing ;
   He lends me every lovely thing,
   Yet cruel he my heart doth sting :
      Whist, wanton, will ye ?

Else I with roses every day
      Will whip you hence,

And bind you, when you long to play,
　　　　　For your offence;
I'll shut my eyes to keep you in;
I'll make you fast it for your sin;
I'll count your power not worth a pin;
—Alas! what hereby shall I win,
　　　　　If he gainsay me?

What if I beat the wanton boy
　　　　　With many a rod?
He will repay me with annoy,
　　　　　Because a god.
Then sit thou safely on my knee,
And let thy bower my bosom be;
Lurk in mine eyes, I like of thee,
O Cupid! so thou pity me,
　　　　　Spare not, but play thee!

　　　　　　　　　　　T. Lodge

LXXII

CUPID AND CAMPASPÉ

Cupid and my Campaspé play'd
At cards for kisses; Cupid paid:
He stakes his quiver, bow, and arrows,
His mother's doves, and team of sparrows;
Loses them too; then down he throws
The coral of his lip, the rose
Growing on's cheek (but none knows how);
With these, the crystal of his brow,
And then the dimple on his chin;
All these did my Campaspé win:
At last he set her both his eyes—
She won, and Cupid blind did rise.
　　　O Love! has she done this to thee?
　　　What shall, alas! become of me?

　　　　　　　　　　　J. Lylye

LXXIII

Pack, clouds, away, and welcome day,
  With night we banish sorrow;
Sweet air blow soft, mount larks aloft
  To give my Love good-morrow!
Wings from the wind to please her mind
  Notes from the lark I'll borrow;
Bird, prune thy wing, nightingale sing,
  To give my Love good-morrow;
      To give my Love good-morrow
      Notes from them both I'll borrow.

Wake from thy nest, Robin-red-breast,
  Sing, birds, in every furrow;
And from each hill, let music shrill
  Give my fair Love good-morrow!
Blackbird and thrush in every bush,
  Stare, linnet, and cock-sparrow!
You pretty elves, amongst yourselves
  Sing my fair Love good-morrow;
      To give my Love good-morrow
      Sing, birds, in every furrow!

                              T. Heywood

LXXIV

PROTHALAMION

Calm was the day, and through the trembling air
Sweet-breathing Zephyrus did softly play—
A gentle spirit, that lightly did delay
Hot Titan's beams, which then did glister fair
When I, (whom sullen care,
Through discontent of my long fruitless stay
In princes' court, and expectation vain
Of idle hopes, which still do fly away
Like empty shadows, did afflict my brain)
Walk'd forth to ease my pain

Along the shore of silver-streaming Thames;
Whose rutty bank, the which his river hems,
Was painted all with variable flowers,
And all the meads adorn'd with dainty gems
Fit to deck maidens' bowers,
And crown their paramours
Against the bridal day, which is not long :
   Sweet Thames ! run softly, till I end my song.

There in a meadow by the river's side
A flock of nymphs I chancéd to espy,
All lovely daughters of the flood thereby,
With goodly greenish locks all loose untied
As each had been a bride ;
And each one had a little wicker basket
Made of fine twigs, entrailéd curiously.
In which they gather'd flowers to fill their flasket,
And with fine fingers cropt full feateously
The tender stalks on high.
Of every sort which in that meadow grew
They gather'd some; the violet, pallid blue,
The little daisy that at evening closes,
The virgin lily and the primrose true,
With store of vermeil roses,
To deck their bridegrooms' posies
Against the bridal day, which was not long :
   Sweet Thames ! run softly, till I end my song.

With that I saw two Swans of goodly hue
Come softly swimming down along the Lee;
Two fairer birds I yet did never see;
The snow which doth the top of Pindus strow
Did never whiter show,
Nor Jove himself, when he a swan would be
For love of Leda, whiter did appear;
Yet Leda was (they say) as white as he,
Yet not so white as these, nor nothing near;
So purely white they were
That even the gentle stream, the which them bare,
Seem'd foul to them, and bade his billows spare
To wet their silken feathers, lest they might
Soil their fair plumes with water not so fair,

And mar their beauties bright
That shone as Heaven's light
Against their bridal day, which was not long :
   Sweet Thames ! run softly, till I end my song.

Eftsoons the nymphs, which now had flowers their fill,
Ran all in haste to see that silver brood
As they came floating on the crystal flood ;
Whom when they saw, they stood amazéd still
Their wondering eyes to fill ;
Them seem'd they never saw a sight so fair
Of fowls, so lovely, that they sure did deem
Them heavenly born, or to be that same pair
Which through the sky draw Venus' silver team :
For sure they did not seem
To be begot of any earthly seed,
But rather Angels, or of Angels' breed ;
Yet were they bred of summer's heat, they say,
In sweetest season, when each flower and weed
The earth did fresh array ;
So fresh they seem'd as day,
Ev'n as their bridal day, which was not long :
   Sweet Thames ! run softly, till I end my song.

Then forth they all out of their baskets drew
Great store of flowers, the honour of the field,
That to the sense did fragrant odours yield,
All which upon those goodly birds they threw
And all the waves did strew,
That like old Peneus' waters they did seem
When down along by pleasant Tempe's shore
Scatter'd with flowers, through Thessaly they stream,
That they appear, through lilies' plenteous store,
Like a bride's chamber-floor.
Two of those nymphs meanwhile two garlands bound
Of freshest flowers which in that mead they found,
The which presenting all in trim array,
Their snowy foreheads therewithal they crown'd ;
Whilst one did sing this lay
Prepared against that day,
Against their bridal day, which was not long :
   Sweet Thames ! run softly till I end my song.

' Ye gentle birds ! the world's fair ornament,
And Heaven's glory, whom this happy hour
Doth lead unto your lovers' blissful bower,
Joy may you have, and gentle heart's content
Of your love's complement;
And let fair Venus, that is queen of love,
With her heart-quelling son upon you smile.
Whose smile, they say, hath virtue to remove
All love's dislike, and friendship's faulty guile
For ever to assoil.
Let endless peace your steadfast hearts accord,
And blesséd plenty wait upon your board;
And let your bed with pleasures chaste abound,
That fruitful issue may to you afford
Which may your foes confound,
And make your joys redound
Upon your bridal day, which is not long :
    Sweet Thames ! run softly, till I end my song.'

So ended she; and all the rest around
To her redoubled that her undersong,
Which said their bridal day should not be long :
And gentle Echo from the neighbour ground
Their accents did resound.
So forth those joyous birds did pass along
Adown the Lee that to them murmur'd low,
As he would speak but that he lack'd a tongue;
Yet did by signs his glad affection show,
Making his stream run slow.
And all the fowl which in his flood did dwell
'Gan flock about these twain, that did excel
The rest, so far as Cynthia doth shend
The lesser stars.   So they, enrangéd well,
Did on those two attend,
And their best service lend
Against their wedding day, which was not long :
    Sweet Thames ! run softly, till I end my song

At length they all to merry London came,
To merry London, my most kindly nurse,
That to me gave this life's first native source,
Though from another place I take my name,

An house of ancient fame :
There when they came whereas those bricky towers
The which on Thames' broad agéd back do ride,
Where now the studious lawyers have their bowers,
There whilome wont the Templar-knights to bide,
Till they decay'd through pride;
Next whereunto there stands a stately place,
Where oft I gainéd gifts and goodly grace
Of that great lord, which therein wont to dwell,
Whose want too well now feels my friendless case;
But ah ! here fits not well
Old woes, but joys to tell
Against the bridal day, which is not long :
  Sweet Thames ! run softly, till I end my song.

Yet therein now doth lodge a noble peer,
Great England's glory and the world's wide wonder,
Whose dreadful name late through all Spain did
    thunder,
And Hercules' two pillars standing near
Did make to quake and fear :
Fair branch of honour, flower of chivalry !
That fillest England with thy triumphs' fame
Joy have thou of thy noble victory,
And endless happiness of thine own name
That promiseth the same ;
That through thy prowess and victorious arms
Thy country may be freed from foreign harms,
And great Elisa's glorious name may ring
Through all the world, fill'd with thy wide alarms,
Which some brave Muse may sing
To ages following :
Upon the bridal day, which is not long .
  Sweet Thames ! run softly, till I end my song.

From those high towers this noble lord issúing
Like radiant Hesper, when his golden hair
In th' ocean billows he hath bathéd fair,
Descended to the river's open viewing
With a great train ensuing.
Above the rest were goodly to be seen
Two gentle knights of lovely face and feature,

Beseeming well the bower of any queen,
With gifts of wit and ornaments of nature,
Fit for so goodly stature,
That like the twins of Jove they seem'd in sight
Which deck the baldric of the Heavens bright;
They two, forth pacing to the river's side,
Received those two fair brides, their love's delight;
Which, at th' appointed tide,
Each one did make his bride
Against their bridal day, which is not long:
   Sweet Thames! run softly, till I end my song.

E. Spenser

LXXV

THE HAPPY HEART

Art thou poor, yet hast thou golden slumbers?
      O sweet content!
Art thou rich, yet is thy mind perplex'd?
      O punishment!
Dost thou laugh to see how fools are vex'd
To add to golden numbers, golden numbers?
O sweet content! O sweet, O sweet content!
  Work apace, apace, apace, apace;
  Honest labour bears a lovely face;
Then hey nonny nonny, hey nonny nonny!

Canst drink the waters of the crispéd spring?
      O sweet content!
Swimm'st thou in wealth, yet sink'st in thine own
    tears?
      O punishment!
Then he that patiently want's burden bears
No burden bears, but is a king, a king!
O sweet content! O sweet, O sweet content!
  Work apace, apace, apace, apace;
  Honest labour bears a lovely face;
Then hey nonny nonny, hey nonny nonny!

T. Dekker

LXXVI

SIC TRANSIT

Come, cheerful day, part of my life to me;
   For while thou view'st me with thy fading light
Part of my life doth still depart with thee,
   And I still onward haste to my last night:
Time's fatal wings do ever forward fly—
So every day we live a day we die.

But O ye nights, ordain'd for barren rest,
   How are my days deprived of life in you
When heavy sleep my soul hath dispossest,
   By feignéd death life sweetly to renew!
Part of my life, in that, you life deny:
So every day we live, a day we die.

T. Campion

LXXVII

This Life, which seems so fair,
Is like a bubble blown up in the air
By sporting children's breath,
Who chase it everywhere
And strive who can most motion it bequeath.
And though it sometimes seem of its own might
Like to an eye of gold to be fix'd there,
And firm to hover in that empty height,
That only is because it is so light.
—But in that pomp it doth not long appear;
For when 'tis most admired, in a thought,
Because it erst was nought, it turns to nought.

W. Drummond

LXXVIII

SOUL AND BODY

Poor Soul, the centre of my sinful earth,
[Foil'd by] those rebel powers that thee array,
Why dost thou pine within, and suffer dearth,
Painting thy outward walls so costly gay?

Why so large cost, having so short a lease,
Dost thou upon thy fading mansion spend?
Shall worms, inheritors of this excess,
Eat up thy charge? is this thy body's end?

Then, Soul, live thou upon thy servant's loss,
And let that pine to aggravate thy store;
Buy terms divine in selling hours of dross;
Within be fed, without be rich no more:—

So shalt thou feed on death, that feeds on men,
And death once dead, there's no more dying then.

W. Shakespeare

LXXIX

The man of life upright,
    Whose guiltless heart is free
From all dishonest deeds,
    Or thought of vanity;

The man whose silent days
    In harmless joys are spent,
Whom hopes cannot delude
    Nor sorrow discontent:

That man needs neither towers
    Nor armour for defence,
Nor secret vaults to fly
    From thunder's violence:

He only can behold
　　With unaffrighted eyes
The horrors of the deep
　　And terrors of the skies.

Thus scorning all the cares
　　That fate or fortune brings,
He makes the heaven his book,
　　His wisdom heavenly things;

Good thoughts his only friends,
　　His wealth a well-spent age,
The earth his sober inn
　　And quiet pilgrimage.

　　　　　　　　　　T. Campion

LXXX

THE LESSONS OF NATURE

Of this fair volume which we World do name
If we the sheets and leaves could turn with care,
Of Him who it corrects, and did it frame,
We clear might read the art and wisdom rare:

Find out His power which wildest powers doth tame,
His providence extending everywhere,
His justice which proud rebels doth not spare,
In every page, no period of the same.

But silly we, like foolish children, rest
Well pleased with colour'd vellum, leaves of gold,
Fair dangling ribbands, leaving what is best,
On the great Writer's sense ne'er taking hold;

Or if by chance we stay our minds on aught,
It is some picture on the margin wrought.

　　　　　　　　　　W. Drummond

LXXXI

Doth then the world go thus, doth all thus move?
Is this the justice which on Earth we find?
Is this that firm decree which all doth bind?
Are these your influences, Powers above?

Those souls which vice's moody mists most blind,
Blind Fortune, blindly, most their friend doth prove;
And they who thee, poor idol Virtue! love,
Ply like a feather toss'd by storm and wind.

Ah! if a Providence doth sway this all
Why should best minds groan under most distress?
Or why should pride humility make thrall,
And injuries the innocent oppress?

Heavens! hinder, stop this fate; or grant a time
When good may have, as well as bad, their prime!

W. Drummond

LXXXII

THE WORLD'S WAY

Tired with all these, for restful death I cry—
As, to behold desert a beggar born,
And needy nothing trimm'd in jollity,
And purest faith unhappily forsworn,

And gilded honour shamefully misplaced,
And maiden virtue rudely strumpeted,
And right perfection wrongfully disgraced,
And strength by limping sway disabled,

And art made tongue-tied by authority,
And folly, doctor-like, controlling skill,
And simple truth miscall'd simplicity,
And captive Good attending captain Ill:—

—Tired with all these, from these would I be gone,
Save that, to die, I leave my Love alone.

W. Shakespeare

LXXXIII

A WISH

Happy were he could finish forth his fate
In some unhaunted desert, where, obscure
From all society, from love and hate
Of worldly folk, there should he sleep secure;

Then wake again, and yield God ever praise;
Content with hip, with haws, and brambleberry;
In contemplation passing still his days,
And change of holy thoughts to make him merry;

Who, when he dies, his tomb might be the bush
Where harmless robin resteth with the thrush:
       —Happy were he!

           R. Devereux, Earl of Essex

LXXXIV

SAINT JOHN BAPTIST

The last and greatest Herald of Heaven's King
Girt with rough skins, hies to the deserts wild,
Among that savage brood the woods forth bring,
Which he more harmless found than man, and mild

His food was locusts, and what there doth spring,
With honey that from virgin hives distill'd;
Parch'd body, hollow eyes, some uncouth thing
Made him appear, long since from earth exiled.

There burst he forth: All ye whose hopes rely
On God, with me amidst these deserts mourn,
Repent, repent, and from old errors turn!
—Who listen'd to his voice, obey'd his cry?

Only the echoes, which he made relent,
Rung from their flinty caves, Repent! Repent!

           W. Drummond

The Golden Treasury

Book Second

LXXXV

ODE ON THE MORNING OF CHRIST'S NATIVITY

This is the month, and this the happy morn
Wherein the Son of Heaven's Eternal King
Of wedded maid and virgin mother born,
Our great redemption from above did bring;
For so the holy sages once did sing
That He our deadly forfeit should release,
And with His Father work us a perpetual peace.

That glorious Form, that Light unsufferable,
And that far-beaming blaze of Majesty
Wherewith He wont at Heaven's high council-table
To sit the midst of Trinal Unity,
He laid aside; and, here with us to be,
Forsook the courts of everlasting day,
And chose with us a darksome house of mortal clay.

Say, heavenly Muse, shall not thy sacred vein
Afford a present to the Infant God?
Hast thou no verse, no hymn, or solemn strain
To welcome Him to this His new abode,
Now while the heaven, by the sun's team untrod,
Hath took no print of the approaching light,
And all the spangled host keep watch in squadrons
          bright?

See how from far, upon the eastern road,
The star-led wizards haste with odours sweet:
O run, prevent them with thy humble ode
And lay it lowly at His blessèd feet;
Have thou the honour first thy Lord to greet,
And join thy voice unto the Angel quire
From out His secret altar touch'd with hallow'd fire.

THE HYMN

It was the winter wild
While the heaven-born Child
All meanly wrapt in the rude manger lies;
Nature in awe to Him
Had doff'd her gaudy trim,
With her great Master so to sympathize:
It was no season then for her
To wanton with the sun, her lusty paramour.

Only with speeches fair
She woos the gentle air
To hide her guilty front with innocent snow;
And on her naked shame,
Pollute with sinful blame,
The saintly veil of maiden white to throw;
Confounded, that her Maker's eyes
Should look so near upon her foul deformities.

But He, her fears to cease,
Sent down the meek-eyed Peace;
She, crown'd with olive green, came softly sliding
Down through the turning sphere,
His ready harbinger,
With turtle wing the amorous clouds dividing;
And waving wide her myrtle wand,
She strikes a universal peace through sea and land.

No war, or battle's sound
Was heard the world around:
The idle spear and shield were high uphung;
The hookèd chariot stood

Unstain'd with hostile blood;
The trumpet spake not to the arméd throng;
And kings sat still with awful eye,
As if they surely knew their sovran Lord was by.

But peaceful was the night
Wherein the Prince of Light
His reign of peace upon the earth began :
The winds, with wonder whist,
Smoothly the waters kist
Whispering new joys to the mild oceán—
Who now hath quite forgot to rave,
While birds of calm sit brooding on the charméd
      wave.

The stars, with deep amaze,
Stand fix'd in steadfast gaze,
Bending one way their precious influence;
And will not take their flight
For all the morning light,
Or Lucifer that often warn'd them thence;
But in their glimmering orbs did glow
Until their Lord Himself bespake, and bid them go.

And though the shady gloom
Had given day her room,
The sun himself withheld his wonted speed,
And hid his head for shame,
As his inferior flame
The new-enlighten'd world no more should need;
He saw a greater Sun appear
Than his bright throne, or burning axletree could
      bear.

The shepherds on the lawn
Or ere the point of dawn
Sate simply chatting in a rustic row;
Full little thought they than
That the mighty Pan
Was kindly come to live with them below;
Perhaps their loves, or else their sheep
Was all that did their silly thoughts so busy keep :—

When such music sweet
Their hearts and ears did greet

As never was by mortal finger strook—.
Divinely-warbled voice
Answering the stringéd noise,
As all their souls in blissful rapture took :
The air, such pleasure loth to lose,
With thousand echoes still prolongs each heavenly
    close.

Nature, that heard such sound
Beneath the hollow round
Of Cynthia's seat the airy region thrilling,
Now was almost won
To think her part was done,
And that her reign had here its last fulfilling ;
She knew such harmony alone
Could hold all Heaven and Earth in happier union.

At last surrounds their sight
A globe of circular light
That with long beams the shamefaced night array'd ;
The helméd Cherubim
And sworded Seraphim
Are seen in glittering ranks with wings display'd,
Harping in loud and solemn quire
With unexpressive notes, to Heaven's new-born Heir.

Such music (as 'tis said)
Before was never made
But when of old the Sons of Morning sung,
While the Creator great
His constellations set
And the well-balanced world on hinges hung ;
And cast the dark foundations deep,
And bid the weltering waves their oozy channel keep.

Ring out, ye crystal spheres !
Once bless our human ears,
If ye have power to touch our senses so ;
And let your silver chime
Move in melodious time ;
And let the bass of heaven's deep organ blow ;
And with your ninefold harmony
Make up full consort to the angelic symphony.

For if such holy song
Enwrap our fancy long,
Time will run back, and fetch the age of gold;
And speckled Vanity
Will sicken soon and die,
And leprous Sin will melt from earthly mould;
And Hell itself will pass away,
And leave her dolorous mansions to the peering day.

Yea, Truth and Justice then
Will down return to men,
Orb'd in a rainbow; and, like glories wearing,
Mercy will sit between
Throned in celestial sheen,
With radiant feet the tissued clouds down steering;
And Heaven, as at some festival,
Will open wide the gates of her high palace-hall.

But wisest Fate says No;
This must not yet be so;
The Babe yet lies in smiling infancy
That on the bitter cross
Must redeem our loss;
So both Himself and us to glorify:
Yet first, to those ychain'd in sleep
The wakeful trump of doom must thunder through
    the deep;

With such a horrid clang
As on Mount Sinai rang
While the red fire and smouldering clouds outbrake:
The aged Earth aghast
With terror of that blast
Shall from the surface to the centre shake,
When, at the world's last session,
The dreadful Judge in middle air shall spread His
    throne.

And then at last our bliss
Full and perfect is,
But now begins; for from this happy day
The old Dragon under ground,
In straiter limits bound,
Not half so far casts his usurpéd sway;

And, wroth to see his kingdom fail,
Swinges the scaly horror of his folded tail.

The Oracles are dumb;
No voice or hideous hum
Runs through the archéd roof in words deceiving.
Apollo from his shrine
Can no more divine,
With hollow shriek the steep of Delphos leaving :
No nightly trance or breathéd spell
Inspires the pale-eyed priest from the prophetic cell.

The lonely mountains o'er
And the resounding shore
A voice of weeping heard, and loud lament;
From haunted spring and dale
Edged with poplar pale
The parting Genius is with sighing sent;
With flower-inwoven tresses torn
The Nymphs in twilight shade of tangled thickets
    mourn.

In consecrated earth
And on the holy hearth
The Lars and Lemurés moan with midnight plaint;
In urns, and altars round
A drear and dying sound
Affrights the Flamens at their service quaint;
And the chill marble seems to sweat,
While each peculiar Power foregoes his wonted seat.

Peor and Baalim
Forsake their temples dim,
With that twice-batter'd god of Palestine;
And moonéd Ashtaroth
Heaven's queen and mother both,
Now sits not girt with tapers' holy shine;
The Lybic Hammon shrinks his horn :
In vain the Tyrian maids their wounded Thammuz
    mourn.

And sullen Moloch, fled,
Hath left in shadows dread
His burning idol all of blackest hue;

In vain with cymbals' ring
They call the grisly king,
In dismal dance about the furnace blue;
The brutish gods of Nile as fast,
Isis, and Orus, and the dog Anubis, haste.

Nor is Osiris seen
In Memphian grove, or green,
Trampling the unshower'd grass with lowings loud:
Nor can he be at rest
Within his sacred chest;
Nought but profoundest Hell can be his shroud;
In vain with timbrell'd anthems dark
The sable-stoléd sorcerers bear his worshipt ark.

He feels from Juda's land
The dreaded Infant's hand;
The rays of Bethlehem blind his dusky eyn;
Nor all the gods beside
Longer dare abide,
Not Typhon huge ending in snaky twine:
Our Babe, to show His Godhead true,
Can in His swaddling bands control the damnéd crew.

So, when the sun in bed
Curtain'd with cloudy red
Pillows his chin upon an orient wave,
The flocking shadows pale
Troop to the infernal jail,
Each fetter'd ghost slips to his several grave;
And the yellow-skirted fays
Fly after the night-steeds, leaving their moon-loved
    maze.

But see! the Virgin blest
Hath laid her Babe to rest;
Time is, our tedious song should here have ending:
Heaven's youngest-teeméd star
Hath fix'd her polish'd car,
Her sleeping Lord with hand-maid lamp attending:
And all about the courtly stable
Bright-harness'd Angels sit in order serviceable.

                                                    J. Milton

LXXXVI

SONG FOR ST. CECILIA'S DAY, 1687

From Harmony, from heavenly Harmony
    This universal frame began :
     When Nature underneath a heap
      Of jarring atoms lay
    And could not heave her head,
The tuneful voice was heard from high,
    Arise, ye more than dead !
Then cold and hot and moist and dry
In order to their stations leap,
    And Music's power obey.
From harmony, from heavenly harmony
    This universal frame began :
    From harmony to harmony
Through all the compass of the notes it ran,
The diapason closing full in Man.

What passion cannot Music raise and quell ?
    When Jubal struck the chorded shell
   His listening brethren stood around,
   And, wondering, on their faces fell
   To worship that celestial sound.
Less than a god they thought there could not dwell
    Within the hollow of that shell
    That spoke so sweetly and so well.
What passion cannot Music raise and quell ?

   The trumpet's loud clangor
    Excites us to arms,
  With shrill notes of anger
    And mortal alarms.
  The double double double beat
   Of the thundering drum
   Cries ' Hark ! the foes come ;
Charge, charge, 'tis too late to retreat ! '

   The soft complaining flute
    In dying notes discovers

The woes of hopeless lovers,
Whose dirge is whisper'd by the warbling lute.

Sharp violins proclaim
Their jealous pangs and desperation,
Fury, frantic indignation,
Depth of pains, and height of passion
For the fair disdainful dame.

But oh! what art can teach,
What human voice can reach
The sacred organ's praise?
Notes inspiring holy love,
Notes that wing their heavenly ways
To mend the choirs above.

Orpheus could lead the savage race,
And trees unrooted left their place
Sequacious of the lyre:
But bright Cecilia raised the wonder higher:
When to her Organ vocal breath was given
An Angel heard, and straight appear'd—
Mistaking Earth for Heaven.

Grand Chorus

As from the power of sacred lays
The spheres began to move,
And sung the great Creator's praise
To all the blest above;
So when the last and dreadful hour
This crumbling pageant shall devour,
The trumpet shall be heard on high,
The dead shall live, the living die,
And Music shall untune the sky.

J. Dryden

LXXXVII

ON THE LATE MASSACRE IN PIEDMONT

Avenge, O Lord! Thy slaughter'd saints, whose bones
Lie scatter'd on the Alpine mountains cold;
Even them who kept Thy truth so pure of old
When all our fathers worshipt stocks and stones,

Forget not : In Thy book record their groans
Who were Thy sheep, and in their ancient fold
Slain by the bloody Piemontese, that roll'd
Mother with infant down the rocks. Their moans

The vales redoubled to the hills, and they
To Heaven. Their martyr'd blood and ashes sow
O'er all the Italian fields, where still doth sway

The triple Tyrant : that from these may grow
A hundred-fold, who, having learnt Thy way,
Early may fly the Babylonian woe.

J. Milton

LXXXVIII

HORATIAN ODE UPON CROMWELL'S RETURN FROM IRELAND

The forward youth that would appear,
Must now forsake his Muses dear,
    Nor in the shadows sing
    His numbers languishing.

'Tis time to leave the books in dust,
And oil the unuséd armour's rust,
    Removing from the wall
    The corslet of the hall.

So restless Cromwell could not cease
In the inglorious arts of peace,
    But through adventurous war
    Urgéd his active star :

And like the three-fork'd lightning, first
Breaking the clouds where it was nurst,
    Did thorough his own Side
    His fiery way divide :

For 'tis all one to courage high,
The emulous, or enemy ;
    And with such, to enclose
    Is more than to oppose ;

Then burning through the air he went
And palaces and temples rent;
    And Caesar's head at last
    Did through his laurels blast.

'Tis madness to resist or blame
The face of angry heaven's flame;
    And if we would speak true,
    Much to the Man is due

Who, from his private gardens, where
He lived reservéd and austere,
    (As if his highest plot
    To plant the bergamot,)

Could by industrious valour climb
To ruin the great work of time,
    And cast the Kingdoms old
    Into another mould;

Though Justice against Fate complain,
And plead the ancient Rights in vain
    But those do hold or break
    As men are strong or weak;

Nature, that hateth emptiness,
Allows of penetration less
    And therefore must make room
    Where greater spirits come.

What field of all the civil war
Where his were not the deepest scar?
    And Hampton shows what part
    He had of wiser art,

Where, twining subtle fears with hope,
He wove a net of such a scope
    That Charles himself might chase
    To Carisbrook's narrow case,

That thence the Royal actor borne
The tragic scaffold might adorn:
    While round the arméd bands
    Did clap their bloody hands.

He nothing common did or mean
Upon that memorable scene,
    But with his keener eye
    The axe's edge did try;

Nor call'd the Gods, with vulgar spite,
To vindicate his helpless right;
    But bow'd his comely head
    Down, as upon a bed.

—This was that memorable hour
Which first assured the forcéd power;
    So when they did design
    The Capitol's first line,

A Bleeding Head, where they begun,
Did fright the architects to run;
    And yet in that the State
    Foresaw its happy fate!

And now the Irish are ashamed
To see themselves in one year tamed:
    So much one man can do
    That does both act and know.

They can affirm his praises best,
And have, though overcome, confest
    How good he is, how just
    And fit for highest trust.

Nor yet grown stiffer with command,
But still in the Republic's hand—
    How fit he is to sway
    That can so well obey!

He to the Commons' feet presents
A Kingdom for his first year's rents,
    And (what he may) forbears
    His fame, to make it theirs:

And has his sword and spoils ungirt
To lay them at the Public's skirt.
    So when the falcon high
    Falls heavy from the sky,

She, having kill'd, no more doth search
But on the next green bough to perch,
    Where, when he first does lure,
    The falconer has her sure.

—What may not then our Isle presume
While victory his crest does plume?
    What may not others fear
    If thus he crowns each year?

As Caesar he, ere long, to Gaul,
To Italy an Hannibal,
    And to all States not free
    Shall climacteric be.

The Pict no shelter now shall find
Within his parti-colour'd mind,
    But from this valour sad
    Shrink underneath the plaid—

Happy, if in the tufted brake
The English hunter him mistake,
    Nor lay his hounds in near
    The Caledonian deer.

But Thou, the War's and Fortune's son,
March indefatigably on;
    And for the last effect
    Still keep the sword erect:

Besides the force it has to fright
The spirits of the shady night,
    The same arts that did gain
    A power, must it maintain.

                    A. Marvell

LXXXIX

LYCIDAS

Elegy on a Friend drowned in the Irish Channel
                1637

Yet once more, O ye laurels, and once more
Ye myrtles brown, with ivy never sere,
I come to pluck your berries harsh and crude,
And with forced fingers rude

Shatter your leaves before the mellowing year.
Bitter constraint and sad occasion dear
Compels me to disturb your season due :
For Lycidas is dead, dead ere his prime,
Young Lycidas, and hath not left his peer.
Who would not sing for Lycidas ? he knew
Himself to sing, and build the lofty rhyme.
He must not float upon his watery bier
Unwept, and welter to the parching wind,
Without the meed of some melodious tear.

Begin then, Sisters of the sacred well
That from beneath the seat of Jove doth spring ;
Begin, and somewhat loudly sweep the string.
Hence with denial vain and coy excuse :
So may some gentle Muse
With lucky words favour my destined urn ;
And as he passes, turn
And bid fair peace be to my sable shroud.

For we were nursed upon the self-same hill,
Fed the same flock by fountain, shade, and rill :
Together both, ere the high lawns appear'd
Under the opening eyelids of the Morn,
We drove a-field, and both together heard
What time the gray-fly winds her sultry horn,
Battening our flocks with the fresh dews of night,
Oft till the star that rose at evening bright
Toward heaven's descent had sloped his westering
    wheel.
Meanwhile the rural ditties were not mute,
Temper'd to the oaten flute,
Rough Satyrs danced, and Fauns with cloven heel
From the glad sound would not be absent long ;
And old Damoetas loved to hear our song.

But, oh ! the heavy change, now thou art gone,
Now thou art gone, and never must return !
Thee, Shepherd, thee the woods and desert caves
With wild thyme and the gadding vine o'ergrown,
And all their echoes, mourn :
The willows and the hazel copses green
Shall now no more be seen
Fanning their joyous leaves to thy soft lays :—

As killing as the canker to the rose,
Or taint-worm to the weanling herds that graze,
Or frost to flowers, that their gay wardrobe wear
When first the white-thorn blows;
Such, Lycidas, thy loss to shepherd's ear.

  Where were ye, Nymphs, when the remorseless deep
Closed o'er the head of your loved Lycidas?
For neither were ye playing on the steep
Where your old bards, the famous Druids, lie,
Nor on the shaggy top of Mona high,
Nor yet where Deva spreads her wizard stream:
Ay me! I fondly dream—
Had ye been there . . . For what could that have
    done?
What could the Muse herself that Orpheus bore,
The Muse herself, for her enchanting son,
Whom universal nature did lament,
When by the rout that made the hideous roar
His gory visage down the stream was sent,
Down the swift Hebrus to the Lesbian shore?

  Alas! what boots it with uncessant care
To tend the homely, slighted, shepherd's trade
And strictly meditate the thankless Muse?
Were it not better done, as others use,
To sport with Amaryllis in the shade,
Or with the tangles of Neaera's hair?
Fame is the spur that the clear spirit doth raise
(That last infirmity of noble mind)
To scorn delights, and live laborious days;
But the fair guerdon when we hope to find,
And think to burst out into sudden blaze,
Comes the blind Fury with the abhorréd shears
And slits the thin-spun life.   ' But not the praise '
Phoebus replied, and touch'd my trembling ears;
' Fame is no plant that grows on mortal soil,
Nor in the glistering foil
Set off to the world, nor in broad rumour lies:
But lives and spreads aloft by those pure eyes
And perfect witness of all-judging Jove;
As he pronounces lastly on each deed,
Of so much fame in heaven expect thy meed.'

O fountain Arethuse, and thou honour'd flood
Smooth-sliding Mincius, crown'd with vocal reeds,
That strain I heard was of a higher mood.
But now my oat proceeds,
And listens to the herald of the sea
That came in Neptune's plea;
He ask'd the waves, and ask'd the felon winds,
What hard mishap hath doom'd this gentle swain?
And question'd every gust of ruggéd wings
That blows from off each beakéd promontory:
They knew not of his story;
And sage Hippotadés their answer brings,
That not a blast was from his dungeon stray'd;
The air was calm, and on the level brine
Sleek Panopé with all her sisters play'd.
It was that fatal and perfidious bark
Built in the eclipse, and rigg'd with curses dark,
That sunk so low that sacred head of thine.

Next Camus, reverend sire, went footing slow,
His mantle hairy, and his bonnet sedge
Inwrought with figures dim, and on the edge
Like to that sanguine flower inscribed with woe:
' Ah! who hath reft,' quoth he, ' my dearest pledge!'
Last came, and last did go
The Pilot of the Galilean lake;
Two massy keys he bore of metals twain
(The golden opes, the iron shuts amain);
He shook his mitred locks, and stern bespake:
' How well could I have spared for thee, young swain,
Enow of such, as for their bellies' sake
Creep and intrude and climb into the fold!
Of other care they little reckoning make
Than how to scramble at the shearers' feast,
And shove away the worthy bidden guest.
Blind mouths! that scarce themselves know how to
      hold
A sheep-hook, or have learn'd aught else the least
That to the faithful herdman's art belongs!
What recks it them? What need they? They are
      sped;
And when they list, their lean and flashy songs

Grate on their scrannel pipes of wretched straw;
The hungry sheep look up, and are not fed,
But swoln with wind and the rank mist they draw
Rot inwardly, and foul contagion spread:
Besides what the grim wolf with privy paw
Daily devours apace, and nothing said:
—But that two-handed engine at the door
Stands ready to smite once, and smite no more.'

Return, Alphéus; the dread voice is past
That shrunk thy streams; return, Sicilian Muse,
And call the vales, and bid them hither cast
Their bells and flowerets of a thousand hues.
Ye valleys low, where the mild whispers use
Of shades, and wanton winds, and gushing brooks
On whose fresh lap the swart star sparely looks;
Throw hither all your quaint enamell'd eyes
That on the green turf suck the honey'd showers
And purple all the ground with vernal flowers.
Bring the rathe primrose that forsaken dies,
The tufted crow-toe, and pale jessamine,
The white pink, and the pansy freak'd with jet,
The glowing violet,
The musk-rose, and the well-attired woodbine,
With cowslips wan that hang the pensive head,
And every flower that sad embroidery wears:
Bid amarantus all his beauty shed,
And daffadillies fill their cups with tears
To strew the laureat hearse where Lycid lies.
For so to interpose a little ease,
Let our frail thoughts dally with false surmise:—
Ay me! whilst thee the shores and sounding seas
Wash far away,—where'er thy bones are hurl'd,
Whether beyond the stormy Hebrides
Where thou perhaps, under the whelming tide,
Visitest the bottom of the monstrous world;
Or whether thou, to our moist vows denied,
Sleep'st by the fable of Bellerus old,
Where the great Vision of the guarded mount
Looks toward Namancos and Bayona's hold,
—Look homeward, Angel, now, and melt with ruth.
—And, O ye dolphins, waft the hapless youth!

Weep no more, woeful shepherds, weep no more,
For Lycidas, your sorrow, is not dead,
Sunk though he be beneath the watery floor :
So sinks the day-star in the ocean bed,
And yet anon repairs his drooping head
And tricks his beams, and with new-spangled ore
Flames in the forehead of the morning sky :
So Lycidas sunk low, but mounted high
Through the dear might of Him that walk'd the
      waves;
Where, other groves and other streams along,
With nectar pure his oozy locks he laves,
And hears the unexpressive nuptial song
In the blest kingdoms meek of joy and love.
There entertain him all the Saints above
In solemn troops, and sweet societies,
That sing, and singing, in their glory move,
And wipe the tears for ever from his eyes.
Now, Lycidas, the shepherds weep no more;
Henceforth thou art the Genius of the shore
In thy large recompense, and shalt be good
To all that wander in that perilous flood.

Thus sang the uncouth swain to the oaks and rills,
While the still morn went out with sandals gray;
He touch'd the tender stops of various quills,
With eager thought warbling his Doric lay :
And now the sun had stretch'd out all the hills,
And now was dropt into the western bay :
At last he rose, and twitch'd his mantle blue :
To-morrow to fresh woods, and pastures new.

J. Milton

xc

ON THE TOMBS IN WESTMINSTER ABBEY

Mortality, behold and fear
What a change of flesh is here !
Think how many royal bones
Sleep within these heaps of stones;
Here they lie, had realms and lands,
Who now want strength to stir their hands.

Where from their pulpits seal'd with dust
They preach, ' In greatness is no trust.'
Here's an acre sown indeed
With the richest royallest seed
That the earth did e'er suck in
Since the first man died for sin :
Here the bones of birth have cried
' Though gods they were, as men they died ! '
Here are sands, ignoble things,
Dropt from the ruin'd sides of kings :
Here's a world of pomp and state
Buried in dust, once dead by fate.

F. Beaumont

XCI

THE LAST CONQUEROR

Victorious men of earth, no more
  Proclaim how wide your empires are ;
Though you bind-in every shore
  And your triumphs reach as far
    As night or day,
  Yet you, proud monarchs, must obey
And mingle with forgotten ashes, when
Death calls ye to the crowd of common men.

Devouring Famine, Plague, and War,
  Each able to undo mankind,
Death's servile emissaries are;
  Nor to these alone confined,
    He hath at will
  More quaint and subtle ways to kill;
A smile or kiss, as he will use the art,
Shall have the cunning skill to break a heart.

J. Shirley

XCII

DEATH THE LEVELLER

The glories of our blood and state
  Are shadows, not substantial things;
There is no armour against fate;
  Death lays his icy hand on kings :

Sceptre and Crown
    Must tumble down,
And in the dust be equal made
With the poor crooked scythe and spade.

Some men with swords may reap the field,
    And plant fresh laurels where they kill:
But their strong nerves at last must yield;
    They tame but one another still:
        Early or late
        They stoop to fate,
And must give up their murmuring breath
When they, pale captives, creep to death.

The garlands wither on your brow;
    Then boast no more your mighty deeds;
Upon Death's purple altar now
    See where the victor-victim bleeds:
        Your heads must come
        To the cold tomb;
Only the actions of the just
Smell sweet, and blossom in their dust.

                              J. Shirley

XCIII

WHEN THE ASSAULT WAS INTENDED TO THE CITY

Captain, or Colonel, or Knight in Arms,
Whose chance on these defenceless doors may seize,
If deed of honour did thee ever please,
Guard them, and him within protect from harms.

He can requite thee; for he knows the charms
That call fame on such gentle acts as these,
And he can spread thy name o'er lands and seas,
Whatever clime the sun's bright circle warms.

Lift not thy spear against the Muses' bower:
The great Emathian conqueror bid spare
The house of Pindarus, when temple and tower

Went to the ground : and the repeated air
Of sad Electra's poet had the power
To save the Athenian walls from ruin bare.

J. Milton

XCIV

ON HIS BLINDNESS

When I consider how my light is spent
Ere half my days, in this dark world and wide,
And that one talent which is death to hide
Lodged with me useless, though my soul more bent

To serve therewith my Maker, and present
My true account, lest He returning chide,—
Doth God exact day-labour, light denied ?
I fondly ask :—But Patience, to prevent

That murmur, soon replies ; God doth not need
Either man's work, or His own gifts : who best
Bear His mild yoke, they serve Him best : His state

Is kingly ; thousands at His bidding speed
And post o'er land and ocean without rest :—
They also serve who only stand and wait.

J. Milton

XCV

CHARACTER OF A HAPPY LIFE

How happy is he born and taught
That serveth not another's will ;
Whose armour is his honest thought
And simple truth his utmost skill !

Whose passions not his masters are,
Whose soul is still prepared for death,
Untied unto the world by care
Of public fame, or private breath ;

Who envies none that chance doth raise
Nor vice; Who never understood
How deepest wounds are given by praise;
Nor rules of state, but rules of good :

Who hath his life from rumours freed,
Whose conscience is his strong retreat;
Whose state can neither flatterers feed,
Nor ruin make oppressors great;

Who God doth late and early pray
More of His grace than gifts to lend;
And entertains the harmless day
With a religious book or friend;

—This man is freed from servile bands
Of hope to rise, or fear to fall;
Lord of himself, though not of lands;
And having nothing, yet hath all.

Sir H. Wotton

XCVI

THE NOBLE NATURE

It is not growing like a tree
    In bulk, doth make Man better be;
Or standing long an oak, three hundred year,
To fall a log at last, dry, bald, and sere :
        A lily of a day
        Is fairer far in May,
    Although it fall and die that night—
    It was the plant and flower of Light.
In small proportions we just beauties see;
And in short measures life may perfect be.

B. Jonson

XCVII

THE GIFTS OF GOD

When God at first made Man,
Having a glass of blessings standing by;
Let us (said He) pour on him all we can:
Let the world's riches, which dispersèd lie,
　　　Contract into a span.

So strength first made a way;
Then beauty flow'd, then wisdom, honour, pleasure:
When almost all was out, God made a stay,
Perceiving that alone, of all His treasure,
　　　Rest in the bottom lay.

For if I should (said He)
Bestow this jewel also on My creature,
He would adore My gifts instead of Me,
And rest in Nature, not the God of Nature,
　　　So both should losers be.

Yet let him keep the rest,
But keep them with repining restlessness:
Let him be rich and weary, that at least,
If goodness lead him not, yet weariness
　　　May toss him to My breast.

　　　　　　　　　　G. Herbert.

XCVIII

THE RETREAT

Happy those early days, when I
Shined in my Angel-infancy!
Before I understood this place
Appointed for my second race,
Or taught my soul to fancy aught
But a white, celestial thought;
When yet I had not walk'd above
A mile or two from my first Love,

And looking back, at that short space
Could see a glimpse of His bright face;
When on some gilded cloud or flower
My gazing soul would dwell an hour,
And in those weaker glories spy
Some shadows of eternity;
Before I taught my tongue to wound
My conscience with a sinful sound,
Or had the black art to dispense
A several sin to every sense,
But felt through all this fleshly dress
Bright shoots of everlastingness.

O how I long to travel back,
And tread again that ancient track!
That I might once more reach that plain
Where first I left my glorious train;
From whence th' enlighten'd spirit sees
That shady City of palm trees!
But ah! my soul with too much stay
Is drunk, and staggers in the way:—
Some men a forward motion love,
But I by backward steps would move;
And when this dust falls to the urn,
In that state I came, return.

H. Vaughan

XCIX

TO MR. LAWRENCE

Lawrence, of virtuous father virtuous son,
Now that the fields are dank and ways are mire,
Where shall we sometimes meet, and by the fire
Help waste a sullen day, what may be won

From the hard season gaining? Time will run
On smoother, till Favonius re-inspire
The frozen earth, and clothe in fresh attire
The lily and rose, that neither sow'd nor spun.

What neat repast shall feast us, light and choice,
Of Attic taste, with wine, whence we may rise
To hear the lute well touch'd, or artful voice

Warble immortal notes and Tuscan air?
He who of those delights can judge, and spare
To interpose them oft, is not unwise.

J. Milton

c

TO CYRIACK SKINNER

Cyriack, whose grandsire, on the royal bench
Of British Themis, with no mean applause
Pronounced, and in his volumes taught, our laws,
Which others at their bar so often wrench;

To-day deep thoughts resolve with me to drench
In mirth, that after no repenting draws;
Let Euclid rest, and Archimedes pause,
And what the Swede intend, and what the French.

To measure life learn thou betimes, and know
Toward solid good what leads the nearest way;
For other things mild Heaven a time ordains,

And disapproves that care, though wise in show,
That with superfluous burden loads the day,
And, when God sends a cheerful hour, refrains.

J. Milton

CI

A HYMN IN PRAISE OF NEPTUNE

Of Neptune's empire let us sing,
At whose command the waves obey;
To whom the rivers tribute pay,
Down the high mountains sliding;
To whom the scaly nation yields
Homage for the crystal fields
Wherein they dwell;

And every sea-god pays a gem
Yearly out of his watery cell,
To deck great Neptune's diadem.

The Tritons dancing in a ring,
Before his palace gates do make
The water with their echoes quake,
Like the great thunder sounding :
The sea-nymphs chaunt their accents shrill,
And the Syrens taught to kill
        With their sweet voice,
Make every echoing rock reply,
Unto their gentle murmuring noise,
The praise of Neptune's empery.

T. Campion

CII

HYMN TO DIANA

Queen and Huntress, chaste and fair,
    Now the sun is laid to sleep,
Seated in thy silver chair
    State in wonted manner keep :
        Hesperus entreats thy light,
        Goddess excellently bright.

Earth, let not thy envious shade
    Dare itself to interpose ;
Cynthia's shining orb was made
    Heaven to clear when day did close :
        Bless us then with wishéd sight,
        Goddess excellently bright.

Lay thy bow of pearl apart
    And thy crystal-shining quiver ;
Give unto the flying hart
Space to breathe, how short soever :
        Thou that mak'st a day of night,
        Goddess excellently bright !

B. Jonson

WISHES FOR THE SUPPOSED MISTRESS

Whoe'er she be,
That not impossible She
That shall command my heart and me;

Where'er she lie,
Lock'd up from mortal eye
In shady leaves of destiny:

Till that ripe birth
Of studied Fate stand forth,
And teach her fair steps tread our earth;

Till that divine
Idea take a shrine
Of crystal flesh, through which to shine:

—Meet you her, my Wishes,
Bespeak her to my blisses,
And be ye call'd, my absent kisses.

   I wish her beauty
That owes not all its duty
To gaudy tire, or glist'ring shoe-tie:

Something more than
Taffata or tissue can,
Or rampant feather, or rich fan.

A face that's best
By its own beauty drest,
And can alone commend the rest:

A face made up
Out of no other shop
Than what Nature's white hand sets ope.

Sidneian showers
Of sweet discourse, whose powers
Can crown old Winter's head with flowers.

Whate'er delight
Can make day's forehead bright
Or give down to the wings of night.

Soft silken hours,
Open suns, shady bowers;
'Bove all, nothing within that lowers.

Days, that need borrow
No part of their good morrow
From a fore-spent night of sorrow:

Days, that in spite
Of darkness, by the light
Of a clear mind are day all night.

Life, that dares send
A challenge to his end,
And when it comes, say, ' Welcome, friend.'

I wish her store
Of worth may leave her poor
Of wishes; and I wish——no more.

   Now, if Time knows
That Her, whose radiant brows
Weave them a garland of my vows;

Her that dares be
What these lines wish to see:
I seek no further, it is She.

'Tis She, and here
Lo! I unclothe and clear
My wishes' cloudy character.

Such worth as this is
Shall fix my flying wishes,
And determine them to kisses.

Let her full glory,
My fancies, fly before ye;
Be ye my fictions:—but her story.

                                   R. Crashaw

CIV

THE GREAT ADVENTURER

Over the mountains
And over the waves,
Under the fountains
And under the graves;
Under floods that are deepest,
Which Neptune obey;
Over rocks that are steepest
Love will find out the way.

Where there is no place
For the glow-worm to lie;
Where there is no space
For receipt of a fly;
Where the midge dares not venture
Lest herself fast she lay;
If love come, he will enter
And soon find out his way.

You may esteem him
A child for his might;
Or you may deem him
A coward from his flight;
But if she whom love doth honour
Be conceal'd from the day,
Set a thousand guards upon her,
Love will find out the way.

Some think to lose him
By having him confined;
And some do suppose him,
Poor thing, to be blind;
But if ne'er so close ye wall him,
Do the best that you may,
Blind love, if so ye call him,
Will find out his way.

You may train the eagle
To stoop to your fist;
Or you may inveigle
The phoenix of the east;
The lioness, ye may move her
To give o'er her prey;
But you'll ne'er stop a lover:
He will find out his way.

Anon.

THE PICTURE OF LITTLE T.C. IN A PROSPECT OF FLOWERS

See with what simplicity
This nymph begins her golden days!
In the green grass she loves to lie,
And there with her fair aspect tames
The wilder flowers, and gives them names;
But only with the roses plays,
And them does tell
What colours best become them, and what smell.

Who can foretell for what high cause
This darling of the Gods was born?
Yet this is she whose chaster laws
The wanton Love shall one day fear,
And, under her command severe,
See his bow broke, and ensigns torn.
Happy who can
Appease this virtuous enemy of man!

O then let me in time compound
And parley with those conquering eyes,
Ere they have tried their force to wound;
Ere with their glancing wheels they drive
In triumph over hearts that strive,
And them that yield but more despise:
Let me be laid,
Where I may see the glories from some shade.

Mean time, whilst every verdant thing
Itself does at thy beauty charm,
Reform the errors of the Spring;
Make that the tulips may have share
Of sweetness, seeing they are fair,
And roses of their thorns disarm;
           But most procure
That violets may a longer age endure.

But O young beauty of the woods,
Whom Nature courts with fruits and flowers,
Gather the flowers, but spare the buds;
Lest FLORA, angry at thy crime
To kill her infants in their prime,
Should quickly make th' example yours;
           And ere we see—
Nip in the blossom—all our hopes and thee.

A. Marvell

CVI

CHILD AND MAIDEN

Ah, Chloris! could I now but sit
    As unconcern'd as when
Your infant beauty could beget
    No happiness or pain!
When I the dawn used to admire,
    And praised the coming day,
I little thought the rising fire
    Would take my rest away.

Your charms in harmless childhood lay
    Like metals in the mine;
Age from no face takes more away
    Than youth conceal'd in thine.
But as your charms insensibly
    To their perfection prest,
So love as unperceived did fly,
    And center'd in my breast.

My passion with your beauty grew,
   While Cupid at my heart,
Still as his mother favour'd you,
   Threw a new flaming dart:
Each gloried in their wanton part ;
   To make a lover, he
Employ'd the utmost of his art—
   To make a beauty, she.

               Sir C. Sedley

CVII

CONSTANCY

I cannot change, as others do,
   Though you unjustly scorn,
Since that poor swain that sighs for you.
   For you alone was born;
No, Phyllis, no, your heart to move
   A surer way I'll try,—
And to revenge my slighted love,
   Will still love on, and die.

When, kill'd with grief, Amintas lies,
   And you to mind shall call
The sighs that now unpitied rise,
   The tears that vainly fall,
That welcome hour that ends his smart
   Will then begin your pain,
For such a faithful tender heart
   Can never break in vain.

       J. Wilmot, Earl of Rochester

CVIII

COUNSEL TO GIRLS

Gather ye rose-buds while ye may,
   Old Time is still a-flying :
And this same flower that smiles to-day
   To-morrow will be dying.

The glorious Lamp of Heaven, the Sun,
    The higher he's a-getting
The sooner will his race be run,
    And nearer he's to setting.

That age is best which is the first,
    When youth and blood are warmer;
But being spent, the worse, and worst
    Times, still succeed the former.

Then be not coy, but use your time;
    And while ye may, go marry:
For having lost but once your prime,
    You may for ever tarry.
                              R. Herrick

CIX

TO LUCASTA, ON GOING TO THE WARS

Tell me not, Sweet, I am unkind
    That from the nunnery
Of thy chaste breast and quiet mind,
    To war and arms I fly.

True, a new mistress now I chase,
    The first foe in the field;
And with a stronger faith embrace
    A sword, a horse, a shield.

Yet this inconstancy is such
    As you too shall adore;
I could not love thee, Dear, so much,
    Loved I not Honour more.
                          Colonel Lovelace

CX

ELIZABETH OF BOHEMIA

You meaner beauties of the night,
    That poorly satisfy our eyes
More by your number than your light,

You common people of the skies,
What are you, when the Moon shall rise?

You curious chanters of the wood
  That warble forth dame Nature's lays,
Thinking your passions understood
  By your weak accents; what's your praise
When Philomel her voice doth raise?

You violets that first appear,
  By your pure purple mantles known
Like the proud virgins of the year,
  As if the spring were all your own,—
What are you, when the Rose is blown?

So when my Mistress shall be seen
  In form and beauty of her mind,
By virtue first, then choice, a Queen,
  Tell me, if she were not design'd
Th' eclipse and glory of her kind?

                    Sir H. Wotton

CXI

TO THE LADY MARGARET LEY

Daughter to that good Earl, once President
Of England's Council and her Treasury,
Who lived in both, unstain'd with gold or fee,
And left them both, more in himself content,

Till the sad breaking of that Parliament
Broke him, as that dishonest victory
At Chaeroneia, fatal to liberty,
Kill'd with report that old man eloquent;—

Though later born than to have known the days
Wherein your father flourish'd, yet by you,
Madam, methinks I see him living yet;

So well your words his noble virtues praise,
That all both judge you to relate them true,
And to possess them, honour'd Margaret.

                    J. Milton

CXII

THE TRUE BEAUTY

He that loves a rosy cheek
  Or a coral lip admires,
Or from star-like eyes doth seek
  Fuel to maintain his fires;
As old Time makes these decay,
So his flames must waste away.

But a smooth and steadfast mind,
  Gentle thoughts, and calm desires,
Hearts with equal love combined,
  Kindle never-dying fires :—
Where these are not, I despise
Lovely cheeks or lips or eyes.

                              T. Carew

CXIII

TO DIANEME

Sweet, be not proud of those two eyes
Which starlike sparkle in their skies;
Nor be you proud, that you can see
All hearts your captives; yours yet free :
Be you not proud of that rich hair
Which wantons with the lovesick air;
Whenas that ruby which you wear,
Sunk from the tip of your soft ear,
Will last to be a precious stone
When all your world of beauty's gone.

                              R. Herrick

CXIV

Love in thy youth, fair Maid, be wise;
  Old Time will make thee colder,
And though each morning new arise
  Yet we each day grow older.

Thou as Heaven art fair and young,
    Thine eyes like twin stars shining;
But ere another day be sprung
    All these will be declining.
Then winter comes with all his fears,
    And all thy sweets shall borrow;
Too late then wilt thou shower thy tears,—
    And I too late shall sorrow!

Anon.

CXV

    Go, lovely Rose!
Tell her, that wastes her time and me,
    That now she knows,
When I resemble her to thee,
How sweet and fair she seems to be.

    Tell her that's young
And shuns to have her graces spied,
    That hadst thou sprung
In deserts, where no men abide,
Thou must have uncommended died.

    Small is the worth
Of beauty from the light retired:
    Bid her come forth,
Suffer herself to be desired,
And not blush so to be admired.

    Then die! that she
The common fate of all things rare
    May read in thee:
How small a part of time they share
That are so wondrous sweet and fair!

E. Waller

CXVI

TO CELIA

Drink to me only with thine eyes,
    And I will pledge with mine;
Or leave a kiss but in the cup
    And I'll not look for wine.
The thirst that from the soul doth rise
    Doth ask a drink divine;
But might I of Jove's nectar sup,
    I would not change for thine.

I sent thee late a rosy wreath,
    Not so much honouring thee
As giving it a hope that there
    It could not wither'd be;
But thou thereon didst only breathe
    And sent'st it back to me;
Since when it grows, and smells, I swear,
    Not of itself but thee!

                B. Jonson

CXVII

CHERRY-RIPE

There is a garden in her face
    Where roses and white lilies blow;
A heavenly paradise is that place,
    Wherein all pleasant fruits do grow;
There cherries grow that none may buy,
Till Cherry-Ripe themselves do cry.

Those cherries fairly do enclose
    Of orient pearl a double row,
Which when her lovely laughter shows,
    They look like rose-buds fill'd with snow:
Yet them no peer nor prince may buy,
Till Cherry-Ripe themselves do cry.

Her eyes like angels watch them still;
   Her brows like bended bows do stand,
Threat'ning with piercing frowns to kill
   All that approach with eye or hand
These sacred cherries to come nigh,
Till Cherry-Ripe themselves do cry!

Anon.

CXVIII

CORINNA'S MAYING

Get up, get up for shame! The blooming morn
Upon her wings presents the god unshorn.
   See how Aurora throws her fair
   Fresh-quilted colours through the air:
   Get up, sweet Slug-a-bed, and see
   The dew bespangling herb and tree.
Each flower has wept, and bow'd toward the east,
Above an hour since; yet you not drest,
   Nay! not so much as out of bed?
   When all the birds have matins said,
   And sung their thankful hymns: 'tis sin,
   Nay, profanation, to keep in,—
Whenas a thousand virgins on this day,
Spring, sooner than the lark, to fetch-in May.

Rise; and put on your foliage, and be seen
To come forth, like the Spring-time, fresh and green,
   And sweet as Flora. Take no care
   For jewels for your gown, or hair:
   Fear not; the leaves will strew
   Gems in abundance upon you:
Besides, the childhood of the day has kept,
Against you come, some orient pearls unwept:
   Come, and receive them while the light
   Hangs on the dew-locks of the night:
   And Titan on the eastern hill
   Retires himself, or else stands still
Till you come forth. Wash, dress, be brief in
   praying:
Few beads are best, when once we go a Maying.

Come, my Corinna, come; and coming, mark
How each field turns a street; each street a park
    Made green, and trimm'd with trees : see how
    Devotion gives each house a bough
    Or branch : Each porch, each door, ere this,
    An ark, a tabernacle is,
Made up of white-thorn neatly interwove;
As if here were those cooler shades of love.
    Can such delights be in the street,
    And open fields, and we not see't?
    Come, we'll abroad : and let's obey
    The proclamation made for May :
And sin no more, as we have done, by staying;
But, my Corinna, come, let's go a Maying.

There's not a budding boy, or girl, this day,
But is got up, and gone to bring in May.
    A deal of youth, ere this, is come
    Back, and with white-thorn laden home.
    Some have despatched their cakes and cream,
    Before that we have left to dream :
And some have wept, and woo'd, and plighted troth,
And chose their priest, ere we can cast off sloth :
    Many a green-gown has been given;
    Many a kiss, both odd and even :
    Many a glance too has been sent
    From out the eye, Love's firmament :
Many a jest told of the keys betraying
This night, and locks pick'd :—Yet we're not a
    Maying.

—Come, let us go, while we are in our prime;
And take the harmless folly of the time !
    We shall grow old apace, and die
    Before we know our liberty.
    Our life is short; and our days run
    As fast away as does the sun :—
And as a vapour, or a drop of rain
Once lost, can ne'er be found again :
    So when or you or I are made
    A fable, song, or fleeting shade;

All love, all liking, all delight
  Lies drown'd with us in endless night.
Then while time serves, and we are but decaying,
Come, my Corinna! come, let's go a Maying.

R. Herrick

CXIX

THE POETRY OF DRESS

I

A sweet disorder in the dress
Kindles in clothes a wantonness :—
A lawn about the shoulders thrown
Into a fine distractión,—
An erring lace, which here and there
Enthrals the crimson stomacher,—
A cuff neglectful, and thereby
Ribbands to flow confusedly,—
A winning wave, deserving note,
In the tempestuous petticoat,—
A careless shoe-string, in whose tie
I see a wild civility,—
Do more bewitch me, than when art
Is too precise in every part.

R. Herrick

CXX

2

Whenas in silks my Julia goes
Then, then (methinks) how sweetly flows
That liquefaction of her clothes.

Next, when I cast mine eyes and see
That brave vibration each way free;
O how that glittering taketh me !

R. Herrick

CXXI

3

My Love in her attire doth shew her wit,
　It doth so well become her :
For every season she hath dressings fit,
　For Winter, Spring, and Summer.
No beauty she doth miss
When all her robes are on :
But Beauty's self she is
When all her robes are gone.

Anon.

CXXII

ON A GIRDLE

That which her slender waist confined
Shall now my joyful temples bind :
No monarch but would give his crown
His arms might do what this has done.

It was my Heaven's extremest sphere,
The pale which held that lovely deer :
My joy, my grief, my hope, my love
Did all within this circle move.

A narrow compass ! and yet there
Dwelt all that's good, and all that's fair :
Give me but what this ribband bound,
Take all the rest the Sun goes round.

E. Waller

CXXIII

A MYSTICAL ECSTASY

E'en like two little bank-dividing brooks,
　　That wash the pebbles with their wanton
　streams,
And having ranged and search'd a thousand nooks,
　　Meet both at length in silver-breasted Thames,
　　Where in a greater current they conjoin :
So I my Best-Belovéd's am ; so He is mine.

E'en so we met; and after long pursuit,
    E'en so we join'd; we both became entire;
No need for either to renew a suit,
    For I was flax and he was flames of fire:
    Our firm-united souls did more than twine;
So I my Best-Belovéd's am; so He is mine.

If all those glittering Monarchs that command
    The servile quarters of this earthly ball,
Should tender, in exchange, their shares of land,
    I would not change my fortunes for them all:
    Their wealth is but a counter to my coin:
The world's but theirs; but my Belovéd's mine.

F. Quarles

CXXIV

TO ANTHEA WHO MAY COMMAND HIM ANY THING

Bid me to live, and I will live
    Thy Protestant to be:
Or bid me love, and I will give
    A loving heart to thee.

A heart as soft, a heart as kind,
    A heart as sound and free
As in the whole world thou canst find,
    That heart I'll give to thee.

Bid that heart stay, and it will stay,
    To honour thy decree:
Or bid it languish quite away,
    And 't shall do so for thee.

Bid me to weep, and I will weep
    While I have eyes to see:
And having none, yet I will keep
    A heart to weep for thee.

Bid me despair, and I'll despair,
    Under that cypress tree:
Or bid me die, and I will dare
    E'en Death, to die for thee.

Thou art my life, my love, my heart,
　The very eyes of me,
And hast command of every part,
　To live and die for thee.

R. Herrick

CXXV

Love not me for comely grace,
For my pleasing eye or face,
Nor for any outward part,
No, nor for my constant heart,—
　For those may fail, or turn to ill,
　So thou and I shall sever :
Keep therefore a true woman's eye,
And love me still, but know not why—
　So hast thou the same reason still
　　To doat upon me ever !

Anon.

CXXVI

Not, Celia, that I juster am
　Or better than the rest;
For I would change each hour, like them,
　Were not my heart at rest.

But I am tied to very thee
　By every thought I have;
Thy face I only care to see,
　Thy heart I only crave.

All that in woman is adored
　In thy dear self I find—
For the whole sex can but afford
　The handsome and the kind.

Why then should I seek further store,
　And still make love anew ?
When change itself can give no more,
　'Tis easy to be true.

Sir C. Sedley

CXXVII

TO ALTHEA FROM PRISON

When Love with unconfinéd wings
    Hovers within my gates,
And my divine Althea brings
    To whisper at the grates;
When I lie tangled in her hair
    And fetter'd to her eye,
The Gods that wanton in the air
    Know no such liberty.

When flowing cups run swiftly round
    With no allaying Thames,
Our careless heads with roses bound,
    Our hearts with loyal flames;
When thirsty grief in wine we steep,
    When healths and draughts go free—
Fishes that tipple in the deep
    Know no such liberty.

When, (like committed linnets), I
    With shriller throat shall sing
The sweetness, mercy, majesty
    And glories of my King;
When I shall voice aloud how good
    He is, how great should be,
Enlargéd winds, that curl the flood,
    Know no such liberty.

Stone walls do not a prison make,
    Nor iron bars a cage;
Minds innocent and quiet take
    That for an hermitage;
If I have freedom in my love
    And in my soul am free,
Angels alone, that soar above,
    Enjoy such liberty.

                              Colonel Lovelace

CXXVIII

TO LUCASTA, GOING BEYOND THE SEAS

If to be absent were to be
    Away from thee;
  Or that when I am gone
  You or I were alone;
Then, my Lucasta, might I crave
Pity from blustering wind, or swallowing wave.

But I'll not sigh one blast or gale
    To swell my sail,
  Or pay a tear to 'suage
  The foaming blue-god's rage;
For whether he will let me pass
Or no, I'm still as happy as I was.

Though seas and land betwixt us both,
    Our faith and troth,
  Like separated souls,
  All time and space controls :
Above the highest sphere we meet
Unseen, unknown, and greet as Angels greet.

So then we do anticipate
    Our after-fate,
  And are alive i' the skies,
  If thus our lips and eyes
Can speak like spirits unconfined
In Heaven, their earthy bodies left behind.

Colonel Lovelace

CXXIX

ENCOURAGEMENTS TO A LOVER

Why so pale and wan, fond lover ?
    Prythee, why so pale ?
Will, if looking well can't move her,
    Looking ill prevail ?
    Prythee, why so pale ?

Why so dull and mute, young sinner?
    Prythee, why so mute?
Will, when speaking well can't win her,
    Saying nothing do't?
    Prythee, why so mute?

Quit, quit, for shame! this will not move,
    This cannot take her;
If of herself she will not love,
    Nothing can make her:
    The D—l take her!

              Sir J. Suckling

CXXX

A SUPPLICATION

Awake, awake, my Lyre!
And tell thy silent master's humble tale
    In sounds that may prevail;
Sounds that gentle thoughts inspire:
    Though so exalted she
    And I so lowly be
Tell her, such different notes make all thy harmony.

Hark, how the strings awake!
And, though the moving hand approach not near,
    Themselves with awful fear
  A kind of numerous trembling make.
    Now all thy forces try;
    Now all thy charms apply;
Revenge upon her ear the conquests of her eye.

Weak Lyre! thy virtue sure
Is useless here, since thou art only found
    To cure, but not to wound,
  And she to wound, but not to cure.
    Too weak too wilt thou prove
    My passion to remove;
Physic to other ills, thou'rt nourishment to Love.

Sleep, sleep again, my Lyre !
For thou canst never tell my humble tale
   In sounds that will prevail,
  Nor gentle thoughts in her inspire;
    All thy vain mirth lay by,
   Bid thy strings silent lie,
Sleep, sleep again, my Lyre, and let thy master die.

                  A. Cowley

CXXXI

THE MANLY HEART

  Shall I, wasting in despair,
  Die because a woman's fair ?
  Or make pale my cheeks with care
  'Cause another's rosy are ?
  Be she fairer than the day
  Or the flowery meads in May—
     If she think not well of me
     What care I how fair she be ?

  Shall my silly heart be pined
  'Cause I see a woman kind;
  Or a well disposéd nature
  Joinéd with a lovely feature ?
  Be she meeker, kinder, than
  Turtle-dove or pelican,
     If she be not so to me
     What care I how kind she be ?

  Shall a woman's virtues move
  Me to perish for her love ?
  Or her well-deservings known
  Make me quite forget mine own ?
  Be she with that goodness blest
  Which may merit name of Best;
     If she be not such to me,
     What care I how good she be ?

'Cause her fortune seems too high,
Shall I play the fool and die?
She that bears a noble mind
If not outward helps she find,
Thinks what with them he would do
Who without them dares her woo;
    And unless that mind I see,
    What care I how great she be?

Great or good, or kind or fair,
I will ne'er the more despair;
If she love me, this believe,
I will die ere she shall grieve;
If she slight me when I woo,
I can scorn and let her go;
    For if she be not for me,
    What care I for whom she be?

G. Wither

CXXXII

MELANCHOLY

Hence, all you vain delights,
As short as are the nights
Wherein you spend your folly:
There's nought in this life sweet
If man were wise to see't,
But only melancholy,
O sweetest Melancholy!
Welcome, folded arms, and fixéd eyes,
A sigh that piercing mortifies,
A look that's fasten'd to the ground,
A tongue chain'd up without a sound!
Fountain-heads and pathless groves,
Places which pale passion loves!
Moonlight walks, when all the fowls
Are warmly housed save bats and owls!
A midnight bell, a parting groan!
These are the sounds we feed upon;
Then stretch our bones in a still gloomy valley;
Nothing's so dainty sweet as lovely melancholy.

J. Fletcher

CXXXIII

FORSAKEN

O waly waly up the bank,
  And waly waly down the brae,
And waly waly yon burn-side
  Where I and my Love wont to gae!
I leant my back unto an aik,
  I thought it was a trusty tree;
But first it bow'd, and syne it brak,
  Sae my true Love did lichtly me.

O waly waly, but love be bonny
  A little time while it is new;
But when 'tis auld, it waxeth cauld
  And fades awa' like morning dew.
O wherefore should I busk my head?
  Or wherefore should I kame my hair?
For my true Love has me forsook,
  And says he'll never loe me mair.

Now Arthur-seat sall be my bed;
  The sheets shall ne'er be prest by me:
Saint Anton's well sall be my drink,
  Since my true Love has forsaken me.
Marti'mas wind, when wilt thou blaw
  And shake the green leaves aff the tree?
O gentle Death, when wilt thou come?
  For of my life I am wearíe.

'Tis not the frost, that freezes fell,
  Nor blawing snaw's inclemencie;
'Tis not sic cauld that makes me cry,
  But my Love's heart grown cauld to me.
When we came in by Glasgow town
  We were a comely sight to see;
My Love was clad in the black velvét,
  And I mysell in cramasie.

But had I wist, before I kist,
   That love had been sae ill to win;
I had lockt my heart in a case of gowd
   And pinn'd it with a siller pin.
And, O! if my young babe were born,
   And set upon the nurse's knee,
And I myself were dead and gane,
   And the green grass growing over me!

                      Anon.

CXXXIV

Upon my lap my sovereign sits
And sucks upon my breast;
Meantime his love maintains my life
And gives my sense her rest.
    Sing lullaby, my little boy,
    Sing lullaby, mine only joy!

When thou hast taken thy repast,
Repose, my babe, on me;
So may thy mother and thy nurse
Thy cradle also be.
    Sing lullaby, my little boy,
    Sing lullaby, mine only joy!

I grieve that duty doth not work
All that my wishing would,
Because I would not be to thee
But in the best I should.
    Sing lullaby, my little boy,
    Sing lullaby, mine only joy!

Yet as I am, and as I may,
I must and will be thine,
Though all too little for thy self
Vouchsafing to be mine.
    Sing lullaby, my little boy,
    Sing lullaby, mine only joy!

                      Anon.

CXXXV

FAIR HELEN

I wish I were where Helen lies;
Night and day on me she cries;
O that I were where Helen lies
    On fair Kirconnell lea !

Curst be the heart that thought the thought,
And curst the hand that fired the shot,
When in my arms burd Helen dropt,
    And died to succour me !

O think na but my heart was sair
When my Love dropt down and spak nae mair !
I laid her down wi' meikle care
    On fair Kirconnell lea.

As I went down the water-side,
None but my foe to be my guide,
None but my foe to be my guide,
    On fair Kirconnell lea ;

I lighted down my sword to draw,
I hackéd him in pieces sma',
I hackéd him in pieces sma',
    For her sake that died for me.

O Helen fair, beyond compare !
I'll make a garland of thy hair
Shall bind my heart for evermair
    Until the day I die.

O that I were where Helen lies !
Night and day on me she cries;
Out of my bed she bids me rise,
    Says, ' Haste and come to me ! '

O Helen fair ! O Helen chaste !
If I were with thee, I were blest,
Where thou lies low and takes thy rest
    On fair Kirconnell lea.

I wish my grave were growing green,
A winding-sheet drawn ower my een,
And I in Helen's arms lying,
    On fair Kirconnell lea.

I wish I were where Helen lies;
Night and day on me she cries;
And I am weary of the skies,
    Since my Love died for me.

Anon.

CXXXVI

THE TWA CORBIES

As I was walking all alane
I heard twa corbies making a mane;
The tane unto the t'other say,
' Where sall we gang and dine to-day?

' —In behint yon auld fail dyke,
I wot there lies a new-slain Knight;
And naebody kens that he lies there,
But his hawk, his hound, and lady fair.

' His hound is to the hunting gane,
His hawk to fetch the wild-fowl hame,
His lady's ta'en another mate,
So we may mak our dinner sweet.

' Ye'll sit on his white hause-bane,
And I'll pick out his bonnie blue een;
Wi' ae lock o' his gowden hair
We'll theek our nest when it grows bare.

' Mony a one for him makes mane,
But nane sall ken where he is gane;
O'er his white banes, when they are bare,
The wind sall blaw for evermair.'

Anon.

CXXXVII

ON THE DEATH OF MR. WILLIAM HERVEY

It was a dismal and a fearful night,—
Scarce could the Morn drive on th' unwilling light,
When sleep, death's image, left my troubled breast,
      By something liker death possest.
My eyes with tears did uncommanded flow,
      And on my soul hung the dull weight
      Of some intolerable fate.
What bell was that?   Ah me!   Too much I know!

My sweet companion, and my gentle peer,
Why hast thou left me thus unkindly here,
Thy end for ever, and my life, to moan?
      O thou hast left me all alone!
Thy soul and body, when death's agony
      Besieged around thy noble heart,
      Did not with more reluctance part
Than I, my dearest friend, do part from thee.

Ye fields of Cambridge, our dear Cambridge, say,
Have ye not seen us walking every day?
Was there a tree about which did not know
      The love betwixt us two?
Henceforth, ye gentle trees, for ever fade,
      Or your sad branches thicker join,
      And into darksome shades combine,
Dark as the grave wherein my friend is laid.

Large was his soul; as large a soul as e'er
Submitted to inform a body here;
High as the place 'twas shortly in Heaven to have,
      But low and humble as his grave;
So high that all the virtues there did come
      As to the chiefest seat
      Conspicuous, and great;
So low that for me too it made a room.

Knowledge he only sought, and so soon caught,
As if for him knowledge had rather sought;
Nor did more learning ever crowded lie
    In such a short mortality.
Whene'er the skilful youth discoursed or writ,
    Still did the notions throng
      About his eloquent tongue;
Nor could his ink flow faster than his wit.

His mirth was the pure spirits of various wit,
Yet never did his God or friends forget.
And when deep talk and wisdom came in view,
    Retired, and gave to them their due.
For the rich help of books he always took,
    Though his own searching mind before
      Was so with notions written o'er,
As if wise Nature had made that her book.

With as much zeal, devotion, piety,
He always lived, as other saints do die.
Still with his soul severe account he kept,
    Weeping all debts out ere he slept.
Then down in peace and innocence he lay,
    Like the sun's laborious light,
      Which still in water sets at night,
Unsullied with his journey of the day.

A. Cowley

CXXXVIII

FRIENDS IN PARADISE

They are all gone into the world of light !
    And I alone sit lingering here;
Their very memory is fair and bright,
    And my sad thoughts doth clear :—

It glows and glitters in my cloudy breast,
    Like stars upon some gloomy grove,
Or those faint beams in which this hill is drest,
    After the sun's remove.

I see them walking in an air of glory,
    Whose light doth trample on my days :
My days, which are at best but dull and hoary,
    Mere glimmering and decays.

O holy Hope ! and high Humility,
    High as the heavens above !
These are your walks, and you have shew'd them
    me,
    To kindle my cold love.

Dear, beauteous Death ! the jewel of the just,
    Shining no where, but in the dark ;
What mysteries do lie beyond thy dust,
    Could man outlook that mark !

He that hath found some fledged bird's nest, may
    know
    At first sight, if the bird be flown ;
But what fair well or grove he sings in now,
    That is to him unknown.

And yet, as Angels in some brighter dreams
    Call to the soul, when man doth sleep ;
So some strange thoughts transcend our wonted
    themes,
    And into glory peep.
                    H. Vaughan

CXXXIX

TO BLOSSOMS

    Fair pledges of a fruitful tree,
        Why do ye fall so fast ?
        Your date is not so past,
    But you may stay yet here awhile
        To blush and gently smile,
        And go at last.

What, were ye born to be
    An hour or half's delight,
    And so to bid good-night?
'Twas pity Nature brought ye forth
    Merely to show your worth,
      And lose you quite.

But you are lovely leaves, where we
    May read how soon things have
    Their end, though ne'er so brave :
And after they have shown their pride
    Like you, awhile, they glide
      Into the grave.
                R. Herrick

CXL

TO DAFFODILS

Fair Daffodils, we weep to see
    You haste away so soon :
As yet the early-rising Sun
    Has not attain'd his noon.
      Stay, stay,
    Until the hasting day
      Has run
    But to the even-song;
And, having pray'd together, we
    Will go with you along.

We have short time to stay, as you,
    We have as short a Spring;
As quick a growth to meet decay
    As you, or any thing.
      We die,
    As your hours do, and dry
      Away
    Like to the Summer's rain;
Or as the pearls of morning's dew
    Ne'er to be found again.
                R. Herrick

CXLI

THE GIRL DESCRIBES HER FAWN

With sweetest milk and sugar first
I it at my own fingers nursed;
And as it grew, so every day
It wax'd more white and sweet than they—
It had so sweet a breath! and oft
I blush'd to see its foot more soft
And white,—shall I say,—than my hand?
Nay, any lady's of the land!

It is a wondrous thing how fleet
'Twas on those little silver feet:
With what a pretty skipping grace
It oft would challenge me the race :—
And when 't had left me far away
'Twould stay, and run again, and stay:
For it was nimbler much than hinds,
And trod as if on the four winds.

I have a garden of my own,
But so with roses overgrown
And lilies, that you would it guess
To be a little wilderness:
And all the spring-time of the year
It only lovéd to be there.
Among the beds of lilies I
Have sought it oft, where it should lie;
Yet could not, till itself would rise,
Find it, although before mine eyes :—
For in the flaxen lilies' shade
It like a bank of lilies laid.

Upon the roses it would feed
Until its lips e'en seem'd to bleed :
And then to me 'twould boldly trip,
And print those roses on my lip.
But all its chief delight was still
On roses thus itself to fill,
And its pure virgin limbs to fold
In whitest sheets of lilies cold :—
Had it lived long, it would have been
Lilies without—roses within.

A. Marvell

CXLII

THOUGHTS IN A GARDEN

How vainly men themselves amaze
To win the palm, the oak, or bays,
And their uncessant labours see
Crown'd from some single herb or tree,
Whose short and narrow-vergéd shade
Does prudently their toils upbraid;
While all the flowers and trees do close
To weave the garlands of Repose.

Fair Quiet, have I found thee here,
And Innocence thy sister dear !
Mistaken long, I sought you then
In busy companies of men :
Your sacred plants, if here below,
Only among the plants will grow :
Society is all but rude
To this delicious solitude.

No white nor red was ever seen
So amorous as this lovely green.
Fond lovers, cruel as their flame,
Cut in these trees their mistress' name :
Little, alas, they know or heed
How far these beauties hers exceed !
Fair trees ! wheres'e'er your barks I wound,
No name shall but your own be found.

When we have run our passions' heat
Love hither makes his best retreat:
The gods, who mortal beauty chase,
Still in a tree did end their race;
Apollo hunted Daphne so
Only that she might laurel grow;
And Pan did after Syrinx speed
Not as a nymph, but for a reed.

What wondrous life is this I lead!
Ripe apples drop about my head;
The luscious clusters of the vine
Upon my mouth do crush their wine;
The nectarine and curious peach
Into my hands themselves do reach;
Stumbling on melons, as I pass,
Ensnared with flowers, I fall on grass.

Meanwhile the mind from pleasure less
Withdraws into its happiness;
The mind, that ocean where each kind
Does straight its own resemblance find:
Yet it creates, transcending these,
Far other worlds, and other seas;
Annihilating all that's made
To a green thought in a green shade.

Here at the fountain's sliding foot
Or at some fruit-tree's mossy root,
Casting the body's vest aside
My soul into the boughs does glide;
There, like a bird, it sits and sings,
Then whets and claps its silver wings,
And, till prepared for longer flight,
Waves in its plumes the various light.

Such was that happy Garden-state
While man there walk'd without a mate:
After a place so pure and sweet,
What other help could yet be meet!
But 'twas beyond a mortal's share
To wander solitary there:

Two paradises 'twere in one,
To live in Paradise alone.

How well the skilful gardener drew
Of flowers and herbs this dial new !
Where, from above, the milder sun
Does through a fragrant zodiac run :
And, as it works, th' industrious bee
Computes its time as well as we.
How could such sweet and wholesome hours
Be reckon'd, but with herbs and flowers !

A. Marvell

CXLIII

FORTUNATI NIMIUM

Jack and Joan, they think no ill,
But loving live, and merry still;
Do their week-day's work, and pray
Devoutly on the holy-day :
Skip and trip it on the green,
And help to choose the Summer Queen;
Lash out at a country feast
Their silver penny with the best.

Well can they judge of nappy ale,
And tell at large a winter tale;
Climb up to the apple loft,
And turn the crabs till they be soft.
Tib is all the father's joy,
And little Tom the mother's boy :—
All their pleasure is, Content,
And care, to pay their yearly rent.

Joan can call by name her cows
And deck her windows with green boughs;
She can wreaths and tutties make,
And trim with plums a bridal cake.
Jack knows what brings gain or loss,
And his long flail can stoutly toss :
Makes the hedge which others break,
And ever thinks what he doth speak.

—Now, you courtly dames and knights,
That study only strange delights,
Though you scorn the homespun gray,
And revel in your rich array;
Though your tongues dissemble deep
And can your heads from danger keep;
Yet, for all your pomp and train,
Securer lives the silly swain !

T. Campion

CXLIV

L'ALLEGRO

Hence, loathéd Melancholy,
  Of Cerberus and blackest Midnight born
In Stygian cave forlorn
  'Mongst horrid shapes, and shrieks, and sights
    unholy !
Find out some uncouth cell
  Where brooding Darkness spreads his jealous wings
And the night-raven sings;
  There under ebon shades, and low-brow'd rocks
As ragged as thy locks,
  In dark Cimmerian desert ever dwell.

    But come, thou Goddess fair and free,
  In heaven yclept Euphrosyne,
  And by men, heart-easing Mirth,
  Whom lovely Venus at a birth
  With two sister Graces more
  To ivy-crownéd Bacchus bore;
  Or whether (as some sager sing)
  The frolic wind that breathes the spring
  Zephyr, with Aurora playing,
  As he met her once a-Maying—
  There on beds of violets blue
  And fresh-blown roses wash'd in dew
  Fill'd her with thee, a daughter fair,
  So buxom, blithe, and debonair.

Haste thee, Nymph, and bring with thee
Jest, and youthful jollity,
Quips, and cranks, and wanton wiles,
Nods, and becks, and wreathèd smiles
Such as hang on Hebe's cheek,
And love to live in dimple sleek;
Sport that wrinkled Care derides,
And Laughter holding both his sides :—
Come, and trip it as you go
On the light fantastic toe;
And in thy right hand lead with thee
The mountain-nymph, sweet Liberty;
And if I give thee honour due
Mirth, admit me of thy crew,
To live with her, and live with thee
In unreprovèd pleasures free;
To hear the lark begin his flight
And singing startle the dull night
From his watch-tower in the skies,
Till the dappled dawn doth rise;
Then to come, in spite of sorrow,
And at my window bid good-morrow
Through the sweetbriar, or the vine,
Or the twisted eglantine:
While the cock with lively din
Scatters the rear of darkness thin,
And to the stack, or the barn-door,
Stoutly struts his dames before:
Oft listening how the hounds and horn
Cheerly rouse the slumbering morn,
From the side of some hoar hill,
Through the high wood echoing shrill:
Sometime walking, not unseen,
By hedge-row elms, on hillocks green,
Right against the eastern gate
Where the great Sun begins his state
Robed in flames and amber light,
The clouds in thousand liveries dight;
While the ploughman, near at hand,
Whistles o'er the furrow'd land,
And the milkmaid singeth blithe,
And the mower whets his scythe,

And every shepherd tells his tale
Under the hawthorn in the dale.
   Straight mine eye hath caught new pleasures
Whilst the landscape round it measures;
Russet lawns, and fallows gray,
Where the nibbling flocks do stray;
Mountains, on whose barren breast
The labouring clouds do often rest;
Meadows trim with daisies pied,
Shallow brooks, and rivers wide;
Towers and battlements it sees
Bosom'd high in tufted trees,
Where perhaps some Beauty lies,
The Cynosure of neighbouring eyes.
   Hard by, a cottage chimney smokes
From betwixt two aged oaks,
Where Corydon and Thyrsis, met,
Are at their savoury dinner set
Of herbs, and other country messes
Which the neat-handed Phillis dresses;
And then in haste her bower she leaves
With Thestylis to bind the sheaves;
Or, if the earlier season lead,
To the tann'd haycock in the mead.
   Sometimes with secure delight
The upland hamlets will invite,
When the merry bells ring round,
And the jocund rebecks sound
To many a youth and many a maid,
Dancing in the chequer'd shade;
And young and old come forth to play
On a sun-shine holyday,
Till the live-long day-light fail:
Then to the spicy nut-brown ale,
With stories told of many a feat,
How Faery Mab the junkets eat :—
She was pinch'd, and pull'd, she said;
And he, by Friar's lantern led;
Tells how the drudging Goblin sweat
To earn his cream-bowl duly set,
When in one night, ere glimpse of morn,
His shadowy flail hath thresh'd the corn

That ten day-labourers could not end;
Then lies him down the lubber fiend,
And, stretch'd out all the chimney's length,
Basks at the fire his hairy strength;
And crop-full out of doors he flings,
Ere the first cock his matin rings.
  Thus done the tales, to bed they creep,
By whispering winds soon lull'd asleep.
  Tower'd cities please us then
And the busy hum of men,
Where throngs of knights and barons bold,
In weeds of peace, high triumphs hold,
With store of ladies, whose bright eyes
Rain influence, and judge the prize
Of wit or arms, while both contend
To win her grace, whom all commend.
There let Hymen oft appear
In saffron robe, with taper clear,
And pomp, and feast, and revelry,
With mask, and antique pageantry;
Such sights as youthful poets dream
On summer eves by haunted stream.
Then to the well-trod stage anon,
If Jonson's learned sock be on,
Or sweetest Shakespeare, Fancy's child,
Warble his native wood-notes wild.
  And ever against eating cares
Lap me in soft Lydian airs
Married to immortal verse,
Such as the meeting soul may pierce
In notes, with many a winding bout
Of linkéd sweetness long drawn out,
With wanton heed and giddy cunning,
The melting voice through mazes running,
Untwisting all the chains that tie
The hidden soul of harmony;
That Orpheus' self may heave his head
From golden slumber, on a bed
Of heap'd Elysian flowers, and hear
Such strains as would have won the ear
Of Pluto, to have quite set free
His half-regain'd Eurydice.

These delights if thou canst give,
Mirth, with thee I mean to live.

J. Milton

CXLV

IL PENSEROSO

Hence, vain deluding Joys,
  The brood of Folly without father bred !
How little you bestead
  Or fill the fixéd mind with all your toys !
Dwell in some idle brain,
  And fancies fond with gaudy shapes possess
As thick and numberless
  As the gay motes that people the sunbeams,
Or likest hovering dreams,
  The fickle pensioners of Morpheus' train.

    But hail, thou goddess sage and holy,
Hail, divinest Melancholy !
Whose saintly visage is too bright
To hit the sense of human sight,
And therefore to our weaker view
O'erlaid with black, staid Wisdom's hue;
Black, but such as in esteem
Prince Memnon's sister might beseem,
Or that starr'd Ethiop queen that strove
To set her beauty's praise above
The sea-nymphs, and their powers offended :
Yet thou art higher far descended :
Thee bright-hair'd Vesta, long of yore,
To solitary Saturn bore;
His daughter she; in Saturn's reign
Such mixture was not held a stain :
Oft in glimmering bowers and glades
He met her, and in secret shades
Of woody Ida's inmost grove,
While yet there was no fear of Jove.

Come, pensive Nun, devout and pure,
Sober, steadfast, and demure,
All in a robe of darkest grain
Flowing with majestic train,
And sable stole of Cipres lawn
Over thy decent shoulders drawn :
Come, but keep thy wonted state,
With even step, and musing gait,
And looks commercing with the skies,
Thy rapt soul sitting in thine eyes :
There, held in holy passion still,
Forget thyself to marble, till
With a sad leaden downward cast
Thou fix them on the earth as fast :
And join with thee calm Peace, and Quiet,
Spare Fast, that oft with gods doth diet,
And hears the Muses in a ring
Aye round about Jove's altar sing :
And add to these retired Leisure
That in trim gardens takes his pleasure :—
But first and chiefest, with thee bring
Him that yon soars on golden wing
Guiding the fiery-wheeléd throne,
The cherub Contemplatión ;
And the mute Silence hist along,
'Less Philomel will deign a song
In her sweetest saddest plight
Smoothing the rugged brow of Night,
While Cynthia checks her dragon yoke
Gently o'er the accustom'd oak.
—Sweet bird, that shunn'st the noise of folly,
Most musical, most melancholy !
Thee, chauntress, oft, the woods among
I woo, to hear thy even-song ;
And missing thee, I walk unseen
On the dry smooth-shaven green,
To behold the wandering Moon
Riding near her highest noon,
Like one that had been led astray
Through the heaven's wide pathless way,
And oft, as if her head she bow'd,
Stooping through a fleecy cloud.

Oft, on a plat of rising ground
I hear the far-off Curfeu sound
Over some wide-water'd shore,
Swinging slow with sullen roar:
Or, if the air will not permit,
Some still removéd place will fit,
Where glowing embers through the room
Teach light to counterfeit a gloom;
Far from all resort of mirth,
Save the cricket on the hearth,
Or the bellman's drowsy charm
To bless the doors from nightly harm.
  Or let my lamp at midnight hour
Be seen in some high lonely tower,
Where I may oft out-watch the Bear
With thrice-great Hermes, or unsphere
The spirit of Plato, to unfold
What worlds or what vast regions hold
The immortal mind, that hath forsook
Her mansion in this fleshly nook:
And of those demons that are found
In fire, air, flood, or under ground,
Whose power hath a true consent
With planet, or with element.
Sometime let gorgeous Tragedy
In scepter'd pall come sweeping by,
Presenting Thebes, or Pelops' line,
Or the tale of Troy divine;
Or what (though rare) of later age
Ennobled hath the buskin'd stage.
  But, O sad Virgin, that thy power
Might raise Musaeus from his bower,
Or bid the soul of Orpheus sing
Such notes as, warbled to the string,
Drew iron tears down Pluto's cheek
And made Hell grant what Love did seek!
Or call up him that left half-told
The story of Cambuscan bold,
Of Camball, and of Algarsife,
And who had Canacé to wife
That own'd the virtuous ring and glass;
And of the wondrous horse of brass

On which the Tartar king did ride :
And if aught else great bards beside
In sage and solemn tunes have sung
Of turneys, and of trophies hung,
Of forests, and enchantments drear,
Where more is meant than meets the ear.
   Thus, Night, oft see me in thy pale career,
Till civil-suited Morn appear,
Not trick'd and frounced as she was wont
With the Attic Boy to hunt,
But kercheft in a comely cloud
While rocking winds are piping loud,
Or usher'd with a shower still,
When the gust hath blown his fill,
Ending on the rustling leaves
With minute drops from off the eaves.
And when the sun begins to fling
His flaring beams, me, goddess, bring
To archéd walks of twilight groves,
And shadows brown, that Sylvan loves,
Of pine, or monumental oak,
Where the rude axe, with heavéd stroke,
Was never heard the nymphs to daunt
Or fright them from their hallow'd haunt.
There in close covert by some brook
Where no profaner eye may look,
Hide me from day's garish eye,
While the bee with honey'd thigh
That at her flowery work doth sing,
And the waters murmuring,
With such consort as they keep
Entice the dewy-feather'd Sleep ;
And let some strange mysterious dream
Wave at his wings in airy stream
Of lively portraiture display'd,
Softly on my eyelids laid :
And, as I wake, sweet music breathe
Above, about, or underneath,
Sent by some Spirit to mortals good,
Or the unseen Genius of the wood.
   But let my due feet never fail
To walk the studious cloister's pale,

And love the high-embowéd roof,
With antique pillars massy proof,
And storied windows richly dight
Casting a dim religious light.
There let the pealing organ blow
To the full-voiced quire below
In service high and anthems clear,
As may with sweetness, through mine ear,
Dissolve me into ecstasies,
And bring all Heaven before mine eyes.
　And may at last my weary age
Find out the peaceful hermitage,
The hairy gown and mossy cell
Where I may sit and rightly spell
Of every star that heaven doth shew,
And every herb that sips the dew;
Till old experience do attain
To something like prophetic strain.

These pleasures, Melancholy, give,
And I with thee will choose to live.

J. Milton

CXLVI

SONG OF THE EMIGRANTS IN BERMUDA

Where the remote Bermudas ride
In the ocean's bosom unespied,
From a small boat that row'd along
The listening winds received this song.
　' What should we do but sing His praise
That led us through the watery maze
Where He the huge sea-monsters wracks,
That lift the deep upon their backs,
Unto an isle so long unknown,
And yet far kinder than our own?
He lands us on a grassy stage,
Safe from the storms, and prelate's rage;
He gave us this eternal Spring
Which here enamels everything,

And sends the fowls to us in care
On daily visits through the air.
He hangs in shades the orange bright
Like golden lamps in a green night,
And does in the pomegranates close
Jewels more rich than Ormus shows :
He makes the figs our mouths to meet
And throws the melons at our feet;
But apples plants of such a price,
No tree could ever bear them twice.
With cedars chosen by His hand
From Lebanon He stores the land;
And makes the hollow seas that roar
Proclaim the ambergris on shore.
He cast (of which we rather boast)
The Gospel's pearl upon our coast;
And in these rocks for us did frame
A temple where to sound His name.
Oh ! let our voice His praise exalt
Till it arrive at Heaven's vault,
Which thence (perhaps) rebounding may
Echo beyond the Mexique bay ! '
—Thus sung they in the English boat
A holy and a cheerful note :
And all the way, to guide their chime,
With falling oars they kept the time.

A. Marvell

CXLVII

AT A SOLEMN MUSIC

Blest pair of Sirens, pledges of Heaven's joy,
Sphere-born harmonious Sisters, Voice and Verse !
Wed your divine sounds, and mixt power employ,
Dead things with inbreathed sense able to pierce;
And to our high-raised phantasy present
That undisturbéd Song of pure concent
Aye sung before the sapphire-colour'd throne
    To Him that sits thereon,

With saintly shout and solemn jubilee;
Where the bright Seraphim in burning row
Their loud uplifted angel-trumpets blow;
And the Cherubic host in thousand quires
Touch their immortal harps of golden wires,
With those just Spirits that wear victorious palms,
        Hymns devout and holy psalms
        Singing everlastingly:
That we on Earth, with undiscording voice
May rightly answer that melodious noise;
As once we did, till disproportion'd sin
Jarr'd against nature's chime, and with harsh din
Broke the fair music that all creatures made
To their great Lord, whose love their motion sway'd
In perfect diapason, whilst they stood
In first obedience, and their state of good.
O may we soon again renew that Song,
And keep in tune with Heaven, till God ere long
To His celestial consort us unite,
To live with Him, and sing in endless morn of light !

J. Milton

CXLVIII

NOX NOCTI INDICAT SCIENTIAM

When I survey the bright
        Celestial sphere :
So rich with jewels hung, that night
Doth like an Ethiop bride appear;

My soul her wings doth spread,
        And heaven-ward flies,
The Almighty's mysteries to read
In the large volumes of the skies.

For the bright firmament
        Shoots forth no flame
So silent, but is eloquent
In speaking the Creator's name.

No unregarded star
    Contracts its light
Into so small a character,
Removed far from our human sight,

    But if we steadfast look,
      We shall discern
In it as in some holy book,
How man may heavenly knowledge learn.

    It tells the Conqueror,
      That far-stretch'd power
Which his proud dangers traffic for,
Is but the triumph of an hour.

    That from the farthest North
      Some nation may
Yet undiscover'd issue forth,
And o'er his new-got conquest sway.

    Some nation yet shut in
      With hills of ice,
May be let out to scourge his sin,
Till they shall equal him in vice.

    And then they likewise shall
      Their ruin have;
For as yourselves your Empires fall,
And every Kingdom hath a grave.

    Thus those celestial fires,
      Though seeming mute,
The fallacy of our desires
And all the pride of life, confute.

    For they have watch'd since first
      The World had birth :
And found sin in itself accursed,
And nothing permanent on earth.

                        W. Habington

CXLIX

HYMN TO DARKNESS

Hail thou most sacred venerable thing!
    What Muse is worthy thee to sing?
Thee, from whose pregnant universal womb
All things, ev'n Light, thy rival, first did come.
What dares he not attempt that sings of thee,
    Thou first and greatest mystery?
Who can the secrets of thy essence tell?
Thou, like the light of God, art inaccessible.

Before great Love this monument did raise,
    This ample theatre of praise;
Before the folding circles of the sky
Were tuned by Him, Who is all harmony;
Before the morning Stars their hymn began,
    Before the council held for man,
Before the birth of either time or place,
Thou reign'st unquestion'd monarch in the empty
      space.

Thy native lot thou didst to Light resign,
    But still half of the globe is thine.
Here with a quiet, but yet awful hand,
Like the best emperors thou dost command.
To thee the stars above their brightness owe,
    And mortals their repose below:
To thy protection fear and sorrow flee,
And those that weary are of light, find rest in thee.

                J. Norris of Bemerton

CL

A VISION

I saw Eternity the other night,
Like a great ring of pure and endless light,
    All calm, as it was bright :—
And round beneath it, Time, in hours, days, years,
    Driven by the spheres,
Like a vast shadow moved; in which the World
    And all her train were hurl'd.

H. Vaughan

CLI

ALEXANDER'S FEAST, OR, THE POWER OF MUSIC

'Twas at the royal feast for Persia won
  By Philip's warlike son—
  Aloft in awful state
  The godlike hero sate
  On his imperial throne;
  His valiant peers were placed around,
  Their brows with roses and with myrtles bound,
  (So should desert in arms be crown'd);
  The lovely Thais by his side
  Sate like a blooming Eastern bride
  In flower of youth and beauty's pride :—
  Happy, happy, happy pair !
  None but the brave
  None but the brave
  None but the brave deserves the fair !

  Timotheus placed on high
Amid the tuneful quire
With flying fingers touch'd the lyre :
The trembling notes ascend the sky
And heavenly joys inspire.
The song began from Jove
Who left his blissful seats above—

Such is the power of mighty love !
A dragon's fiery form belied the god ;
Sublime on radiant spires he rode
When he to fair Olympia prest,
And while he sought her snowy breast,
Then round her slender waist he curl'd,
And stamp'd an image of himself, a sovereign of the
    world.
—The listening crowd admire the lofty sound ;
A present deity ! they shout around :
A present deity ! the vaulted roofs rebound :
With ravish'd ears
The monarch hears,
Assumes the god ;
Affects to nod
And seems to shake the spheres.

    The praise of Bacchus then the sweet musician
        sung,
Of Bacchus ever fair and ever young :
The jolly god in triumph comes ;
Sound the trumpets, beat the drums !
Flush'd with a purple grace
He shows his honest face :
Now give the hautboys breath ; he comes, he comes !
Bacchus, ever fair and young,
Drinking joys did first ordain ;
Bacchus' blessings are a treasure,
Drinking is the soldier's pleasure :
Rich the treasure,
Sweet the pleasure,
Sweet is pleasure after pain.

    Soothed with the sound, the king grew vain ;
Fought all his battles o'er again,
And thrice he routed all his foes, and thrice he slew
    the slain !
The master saw the madness rise,
His glowing cheeks, his ardent eyes ;
And while he Heaven and Earth defied
Changed his hand and check'd his pride.
He chose a mournful Muse
Soft pity to infuse :

He sung Darius great and good,
By too severe a fate
Fallen, fallen, fallen, fallen,
Fallen from his high estate,
And weltering in his blood;
Deserted at his utmost need
By those his former bounty fed;
On the bare earth exposed he lies
With not a friend to close his eyes.
—With downcast looks the joyless victor sate,
Revolving in his alter'd soul
The various turns of Chance below;
And now and then a sigh he stole,
And tears began to flow.

The mighty master smiled to see
That love was in the next degree;
'Twas but a kindred-sound to move,
For pity melts the mind to love.
Softly sweet, in Lydian measures
Soon he soothed his soul to pleasures.
War, he sung, is toil and trouble,
Honour but an empty bubble;
Never ending, still beginning,
Fighting still, and still destroying;
If the world be worth thy winning,
Think, O think, it worth enjoying:
Lovely Thais sits beside thee,
Take the good the gods provide thee!
—The many rend the skies with loud applause;
So Love was crown'd, but Music won the cause.
The prince, unable to conceal his pain,
Gazed on the fair
Who caused his care,
And sigh'd and look'd, sigh d and look'd,
Sigh'd and look'd, and sigh'd again:
At length with love and wine at once opprest
The vanquish'd victor sunk upon her breast.

Now strike the golden lyre again:
A louder yet, and yet a louder strain!
Break his bands of sleep asunder
And rouse him like a rattling peal of thunder.

Hark, hark ! the horrid sound
Has raised up his head :
As awaked from the dead
And amazed he stares around.
Revenge, revenge, Timotheus cries,
See the Furies arise !
See the snakes that they rear
How they hiss in their hair,
And the sparkles that flash from their eyes !
Behold a ghastly band,
Each a torch in his hand !
Those are Grecian ghosts, that in battle were slain
And unburied remain
Inglorious on the plain :
Give the vengeance due
To the valiant crew !
Behold how they toss their torches on high,
How they point to the Persian abodes
And glittering temples of their hostile gods.
—The princes applaud with a furious joy :
And the King seized a flambeau with zeal to
        destroy ;
Thais led the way
To light him to his prey,
And like another Helen, fired another Troy !

    —Thus, long ago,
Ere heaving bellows learn'd to blow,
While organs yet were mute,
Timotheus, to his breathing flute
And sounding lyre
Could swell the soul to rage, or kindle soft desire.
At last divine Cecilia came,
Inventress of the vocal frame ;
The sweet enthusiast from her sacred store
Enlarged the former narrow bounds,
And added length to solemn sounds,
With Nature's mother-wit, and arts unknown before
—Let old Timotheus yield the prize
Or both divide the crown ;
He raised a mortal to the skies ;
She drew an angel down !

                                J. Dryden

The Golden Treasury

Book Third

ODE ON THE PLEASURE ARISING FROM VICISSITUDE

Now the golden Morn aloft
  Waves her dew-bespangled wing,
With vermeil cheek and whisper soft
  She woos the tardy Spring :
Till April starts, and calls around
The sleeping fragrance from the ground,
And lightly o'er the living scene
Scatters his freshest, tenderest green.

New-born flocks, in rustic dance,
  Frisking ply their feeble feet;
Forgetful of their wintry trance
  The birds his presence greet :
But chief, the sky-lark warbles high
His trembling thrilling ecstasy;
And lessening from the dazzled sight,
Melts into air and liquid light.

Yesterday the sullen year
  Saw the snowy whirlwind fly;
Mute was the music of the air,
  The herd stood drooping by :
Their raptures now that wildly flow
No yesterday nor morrow know;
'Tis Man alone that joy descries
With forward and reverted eyes.

Smiles on past misfortune's brow
   Soft reflection's hand can trace,
And o'er the cheek of sorrow throw
   A melancholy grace;
While hope prolongs our happier hour,
Or deepest shades, that dimly lour
And blacken round our weary way,
Gilds with a gleam of distant day.

Still, where rosy pleasure leads,
   See a kindred grief pursue;
Behind the steps that misery treads
   Approaching comfort view:
The hues of bliss more brightly glow
Chastised by sabler tints of woe,
And blended form, with artful strife
The strength and harmony of life.

See the wretch that long has tost
   On the thorny bed of pain,
At length repair his vigour lost
   And breathe and walk again:
The meanest floweret of the vale,
The simplest note that swells the gale,
The common sun, the air, the skies,
To him are opening Paradise.

            T. Gray

CLIII

ODE TO SIMPLICITY

O Thou, by Nature taught
   To breathe her genuine thought
In numbers warmly pure, and sweetly strong;
   Who first, on mountains wild,
   In Fancy, loveliest child,
Thy babe, or Pleasure's, nursed the powers of song!

   Thou, who with hermit heart,
   Disdain'st the wealth of art,
And gauds, and pageant weeds, and trailing pall,
   But com'st, a decent maid
   In Attic robe array'd,
O chaste, unboastful Nymph, to thee I call!

By all the honey'd store
On Hybla's thymy shore,
By all her blooms and mingled murmurs dear;
By her whose love-lorn woe
In evening musings slow
Soothed sweetly sad Electra's poet's ear:

By old Cephisus deep,
Who spread his wavy sweep
In warbled wanderings round thy green retreat;
On whose enamell'd side,
When holy Freedom died,
No equal haunt allured thy future feet:—

O sister meek of Truth,
To my admiring youth
Thy sober aid and native charms infuse!
The flowers that sweetest breathe,
Though Beauty cull'd the wreath,
Still ask thy hand to range their order'd hues.

While Rome could none esteem
But Virtue's patriot theme,
You loved her hills, and led her laureat band;
But stay'd to sing alone
To one distinguish'd throne;
And turn'd thy face, and fled her alter'd land.

No more, in hall or bower,
The Passions own thy power;
Love, only Love, her forceless numbers mean:
For thou hast left her shrine;
Nor olive more, nor vine,
Shall gain thy feet to bless the servile scene.

Though taste, though genius, bless
To some divine excess,
Faints the cold work till thou inspire the whole;
What each, what all supply
May court, may charm our eye;
Thou, only thou, canst raise the meeting soul!

Of these let others ask
To aid some mighty task;

I only seek to find thy temperate vale;
    Where oft my reed might sound
    To maids and shepherds round,
And all thy sons, O Nature ! learn my tale.
W. Collins

CLIV

SOLITUDE

Happy the man, whose wish and care
A few paternal acres bound,
Content to breathe his native air
    In his own ground.

Whose herds with milk, whose fields with bread,
Whose flocks supply him with attire;
Whose trees in summer yield him shade,
    In winter fire.

Blest, who can unconcern'dly find
Hours, days, and years, slide soft away
In health of body, peace of mind,
    Quiet by day,

Sound sleep by night; study and ease
Together mixt, sweet recreation,
And innocence, which most does please
    With meditation.

Thus let me live, unseen, unknown;
Thus unlamented let me die;
Steal from the world, and not a stone
    Tell where I lie.

A. Pope

CLV

THE BLIND BOY

O say what is that thing call'd Light,
    Which I must ne'er enjoy;
What are the blessings of the sight,
    O tell your poor blind boy !

You talk of wondrous things you see,
    You say the sun shines bright;
I feel him warm, but how can he
    Or make it day or night?

My day or night myself I make
    Whene'er I sleep or play;
And could I ever keep awake
    With me 'twere always day.

With heavy sighs I often hear
    You mourn my hapless woe;
But sure with patience I can bear
    A loss I ne'er can know.

Then let not what I cannot have
    My cheer of mind destroy:
Whilst thus I sing, I am a king,
    Although a poor blind boy.

            C. Cibber

CLVI

ON A FAVOURITE CAT, DROWNED IN A TUB OF GOLD FISHES

'Twas on a lofty vase's side,
Where China's gayest art had dyed
    The azure flowers that blow,
Demurest of the tabby kind
The pensive Selima, reclined,
    Gazed on the lake below.

Her conscious tail her joy declared:
The fair round face, the snowy beard,
    The velvet of her paws,
Her coat that with the tortoise vies,
Her ears of jet, and emerald eyes—
    She saw, and purr'd applause.

Still had she gazed, but 'midst the tide
Two angel forms were seen to glide,

The Genii of the stream :
Their scaly armour's Tyrian hue
Through richest purple, to the view
Betray'd a golden gleam.

The hapless Nymph with wonder saw :
A whisker first, and then a claw
With many an ardent wish
She stretch'd, in vain, to reach the prize—
What female heart can gold despise ?
What Cat's averse to fish ?

Presumptuous maid ! with looks intent
Again she stretch'd, again she bent,
Nor knew the gulf between—
Malignant Fate sat by and smiled—
The slippery verge her feet beguiled ;
She tumbled headlong in !

Eight times emerging from the flood
She mew'd to every watery God
Some speedy aid to send :—
No Dolphin came, no Nereid stirr'd,
Nor cruel Tom nor Susan heard—
A favourite has no friend !

From hence, ye Beauties ! undeceived
Know one false step is ne'er retrieved,
And be with caution bold :
Not all that tempts your wandering eyes
And heedless hearts, is lawful prize,
Nor all that glisters, gold !

                                   T. Gray

CLVII

TO CHARLOTTE PULTENEY

Timely blossom, Infant fair,
Fondling of a happy pair,
Every morn and every night
Their solicitous delight,
Sleeping, waking, still at ease,

Pleasing, without skill to please ;
Little gossip, blithe and hale,
Tattling many a broken tale,
Singing many a tuneless song,
Lavish of a heedless tongue ;
Simple maiden, void of art,
Babbling out the very heart,
Yet abandon'd to thy will,
Yet imagining no ill,
Yet too innocent to blush ;
Like the linnet in the bush
To the mother-linnet's note
Moduling her slender throat ;
Chirping forth thy petty joys,
Wanton in the change of toys,
Like the linnet green, in May
Flitting to each bloomy spray ;
Wearied then and glad of rest,
Like the linnet in the nest :—
This thy present happy lot
This, in time will be forgot :
Other pleasures, other cares,
Ever-busy Time prepares ;
And thou shalt in thy daughter see.
This picture, once, resembled thee.

A. Philips

CLVIII

RULE BRITANNIA

When Britain first at Heaven's command
   Arose from out the azure main,
This was the charter of her land,
   And guardian angels sung the strain :
Rule, Britannia ! Britannia rule the waves !
   Britons never shall be slaves.

The nations not so blest as thee
   Must in their turn to tyrants fall,
Whilst thou shalt flourish great and free
   The dread and envy of them all.

Still more majestic shalt thou rise,
  More dreadful from each foreign stroke;
As the loud blast that tears the skies
  Serves but to root thy native oak.

Thee haughty tyrants ne'er shall tame;
  All their attempts to bend thee down
Will but arouse thy generous flame,
  And work their woe and thy renown.

To thee belongs the rural reign;
  Thy cities shall with commerce shine;
All thine shall be the subject main,
  And every shore it circles thine!

The Muses, still with Freedom found,
  Shall to thy happy coast repair;
Blest Isle, with matchless beauty crown'd
  And manly hearts to guard the fair:—
Rule, Britannia! Britannia rule the waves!
  Britons never shall be slaves!

J. Thomson

CLIX

THE BARD

Pindaric Ode

' Ruin seize thee, ruthless King!
  Confusion on thy banners wait;
Tho' fann'd by Conquest's crimson wing
  They mock the air with idle state.
Helm, nor hauberk's twisted mail,
Nor e'en thy virtues, Tyrant, shall avail
To save thy secret soul from nightly fears,
From Cambria's curse, from Cambria's tears!'
—Such were the sounds that o'er the crested pride
  Of the first Edward scatter'd wild dismay,
As down the steep of Snowdon's shaggy side
  He wound with toilsome march his long array:—
Stout Glo'ster stood aghast in speechless trance;

' To arms ! ' cried Mortimer, and couch'd his quiver-
       ing lance.

  On a rock, whose haughty brow
Frowns o'er old Conway's foaming flood,
  Robed in the sable garb of woe
With haggard eyes the Poet stood;
(Loose his beard and hoary hair
Stream'd like a meteor to the troubled air)
And with a master's hand and prophet's fire
Struck the deep sorrows of his lyre :
  ' Hark, how each giant-oak and desert-cave
Sighs to the torrent's awful voice beneath !
O'er thee, oh King ! their hundred arms they wave,
  Revenge on thee in hoarser murmurs breathe;
Vocal no more, since Cambria's fatal day,
To high-born Hoel's harp, or soft Llewellyn's lay.

  ' Cold is Cadwallo's tongue,
  That hush'd the stormy main :
Brave Urien sleeps upon his craggy bed :
  Mountains, ye mourn in vain
  Modred, whose magic song
Made huge Plinlimmon bow his cloud-topt head.
  On dreary Arvon's shore they lie
Smear'd with gore and ghastly pale :
Far, far aloof the affrighted ravens sail;
  The famish'd eagle screams, and passes by.
Dear lost companions of my tuneful art,
  Dear as the light that visits these sad eyes,
Dear as the ruddy drops that warm my heart,
  Ye died amidst your dying country's cries—
No more I weep; They do not sleep;
  On yonder cliffs, a griesly band,
I see them sit; They linger yet,
  Avengers of their native land :
With me in dreadful harmony they join,
And weave with bloody hands the tissue of thy line.

  Weave the warp and weave the woof
    The winding sheet of Edward's race :
Give ample room and verge enough
    The characters of hell to trace.

Mark the year, and mark the night,
When Severn shall re-echo with affright
The shrieks of death thro' Berkley's roof that ring,
Shrieks of an agonizing king!
  She-wolf of France, with unrelenting fangs
That tear'st the bowels of thy mangled mate,
  From thee be born, who o'er thy country hangs
The scourge of heaven! What terrors round him
    wait!
Amazement in his van, with flight combined,
And sorrow's faded form, and solitude behind.

' *Mighty victor, mighty lord,*
  Low on his funeral couch he lies!
No pitying heart, no eye, afford
  A tear to grace his obsequies.
Is the sable warrior fled?
Thy son is gone. He rests among the dead.
The swarm that in thy noon-tide beam were born?
—Gone to salute the rising morn.
Fair laughs the Morn, and soft the zephyr blows,
  While proudly riding o'er the azure realm
In gallant trim the gilded vessel goes:
  Youth on the prow, and Pleasure at the helm:
Regardless of the sweeping whirlwind's sway,
That hush'd in grim repose expects his evening prey.

  ' *Fill high the sparkling bowl,*
The rich repast prepare;
  Reft of a crown, he yet may share the feast:
Close by the regal chair
    Fell Thirst and Famine scowl
  A baleful smile upon their baffled guest,
Heard ye the din of battle bray,
  Lance to lance, and horse to horse?
  Long years of havock urge their destined course,
And thro' the kindred squadrons mow their way.
Ye towers of Julius, London's lasting shame,
With many a foul and midnight murder fed,
  Revere his consort's faith, his father's fame,
And spare the meek usurper's holy head!
Above, below, the rose of snow,

Twined with her blushing foe, we spread :
The bristled boar in infant-gore
   Wallows beneath the thorny shade.
Now, brothers, bending o'er the accursèd loom,
Stamp we our vengeance deep, and ratify his doom.

' *Edward, lo ! to sudden fate*
   (*Weave we the woof ; The thread is spun ;*)
Half of thy heart we consecrate.
   (*The web is wove ; The work is done.*)
—Stay, oh stay ! nor thus forlorn
Leave me unbless'd, unpitied, here to mourn :
In yon bright track that fires the western skies
They melt, they vanish from my eyes.
But oh ! what solemn scenes on Snowdon's height
   Descending slow their glittering skirts unroll ?
Visions of glory, spare my aching sight,
Ye unborn ages, crowd not on my soul !
No more our long-lost Arthur we bewail :—
All hail, ye genuine kings ! Britannia's issue, hail !

   ' Girt with many a baron bold
Sublime their starry fronts they rear;
   And gorgeous dames, and statesmen old
In bearded majesty, appear.
In the midst a form divine !
Her eye proclaims her of the Briton-line :
Her lion-port, her awe-commanding face
Attemper'd sweet to virgin-grace.
What strings symphonious tremble in the air,
   What strains of vocal transport round her play ?
Hear from the grave, great Taliessin, hear;
   They breathe a soul to animate thy clay.
Bright Rapture calls, and soaring as she sings,
Waves in the eye of heaven her many-colour'd wings.

' The verse adorn again
   Fierce war, and faithful love,
And truth severe, by fairy fiction drest.
   In buskin'd measures move
Pale grief, and pleasing pain,
With horror, tyrant of the throbbing breast.
A voice as of the cherub-choir

Gales from blooming Eden bear,
  And distant warblings lessen on my ear
That lost in long futurity expire.
Fond impious man, think'st thou yon sanguine cloud
  Raised by thy breath, has quench'd the orb of day?
To-morrow he repairs the golden flood
  And warms the nations with redoubled ray.
Enough for me: with joy I see
  The different doom our fates assign:
Be thine despair and sceptred care,
  To triumph and to die are mine.
—He spoke, and headlong from the mountain's
        height
Deep in the roaring tide he plunged to endless night.

T. Gray

CLX

ODE WRITTEN IN 1746

How sleep the brave, who sink to rest
By all their country's wishes blest!
When Spring, with dewy fingers cold,
Returns to deck their hallow'd mould,
She there shall dress a sweeter sod
Than Fancy's feet have ever trod.

By fairy hands their knell is rung,
By forms unseen their dirge is sung:
There Honour comes, a pilgrim gray,
To bless the turf that wraps their clay;
And Freedom shall awhile repair
To dwell a weeping hermit there!

W. Collins

CLXI

LAMENT FOR CULLODEN

The lovely lass o' Inverness,
Nae joy nor pleasure can she see;
For e'en and morn she cries, Alas!
And aye the saut tear blins her ee:
Drumossie moor—Drumossie day—

A waefu' day it was to me !
For there I lost my father dear,
My father dear, and brethren three.

Their winding-sheet the bluidy clay,
Their graves are growing green to see;
And by them lies the dearest lad
That ever blest a woman's ee !
Now wae to thee, thou cruel lord,
A bluidy man I trow thou be;
For mony a heart thou hast made sair
That ne'er did wrang to thine or thee.

R. Burns

CLXII

LAMENT FOR FLODDEN

I've heard them lilting at our ewe-milking,
    Lasses a' lilting before dawn o' day;
But now they are moaning on ilka green loaning—
    The Flowers of the Forest are a' wede away.

At bughts, in the morning, nae blythe lads are
        scorning,
    Lasses are lonely and dowie and wae;
Nae daffin', nae gabbin', but sighing and sabbing,
    Ilk ane lifts her leglin and hies her away.

In har'st, at the shearing, nae youths now are jeering,
    Bandsters are lyart, and runkled, and gray;
At fair or at preaching, nae wooing, nae fleeching—
    The Flowers of the Forest are a' wede away.

At e'en, in the gloaming, nae younkers are roaming
    'Bout stacks wi' the lasses at bogle to play;
But ilk ane sits drearie, lamenting her dearie—
    The Flowers of the Forest are weded away.

Dool and wae for the order, sent our lads to the
        Border !
    The English, for ance, by guile wan the day;
The Flowers of the Forest, that fought aye the
        foremost,
    The prime of our land, are cauld in the clay.

We'll hear nae mair lilting at the ewe-milking;
  Women and bairns are heartless and wae;
Sighing and moaning on ilka green loaning—
  The Flowers of the Forest are a' wede away.

J. Elliott

CLXIII

THE BRAES OF YARROW

Thy braes were bonny, Yarrow stream,
When first on them I met my lover;
Thy braes how dreary, Yarrow stream,
When now thy waves his body cover!
For ever now, O Yarrow stream!
Thou art to me a stream of sorrow;
For never on thy banks shall I
Behold my Love, the flower of Yarrow!

He promised me a milk-white steed
To bear me to his father's bowers;
He promised me a little page
To squire me to his father's towers;
He promised me a wedding-ring,—
The wedding-day was fix'd to-morrow;—
Now he is wedded to his grave,
Alas, his watery grave, in Yarrow!

Sweet were his words when last we met;
My passion I as freely told him;
Clasp'd in his arms, I little thought
That I should never more behold him!
Scarce was he gone, I saw his ghost;
It vanish'd with a shriek of sorrow;
Thrice did the water-wraith ascend,
And gave a doleful groan thro' Yarrow.

His mother from the window look'd
With all the longing of a mother;
His little sister weeping walk'd
The green-wood path to meet her brother;
They sought him east, they sought him west,
They sought him all the forest thorough;
They only saw the cloud of night,
They only heard the roar of Yarrow.

No longer from thy window look—
Thou hast no son, thou tender mother!
No longer walk, thou lovely maid;
Alas, thou hast no more a brother!
No longer seek him east or west
And search no more the forest thorough;
For, wandering in the night so dark,
He fell a lifeless corpse in Yarrow.

The tear shall never leave my cheek,
No other youth shall be my marrow—
I'll seek thy body in the stream,
And then with thee I'll sleep in Yarrow.
—The tear did never leave her cheek,
No other youth became her marrow;
She found his body in the stream,
And now with him she sleeps in Yarrow.

J. Logan

CLXIV

WILLY DROWNED IN YARROW

Down in yon garden sweet and gay
  Where bonnie grows the lily,
I heard a fair maid sighing say,
  ' My wish be wi' sweet Willie!

' Willie's rare, and Willie's fair,
  And Willie's wondrous bonny;
And Willie hecht to marry me
  Gin e'er he married ony.

' O gentle wind, that bloweth south,
  From where my Love repaireth,
Convey a kiss frae his dear mouth
  And tell me how he fareth!

' O tell sweet Willie to come doun
  And hear the mavis singing,
And see the birds on ilka bush
  And leaves around them hinging.

' The lav'rock there, wi' her white breast
    And gentle throat sae narrow;
There's sport eneuch for gentlemen
    On Leader haughs and Yarrow.

' O Leader haughs are wide and braid
    And Yarrow haughs are bonny;
There Willie hecht to marry me
    If e'er he married ony.

' But Willie's gone, whom I thought on,
    And does not hear me weeping;
Draws many a tear frae true love's e'e
    When other maids are sleeping.

' Yestreen I made my bed fu' braid,
    The night I'll mak' it narrow,
For a' the live-lang winter night
    I lie twined o' my marrow.

' O came ye by yon water-side?
    Pou'd you the rose or lily?
Or came you by yon meadow green,
    Or saw you my sweet Willie? '

She sought him up, she sought him down,
    She sought him braid and narrow;
Syne, in the cleaving of a craig,
    She found him drown'd in Yarrow!

Anon.

CLXV

LOSS OF THE ROYAL GEORGE

Toll for the Brave!
The brave that are no more!
All sunk beneath the wave
Fast by their native shore!

Eight hundred of the brave
Whose courage well was tried,
Had made the vessel heel
And laid her on her side.

A land-breeze shook the shrouds
And she was overset;
Down went the Royal George,
With all her crew complete.

Toll for the brave!
Brave Kempenfelt is gone;
His last sea-fight is fought,
His work of glory done.

It was not in the battle;
No tempest gave the shock;
She sprang no fatal leak,
She ran upon no rock.

His sword was in its sheath,
His fingers held the pen,
When Kempenfelt went down
With twice four hundred men.

—Weigh the vessel up
Once dreaded by our foes!
And mingle with our cup
The tears that England owes.

Her timbers yet are sound,
And she may float again
Full charged with England's thunder,
And plough the distant main:

But Kempenfelt is gone,
His victories are o'er;
And he and his eight hundred
Shall plough the wave no more.

W. Cowper

CLXVI

BLACK-EYED SUSAN

All in the Downs the fleet was moor'd,
  The streamers waving in the wind,
When black-eyed Susan came aboard;
  ' O! where shall I my true-love find?
Tell me, ye jovial sailors, tell me true
If my sweet William sails among the crew.

William, who high upon the yard
  Rock'd with the billow to and fro,
Soon as her well-known voice he heard
  He sigh'd, and cast his eyes below :
The cord slides swiftly through his glowing hands,
And quick as lightning on the deck he stands.

So the sweet lark, high poised in air,
  Shuts close his pinions to his breast
If chance his mate's shrill call he hear,
  And drops at once into her nest :—
The noblest captain in the British fleet
Might envy William's lip those kisses sweet.

' O Susan, Susan, lovely dear,
  My vows shall ever true remain ;
Let me kiss off that falling tear;
  We only part to meet again.
Change as ye list, ye winds; my heart shall be
The faithful compass that still points to thee.

' Believe not what the landmen say
  Who tempt with doubts thy constant mind :
They'll tell thee, sailors, when away,
  In every port a mistress find :
Yes, yes, believe them when they tell thee so,
For Thou art present wheresoe'er I go.

' If to fair India's coast we sail,
  Thy eyes are seen in diamonds bright,
Thy breath is Afric's spicy gale,
  Thy skin is ivory so white.
Thus every beauteous object that I view
Wakes in my soul some charm of lovely Sue.

' Though battle call me from thy arms
  Let not my pretty Susan mourn;
Though cannons roar, yet safe from harms
  William shall to his Dear return.
Love turns aside the balls that round me fly,
Lest precious tears should drop from Susan's eye.

The boatswain gave the dreadful word,
  The sails their swelling bosom spread,
No longer must she stay aboard;

They kiss'd, she sigh'd, he hung his head.
Her lessening boat unwilling rows to land;
  'Adieu!' she cries; and waved her lily hand.

J. Gay

CLXVII

SALLY IN OUR ALLEY

Of all the girls that are so smart
  There's none like pretty Sally;
She is the darling of my heart,
  And she lives in our alley.
There is no lady in the land
  Is half so sweet as Sally;
She is the darling of my heart,
  And she lives in our alley.

Her father he makes cabbage-nets
  And through the streets does cry 'em;
Her mother she sells laces long
  To such as please to buy 'em:
But sure such folks could ne'er beget
  So sweet a girl as Sally!
She is the darling of my heart,
  And she lives in our alley.

When she is by, I leave my work,
  I love her so sincerely;
My master comes like any Turk,
  And bangs me most severely—
But let him bang his bellyful,
  I'll bear it all for Sally;
She is the darling of my heart,
  And she lives in our alley.

Of all the days that's in the week
  I dearly love but one day—
And that's the day that comes betwixt
  A Saturday and Monday;
For then I'm drest all in my best
  To walk abroad with Sally;
She is the darling of my heart,
  And she lives in our alley.

My master carries me to church,
  And often am I blamed
Because I leave him in the lurch
  As soon as text is named;
I leave the church in sermon-time
  And slink away to Sally;
She is the darling of my heart,
  And she lives in our alley.

When Christmas comes about again
  O then I shall have money;
I'll hoard it up, and box it all,
  I'll give it to my honey;
I would it were ten thousand pound,
  I'd give it all to Sally;
She is the darling of my heart,
  And she lives in our alley.

My master and the neighbours all
  Make game of me and Sally,
And, but for her, I'd better be
  A slave and row a galley;
But when my seven long years are out
  O then I'll marry Sally,—
O then we'll wed, and then we'll bed . . .
  But not in our alley!

                              H. Carey

CLXVIII

A FAREWELL

Go fetch to me a pint o' wine,
  An' fill it in a silver tassie;
That I may drink before I go
  A service to my bonnie lassie:
The boat rocks at the pier o' Leith,
  Fu' loud the wind blaws frae the ferry,
The ship rides by the Berwick-law,
  And I maun leave my bonnie Mary.

The trumpets sound, the banners fly,
  The glittering spears are rankéd ready;
The shouts o' war are heard afar,
  The battle closes thick and bloody;
But it's not the roar o' sea or shore
  Wad make me langer wish to tarry;
Nor shout o' war that's heard afar—
  It's leaving thee, my bonnie Mary.

R. Burns

CLXIX

If doughty deeds my lady please
  Right soon I'll mount my steed;
And strong his arm, and fast his seat
  That bears frae me the meed.
I'll wear thy colours in my cap
  Thy picture at my heart;
And he that bends not to thine eye
  Shall rue it to his smart!
    Then tell me how to woo thee, Love;
      O tell me how to woo thee!
    For thy dear sake, nae care I'll take
      Tho' ne'er another trow me.

If gay attire delight thine eye
  I'll dight me in array;
I'll tend thy chamber door all night,
  And squire thee all the day.
If sweetest sounds can win thine ear,
  These sounds I'll strive to catch;
Thy voice I'll steal to woo thysell,
  That voice that nane can match.

But if fond love thy heart can gain,
  I never broke a vow;
Nae maiden lays her skaith to me,
  I never loved but you.
For you alone I ride the ring,
  For you I wear the blue;
For you alone I strive to sing,
  O tell me how to woo!

Then tell me how to woo thee, Love;
  O tell me how to woo thee!
For thy dear sake, nae care I'll take,
  Tho' ne'er another trow me.

R. Graham of Gartmore

CLXX

TO A YOUNG LADY

Sweet stream, that winds through yonder glade,
Apt emblem of a virtuous maid—
Silent and chaste she steals along,
Far from the world's gay busy throng:
With gentle yet prevailing force,
Intent upon her destined course;
Graceful and useful all she does,
Blessing and blest where'er she goes;
Pure-bosom'd as that watery glass,
And Heaven reflected in her face.

W. Cowper

CLXXI

THE SLEEPING BEAUTY

Sleep on, and dream of Heaven awhile—
Tho' shut so close thy laughing eyes,
Thy rosy lips still wear a smile
And move, and breathe delicious sighs!

Ah, now soft blushes tinge her cheeks
And mantle o'er her neck of snow:
Ah, now she murmurs, now she speaks
What most I wish—and fear to know!

She starts, she trembles, and she weeps!
Her fair hands folded on her breast:
—And now, how like a saint she sleeps!
A seraph in the realms of rest!

Sleep on secure !   Above controul
Thy thoughts belong to Heaven and thee :
And may the secret of thy soul
Remain within its sanctuary !

S. Rogers

CLXXII

For ever, Fortune, wilt thou prove
An unrelenting foe to Love,
And when we meet a mutual heart
Come in between, and bid us part ?

Bid us sigh on from day to day,
And wish and wish the soul away;
Till youth and genial years are flown,
And all the life of life is gone ?

But busy, busy, still art thou,
To bind the loveless joyless vow,
The heart from pleasure to delude,
To join the gentle to the rude.

For once, O Fortune, hear my prayer,
And I absolve thy future care;
All other blessings I resign,
Make but the dear Amanda mine.

J. Thomson

CLXXIII

The merchant, to secure his treasure,
Conveys it in a borrow'd name :
Euphelia serves to grace my measure,
But Cloe is my real flame.

My softest verse, my darling lyre
Upon Euphelia's toilet lay—
When Cloe noted her desire
That I should sing, that I should play.

My lyre I tune, my voice I raise,
But with my numbers mix my sighs;
And whilst I sing Euphelia's praise,
I fix my soul on Cloe's eyes.

Fair Cloe blush'd : Euphelia frown'd :
I sung, and gazed ; I play'd, and trembled :
And Venus to the Loves around
Remark'd how ill we all dissembled.

M. Prior

CLXXIV

LOVE'S SECRET

Never seek to tell thy love,
   Love that never told can be ;
For the gentle wind doth move
   Silently, invisibly.

I told my love, I told my love,
   I told her all my heart,
Trembling, cold, in ghastly fears :—
   Ah ! she did depart.

Soon after she was gone from me
   A traveller came by,
Silently, invisibly :
   He took her with a sigh.

W. Blake

CLXXV

When lovely woman stoops to folly
And finds too late that men betray,—
What charm can soothe her melancholy,
What art can wash her guilt away ?

The only art her guilt to cover,
To hide her shame from every eye,
To give repentance to her lover
And wring his bosom, is—to die.

O. Goldsmith

CLXXVI

Ye banks and braes o' bonnie Doon
  How can ye blume sae fair!
How can ye chant, ye little birds,
  And I sae fu' o' care!

Thou'll break my heart, thou bonnie bird
  That sings upon the bough;
Thou minds me o' the happy days
  When my fause Luve was true.

Thou'll break my heart, thou bonnie bird
  That sings beside thy mate;
For sae I sat, and sae I sang,
  And wist na o' my fate.

Aft hae I roved by bonnie Doon
  To see the woodbine twine,
And ilka bird sang o' its love;
  And sae did I o' mine.

Wi' lightsome heart I pu'd a rose,
  Frae aff its thorny tree;
And my fause luver staw the rose,
  But left the thorn wi' me.

R. Burns

CLXXVII

THE PROGRESS OF POESY

A Pindaric Ode

Awake, Aeolian lyre, awake,
And give to rapture all thy trembling strings.
From Helicon's harmonious springs
    A thousand rills their mazy progress take:
The laughing flowers that round them blow
Drink life and fragrance as they flow.
Now the rich stream of music winds along
Deep, majestic, smooth, and strong,

Thro' verdant vales, and Ceres' golden reign;
Now rolling down the steep amain
Headlong, impetuous, see it pour:
The rocks and nodding groves re-bellow to the
    roar.

Oh! Sovereign of the willing soul,
Parent of sweet and solemn-breathing airs,
Enchanting shell! the sullen Cares
    And frantic Passions hear thy soft controul,
On Thracia's hills the Lord of War
Has curb'd the fury of his car
And dropt his thirsty lance at thy command.
Perching on the sceptred hand
Of Jove, thy magic lulls the feather'd king
With ruffled plumes, and flagging wing:
Quench'd in dark clouds of slumber lie
The terror of his beak, and lightnings of his eye.

Thee the voice, the dance, obey
Temper'd to thy warbled lay.
O'er Idalia's velvet-green
The rosy-crownéd Loves are seen
On Cytherea's day;
With antic Sport, and blue-eyed Pleasures,
Frisking light in frolic measures;
Now pursuing, now retreating,
    Now in circling troops they meet:
To brisk notes in cadence beating
    Glance their many-twinkling feet.
Slow melting strains their Queen's approach declare:
    Where'er she turns, the Graces homage pay:
With arms sublime that float upon the air
    In gliding state she wins her easy way:
O'er her warm cheek and rising bosom move
The bloom of young Desire and purple light of Love.

Man's feeble race what ills await!
Labour, and Penury, the racks of Pain,
Disease, and Sorrow's weeping train,
    And Death, sad refuge from the storms of fate!
The fond complaint, my song, disprove,
And justify the laws of Jove.

Say, has he given in vain the heavenly Muse?
Night, and all her sickly dews,
Her spectres wan, and birds of boding cry
He gives to range the dreary sky:
Till down the eastern cliffs afar
Hyperion's march they spy, and glittering shafts of
      war.

  In climes beyond the solar road
Where shaggy forms o'er ice-built mountains roam,
The Muse has broke the twilight gloom
    To cheer the shivering native's dull abode.
And oft, beneath the odorous shade
Of Chili's boundless forests laid,
She deigns to hear the savage youth repeat
In loose numbers wildly sweet
Their feather-cinctured chiefs, and dusky loves.
Her track, where'er the goddess roves,
Glory pursue, and generous Shame,
Th' unconquerable Mind, and Freedom's holy flame.

Woods, that wave o'er Delphi's steep,
Isles, that crown th' Aegean deep,
Fields that cool Ilissus laves,
Or where Maeander's amber waves
In lingering labyrinths creep,
How do your tuneful echoes languish,
Mute, but to the voice of anguish!
Where each old poetic mountain
   Inspiration breathed around;
Every shade and hallow'd fountain
   Murmur'd deep a solemn sound:
Till the sad Nine, in Greece's evil hour
   Left their Parnassus for the Latian plains.
Alike they scorn the pomp of tyrant Power,
   And coward Vice, that revels in her chains.
When Latium had her lofty spirit lost,
They sought, oh Albion! next, thy sea-encircled coast.

  Far from the sun and summer-gale
In thy green lap was Nature's Darling laid,
What time, where lucid Avon stray'd,
   To him the mighty Mother did unveil

Her awful face : the dauntless child
Stretch'd forth his little arms, and smiled.
' This pencil take ' (she said), ' whose colours clear
Richly paint the vernal year :
Thine, too, these golden keys, immortal Boy !
This can unlock the gates of joy;
Of horror that, and thrilling fears,
Or ope the sacred source of sympathetic tears.'

  Nor second He, that rode sublime
Upon the seraph-wings of Extasy
The secrets of the abyss to spy :
  He pass'd the flaming bounds of place and time :
The living Throne, the sapphire-blaze
Where angels tremble while they gaze,
He saw; but blasted with excess of light,
Closed his eyes in endless night.
Behold where Dryden's less presumptuous car
Wide o'er the fields of glory bear
Two coursers of ethereal race,
With necks in thunder clothed, and long-resounding
      pace.

Hark, his hands the lyre explore !
Bright-eyed Fancy, hovering o'er,
Scatters from her pictured urn
Thoughts that breathe, and words that burn.
  But ah ! 'tis heard no more—
Oh ! lyre divine, what daring spirit
Wakes thee now ? Tho' he inherit
Nor the pride, nor ample pinion,
  That the Theban eagle bear,
Sailing with supreme dominion
Thro' the azure deep of air :
Yet oft before his infant eyes would run
  Such forms as glitter in the Muse's ray
With orient hues, unborrow'd of the sun :
  Yet shall he mount and keep his distant way
Beyond the limits of a vulgar fate :
Beneath the Good how far—but far above the Great.

                                        T. Gray

CLXXVIII

THE PASSIONS

An Ode for Music

When Music, heavenly maid, was young,
While yet in early Greece she sung,
The Passions oft, to hear her shell,
Throng'd around her magic cell
Exulting, trembling, raging, fainting,
Possest beyond the Muse's painting;
By turns they felt the glowing mind
Disturb'd, delighted, raised, refined :
'Till once, 'tis said, when all were fired,
Fill'd with fury, rapt, inspired,
From the supporting myrtles round
They snatch'd her instruments of sound,
And, as they oft had heard apart
Sweet lessons of her forceful art,
Each (for Madness ruled the hour)
Would prove his own expressive power.

First Fear his hand, its skill to try,
  Amid the chords bewilder'd laid,
And back recoil'd, he knew not why,
  E'en at the sound himself had made.

Next Anger rush'd, his eyes on fire,
  In lightnings, own'd his secret stings;
In one rude clash he struck the lyre
  And swept with hurried hand the strings.

With woeful measures wan Despair,
  Low sullen sounds, his grief beguiled;
A solemn, strange, and mingled air,
  'Twas sad by fits, by starts 'twas wild.

But thou, O Hope, with eyes so fair,
  What was thy delighted measure?
Still it whisper'd promised pleasure
  And bade the lovely scenes at distance hail !
Still would her touch the strain prolong;
  And from the rocks, the woods, the vale

She call'd on Echo still through all the song;
  And, where her sweetest theme she chose,
  A soft responsive voice was heard at every close;
And Hope enchanted smiled, and waved her golden
    hair;—

And longer had she sung :—but with a frown
    Revenge impatient rose :
He threw his blood-stain'd sword in thunder down;
    And with a withering look
  The war-denouncing trumpet took
And blew a blast so loud and dread,
Were ne'er prophetic sounds so full of woe !
    And ever and anon he beat
    The doubling drum with furious heat;
And, though sometimes, each dreary pause between,
    Dejected Pity at his side
    Her soul-subduing voice applied,
    Yet still he kept his wild unalter'd mien,
While each strain'd ball of sight seem'd bursting
    from his head.

Thy numbers, Jealousy, to nought were fix'd :
  Sad proof of thy distressful state !
Of differing themes the veering song was mix'd;
  And now it courted Love, now raving call'd on
    Hate.

With eyes up-raised, as one inspired,
Pale Melancholy sat retired;
And from her wild sequester'd seat,
In notes by distance made more sweet,
Pour'd through the mellow horn her pensive soul :
    And dashing soft from rocks around
    Bubbling runnels join'd the sound;
Through glades and glooms the mingled measure
    stole,
  Or, o'er some haunted stream, with fond delay,
    Round an holy calm diffusing,
    Love of peace, and lonely musing,
  In hollow murmurs died away.

But O ! how alter'd was its sprightlier tone
When Cheerfulness, a nymph of healthiest hue,

Her bow across her shoulder flung,
Her buskins gemm'd with morning dew,
Blew an inspiring air, that dale and thicket rung,
  The hunter's call to Faun and Dryad known!
The oak-crown'd Sisters and their chaste-eyed Queen,
  Satyrs and Sylvan Boys, were seen
  Peeping from forth their alleys green:
Brown Exercise rejoiced to hear;
  And Sport leapt up, and seized his beechen spear.

Last came Joy's ecstatic trial:
He, with viny crown advancing,
  First to the lively pipe his hand addrest:
But soon he saw the brisk awakening viol
  Whose sweet entrancing voice he loved the best:
They would have thought who heard the strain
    They saw, in Tempe's vale, her native maids
    Amidst the festal-sounding shades
To some unwearied minstrel dancing;
While, as his flying fingers kiss'd the strings,
  Love framed with Mirth a gay fantastic round:
  Loose were her tresses seen, her zone unbound;
  And he, amidst his frolic play,
  As if he would the charming air repay,
Shook thousand odours from his dewy wings.

O Music! sphere-descended maid,
Friend of Pleasure, Wisdom's aid!
Why, goddess! why, to us denied,
Lay'st thou thy ancient lyre aside?
As in that loved Athenian bower
You learn'd an all-commanding power,
Thy mimic soul, O Nymph endear'd,
Can well recall what then it heard.
Where is the native simple heart
Devote to Virtue, Fancy, Art?
Arise, as in that elder time,
Warm, energic, chaste, sublime!
Thy wonders, in that god-like age,
Fill thy recording Sister's page;—
'Tis said, and I believe the tale,
Thy humblest reed could more prevail,

Had more of strength, diviner rage,
Than all which charms this laggard age;
E'en all at once together found,
Cecilia's mingled world of sound :—
O bid our vain endeavours cease :
Revive the just designs of Greece :
Return in all thy simple state !
Confirm the tales her sons relate !

W. Collins

CLXXIX

THE SONG OF DAVID

He sang of God, the mighty source
Of all things, the stupendous force
  On which all strength depends :
From Whose right arm, beneath Whose eyes,
All period, power, and enterprise
  Commences, reigns, and ends.

The world, the clustering spheres He made,
The glorious light, the soothing shade,
  Dale, champaign, grove and hill :
The multitudinous abyss,
Where secrecy remains in bliss,
  And wisdom hides her skill.

Tell them, I AM, Jehovah said
To Moses : while Earth heard in dread,
  And, smitten to the heart,
At once, above, beneath, around,
All Nature, without voice or sound,
Replied, ' O Lord, THOU ART.'

C. Smart

CLXXX

INFANT JOY

' I have no name;
I am but two days old.'
—What shall I call thee?
' I happy am;
Joy is my name.'
—Sweet joy befall thee!

Pretty joy!
Sweet joy, but two days old;
Sweet joy I call thee:
Thou dost smile:
I sing the while,
Sweet joy befall thee!

W. Blake

CLXXXI

A CRADLE SONG

Sleep, sleep, beauty bright,
Dreaming in the joys of night:
Sleep, sleep; in thy sleep
Little sorrows sit and weep.

Sweet babe, in thy face
Soft desires I can trace,
Secret joys and secret smiles,
Little pretty infant wiles.

As thy softest limbs I feel,
Smiles as of the morning steal
O'er thy cheek, and o'er thy breast
Where thy little heart doth rest.

Oh the cunning wiles that creep
In thy little heart asleep!
When thy little heart doth wake,
Then the dreadful light shall break.

W. Blake

CLXXXII

ODE ON THE SPRING

Lo ! where the rosy-bosom'd Hours,
  Fair Venus' train, appear,
Disclose the long-expecting flowers
  And wake the purple year !
The Attic warbler pours her throat
Responsive to the cuckoo's note,
The untaught harmony of Spring :
While, whispering pleasure as they fly,
Cool Zephyrs thro' the clear blue sky
  Their gather'd fragrance fling.

Where'er the oak's thick branches stretch
  A broader, browner shade,
Where'er the rude and moss-grown beech
  O'er-canopies the glade,
Beside some water's rushy brink
With me the Muse shall sit, and think
(At ease reclined in rustic state)
How vain the ardour of the crowd,
How low, how little are the proud,
  How indigent the great !

Still is the toiling hand of Care ;
  The panting herds repose :
Yet hark, how thro' the peopled air
  The busy murmur glows !
The insect-youth are on the wing,
Eager to taste the honied spring
And float amid the liquid noon :
Some lightly o'er the current skim,
Some show their gaily-gilded trim
  Quick-glancing to the sun.

To Contemplation's sober eye
  Such is the race of Man :
And they that creep, and they that fly
  Shall end where they began.
Alike the Busy and the Gay

But flutter thro' life's little day,
In Fortune's varying colours drest:
Brush'd by the hand of rough Mischance,
Or chill'd by Age, their airy dance
    They leave, in dust to rest.

Methinks I hear in accents low
    The sportive kind reply:
Poor moralist! and what art thou?
    A solitary fly!
Thy joys no glittering female meets,
No hive hast thou of hoarded sweets,
No painted plumage to display:
On hasty wings thy youth is flown;
Thy sun is set, thy spring is gone—
    We frolic while 'tis May.

                    T. Gray

CLXXXIII

THE POPLAR FIELD

The poplars are fell'd; farewell to the shade
And the whispering sound of the cool colonnade;
The winds play no longer and sing in the leaves,
Nor Ouse on his bosom their image receives.

Twelve years have elapsed since I first took a view
Of my favourite field, and the bank where they grew;
And now in the grass behold they are laid,
And the tree is my seat that once lent me a shade!

The blackbird has fled to another retreat
Where the hazels afford him a screen from the heat;
And the scene where his melody charm'd me before
Resounds with his sweet-flowing ditty no more.

My fugitive years are all hasting away,
And I must ere long lie as lowly as they,
With a turf on my breast and a stone at my head,
Ere another such grove shall arise in its stead.

The change both my heart and my fancy employs;
I reflect on the frailty of man and his joys:
Short-lived as we are, yet our pleasures, we see,
Have a still shorter date, and die sooner than we.

W. Cowper

CLXXXIV

TO A MOUSE

*On turning her up in her nest, with the plough,
November, 1785*

Wee, sleekit, cow'rin', tim'rous beastie,
O what a panic's in thy breastie!
Thou need na start awa sae hasty,
Wi' bickering brattle!
I wad be laith to rin an' chase thee
Wi' murd'ring pattle!

I'm truly sorry man's dominion
Has broken Nature's social union,
An' justifies that ill opinion
Which makes thee startle
At me, thy poor earth-born companion,
An' fellow-mortal!

I doubt na, whiles, but thou may thieve;
What then? poor beastie, thou maun live!
A daimen-icker in a thrave
'S a sma' request:
I'll get a blessin' wi' the lave,
And never miss't!

Thy wee bit housie, too, in ruin!
Its silly wa's the win's are strewin:
And naething, now, to big a new ane,
O' foggage green!
An' bleak December's winds ensuin'
Baith snell an' keen!

Thou saw the fields laid bare an waste
An' weary winter comin' fast,
An' cozie here, beneath the blast,
Thou thought to dwell,
Till, crash ! the cruel coulter past
Out thro' thy cell.

That wee bit heap o' leaves an' stibble
Has cost thee mony a weary nibble !
Now thou's turn'd out, for a' thy trouble,
But house or hald,
To thole the winter's sleety dribble
An' cranreuch cauld !

But, Mousie, thou art no thy lane
In proving foresight may be vain :
The best laid schemes o' mice an' men
Gang aft a-gley,
An' lea'e us nought but grief an' pain,
For promised joy.

Still thou art blest, compared wi' me !
The present only toucheth thee :
But, Och ! I backward cast my e'e
On prospects drear !
An' forward, tho' I canna see,
I guess an' fear !

R. Burns

CLXXXV

A WISH

Mine be a cot beside the hill;
A bee-hive's hum shall soothe my ear;
A willowy brook that turns a mill,
With many a fall shall linger near.

The swallow, oft, beneath my thatch
Shall twitter from her clay-built nest;
Oft shall the pilgrim lift the latch,
And share my meal, a welcome guest.

Around my ivied porch shall spring
Each fragrant flower that drinks the dew;
 And Lucy, at her wheel, shall sing
 In russet-gown and apron blue.

The village-church among the trees,
Where first our marriage-vows were given,
 With merry peals shall swell the breeze
 And point with taper spire to Heaven.

S. Rogers

CLXXXVI

ODE TO EVENING

If aught of oaten stop or pastoral song
May hope, O pensive Eve, to soothe thine ear
 Like thy own solemn springs,
 Thy springs, and dying gales;

O Nymph reserved,—while now the bright-hair'd
          sun
Sits in yon western tent, whose cloudy skirts,
 With brede ethereal wove,
 O'erhang his wavy bed;

Now air is hush'd, save where the weak-eyed bat
With short shrill shriek flits by on leathern wing,
 Or where the beetle winds
 His small but sullen horn,

As oft he rises midst the twilight path,
Against the pilgrim borne in heedless hum,—
 Now teach me, maid composed,
 To breathe some soften'd strain

Whose numbers, stealing through thy darkening vale,
May not unseemly with its stillness suit;
 As, musing slow, I hail
 Thy genial loved return.

For when thy folding-star arising shows
His paly circlet, at his warning lamp
    The fragrant Hours, and Elves
      Who slept in buds the day,

And many a Nymph who wreathes her brows with
    sedge
And sheds the freshening dew, and, lovelier still,
    The pensive Pleasures sweet,
      Prepare thy shadowy car.

Then let me rove some wild and heathy scene;
Or find some ruin midst its dreary dells,
    Whose walls more awful nod
      By thy religious gleams.

Or, if chill blustering winds or driving rain
Prevent my willing feet, be mine the hut
    That, from the mountain's side,
      Views wilds, and swelling floods,

And hamlets brown, and dim-discover'd spires;
And hears their simple bell; and marks o'er all
    Thy dewy fingers draw
      The gradual dusky veil.

While Spring shall pour his showers, as oft he wont,
And bathe thy breathing tresses, meekest Eve !
    While Summer loves to sport
      Beneath thy lingering light;

While sallow Autumn fills thy lap with leaves;
Or Winter, yelling through the troublous air,
    Affrights thy shrinking train
      And rudely rends thy robes;

So long, regardful of thy quiet rule,
Shall Fancy, Friendship, Science, smiling Peace,
    Thy gentlest influence own,
      And love thy favourite name !
                    W. Collins

CLXXXVII

ELEGY WRITTEN IN A COUNTRY CHURCHYARD

The curfew tolls the knell of parting day,
The lowing herd wind slowly o'er the lea,
The ploughman homeward plods his weary way,
And leaves the world to darkness and to me.

Now fades the glimmering landscape on the sight,
And all the air a solemn stillness holds,
Save where the beetle wheels his droning flight,
And drowsy tinklings lull the distant folds :

Save that from yonder ivy-mantled tower
The moping owl does to the moon complain
Of such as, wandering near her secret bower,
Molest her ancient solitary reign.

Beneath those rugged elms, that yew-tree's shade
Where heaves the turf in many a mouldering heap,
Each in his narrow cell for ever laid,
The rude forefathers of the hamlet sleep.

The breezy call of incense-breathing morn,
The swallow twittering from the straw-built shed,
The cock's shrill clarion, or the echoing horn,
No more shall rouse them from their lowly bed.

For them no more the blazing hearth shall burn
Or busy housewife ply her evening care :
No children run to lisp their sire's return,
Or climb his knees the envied kiss to share.

Oft did the harvest to their sickle yield,
Their furrow oft the stubborn glebe has broke;
How jocund did they drive their team afield !
How bow'd the woods beneath their sturdy stroke !

Let not ambition mock their useful toil,
Their homely joys, and destiny obscure;
Nor grandeur hear with a disdainful smile
The short and simple annals of the poor.

The boast of heraldry, the pomp of power,
And all that beauty, all that wealth e'er gave
Awaits alike th' inevitable hour :—
The paths of glory lead but to the grave.

Nor you, ye proud, impute to these the fault
If memory o'er their tomb no trophies raise,
Where through the long-drawn aisle and fretted vault
The pealing anthem swells the note of praise.

Can storied urn or animated bust
Back to its mansion call the fleeting breath?
Can honour's voice provoke the silent dust,
Or flattery soothe the dull cold ear of death?

Perhaps in this neglected spot is laid
Some heart once pregnant with celestial fire;
Hands, that the rod of empire might have sway'd,
Or waked to extasy the living lyre :

But knowledge to their eyes her ample page
Rich with the spoils of time, did ne'er unroll;
Chill penury repress'd their noble rage,
And froze the genial current of the soul.

Full many a gem of purest ray serene
The dark unfathom'd caves of ocean bear :
Full many a flower is born to blush unseen,
And waste its sweetness on the desert air.

Some village-Hampden, that with dauntless breast
The little tyrant of his fields withstood,
Some mute inglorious Milton here may rest,
Some Cromwell, guiltless of his country's blood.

Th' applause of listening senates to command,
The threats of pain and ruin to despise,
To scatter plenty o'er a smiling land,
And read their history in a nation's eyes

Their lot forbad : nor circumscribed alone
Their growing virtues, but their crimes confined;
Forbad to wade thro' slaughter to a throne,
And shut the gates of mercy on mankind;

The struggling pangs of conscious truth to hide,
To quench the blushes of ingenuous shame,
Or heap the shrine of luxury and pride
With incense kindled at the Muse's flame.

Far from the madding crowd's ignoble strife
Their sober wishes never learn'd to stray;
Along the cool sequester'd vale of life
They kept the noiseless tenour of their way.

Yet e'en these bones from insult to protect
Some frail memorial still erected nigh,
With uncouth rhymes and shapeless sculpture
    deck'd,
Implores the passing tribute of a sigh.

Their name, their years, spelt by th' unletter'd Muse,
The place of fame and elegy supply :
And many a holy text around she strews,
That teach the rustic moralist to die.

For who, to dumb forgetfulness a prey,
This pleasing anxious being e'er resign'd,
Left the warm precincts of the cheerful day,
Nor cast one longing lingering look behind ?

On some fond breast the parting soul relies,
Some pious drops the closing eye requires;
E'en from the tomb the voice of nature cries,
E'en in our ashes live their wonted fires.

For thee, who, mindful of th' unhonour'd dead,
Dost in these lines their artless tale relate;
If chance, by lonely contemplation led,
Some kindred spirit shall enquire thy fate,—

Haply some hoary-headed swain may say,
' Oft have we seen him at the peep of dawn
Brushing with hasty steps the dews away,
To meet the sun upon the upland lawn;

' There at the foot of yonder nodding beech
That wreathes its old fantastic roots so high,
His listless length at noon-tide would he stretch,
And pore upon the brook that babbles by.

' Hard by yon wood, now smiling as in scorn,
Muttering his wayward fancies he would rove;
Now drooping, woeful-wan, like one forlorn,
Or crazed with care, or cross'd in hopeless love.

' One morn I miss'd him on the custom'd hill,
Along the heath, and near his favourite tree;
Another came; nor yet beside the rill,
Nor up the lawn, nor at the wood was he;

' The next with dirges due in sad array
Slow through the church-way path we saw him
    borne,—
Approach and read (for thou canst read) the lay
Graved on the stone beneath yon aged thorn.'

THE EPITAPH

Here rests his head upon the lap of earth
A youth, to fortune and to fame unknown;
Fair science frown'd not on his humble birth
And melancholy mark'd him for her own.

Large was his bounty, and his soul sincere;
Heaven did a recompense as largely send:
He gave to misery (all he had) a tear,
He gain'd from Heaven ('twas all he wish'd) a friend.

No farther seek his merits to disclose,
Or draw his frailties from their dread abode,
(There they alike in trembling hope repose,)
The bosom of his Father and his God.

T. Gray

CLXXXVIII

MARY MORISON

O Mary, at thy window be,
It is the wish'd, the trysted hour!
Those smiles and glances let me see
That make the miser's treasure poor:
How blithely wad I bide the stoure,
A weary slave frae sun to sun,
Could I the rich reward secure,
The lovely Mary Morison.

Yestreen when to the trembling string
The dance gaed thro' the lighted ha',
To thee my fancy took its wing,—
I sat, but neither heard nor saw:
Tho' this was fair, and that was braw,
And yon the toast of a' the town,
I sigh'd, and said amang them a',
' Ye are na Mary Morison.'

O Mary, canst thou wreck his peace
Wha for thy sake wad gladly dee?
Or canst thou break that heart of his,
Whase only faut is loving thee?
If love for love thou wilt na gie,
At least be pity to me shown;
A thought ungentle canna be
The thought o' Mary Morison.

R. Burns

CLXXXIX

BONNIE LESLEY

O saw ye bonnie Lesley
  As she gaed o'er the border?
She's gane, like Alexander,
  To spread her conquests farther.

To see her is to love her,
  And love but her for ever;
For Nature made her what she is,
  And ne'er made sic anither!

Thou art a queen, Fair Lesley,
  Thy subjects we, before thee;
Thou art divine, Fair Lesley,
  The hearts o' men adore thee.

The Deil he could na scaith thee,
  Or aught that wad belang thee;
He'd look into thy bonnie face,
  And say ' I canna wrang thee!'

The Powers aboon will tent thee;
   Misfortune sha' na steer thee;
Thou'rt like themselves sae lovely
   That ill they'll ne'er let near thee.

Return again, Fair Lesley,
   Return to Caledonie!
That we may brag we hae a lass
   There's nane again sae bonnie.

              R. Burns

CXC

O my Luve's like a red, red rose
   That's newly sprung in June:
O my Luve's like the melodie
   That's sweetly play'd in tune.

As fair art thou, my bonnie lass,
   So deep in luve am I:
And I will luve thee still, my dear,
   Till a' the seas gang dry:

Till a' the seas gang dry, my dear,
   And the rocks melt wi' the sun;
I will luve thee still, my dear,
   While the sands o' life shall run.

And fare thee weel, my only Luve!
   And fare thee weel awhile!
And I will come again, my Luve,
   Tho' it were ten thousand mile.

              R. Burns

CXCI

HIGHLAND MARY

Ye banks and braes and streams around
   The castle o' Montgomery,
Green be your woods, and fair your flowers,
   Your waters never drumlie!

There simmer first unfauld her robes,
    And there the langest tarry;
For there I took the last fareweel
    O' my sweet Highland Mary.

How sweetly bloom'd the gay green birk,
    How rich the hawthorn's blossom,
As underneath their fragrant shade
    I clasp'd her to my bosom!
The golden hours on angel wings
    Flew o'er me and my dearie;
For dear to me as light and life
    Was my sweet Highland Mary.

Wi' mony a vow and lock'd embrace
    Our parting was fu' tender;
And pledging aft to meet again,
    We tore oursels asunder;
But, Oh! fell Death's untimely frost,
    That nipt my flower sae early!
Now green's the sod, and cauld's the clay,
    That wraps my Highland Mary!

O pale, pale now, those rosy lips,
    I aft hae kiss'd sae fondly!
And closed for aye the sparkling glance
    That dwelt on me sae kindly;
And mouldering now in silent dust
    That heart that lo'ed me dearly!
But still within my bosom's core
    Shall live my Highland Mary.

                       R. Burns

CXCII

AULD ROBIN GRAY

When the sheep are in the fauld, and the kye a'
    hame,
And a' the warld to rest are gane,
The waes o' my heart fa' in showers frae my e'e,
While my gudeman lies sound by me.

Young Jamie lo'ed me weel, and sought me for his
    bride;
But saving a croun he had naething else beside;
To make the croun a pund, young Jamie gaed to sea;
And the croun and the pund were baith for me.

He hadna been awa' a week but only twa,
When my father brak his arm, and the cow was
    stown awa;
My mother she fell sick, and my Jamie at the sea—
And auld Robin Gray came a-courtin' me.

My father couldna work, and my mother couldna spin;
I toil'd day and night, but their bread I couldna win;
Auld Rob maintain'd them baith, and wi' tears in his
    e'e
Said, Jennie, for their sakes, O, marry me!

My heart it said nay; I look'd for Jamie back;
But the wind it blew high, and the ship it was a
    wrack;
His ship it was a wrack—why dinna Jamie dee?
Or why do I live to cry, Wae's me?

My father urgit sair : my mother didna speak;
But she look'd in my face till my heart was like to
    break :
They gi'ed him my hand, but my heart was at the sea;
Sae auld Robin Gray he was gudeman to me.

I hadna been a wife a week but only four,
When mournfu' as I sat on the stane at the door,
I saw my Jamie's wraith, for I couldna think it he
Till he said, I'm come hame to marry thee.

O sair, sair did we greet, and muckle did we say;
We took but ae kiss, and I bad him gang away;
I wish that I were dead, but I'm no like to dee;
And why was I born to say, Wae's me!

I gang like a ghaist, and I carena to spin;
I daurna think on Jamie, for that wad be a sin;
But I'll do my best a gude wife aye to be,
For auld Robin Gray he is kind unto me.

                            Lady A. Lindsay

CXCIII

DUNCAN GRAY

Duncan Gray cam here to woo,
    Ha, ha, the wooing o't;
On blythe Yule night when we were **fou,**
    Ha, ha, the wooing o't :
Maggie coost her head fu' high,
Look'd asklent and unco skeigh,
Gart poor Duncan stand abeigh;
    Ha, ha, the wooing o't !

Duncan fleech'd, and Duncan pray'd;
Meg was deaf as Ailsa Craig;
Duncan sigh'd baith out and in,
Grat his een baith bleer't and blin',
Spak o' lowpin ower a linn !

Time and chance are but a tide,
Slighted love is sair to bide;
Shall I, like a fool, quoth he,
For a haughty hizzie dee?
She may gae to—France for me !

How it comes let doctors tell,
Meg grew sick—as he grew well;
Something in her bosom wrings,
For relief a sigh she brings;
And O, her een, they spak sic things !

Duncan was a lad o' grace;
Maggie's was a piteous case;
Duncan couldna be her death,
Swelling pity smoor'd his wrath;
Now they're crouse and canty baith :
    Ha, ha, the wooing o't !

                    R. Burns

CXCIV

THE SAILOR'S WIFE

And are ye sure the news is true?
  And are ye sure he's weel?
Is this a time to think o' wark?
  Ye jades, lay by your wheel;
Is this the time to spin a thread,
  When Colin's at the door?
Reach down my cloak, I'll to the quay,
  And see him come ashore.
For there's nae luck about the house,
  There's nae luck at a';
There's little pleasure in the house
  When our gudeman's awa'.

And gie to me my bigonet,
  My bishop's satin gown;
For I maun tell the baillie's wife
  That Colin's in the town.
My Turkey slippers maun gae on,
  My stockings pearly blue;
It's a' to pleasure our gudeman,
  For he's baith leal and true.

Rise, lass, and mak a clean fireside,
  Put on the muckle pot;
Gie little Kate her button gown
  And Jock his Sunday coat;
And mak their shoon as black as slaes,
  Their hose as white as snaw;
It's a' to please my ain gudeman,
  For he's been long awa.

There's twa fat hens upo' the coop
  Been fed this month and mair;
Mak haste and thraw their necks about,
  That Colin weel may fare;
And spread the table neat and clean,
  Gar ilka thing look braw,
For wha can tell how Colin fared
  When he was far awa?

Sae true his heart, sae smooth his speech,
　His breath like caller air;
His very foot has music in't
　As he comes up the stair—
And will I see his face again?
　And will I hear him speak?
I'm downright dizzy wi' the thought,
　In troth I'm like to greet!

If Colin's weel, and weel content,
　I hae nae mair to crave:
And gin I live to keep him sae,
　I'm blest aboon the lave:
And will I see his face again,
　And will I hear him speak?
I'm downright dizzy wi' the thought,
　In troth I'm like to greet.
For there's nae luck about the house,
　There's nae luck at a';
There's little pleasure in the house
　When our gudeman's awa'.

　　　　　　　　W. J. Mickle

CXCV

ABSENCE

When I think on the happy days
　I spent wi' you, my dearie;
And now what lands between us lie,
　How can I be but eerie!

How slow ye move, ye heavy hours,
　As ye were wae and weary!
It was na sae ye glinted by
　When I was wi' my dearie.

　　　　　　　　Anon

CXCVI

JEAN

Of a' the airts the wind can blaw
   I dearly like the West,
For there the bonnie lassie lives,
   The lassie I lo'e best :
There wild woods grow, and rivers row,
   And mony a hill between;
But day and night my fancy's flight
   Is ever wi' my Jean.

I see her in the dewy flowers,
   I see her sweet and fair :
I hear her in the tunefu' birds,
   I hear her charm the air :
There's not a bonnie flower that springs
   By fountain, shaw, or green,
There's not a bonnie bird that sings
   But minds me o' my Jean.

O blaw ye westlin winds, blaw saft
   Amang the leafy trees;
Wi' balmy gale, frae hill and dale
   Bring hame the laden bees;
And bring the lassie back to me
   That's aye sae neat and clean;
Ae smile o' her wad banish care,
   Sae charming is my Jean.

What sighs and vows amang the knowes
   Hae pass'd atween us twa !
How fond to meet, how wae to part
   That night she gaed awa !
The Powers aboon can only ken
   To whom the heart is seen,
That nane can be sae dear to me
   As my sweet lovely Jean !

R. Burns

CXCVII

JOHN ANDERSON

John Anderson my jo, John,
When we were first acquent
Your locks were like the raven,
Your bonnie brow was brent;
But now your brow is bald, John,
Your locks are like the snow;
But blessings on your frosty pow,
John Anderson my jo.

John Anderson my jo, John,
We clamb the hill thegither,
And mony a canty day, John,
We've had wi' ane anither:
Now we maun totter down, John,
But hand in hand we'll go,
And sleep thegither at the foot,
John Anderson my jo.

                              R. Burns

CXCVIII

THE LAND O' THE LEAL

I'm wearing awa', Jean,
Like snaw when its thaw, Jean,
I'm wearing awa'
    To the land o' the leal.
There's nae sorrow there, Jean,
There's neither cauld nor care, Jean,
The day is aye fair
    In the land o' the leal.

Ye were aye leal and true, Jean,
Your task's ended noo, Jean,
And I'll welcome you
    To the land o' the leal.

Our bonnie bairn's there, Jean,
She was baith guid and fair, Jean :
O we grudged her right sair
  To the land o' the leal !

Then dry that tearfu' e'e, Jean,
My soul langs to be free, Jean,
And angels wait on me
  To the land o' the leal.

Now fare ye weel, my ain Jean,
This warld's care is vain, Jean;
We'll meet and aye be fain
  In the land o' the leal.

Lady Nairne

CXCIX

ODE ON A DISTANT PROSPECT OF ETON COLLEGE

Ye distant spires, ye antique towers
  That crown the watery glade,
Where grateful Science still adores
  Her Henry's holy shade;
And ye, that from the stately brow
Of Windsor's heights th' expanse below
Of grove, of lawn, of mead survey,
Whose turf, whose shade, whose flowers among
Wanders the hoary Thames along
  His silver-winding way :

Ah happy hills ! ah pleasing shade !
  Ah fields beloved in vain !
Where once my careless childhood stray'd,
  A stranger yet to pain !
I feel the gales that from ye blow
A momentary bliss bestow,
As waving fresh their gladsome wing
My weary soul they seem to soothe,
And, redolent of joy and youth,
  To breathe a second spring.

Say, Father Thames, for thou hast seen
  Full many a sprightly race
Disporting on thy margent green
  The paths of pleasure trace;
Who foremost now delight to cleave
With pliant arm, thy glassy wave?
The captive linnet which enthral?
What idle progeny succeed
To chase the rolling circle's speed
  Or urge the flying ball?

While some on earnest business bent
  Their murmuring labours ply
'Gainst graver hours, that bring constraint
  To sweeten liberty:
Some bold adventurers disdain
The limits of their little reign
And unknown regions dare descry:
Still as they run they look behind,
They hear a voice in every wind,
  And snatch a fearful joy.

Gay hope is theirs by fancy fed,
  Less pleasing when possest;
The tear forgot as soon as shed,
  The sunshine of the breast:
Theirs buxom health, of rosy hue,
Wild wit, invention ever new,
And lively cheer, of vigour born;
The thoughtless day, the easy night,
The spirits pure, the slumbers light
  That fly th' approach of morn.

Alas! regardless of their doom
  The little victims play;
No sense have they of ills to come
  Nor care beyond to-day:
Yet see how all around 'em wait
The ministers of human fate
And black Misfortune's baleful train!
Ah show them where in ambush stand
To seize their prey, the murderous band!
  Ah, tell them they are men!

These shall the fury Passions tear,
  The vultures of the mind,
Disdainful Anger, pallid Fear,
  And Shame that sculks behind,
Or pining Love shall waste their youth,
Or Jealousy with rankling tooth
That inly gnaws the secret heart,
And Envy wan, and faded Care,
Grim-visaged comfortless Despair,
  And Sorrow's piercing dart.

Ambition this shall tempt to rise,
  Then whirl the wretch from high
To bitter Scorn a sacrifice
  And grinning Infamy.
The stings of Falsehood those shall try
And hard Unkindness' alter'd eye,
That mocks the tear it forced to flow;
And keen Remorse with blood defiled,
And moody Madness laughing wild
  Amid severest woe.

Lo, in the vale of years beneath
  A griesly troop are seen,
The painful family of Death,
  More hideous than their queen :
This racks the joints, this fires the veins,
That every labouring sinew strains,
Those in the deeper vitals rage :
Lo ! Poverty, to fill the band,
That numbs the soul with icy hand,
  And slow-consuming Age.

To each his sufferings : all are men,
  Condemn'd alike to groan;
The tender for another's pain,
  Th' unfeeling for his own.
Yet, ah ! why should they know their fate,
Since sorrow never comes too late,
And happiness too swiftly flies ?
Thought would destroy their paradise.
No more;—where ignorance is bliss,
  'Tis folly to be wise.

                T. Gray

CC

THE SHRUBBERY

O happy shades ! to me unblest !
  Friendly to peace, but not to me !
How ill the scene that offers rest,
  And heart that cannot rest, agree !

This glassy stream, that spreading pine,
  Those alders quivering to the breeze,
Might soothe a soul less hurt than mine,
  And please, if anything could please.

But fix'd unalterable Care
  Foregoes not what she feels within,
Shows the same sadness everywhere,
  And slights the season and the scene.

For all that pleased in wood or lawn
  While Peace possess'd these silent bowers,
Her animating smile withdrawn,
  Has lost its beauties and its powers.

The saint or moralist should tread
  This moss-grown alley, musing, slow,
They seek like me the secret shade,
  But not, like me, to nourish woe !

Me, fruitful scenes and prospects waste
  Alike admonish not to roam;
These tell me of enjoyments past,
  And those of sorrows yet to come.

                                    W. Cowper

CCI

HYMN TO ADVERSITY

Daughter of Jove, relentless power,
  Thou tamer of the human breast,
Whose iron scourge and torturing hour
  The bad affright, afflict the best !
Bound in thy adamantine chain
The proud are taught to taste of pain,
And purple tyrants vainly groan
With pangs unfelt before, unpitied and alone.

When first thy Sire to send on earth
 Virtue, his darling child, design'd,
To thee he gave the heavenly birth
 And bade to form her infant mind.
Stern, rugged nurse! thy rigid lore
With patience many a year she bore;
What sorrow was, thou bad'st her know,
And from her own she learn'd to melt at others' woe.

Scared at thy frown terrific, fly
 Self-pleasing Folly's idle brood,
Wild Laughter, Noise, and thoughtless Joy,
 And leave us leisure to be good.
Light they disperse, and with them go
The summer friend, the flattering foe;
By vain Prosperity received,
To her they vow their truth, and are again believed.

Wisdom in sable garb array'd
 Immersed in rapturous thought profound,
And Melancholy, silent maid,
 With leaden eye, that loves the ground,
Still on thy solemn steps attend:
Warm Charity, the general friend,
With Justice, to herself severe,
And Pity dropping soft the sadly-pleasing tear

Oh! gently on thy suppliant's head
 Dread goddess, lay thy chastening hand!
Not in thy Gorgon terrors clad,
 Nor circled with the vengeful band
(As by the impious thou art seen)
With thundering voice, and threatening mien,
With screaming Horror's funeral cry,
Despair, and fell Disease, and ghastly Poverty;—

Thy form benign, oh goddess, wear,
 Thy milder influence impart,
Thy philosophic train be there
 To soften, not to wound my heart.
The generous spark extinct revive,
Teach me to love and to forgive,
Exact my own defects to scan,
What others are to feel, and know myself a Man.

        T. Gray

CCII

THE SOLITUDE OF
ALEXANDER SELKIRK

I am monarch of all I survey;
My right there is none to dispute;
From the centre all round to the sea
I am lord of the fowl and the brute.
O Solitude! where are the charms
That sages have seen in thy face?
Better dwell in the midst of alarms,
Than reign in this horrible place.

I am out of humanity's reach,
I must finish my journey alone,
Never hear the sweet music of speech;
I start at the sound of my own.
The beasts that roam over the plain
My form with indifference see;
They are so unacquainted with man,
Their tameness is shocking to me.

Society, Friendship, and Love
Divinely bestow'd upon man,
Oh, had I the wings of a dove
How soon would I taste you again!
My sorrows I then might assuage
In the ways of religion and truth,
Might learn from the wisdom of age,
And be cheer'd by the sallies of youth.

Ye winds that have made me your sport,
Convey to this desolate shore
Some cordial endearing report
Of a land I shall visit no more:
My friends, do they now and then send
A wish or a thought after me?
O tell me I yet have a friend,
Though a friend I am never to see.

How fleet is a glance of the mind !
Compared with the speed of its flight,
The tempest itself lags behind,
And the swift-wingéd arrows of light.
When I think of my own native land
In a moment I seem to be there;
But alas ! recollection at hand
Soon hurries me back to despair.

But the sea-fowl is gone to her nest,
The beast is laid down in his lair;
Even here is a season of rest,
And I to my cabin repair.
There's mercy in every place,
And mercy, encouraging thought !
Gives even affliction a grace
And reconciles man to his lot.

W. Cowper

CCIII

TO MARY UNWIN

Mary ! I want a lyre with other strings,
Such aid from Heaven as some have feign'd they
    drew,
An eloquence scarce given to mortals, new
And undebased by praise of meaner things,

That ere through age or woe I shed my wings
I may record thy worth with honour due,
In verse as musical as thou art true,
And that immortalizes whom it sings :—

But thou hast little need.   There is a Book
By seraphs writ with beams of heavenly light,
On which the eyes of God not rarely look,

A chronicle of actions just and bright—
There all thy deeds, my faithful Mary, shine;
And since thou own'st that praise, I spare thee mine.

W. Cowper

CCIV

TO THE SAME

The twentieth year is well-nigh past
Since first our sky was overcast;
Ah would that this might be the last!
    My Mary!

Thy spirits have a fainter flow,
I see thee daily weaker grow—
'Twas my distress that brought thee low,
    My Mary!

Thy needles, once a shining store,
For my sake restless heretofore,
Now rust disused, and shine no more;
    My Mary!

For though thou gladly wouldst fulfil
The same kind office for me still,
Thy sight now seconds not thy will,
    My Mary!

But well thou play'dst the housewife's part,
And all thy threads with magic art
Have wound themselves about this heart,
    My Mary!

Thy indistinct expressions seem
Like language utter'd in a dream;
Yet me they charm, whate'er the theme,
    My Mary!

Thy silver locks, once auburn bright,
Are still more lovely in my sight
Than golden beams of orient light,
    My Mary!

For could I view nor them nor thee,
What sight worth seeing could I see?
The sun would rise in vain for me,
    My Mary!

Partakers of thy sad decline
Thy hands their little force resign;
Yet, gently prest, press gently mine,
  My Mary!

Such feebleness of limbs thou prov'st
That now at every step thou mov'st
Upheld by two; yet still thou lov'st,
  My Mary!

And still to love, though prest with ill,
In wintry age to feel no chill,
With me is to be lovely still,
  My Mary!

But ah! by constant heed I know
How oft the sadness that I show
Transforms thy smiles to looks of woe,
  My Mary!

And should my future lot be cast
With much resemblance of the past,
Thy worn-out heart will break at last—
  My Mary!
   W. Cowper

CCV

THE CASTAWAY

Obscurest night involved the sky,
 The Atlantic billows roar'd,
When such a destined wretch as I,
 Wash'd headlong from on board,
Of friends, of hope, of all bereft,
His floating home for ever left.

No braver chief could Albion boast
 Than he with whom he went,
Nor ever ship left Albion's coast
 With warmer wishes sent.
He loved them both, but both in vain,
Nor him beheld, nor her again.

Not long beneath the whelming brine,
   Expert to swim, he lay;
Nor soon he felt his strength decline,
   Or courage die away;
But waged with death a lasting strife,
Supported by despair of life.

He shouted : nor his friends had fail'd
   To check the vessel's course,
But so the furious blast prevail'd,
   That, pitiless perforce,
They left their outcast mate behind,
And scudded still before the wind.

Some succour yet they could afford;
   And such as storms allow,
The cask, the coop, the floated cord,
   Delay'd not to bestow.
But he (they knew) nor ship nor shore,
Whate'er they gave, should visit more.

Nor, cruel as it seem'd, could he
   Their haste himself condemn,
Aware that flight, in such a sea,
   Alone could rescue them;
Yet bitter felt it still to die
Deserted, and his friends so nigh.

He long survives, who lives an hour
   In ocean, self-upheld;
And so long he, with unspent power,
   His destiny repell'd;
And ever, as the minutes flew,
Entreated help, or cried ' Adieu ! '

At length, his transient respite past,
   His comrades, who before
Had heard his voice in every blast,
   Could catch the sound no more;
For then, by toil subdued, he drank
The stifling wave, and then he sank.

No poet wept him; but the page
    Of narrative sincere,
That tells his name, his worth, his age,
    Is wet with Anson's tear:
And tears by bards or heroes shed
Alike immortalize the dead.

I therefore purpose not, or dream,
    Descanting on his fate,
To give the melancholy theme
    A more enduring date:
But misery still delights to trace
Its semblance in another's case.

No voice divine the storm allay'd,
    No light propitious shone,
When, snatch'd from all effectual aid,
    We perish'd, each alone:
But I beneath a rougher sea,
And whelm'd in deeper gulfs than he.

                    W. Cowper

CCVI

TOMORROW

In the downhill of life, when I find I'm declining,
    May my fate no less fortunate be
Than a snug elbow-chair will afford for reclining,
    And a cot that o'erlooks the wide sea;
With an ambling pad-pony to pace o'er the lawn,
    While I carol away idle sorrow,
And blithe as the lark that each day hails the dawn
    Look forward with hope for Tomorrow.

With a porch at my door, both for shelter and shade
    too,
    As the sunshine or rain may prevail;
And a small spot of ground for the use of the spade
    too,
    With a barn for the use of the flail:
A cow for my dairy, a dog for my game,
    And a purse when a friend wants to borrow;
I'll envy no Nabob his riches or fame,
    Or what honours may wait him Tomorrow.

From the bleak northern blast may my cot be com-
    pletely
  Secured by a neighbouring hill;
And at night may repose steal upon me more sweetly
  By the sound of a murmuring rill:
And while peace and plenty I find at my board,
  With a heart free from sickness and sorrow,
With my friends may I share what Today may afford,
  And let them spread the table Tomorrow.

And when I at last must throw off this frail cov'ring
  Which I've worn for three-score years and ten,
On the brink of the grave I'll not seek to keep
    hov'ring,
  Nor my thread wish to spin o'er again:
But my face in the glass I'll serenely survey,
  And with smiles count each wrinkle and furrow;
As this old worn-out stuff, which is threadbare Today,
  May become Everlasting Tomorrow.

J. Collins

CCVII

Life! I know not what thou art,
But know that thou and I must part;
And when, or how, or where we met
I own to me's a secret yet.

    Life! we've been long together
Through pleasant and through cloudy weather;
'Tis hard to part when friends are dear—
Perhaps 'twill cost a sigh, a tear;
—Then steal away, give little warning,
  Choose thine own time;
Say not Good Night,—but in some brighter
    clime
  Bid me Good Morning.

A. L. Barbauld

The Golden Treasury

Book Fourth

TO THE MUSES

Whether on Ida's shady brow,
  Or in the chambers of the East,
The chambers of the sun, that now
  From ancient melody have ceased;

Whether in Heaven ye wander fair,
  Or the green corners of the earth,
Or the blue regions of the air,
  Where the melodious winds have birth;

Whether on crystal rocks ye rove
  Beneath the bosom of the sea,
Wandering in many a coral grove,—
  Fair Nine, forsaking Poetry;
How have you left the ancient love

  That bards of old enjoy'd in you!
The languid strings do scarcely move,
  The sound is forced, the notes are few.

                                        W. Blake

CCIX

ODE ON THE POETS

Bards of Passion and of Mirth
Ye have left your souls on earth!
Have ye souls in heaven too,
Double-lived in regions new?

—Yes, and those of heaven commune
With the spheres of sun and moon;
With the noise of fountains wond'rous
And the parle of voices thund'rous;
With the whisper of heaven's trees
And one another, in soft ease
Seated on Elysian lawns
Browsed by none but Dian's fawns;
Underneath large blue-bells tented,
Where the daisies are rose-scented,
And the rose herself has got
Perfume which on earth is not;
Where the nightingale doth sing
Not a senseless, trancéd thing,
But divine melodious truth;
Philosophic numbers smooth;
Tales and golden histories
Of heaven and its mysteries.

Thus ye live on high, and then
On the earth ye live again;
And the souls ye left behind you
Teach us, here, the way to find you,
Where your other souls are joying,
Never slumber'd, never cloying,
Here, your earth-born souls still speak
To mortals, of their little week;
Of their sorrows and delights;
Of their passions and their spites;
Of their glory and their shame;
What doth strengthen and what maim :—
Thus ye teach us, every day,
Wisdom, though fled far away.

Bards of Passion and of Mirth
Ye have left your souls on earth !
Ye have souls in heaven too,
Double-lived in regions new !

J. Keats

CCX

ON FIRST LOOKING INTO CHAPMAN'S HOMER

Much have I travell'd in the realms of gold
And many goodly states and kingdoms seen;
Round many western islands have I been
Which bards in fealty to Apollo hold.

Oft of one wide expanse had I been told
That deep-brow'd Homer ruled as his demesne:
Yet did I never breathe its pure serene
Till I heard Chapman speak out loud and bold:

—Then felt I like some watcher of the skies
When a new planet swims into his ken;
Or like stout Cortez, when with eagle eyes

He stared at the Pacific—and all his men
Look'd at each other with a wild surmise—
Silent, upon a peak in Darien.

J. Keats

CCXI

LOVE

All thoughts, all passions, all delights,
Whatever stirs this mortal frame,
All are but ministers of Love,
    And feed his sacred flame.

Oft in my waking dreams do I
Live o'er again that happy hour,
When midway on the mount I lay,
    Beside the ruin'd tower.

The moonshine stealing o'er the scene
Had blended with the lights of eve;
And she was there, my hope, my joy,
    My own dear Genevieve!

She lean'd against the arméd man,
The statue of the arméd knight;
She stood and listen'd to my lay,
    Amid the lingering light.

Few sorrows hath she of her own,
My hope ! my joy ! my Genevieve !
She loves me best, whene'er I sing
    The songs that make her grieve.

I play'd a soft and doleful air,
I sang an old and moving story—
An old rude song, that suited well
    That ruin wild and hoary.

She listen'd with a flitting blush,
With downcast eyes and modest grace;
For well she knew, I could not choose
    But gaze upon her face.

I told her of the Knight that wore
Upon his shield a burning brand;
And that for ten long years he woo'd
    The Lady of the Land.

I told her how he pined : and ah !
The deep, the low, the pleading tone
With which I sang another's love
    Interpreted my own.

She listen'd with a flitting blush,
With downcast eyes, and modest grace;
And she forgave me, that I gazed
    Too fondly on her face !

But when I told the cruel scorn
That crazed that bold and lovely Knight,
And that he cross'd the mountain-woods,
    Nor rested day nor night;

That sometimes from the savage den,
And sometimes from the darksome shade,
And sometimes starting up at once
    In green and sunny glade,—

There came and look'd him in the face
An angel beautiful and bright;
And that he knew it was a Fiend.
    This miserable Knight!

And that unknowing what he did,
He leap'd amid a murderous band,
And saved from outrage worse than death
    The Lady of the Land;—

And how she wept, and clasp'd his knees;
And how she tended him in vain—
And ever strove to expiate
    The scorn that crazed his brain;—

And that she nursed him in a cave,
And how his madness went away,
When on the yellow forest-leaves
    A dying man he lay;—

His dying words—but when I reach'd
That tenderest strain of all the ditty,
My faltering voice and pausing harp
    Disturb'd her soul with pity!

All impulses of soul and sense
Had thrill'd my guileless Genevieve;
The music and the doleful tale,
    The rich and balmy eve;

And hopes, and fears that kindle hope,
An undistinguishable throng,
And gentle wishes long subdued,
    Subdued and cherish'd long!

She wept with pity and delight,
She blush'd with love, and virgin shame;
And like the murmur of a dream,
    I heard her breathe my name.

Her bosom heaved—she stepp'd aside,
As conscious of my look she stept—
Then suddenly, with timorous eye
    She fled to me and wept.

She half inclosed me with her arms,
She press'd me with a meek embrace;
And bending back her head, look'd up,
    And gazed upon my face.

'Twas partly love, and partly fear,
And partly 'twas a bashful art
That I might rather feel, than see,
    The swelling of her heart.

I calm'd her fears, and she was calm,
And told her love with virgin pride;
And so I won my Genevieve,
    My bright and beauteous Bride.

S. T. Coleridge

CCXII

ALL FOR LOVE

O talk not to me of a name great in story,
The days of our youth are the days of our glory;
And the myrtle and ivy of sweet two-and-twenty
Are worth all your laurels, though ever so plenty.

What are garlands and crowns to the brow that is
    wrinkled?
'Tis but as a dead flower with May-dew be-
    sprinkled:
Then away with all such from the head that is
    hoary—
What care I for the wreaths that can only give glory?

Oh Fame!—if I e'er took delight in thy praises,
'Twas less for the sake of thy high-sounding phrases,
Than to see the bright eyes of the dear one discover
She thought that I was not unworthy to love her.

There chiefly I sought thee, there only I found thee;
Her glance was the best of the rays that surround thee;
When it sparkled o'er aught that was bright in my
    story,
I knew it was love, and I felt it was glory.

Lord Byron

CCXIII

THE OUTLAW

O Brignall banks are wild and fair,
 And Greta woods are green,
And you may gather garlands there
 Would grace a summer-queen.
And as I rode by Dalton-Hall
 Beneath the turrets high,
A Maiden on the castle-wall
 Was singing merrily :
' O Brignall banks are fresh and fair,
 And Greta woods are green ;
I'd rather rove with Edmund there
 Than reign our English queen.'

' If, Maiden, thou wouldst wend with me,
 To leave both tower and town,
Thou first must guess what life lead we
 That dwell by dale and down.
And if thou canst that riddle read,
 As read full well you may,
Then to the greenwood shalt thou speed
 As blithe as Queen of May.'
Yet sung she, ' Brignall banks are fair,
 And Greta woods are green ;
I'd rather rove with Edmund there
 Than reign our English queen.

' I read you, by your bugle-horn
 And by your palfrey good,
I read you for a ranger sworn
 To keep the king's greenwood.'
' A Ranger, lady, winds his horn,
 And 'tis at peep of light ;
His blast is heard at merry morn,
 And mine at dead of night.'
Yet sung she, ' Brignall banks are fair,
 And Greta woods are gay ;
I would I were with Edmund there
 To reign his Queen of May !

'With burnish'd brand and musketoon
    So gallantly you come,
I read you for a bold Dragoon
    That lists the tuck of drum.'
'I list no more the tuck of drum,
    No more the trumpet hear;
But when the beetle sounds his hum
    My comrades take the spear.
And O! though Brignall banks be fair
    And Greta woods be gay,
Yet mickle must the maiden dare
    Would reign my Queen of May!

'Maiden! a nameless life I lead,
    A nameless death I'll die;
The fiend whose lantern lights the mead
    Were better mate than I!
And when I'm with my comrades met
    Beneath the greenwood bough,—
What once we were we all forget
    Nor think what we are now.'

Chorus

'Yet Brignall banks are fresh and fair,
    And Greta woods are green,
And you may gather garlands there
    Would grace a summer-queen.'

Sir W. Scott

CCXIV

There be none of Beauty's daughters
    With a magic like Thee;
And like music on the waters
    Is thy sweet voice to me:
When, as if its sound were causing
    The charmed ocean's pausing,
    The waves lie still and gleaming,
And the lull'd winds seem dreaming:

And the midnight moon is weaving
  Her bright chain o'er the deep,
Whose breast is gently heaving
  As an infant's asleep :
So the spirit bows before thee
To listen and adore thee;
With a full but soft emotion,
Like the swell of Summer's ocean.

Lord Byron

CCXV

THE INDIAN SERENADE

I arise from dreams of Thee
In the first sweet sleep of night,
When the winds are breathing low
And the stars are shining bright :
I arise from dreams of thee,
And a spirit in my feet
Hath led me—who knows how ?
To thy chamber-window, Sweet !

The wandering airs they faint
On the dark, the silent stream—
The champak odours fail
Like sweet thoughts in a dream;
The nightingale's complaint
It dies upon her heart,
As I must die on thine
O belovéd as thou art !

Oh lift me from the grass !
I die, I faint, I fail !
Let thy love in kisses rain
On my lips and eyelids pale.
My cheek is cold and white, alas !
My heart beats loud and fast;
Oh ! press it close to thine again
Where it will break at last.

P. B. Shelley

CCXVI

She walks in beauty, like the night
Of cloudless climes and starry skies,
And all that's best of dark and bright
Meet in her aspect and her eyes;
Thus mellow'd to that tender light
Which heaven to gaudy day denies.

One shade the more, one ray the less,
Had half impair'd the nameless grace
Which waves in every raven tress
Or softly lightens o'er her face,
Where thoughts serenely sweet express
How pure, how dear their dwelling-place.

And on that cheek and o'er that brow
So soft, so calm, yet eloquent,
The smiles that win, the tints that glow
But tell of days in goodness spent,—
A mind at peace with all below,
A heart whose love is innocent.

Lord Byron

CCXVII

She was a Phantom of delight
When first she gleam'd upon my sight;
A lovely Apparition, sent
To be a moment's ornament;
Her eyes as stars of twilight fair;
Like Twilight's, too, her dusky hair;
But all things else about her drawn
From May-time and the cheerful dawn;
A dancing shape, an image gay,
To haunt, to startle, and waylay.

I saw her upon nearer view,
A Spirit, yet a Woman too!
Her houshold motions light and free,
And steps of virgin-liberty;

A countenance in which did meet
Sweet records, promises as sweet;
A creature not too bright or good
For human nature's daily food,
For transient sorrows, simple wiles,
Praise, blame, love, kisses, tears, and smiles.

And now I see with eye serene
The very pulse of the machine;
A being breathing thoughtful breath,
A traveller between life and death:
The reason firm, the temperate will,
Endurance, foresight, strength, and skill;
A perfect Woman, nobly plann'd
To warn, to comfort, and command;
And yet a Spirit still, and bright
With something of an angel-light.

W. Wordsworth

CCXVIII

She is not fair to outward view
    As many maidens be;
Her loveliness I never knew
    Until she smiled on me.
O then I saw her eye was bright,
A well of love, a spring of light.

But now her looks are coy and cold,
    To mine they ne'er reply,
And yet I cease not to behold
    The love-light in her eye:
Her very frowns are fairer far
Than smiles of other maidens are.

H. Coleridge

CCXIX

I fear thy kisses, gentle maiden;
Thou needest not fear mine;
My spirit is too deeply laden
Ever to burthen thine.

I fear thy mien, thy tones, thy motion;
Thou needest not fear mine;
Innocent is the heart's devotion
With which I worship thine.

P. B. Shelley

CCXX

She dwelt among the untrodden ways
　　Beside the springs of Dove;
A maid whom there were none to praise,
　　And very few to love.

A violet by a mossy stone
　　Half-hidden from the eye!
—Fair as a star, when only one
　　Is shining in the sky.

She lived unknown, and few could know
　　When Lucy ceased to be;
But she is in her grave, and, oh,
　　The difference to me!

W. Wordsworth

CCXXI

I travell'd among unknown men
　　In lands beyond the sea;
Nor, England! did I know till then
　　What love I bore to thee.

'Tis past, that melancholy dream !
  Nor will I quit thy shore
A second time; for still I seem
  To love thee more and more.

Among thy mountains did I feel
  The joy of my desire;
And she I cherish'd turn'd her wheel
  Beside an English fire.

Thy mornings show'd, thy nights conceal'd
  The bowers where Lucy play'd;
And thine too is the last green field
  That Lucy's eyes survey'd.

                              W. Wordsworth

CCXXII

THE EDUCATION OF NATURE

Three years she grew in sun and shower;
Then Nature said, ' A lovelier flower
On earth was never sown :
This Child I to myself will take;
She shall be mine, and I will make
A lady of my own.

' Myself will to my darling be
Both law and impulse : and with me
The girl, in rock and plain,
In earth and heaven, in glade and bower,
Shall feel an overseeing power
To kindle or restrain.

' She shall be sportive as the fawn
That wild with glee across the lawn
Or up the mountain springs;
And her's shall be the breathing balm,
And her's the silence and the calm
Of mute insensate things.

The floating clouds their state shall lend
To her; for her the willow bend;
Nor shall she fail to see
Ev'n in the motions of the storm
Grace that shall mould the maiden's form
By silent sympathy.

' The stars of midnight shall be dear
To her; and she shall lean her ear
In many a secret place
Where rivulets dance their wayward round,
And beauty born of murmuring sound
Shall pass into her face.

' And vital feelings of delight
Shall rear her form to stately height,
Her virgin bosom swell;
Such thoughts to Lucy I will give
While she and I together live
Here in this happy dell.'

Thus Nature spake—The work was done—
How soon my Lucy's race was run !
She died, and left to me
This heath, this calm and quiet scene;
The memory of what has been,
And never more will be.

W. Wordsworth

CCXXIII

A slumber did my spirit seal;
　I had no human fears :
She seem'd a thing that could not feel
　The touch of earthly years.

No motion has she now, no force;
　She neither hears nor sees;
Roll'd round in earth's diurnal course
　With rocks, and stones, and trees.

W. Wordsworth

CCXXIV

A LOST LOVE

I meet thy pensive, moonlight face;
    Thy thrilling voice I hear;
And former hours and scenes retrace,
    Too fleeting, and too dear !

Then sighs and tears flow fast and free,
    Though none is nigh to share;
And life has nought beside for me
    So sweet as this despair.

There are crush'd hearts that will not break;
    And mine, methinks, is one;
Or thus I should not weep and wake,
    And thou to slumber gone.

I little thought it thus could be
    In days more sad and fair—
That earth could have a place for me,
    And thou no longer there.

Yet death cannot our hearts divide,
    Or make thee less my own :
'Twere sweeter sleeping at thy side
    Than watching here alone

Yet never, never can we part,
    While Memory holds her reign :
Thine, thine is still this wither'd heart,
    Till we shall meet again.

H. F. Lyte

CCXXV

LORD ULLIN'S DAUGHTER

A Chieftain to the Highlands bound
Cries ' Boatman, do not tarry !
And I'll give thee a silver pound
To row us o'er the ferry ! '

'Now who be ye, would cross Lochgyle,
This dark and stormy water?'
'O I'm the chief of Ulva's isle,
And this, Lord Ullin's daughter.

'And fast before her father's men
Three days we've fled together,
For should he find us in the glen,
My blood would stain the heather.

'His horsemen hard behind us ride—
Should they our steps discover,
Then who will cheer my bonny bride,
When they have slain her lover?'

Out spoke the hardy Highland wight,
'I'll go, my chief, I'm ready :
It is not for your silver bright,
But for your winsome lady :—

'And by my word ! the bonny bird
In danger shall not tarry ;
So though the waves are raging white
I'll row you o'er the ferry.'

By this the storm grew loud apace,
The water-wraith was shrieking ;
And in the scowl of Heaven each face
Grew dark as they were speaking.

But still as wilder blew the wind,
And as the night grew drearer,
Adown the glen rode arméd men,
Their trampling sounded nearer.

'O haste thee, haste !' the lady cries,
'Though tempests round us gather ;
I'll meet the raging of the skies,
But not an angry father.'

The boat has left a stormy land,
A stormy sea before her,—
When, oh ! too strong for human hand
The tempest gather'd o'er her.

And still they row'd amidst the roar
Of waters fast prevailing :
Lord Ullin reach'd that fatal shore,—
His wrath was changed to wailing.

For, sore dismay'd, through storm and shade
His child he did discover :—
One lovely hand she stretch'd for aid,
And one was round her lover.

' Come back ! come back ! ' he cried in grief,
' Across this stormy water :
And I'll forgive your Highland chief,
My daughter !—Oh, my daughter ! '

'Twas vain : the loud waves lash'd the shore,
Return or aid preventing :
The waters wild went o'er his child,
And he was left lamenting.

T. Campbell

CCXXVI

LUCY GRAY

Oft I had heard of Lucy Gray :
And when I cross'd the wild,
I chanced to see at break of day
The solitary child.

No mate, no comrade Lucy knew ;
She dwelt on a wide moor,
The sweetest thing that ever grew
Beside a human door !

You yet may spy the fawn at play,
The hare upon the green ;
But the sweet face of Lucy Gray
Will never more be seen.

' To-night will be a stormy night—
You to the town must go ;
And take a lantern, Child, to light
Your mother through the snow.'

'That, Father ! will I gladly do :
'Tis scarcely afternoon—
The minster-clock has just struck two,
And yonder is the moon ! '

At this the father raised his hook,
And snapp'd a faggot-band ;
He plied his work ;—and Lucy took
The lantern in her hand.

Not blither is the mountain roe :
With many a wanton stroke
Her feet disperse the powdery snow,
That rises up like smoke.

The storm came on before its time :
She wander'd up and down ;
And many a hill did Lucy climb :
But never reach'd the town.

The wretched parents all that night
Went shouting far and wide ;
But there was neither sound nor sight
To serve them for a guide.

At day-break on a hill they stood
That overlook'd the moor ;
And thence they saw the bridge of wood
A furlong from their door.

They wept—and, turning homeward, cried
' In heaven we all shall meet ! '
—When in the snow the mother spied
The print of Lucy's feet.

Then downwards from the steep hill's edge
They track'd the footmarks small ;
And through the broken hawthorn hedge,
And by the long stone-wall :

And then an open field they cross'd :
The marks were still the same ;
They track'd them on, nor ever lost ;
And to the bridge they came :

They follow'd from the snowy bank
Those footmarks, one by one,
Into the middle of the plank;
And further there were none!

—Yet some maintain that to this day
She is a living child;
That you may see sweet Lucy Gray
Upon the lonesome wild.

O'er rough and smooth she trips along,
And never looks behind;
And sings a solitary song
That whistles in the wind.

W. Wordsworth

CCXXVII

JOCK OF HAZELDEAN

Why weep ye by the tide, ladie?
 Why weep ye by the tide?
I'll wed ye to my youngest son,
 And ye sall be his bride:
And ye sall be his bride, ladie,
 Sae comely to be seen '—
But aye she loot the tears down fa'
 For Jock of Hazeldean.

' Now let this wilfu' grief be done,
 And dry that cheek so pale;
Young Frank is chief of Errington
 And lord of Langley-dale;
His step is first in peaceful ha',
 His sword in battle keen '—
But aye she loot the tears down fa'
 For Jock of Hazeldean.

A chain of gold ye sall not lack,
 Nor braid to bind your hair,
Nor mettled hound, nor managed hawk,
 Nor palfrey fresh and fair;

And you the foremost o' them a'
  Shall ride our forest-queen '—
But aye she loot the tears down fa'
  For Jock of Hazeldean.

The kirk was deck'd at morning-tide,
  The tapers glimmer'd fair;
The priest and bridegroom wait the bride,
  And dame and knight are there:
They sought her baith by bower and ha';
  The ladie was not seen!
She's o'er the Border, and awa'
  Wi' Jock of Hazeldean.

Sir W. Scott

CCXXVIII

LOVE'S PHILOSOPHY

The fountains mingle with the river
And the rivers with the ocean,
The winds of heaven mix for ever
With a sweet emotion;
Nothing in the world is single,
All things by a law divine
In one another's being mingle—
Why not I with thine?

See the mountains kiss high heaven
And the waves clasp one another;
No sister-flower would be forgiven
If it disdain'd its brother:
And the sunlight clasps the earth,
And the moonbeams kiss the sea—
What are all these kissings worth,
If thou kiss not me?

P. B. Shelley

CCXXIX

ECHOES

How sweet the answer Echo makes
To Music at night
When, roused by lute or horn, she wakes,
And far away o'er lawns and lakes
Goes answering light !

Yet Love hath echoes truer far
And far more sweet
Than e'er, beneath the moonlight's star,
Of horn or lute or soft guitar
The songs repeat.

'Tis when the sigh,—in youth sincere
And only then,
The sigh that's breathed for one to hear—
Is by that one, that only Dear
Breathed back again.

T. Moore

CCXXX

A SERENADE

Ah ! County Guy, the hour is nigh,
  The sun has left the lea,
The orange-flower perfumes the bower,
  The breeze is on the sea.
The lark, his lay who thrill'd all day,
  Sits hush'd his partner nigh ;
Breeze, bird, and flower confess the hour,
  But where is County Guy ?

The village maid steals through the shade
  Her shepherd's suit to hear ;
To Beauty shy, by lattice high,
  Sings high-born Cavalier.

The star of Love, all stars above,
Now reigns o'er earth and sky,
And high and low the influence know—
But where is County Guy?

Sir W. Scott

CCXXXI

TO THE EVENING STAR

Gem of the crimson-colour'd Even,
Companion of retiring day,
Why at the closing gates of heaven,
Beloved Star, dost thou delay?

So fair thy pensile beauty burns
When soft the tear of twilight flows;
So due thy plighted love returns
To chambers brighter than the rose;

To Peace, to Pleasure, and to Love
So kind a star thou seem'st to be,
Sure some enamour'd orb above
Descends and burns to meet with thee.

Thine is the breathing, blushing hour
When all unheavenly passions fly,
Chased by the soul-subduing power
Of Love's delicious witchery.

O! sacred to the fall of day
Queen of propitious stars, appear,
And early rise, and long delay,
When Caroline herself is here!

Shine on her chosen green resort
Whose trees the sunward summit crown,
And wanton flowers, that well may court
An angel's feet to tread them down:—

Shine on her sweetly scented road
Thou star of evening's purple dome,
That lead'st the nightingale abroad,
And guid'st the pilgrim to his home.

Shine where my charmer's sweeter breath
Embalms the soft exhaling dew,
Where dying winds a sigh bequeath
To kiss the cheek of rosy hue :—

Where, winnow'd by the gentle air,
Her silken tresses darkly flow
And fall upon her brow so fair,
Like shadows on the mountain snow.

Thus, ever thus, at day's decline
In converse sweet to wander far—
O bring with thee my Caroline,
And thou shalt be my Ruling Star !

T. Campbell

CCXXXII

TO THE NIGHT

Swiftly walk over the western wave,
  Spirit of Night !
Out of the misty eastern cave
Where, all the long and lone daylight,
Thou wovest dreams of joy and fear
Which make thee terrible and dear,—
  Swift be thy flight !

Wrap thy form in a mantle gray
  Star-inwrought;
Blind with thine hair the eyes of Day,
Kiss her until she be wearied out :
Then wander o'er city and sea and land,
Touching all with thine opiate wand—
  Come, long-sought !

When I arose and saw the dawn,
  I sigh'd for thee;
When light rode high, and the dew was gone,
And noon lay heavy on flower and tree,
And the weary Day turn'd to his rest
Lingering like an unloved guest,
  I sigh'd for thee.

Thy brother Death came, and cried
   Wouldst thou me?
Thy sweet child Sleep, the filmy-eyed,
Murmur'd like a noon-tide bee
Shall I nestle near thy side?
Wouldst thou me?—And I replied
   No, not thee!

Death will come when thou art dead,
   Soon, too soon—
Sleep will come when thou art fled;
Of neither would I ask the boon
I ask of thee, belovèd Night—
Swift be thine approaching flight,
   Come soon, soon!
       P. B. Shelley

CCXXXIII

TO A DISTANT FRIEND

Why art thou silent? Is thy love a plant
Of such weak fibre that the treacherous air
Of absence withers what was once so fair?
Is there no debt to pay, no boon to grant?

Yet have my thoughts for thee been vigilant,
Bound to thy service with unceasing care—
The mind's least generous wish a mendicant
For nought but what thy happiness could spare.

Speak!—though this soft warm heart, once free to
  hold
A thousand tender pleasures, thine and mine,
Be left more desolate, more dreary cold

Than a forsaken bird's-nest fill'd with snow
'Mid its own bush of leafless eglantine—
Speak, that my torturing doubts their end may know!
       W. Wordsworth

CCXXXIV

When we two parted
In silence and tears,
Half broken-hearted,
To sever for years,
Pale grew thy cheek and cold,
Colder thy kiss;
Truly that hour foretold
Sorrow to this!

The dew of the morning
Sunk chill on my brow;
It felt like the warning
Of what I feel now.
Thy vows are all broken,
And light is thy fame:
I hear thy name spoken
And share in its shame.

They name thee before me,
A knell to mine ear;
A shudder comes o'er me—
Why wert thou so dear?
They know not I knew thee
Who knew thee too well:
Long, long shall I rue thee,
Too deeply to tell.

In secret we met:
In silence I grieve
That thy heart could forget,
Thy spirit deceive.
If I should meet thee
After long years,
How should I greet thee?—
With silence and tears.

Lord Byron

CCXXXV

HAPPY INSENSIBILITY

In a drear-nighted December,
Too happy, happy tree,
Thy branches ne'er remember
Their green felicity :
The north cannot undo them
With a sleety whistle through them,
Nor frozen thawings glue them
From budding at the prime.

In a drear-nighted December,
Too happy, happy brook,
Thy bubblings ne'er remember
Apollo's summer look;
But with a sweet forgetting
They stay their crystal fretting,
Never, never petting
About the frozen time.

Ah ! would 'twere so with many
A gentle girl and boy !
But were there ever any
Writhed not at passéd joy ?
To know the change and feel it,
When there is none to heal it
Nor numbéd sense to steal it—
Was never said in rhyme.

J. Keats

CCXXXVI

Where shall the lover rest
  Whom the fates sever
From his true maiden's breast
  Parted for ever ?

Where, through groves deep and high
   Sounds the far billow,
Where early violets die
   Under the willow.
      Eleu loro
   Soft shall be his pillow.

There through the summer day
   Cool streams are laving;
There, while the tempests sway,
   Scarce are boughs waving;
There thy rest shalt thou take,
   Parted for ever,
Never again to wake
   Never, O never!
      Eleu loro
   Never, O never!

Where shall the traitor rest,
   He, the deceiver,
Who could win maiden's breast,
   Ruin, and leave her?
In the lost battle,
   Borne down by the flying,
Where mingles war's rattle
   With groans of the dying;
      Eleu loro
   There shall he be lying.

Her wing shall the eagle flap
   O'er the falsehearted;
His warm blood the wolf shall lap
   Ere life be parted:
Shame and dishonour sit
   By his grave ever;
Blessing shall hallow it
   Never, O never!
      Eleu loro
   Never, O never!
            Sir W. Scott

CCXXXVII

LA BELLE DAME SANS MERCI

' O what can ail thee, knight-at-arms,
   Alone and palely loitering ?
The sedge has wither'd from the lake,
   And no birds sing.

' O what can ail thee, knight-at-arms !
   So haggard and so woe-begone ?
The squirrel's granary is full,
   And the harvest's done.

' I see a lily on thy brow
   With anguish moist and fever-dew,
And on thy cheeks a fading rose
   Fast withereth too.'

I met a lady in the meads,
   Full beautiful—a faery's child,
Her hair was long, her foot was light,
   And her eyes were wild.

' I made a garland for her head,
   And bracelets too, and fragrant zone;
She look'd at me as she did love,
   And made sweet moan.

' I set her on my pacing steed
   And nothing else saw all day long,
For sidelong would she bend, and sing
   A faery's song.

' She found me roots of relish sweet
   And honey wild and manna-dew,
And sure in language strange she said
   " I love thee true."

' She took me to her elfin grot,
   And there she wept and sigh'd full sore;
And there I shut her wild wild eyes
   With kisses four.

'And there she lulléd me asleep,
  And there I dream'd—Ah! woe betide!
The latest dream I ever dream'd
  On the cold hill's side.

' I saw pale kings and princes too,
  Pale warriors, death-pale were they all:
They cried—" La belle Dame sans Merci
  Hath thee in thrall! "

I saw their starved lips in the gloam
  With horrid warning gapéd wide,
And I awoke and found me here
  On the cold hill's side.

And this is why I sojourn here
  Alone and palely loitering,
Though the sedge is wither'd from the lake,
  And no birds sing.'

                                J. Keats

CCXXXVIII

THE ROVER

A weary lot is thine, fair maid,
  A weary lot is thine!
To pull the thorn thy brow to braid,
  And press the rue for wine.
A lightsome eye, a soldier's mien,
  A feather of the blue,
A doublet of the Lincoln green—
  No more of me you knew
              My Love!
No more of me you knew.

' This morn is merry June, I trow,
  The rose is budding fain;
But she shall bloom in winter snow
  Ere we two meet again.'

He turn'd his charger as he spake
  Upon the river shore,
He gave the bridle-reins a shake,
  Said ' Adieu for evermore
        My Love !
And adieu for evermore.'
                Sir W. Scott

CCXXXIX

THE FLIGHT OF LOVE

When the lamp is shatter'd
The light in the dust lies dead—
When the cloud is scatter'd,
The rainbow's glory is shed.
When the lute is broken,
Sweet tones are remember'd not ;
When the lips have spoken,
Loved accents are soon forgot.

As music and splendour
Survive not the lamp and the lute,
The heart's echoes render
No song when the spirit is mute—
No song but sad dirges,
Like the wind through a ruin'd cell,
Or the mournful surges
That ring the dead seaman's knell.

When hearts have once mingled,
Love first leaves the well-built nest ;
The weak one is singled
To endure what it once possesst.
O Love ! who bewailest
The frailty of all things here,
Why choose you the frailest
For your cradle, your home, and your bier ?

Its passions will rock thee
As the storms rock the ravens on high;
Bright reason will mock thee
Like the sun from a wintry sky.
From thy nest every rafter
Will rot, and thine eagle home
Leave thee naked to laughter,
When leaves fall and cold winds come.

P. B. Shelley

CCXL

THE MAID OF NEIDPATH

O lovers' eyes are sharp to see,
   And lovers' ears in hearing;
And love, in life's extremity,
   Can lend an hour of cheering.
Disease had been in Mary's bower
   And slow decay from mourning,
Though now she sits on Neidpath's tower
   To watch her Love's returning.

All sunk and dim her eyes so bright,
   Her form decay'd by pining,
Till through her wasted hand, at night,
   You saw the taper shining.
By fits a sultry hectic hue
   Across her cheek was flying;
By fits so ashy pale she grew
   Her maidens thought her dying.

Yet keenest powers to see and hear
   Seem'd in her frame residing;
Before the watch-dog prick'd his ear
   She heard her lover's riding;
Ere scarce a distant form was kenn'd
   She knew and waved to greet him,
And o'er the battlement did bend
   As on the wing to meet him.

He came—he pass'd—an heedless gaze
    As o'er some stranger glancing;
Her welcome, spoke in faltering phrase,
    Lost in his courser's prancing—
The castle-arch, whose hollow tone
    Returns each whisper spoken,
Could scarcely catch the feeble moan
    Which told her heart was broken.
                  Sir W. Scott

CCXLI

Earl March look'd on his dying child,
    And, smit with grief to view her—
The youth, he cried, whom I exiled
    Shall be restcred to woo her.

She's at the window many an hour
    His coming to discover :
And he look'd up to Ellen's bower
    And she look'd on her lover—

But ah ! so pale, he knew her not,
    Though her smile on him was dwelling—
And am I then forgot—forgot ?
    It broke the heart of Ellen.

In vain he weeps, in vain he sighs,
    Her cheek is cold as ashes;
Nor love's own kiss shall wake those eyes
    To lift their silken lashes.
                  T. Campbell

CCXLII

Bright Star ! would I were steadfast as thou art—
Not in lone splendour hung aloft the night,
And watching, with eternal lids apart,
Like Nature's patient sleepless Eremite.

The moving waters at their priestlike task
Of pure ablution round earth's human shores,
Or gazing on the new soft fallen mask
Of snow upon the mountains and the moors :—

No—yet still steadfast, still unchangeable,
Pillow'd upon my fair Love's ripening breast
To feel for ever its soft fall and swell,
Awake for ever in a sweet unrest ;

Still, still to hear her tender-taken breath,
And so live ever,—or else swoon to death.

J. Keats

CCXLIII

THE TERROR OF DEATH

When I have fears that I may cease to be
Before my pen has glean'd my teeming brain,
Before high-piléd books, in charact'ry
Hold like rich garners the full-ripen'd grain;

When I behold, upon the night's starr'd face,
Huge cloudy symbols of a high romance,
And think that I may never live to trace
Their shadows, with the magic hand of chance

And when I feel, fair Creature of an hour !
That I shall never look upon thee more,
Never have relish in the faery power
Of unreflecting love—then on the shore

Of the wide world I stand alone, and think
Till Love and Fame to nothingness do sink.

Keats

CCXLIV

DESIDERIA

Surprized by joy—impatient as the wind—
I turn'd to share the transport—Oh! with whom
But Thee—deep buried in the silent tomb,
That spot which no vicissitude can find?

Love, faithful love recall'd thee to my mind—
But how could I forget thee?   Through what power
Even for the least division of an hour
Have I been so beguiled as to be blind

To my most grievous loss!—That thought's return
Was the worst pang that sorrow ever bore
Save one, one only, when I stood forlorn,

Knowing my heart's best treasure was no more;
That neither present time, nor years unborn
Could to my sight that heavenly face restore.

W. Wordsworth

CCXLV

At the mid hour of night, when stars are weeping,
    I fly
To the lone vale we loved, when life shone warm in
    thine eye;
And I think oft, if spirits can steal from the regions
    of air
To revisit past scenes of delight, thou wilt come to
    me there
And tell me our love is remember'd, even in the sky i

Then I sing the wild song it once was rapture to hear
When our voices, commingling, breathed like one on
    the ear;
And as Echo far off through the vale my sad orison
    rolls,

I think, oh my Love ! 'tis thy voice, from the Kingdom of Souls
Faintly answering still the notes that once were so
   dear.

                          T. Moore

CCXLVI

ELEGY ON THYRZA

And thou art dead, as young and fair
   As aught of mortal birth;
And forms so soft and charms so rare
   Too soon return'd to Earth !
Though Earth received them in her bed,
And o'er the spot the crowd may tread
   In carelessness or mirth,
There is an eye which could not brook
A moment on that grave to look.

I will not ask where thou liest low
   Nor gaze upon the spot;
There flowers or weeds at will may grow
   So I behold them not :
It is enough for me to prove
That what I loved, and long must love,
   Like common earth can rot;
To me there needs no stone to tell
'Tis Nothing that I loved so well.

Yet did I love thee to the last,
   As fervently as thou
Who didst not change through all the past
   And canst not alter now.
The love where Death has set his seal
Nor age can chill, nor rival steal,
   Nor falsehood disavow :
And, what were worse, thou canst not see
Or wrong, or change, or fault in me.

The better days of life were ours;
   The worst can be but mine:
The sun that cheers, the storm that lours,
   Shall never more be thine.
The silence of that dreamless sleep
I envy now too much to weep;
   Nor need I to repine
That all those charms have pass'd away
I might have watch'd through long decay.

The flower in ripen'd bloom unmatch'd
   Must fall the earliest prey;
Though by no hand untimely snatch'd,
   The leaves must drop away.
And yet it were a greater grief
To watch it withering, leaf by leaf,
   Than see it pluck'd today;
Since earthly eye but ill can bear
To trace the change to foul from fair.

I know not if I could have borne
   To see thy beauties fade;
The night that follow'd such a morn
   Had worn a deeper shade:
Thy day without a cloud hath past,
And thou wert lovely to the last,
   Extinguish'd, not decay'd;
As stars that shoot along the sky
Shine brightest as they fall from high.

As once I wept, if I could weep,
   My tears might well be shed,
To think I was not near, to keep
   One vigil o'er thy bed:
To gaze, how fondly! on thy face,
To fold thee in a faint embrace,
   Uphold thy drooping head;
And show that love, however vain,
Nor thou nor I can feel again.

Yet how much less it were to gain,
   Though thou hast left me free,
The loveliest things that still remain
   Than thus remember thee!

The all of thine that cannot die
Through dark and dread Eternity
　Returns again to me,
And more thy buried love endears
Than aught except its living years.

Lord Byron

CCXLVII

One word is too often profaned
　For me to profane it,
One feeling too falsely disdain'd
　For thee to disdain it.
One hope is too like despair
　For prudence to smother,
And pity from thee more dear
　Than that from another.

I can give not what men call love;
　But wilt thou accept not
The worship the heart lifts above
　And the Heavens reject not:
The desire of the moth for the star,
　Of the night for the morrow,
The devotion to something afar
　From the sphere of our sorrow?

P. B. Shelley

CCXLVIII

GATHERING SONG OF DONALD THE BLACK

Pibroch of Donuil Dhu
Pibroch of Donuil
Wake thy wild voice anew,
Summon Clan Conuil.

Come away, come away,
  Hark to the summons !
Come in your war-array,
  Gentles and commons.

Come from deep glen, and
  From mountain so rocky ;
The war-pipe and pennon
  Are at Inverlocky.
Come every hill-plaid, and
  True heart that wears one,
Come every steel blade, and
  Strong hand that bears one.

Leave untended the herd,
  The flock without shelter ;
Leave the corpse uninterr'd,
  The bride at the altar ;
Leave the deer, leave the steer,
  Leave nets and barges :
Come with your fighting gear,
  Broadswords and targes.

Come as the winds come, when
  Forests are rended,
Come as the waves come, when
  Navies are stranded :
Faster come, faster come,
  Faster and faster,
Chief, vassal, page and groom,
  Tenant and master.

Fast they come, fast they come ;
  See how they gather !
Wide waves the eagle plume
  Blended with heather.
Cast your plaids, draw your blades,
  Forward each man set !
Pibroch of Donuil Dhu
  Knell for the onset !

                              Sir W. Scott

CCXLIX

A wet sheet and a flowing sea,
  A wind that follows fast
And fills the white and rustling sail
  And bends the gallant mast;
And bends the gallant mast, my boys,
  While like the eagle free
Away the good ship flies, and leaves
  Old England on the lee.

O for a soft and gentle wind!
  I heard a fair one cry;
But give to me the snoring breeze
  And white waves heaving high;
And white waves heaving high, my lads,
  The good ship tight and free—
The world of waters is our home,
  And merry men are we.

There's tempest in yon hornéd moon,
  And lightning in yon cloud;
But hark the music, mariners!
  The wind is piping loud;
The wind is piping loud, my boys,
  The lightning flashes free—
While the hollow oak our palace is,
  Our heritage the sea.

A. Cunningham

CCL

Ye Mariners of England
That guard our native seas!
Whose flag has braved, a thousand years,
The battle and the breeze!
Your glorious standard launch again
To match another foe:

And sweep through the deep,
While the stormy winds do blow;
While the battle rages loud and long
And the stormy winds do blow.

The spirits of your fathers
Shall start from every wave—
For the deck it was their field of fame,
And Ocean was their grave :
Where Blake and mighty Nelson fell
Your manly hearts shall glow,
As ye sweep through the deep,
While the stormy winds do blow;
While the battle rages loud and long
And the stormy winds do blow.

Britannia needs no bulwarks,
No towers along the steep;
Her march is o'er the mountain-waves,
Her home is on the deep.
With thunders from her native oak
She quells the floods below—
As they roar on the shore,
When the stormy winds do blow;
When the battle rages loud and long,
And the stormy winds do blow.

The meteor flag of England
Shall yet terrific burn;
Till danger's troubled night depart
And the star of peace return.
Then, then, ye ocean-warriors !
Our song and feast shall flow
To the fame of your name,
When the storm has ceased to blow;
When the fiery fight is heard no more,
And the storm has ceased to blow.

T. Campbell

CCLI

BATTLE OF THE BALTIC

Of Nelson and the North
Sing the glorious day's renown,
When to battle fierce came forth
All the might of Denmark's crown,
And her arms along the deep proudly shone;
By each gun the lighted brand
In a bold determined hand,
And the Prince of all the land
Let them on.

Like leviathans afloat
Lay their bulwarks on the brine;
While the sign of battle flew
On the lofty British line:
It was ten of April morn by the chime:
As they drifted on their path
There was silence deep as death;
And the boldest held his breath
For a time.

But the might of England flush'd
To anticipate the scene;
And her van the fleeter rush'd
O'er the deadly space between.
' Hearts of oak ! ' our captains cried, when each gun
From its adamantine lips
Spread a death-shade round the ships,
Like the hurricane eclipse
Of the sun.

Again ! again ! again !
And the havoc did not slack,
Till a feeble cheer the Dane
To our cheering sent us back;—
Their shots along the deep slowly boom :—
Then ceased—and all is wail,
As they strike the shatter'd sail;
Or in conflagration pale
Light the gloom.

Out spoke the victor then
As he hail'd them o'er the wave,
' Ye are brothers ! ye are men !
And we conquer but to save :—
So peace instead of death let us bring :
But yield, proud foe, thy fleet
With the crews, at England's feet,
And make submission meet
To our King.'

Then Denmark bless'd our chief
That he gave her wounds repose ;
And the sounds of joy and grief
From her people wildly rose,
As death withdrew his shades from the day
While the sun look'd smiling bright
O'er a wide and woeful sight,
Where the fires of funeral light
Died away.

Now joy, old England, raise !
For the tidings of thy might,
By the festal cities' blaze,
Whilst the wine-cup shines in light ;
And yet amidst that joy and uproar,
Let us think of them that sleep
Full many a fathom deep
By thy wild and stormy steep,
Elsinore !

Brave hearts ! to Britain's pride
Once so faithful and so true,
On the deck of fame that died,
With the gallant good Riou :
Soft sigh the winds of Heaven o'er their grave !
While the billow mournful rolls
And the mermaid's song condoles
Singing glory to the souls
Of the brave !

                                    T. Campbell

CCLII

ODE TO DUTY

Stern Daughter of the Voice of God !
O Duty ! if that name thou love
Who art a light to guide, a rod
To check the erring, and reprove;
Thou who art victory and law
When empty terrors overawe;
From vain temptations dost set free,
And calm'st the weary strife of frail humanity !

There are who ask not if thine eye
Be on them; who, in love and truth
Where no misgiving is, rely
Upon the genial sense of youth :
Glad hearts ! without reproach or blot,
Who do thy work, and know it not :
Oh ! if through confidence misplaced
They fail, thy saving arms, dread Power ! around
    them cast.

Serene will be our days and bright
And happy will our nature be
When love is an unerring light,
And joy its own security.
And they a blissful course may hold
Ev'n now, who, not unwisely bold,
Live in the spirit of this creed;
Yet seek thy firm support, according to their need

I, loving freedom, and untried,
No sport of every random gust,
Yet being to myself a guide,
Too blindly have reposed my trust :
And oft, when in my heart was heard
Thy timely mandate, I deferr'd
The task, in smoother walks to stray;
But thee I now would serve more strictly, if I may.

Through no disturbance of my soul
Or strong compunction in me wrought,
I supplicate for thy controul,
But in the quietness of thought :
Me this uncharter'd freedom tires ;
I feel the weight of chance-desires :
My hopes no more must change their name ;
I long for a repose that ever is the same.

Stern Lawgiver ! yet thou dost wear
The Godhead's most benignant grace ;
Nor know we anything so fair
As is the smile upon thy face :
Flowers laugh before thee on their beds,
And fragrance in thy footing treads ;
Thou dost preserve the Stars from wrong ;
And the most ancient Heavens, through Thee, are
    fresh and strong.

To humbler functions, awful Power !
I call thee : I myself commend
Unto thy guidance from this hour ;
Oh let my weakness have an end !
Give unto me, made lowly wise,
The spirit of self-sacrifice ;
The confidence of reason give ;
And in the light of truth thy Bondman let me live.

                              W. Wordsworth.

CCLIII

ON THE CASTLE OF CHILLON

Eternal Spirit of the chainless Mind !
Brightest in dungeons, Liberty ! thou art,
For there thy habitation is the heart—
The heart which love of Thee alone can bind ;

And when thy sons to fetters are consign'd,
To fetters, and the damp vault's dayless gloom,
Their country conquers with their martyrdom,
And Freedom's fame finds wings on every wind.

Chillon ! thy prison is a holy place
And thy sad floor an altar, for 'twas trod,
Until his very steps have left a trace

Worn as if thy cold pavement were a sod,
By Bonnivard ! May none those marks efface !
For they appeal from tyranny to God.

Lord Byron

CCLIV

ENGLAND AND SWITZERLAND, 1802

Two Voices are there; one is of the Sea,
One of the Mountains; each a mighty voice :
In both from age to age thou didst rejoice,
They were thy chosen music, Liberty !

There came a tyrant, and with holy glee
Thou fought'st against him,—but hast vainly
    striven :
Thou from thy Alpine holds at length art driven,
Where not a torrent murmurs heard by thee.

—Of one deep bliss thine ear hath been bereft;
Then cleave, O cleave to that which still is left—
For, high-soul'd Maid, what sorrow would it be

That Mountain floods should thunder as before,
And Ocean bellow from his rocky shore,
And neither awful Voice be heard by Thee!

W. Wordsworth

CCLV

ON THE EXTINCTION OF THE VENETIAN REPUBLIC

Once did She hold the gorgeous East in fee
And was the safeguard of the West; the worth
Of Venice did not fall below her birth,
Venice, the eldest child of Liberty.

She was a maiden city, bright and free;
No guile seduced, no force could violate;
And when she took unto herself a mate,
She must espouse the everlasting Sea.

And what if she had seen those glories fade,
Those titles vanish, and that strength decay,—
Yet shall some tribute of regret be paid

When her long life hath reach'd its final day:
Men are we, and must grieve when even the shade
Of that which once was great is pass'd away.

W. Wordsworth

CCLVI

LONDON, 1802

O Friend ! I know not which way I must look
For comfort, being, as I am, opprest
To think that now our life is only drest
For show; mean handy-work of craftsman, cook,

Or groom !—We must run glittering like a brook
In the open sunshine, or we are unblest;
The wealthiest man among us is the best:
No grandeur now in nature or in book

Delights us.   Rapine, avarice, expense,
This is idolatry; and these we adore:
Plain living and high thinking are no more:

The homely beauty of the good old cause
Is gone; our peace, our fearful innocence,
And pure religion breathing household laws.

W. Wordsworth

CCLVII

THE SAME

Milton ! thou shouldst be living at this hour :
England hath need of thee : she is a fen
Of stagnant waters : altar, sword, and pen,
Fireside, the heroic wealth of hall and bower,

Have forfeited their ancient English dower
Of inward happiness.   We are selfish men:
Oh! raise us up, return to us again;
And give us manners, virtue, freedom, power.

Thy soul was like a Star, and dwelt apart:
Thou hadst a voice whose sound was like the sea,
Pure as the naked heavens, majestic, free;

So didst thou travel on life's common way
In cheerful godliness; and yet thy heart
The lowliest duties on herself did lay.

W. Wordsworth

CCLVIII

When I have borne in memory what has tamed
Great nations; how ennobling thoughts depart
When men change swords for ledgers, and desert
The student's bower for gold,—some fears unnamed

I had, my Country!—am I to be blamed?
Now, when I think of thee, and what thou art,
Verily, in the bottom of my heart
Of those unfilial fears I am ashamed.

For dearly must we prize thee; we who find
In thee a bulwark for the cause of men;
And I by my affection was beguiled:

What wonder if a Poet now and then,
Among the many movements of his mind,
Felt for thee as a lover or a child!

W. Wordsworth

CCLIX

HOHENLINDEN

On Linden, when the sun was low,
All bloodless lay the untrodden snow;
And dark as winter was the flow
   Of Iser, rolling rapidly.

But Linden saw another sight,
When the drum beat at dead of night
Commanding fires of death to light
    The darkness of her scenery.

By torch and trumpet fast array'd
Each horseman drew his battle-blade,
And furious every charger neigh'd
    To join the dreadful revelry.

Then shook the hills with thunder riven;
Then rush'd the steed, to battle driven;
And louder than the bolts of Heaven
    Far flash'd the red artillery.

But redder yet that light shall glow
On Linden's hills of stainéd snow;
And bloodier yet the torrent flow
    Of Iser, rolling rapidly.

'Tis morn; but scarce yon level sun
Can pierce the war-clouds, rolling dun,
Where furious Frank and fiery Hun
    Shout in their sulphurous canopy.

The combat deepens. On, ye Brave
Who rush to glory, or the grave!
Wave, Munich! all thy banners wave,
    And charge with all thy chivalry!

Few, few shall part, where many meet!
The snow shall be their winding-sheet,
And every turf beneath their feet
    Shall be a soldier's sepulchre.

T. Campbell

CCLX

AFTER BLENHEIM

It was a summer evening,
    Old Kaspar's work was done,
And he before his cottage door
    Was sitting in the sun;
And by him sported on the green
His little grandchild Wilhelmine.

She saw her brother Peterkin
  Roll something large and round
Which he beside the rivulet
  In playing there had found;
He came to ask what he had found
That was so large and smooth and round.

Old Kaspar took it from the boy
  Who stood expectant by;
And then the old man shook his head,
  And with a natural sigh
' 'Tis some poor fellow's skull,' said he,
' Who fell in the great victory.

' I find them in the garden,
  For there's many here about;
And often when I go to plough
  The ploughshare turns them out.
For many thousand men,' said he,
' Were slain in that great victory.'

' Now tell us what 'twas all about,'
  Young Peterkin he cries;
And little Wilhelmine looks up
  With wonder-waiting eyes;
' Now tell us all about the war,
And what they fought each other for.'

' It was the English,' Kaspar cried,
  ' Who put the French to rout;
But what they fought each other for
  I could not well make out.
But every body said,' quoth he,
' That 'twas a famous victory.

' My father lived at Blenheim then,
  Yon little stream hard by;
They burnt his dwelling to the ground,
  And he was forced to fly:
So with his wife and child he fled,
Nor had he where to rest his head.

' With fire and sword the country round
  Was wasted far and wide,

And many a childing mother then
  And newborn baby died :
But things like that, you know, must be
At every famous victory.

' They say it was a shocking sight
  After the field was won ;
For many thousand bodies here
  Lay rotting in the sun :
But things like that, you know, must be
After a famous victory.

' Great praise the Duke of Marlbro' won
  And our good Prince Eugene ; '
' Why 'twas a very wicked thing ! '
  Said little Wilhelmine ;
' Nay . . nay . . my little girl,' quoth he,
' It was a famous victory.

' And every body praised the Duke
  Who this great fight did win.'
' But what good came of it at last ? '
  Quoth little Peterkin :—
' Why that I cannot tell,' said he,
' But 'twas a famous victory.'

                          R. Southey

PRO PATRIA MORI

When he who adores thee has left but the name
  Of his fault and his sorrows behind,
Oh ! say wilt thou weep, when they darken the fame
  Of a life that for thee was resign'd !
Yes, weep, and however my foes may condemn,
  Thy tears shall efface their decree ;
For, Heaven can witness, though guilty to them,
  I have been but too faithful to thee.

With thee were the dreams of my earliest love;
   Every thought of my reason was thine:
In my last humble prayer to the Spirit above
   Thy name shall be mingled with mine!
Oh! blest are the lovers and friends who shall live
   The days of thy glory to see;
But the next dearest blessing that Heaven can give
   Is the pride of thus dying for thee.

T. Moore

CCLXII

*THE BURIAL OF SIR JOHN MOORE
AT CORUNNA*

Not a drum was heard, not a funeral note,
   As his corpse to the rampart we hurried;
Not a soldier discharged his farewell shot
   O'er the grave where our hero we buried.

We buried him darkly at dead of night,
   The sods with our bayonets turning;
By the struggling moonbeam's misty light
   And the lantern dimly burning.

No useless coffin enclosed his breast,
   Not in sheet or in shroud we wound him;
But he lay like a warrior taking his rest,
   With his martial cloak around him.

Few and short were the prayers we said,
   And we spoke not a word of sorrow;
But we steadfastly gazed on the face that was dead,
   And we bitterly thought of the morrow.

We thought, as we hollow'd his narrow bed
   And smoothed down his lonely pillow,
That the foe and the stranger would tread o'er his
      head,
   And we far away on the billow!

Lightly they'll talk of the spirit that's gone
   And o'er his cold ashes upbraid him,—
But little he'll reck, if they let him sleep on
   In the grave where a Briton has laid him.

But half of our heavy task was done
　When the clock struck the hour for retiring :
And we heard the distant and random gun
　That the foe was sullenly firing.

Slowly and sadly we laid him down,
　From the field of his fame fresh and gory;
We carved not a line, and we raised not a stone,
　But we left him alone with his glory.

C. Wolfe

CCLXIII

SIMON LEE THE OLD HUNTSMAN

In the sweet shire of Cardigan,
Not far from pleasant Ivor Hall,
An old man dwells, a little man,—
'Tis said he once was tall.
Full five-and-thirty years he lived
A running huntsman merry;
And still the centre of his cheek
Is red as a ripe cherry.

No man like him the horn could sound,
And hill and valley rang with glee,
When Echo bandied, round and round,
The halloo of Simon Lee.
In those proud days he little cared
For husbandry or tillage;
To blither tasks did Simon rouse
The sleepers of the village.

He all the country could outrun,
Could leave both man and horse behind;
And often, ere the chase was done,
He reel'd and was stone-blind.
And still there's something in the world
At which his heart rejoices;
For when the chiming hounds are out,
He dearly loves their voices.

But oh the heavy change !—bereft
Of health, strength, friends and kindred, see
Old Simon to the world is left
In liveried poverty :—
His master's dead, and no one now
Dwells in the Hall of Ivor;
Men, dogs, and horses, all are dead;
He is the sole survivor.

And he is lean and he is sick,
His body, dwindled and awry,
Rests upon ankles swoln and thick ;
His legs are thin and dry.
One prop he has, and only one,—
His wife, an aged woman,
Lives with him, near the waterfall,
Upon the village common.

Beside their moss-grown hut of clay,
Not twenty paces from the door,
A scrap of land they have, but they
Are poorest of the poor.
This scrap of land he from the heath
Enclosed when he was stronger;
But what to them avails the land
Which he can till no longer?

Oft, working by her husband's side,
Ruth does what Simon cannot do;
For she, with scanty cause for pride,
Is stouter of the two.
And, though you with your utmost skill
From labour could not wean them,
'Tis little, very little, all
That they can do between them.

Few months of life has he in store
As he to you will tell,
For still, the more he works, the more
Do his weak ankles swell.
My gentle Reader, I perceive
How patiently you've waited,
And now I fear that you expect
Some tale will be related.

O Reader ! had you in your mind
Such stores as silent thought can bring,
O gentle Reader ! you would find
A tale in every thing.
What more I have to say is short,
And you must kindly take it :
It is no tale ; but, should you think,
Perhaps a tale you'll make it.

One summer-day I chanced to see
This old Man doing all he could
To unearth the root of an old tree,
A stump of rotten wood.
The mattock totter'd in his hand ;
So vain was his endeavour
That at the root of the old tree
He might have work'd for ever.

' You're overtask'd, good Simon Lee,
Give me your tool,' to him I said ;
And at the word right gladly he
Received my proffer'd aid.
I struck, and with a single blow
The tangled root I sever'd,
At which the poor old man so long
And vainly had endeavour'd.

The tears into his eyes were brought,
And thanks and praises seem'd to run
So fast out of his heart, I thought
They never would have done.
—I've heard of hearts unkind, kind deed
With coldness still returning ;
Alas ! the gratitude of men
Hath oftener left me mourning.

W. Wordsworth

CLXIV

THE OLD FAMILIAR FACES

I have had playmates, I have had companions,
In my days of childhood, in my joyful school-days ;
All, all are gone, the old familiar faces.

I have been laughing, I have been carousing,
Drinking late, sitting late, with my bosom cronies;
All, all are gone, the old familiar faces.

I loved a Love once, fairest among women:
Closed are her doors on me, I must not see her—
All, all are gone, the old familiar faces.

I have a friend, a kinder friend has no man:
Like an ingrate, I left my friend abruptly;
Left him, to muse on the old familiar faces,

Ghost-like I paced round the haunts of my childhood,
Earth seem'd a desert I was bound to traverse,
Seeking to find the old familiar faces.

Friend of my bosom, thou more than a brother,
Why wert not thou born in my father's dwelling?
So might we talk of the old familiar faces,

How some they have died, and some they have left
    me,
And some are taken from me; all are departed;
All, all are gone, the old familiar faces.

                        C. Lamb

CCLXV

THE JOURNEY ONWARDS

As slow our ship her foamy track
    Against the wind was cleaving,
Her trembling pennant still look'd back
    To that dear isle 'twas leaving.
So loth we part from all we love,
    From all the links that bind us;
So turn our hearts, as on we rove,
    To those we've left behind us!

When, round the bowl, of vanish'd years
    We talk with joyous seeming—
With smiles that might as well be tears,
    So faint, so sad their beaming;

While memory brings us back again
    Each early tie that twined us,
Oh, sweet's the cup that circles then
    To those we've left behind us!

And when, in other climes, we meet
    Some isle or vale enchanting,
Where all looks flowery, wild, and sweet,
    And nought but love is wanting;
We think how great had been our bliss
    If Heaven had but assign'd us
To live and die in scenes like this,
    With some we've left behind us!

As travellers oft look back at eve
    When eastward darkly going,
To gaze upon that light they leave
    Still faint behind them glowing,—
So, when the close of pleasure's day
    To gloom hath near consign'd us,
We turn to catch one fading ray
    Of joy that's left behind us.

                              T. Moore

CCLXVI

YOUTH AND AGE

There's not a joy the world can give like that it
    takes away
When the glow of early thought declines in feeling's
    dull decay;
'Tis not on youth's smooth cheek the blush alone,
    which fades so fast,
But the tender bloom of heart is gone, ere youth
    itself be past.

Then the few whose spirits float above the wreck of
    happiness
Are driven o'er the shoals of guilt, or ocean of excess;
The magnet of their course is gone, or only points in
    vain
The shore to which their shiver'd sail shall never
    stretch again.

Then the mortal coldness of the soul like death itself
    comes down;
It cannot feel for others' woes, it dare not dream its
    own;
That heavy chill has frozen o'er the fountain of our
    tears,
And though the eye may sparkle still, 'tis where the
    ice appears.

Though wit may flash from fluent lips, and mirth
    distract the breast,
Through midnight hours that yield no more their
    former hope of rest;
'Tis but as ivy-leaves around the ruin'd turret wreathe,
All green and wildly fresh without, but worn and
    gray beneath.

Oh could I feel as I have felt, or be what I have been,
Or weep as I could once have wept o'er many a
    vanish'd scene,—
As springs in deserts found seem sweet, all brackish
    though they be,
So midst the wither'd waste of life, those tears would
    flow to me!

Lord Byron

CCLXVII

A LESSON

There is a Flower, the lesser Celandine,
That shrinks like many more from cold and rain,
And the first moment that the sun may shine,
Bright as the sun himself, 'tis out again!

When hailstones have been falling, swarm on swarm,
Or blasts the green field and the trees distrest,
Oft have I seen it muffled up from harm
In close self-shelter, like a thing at rest.

But lately, one rough day, this Flower I past,
And recognized it, though an alter'd form,
Now standing forth an offering to the blast,
And buffeted at will by rain and storm.

I stopp'd and said, with inly-mutter'd voice,
'It doth not love the shower, nor seek the cold;
This neither is its courage nor its choice,
But its necessity in being old.

'The sunshine may not cheer it, nor the dew;
It cannot help itself in its decay;
Stiff in its members, wither'd, changed of hue,'—
And, in my spleen, I smiled that it was gray.

To be a prodigal's favourite—then, worse truth,
A miser's pensioner—behold our lot!
O Man! that from thy fair and shining youth
Age might but take the things Youth needed not!

W. Wordsworth

CCLXVIII

PAST AND PRESENT

I remember, I remember
The house where I was born,
The little window where the sun
Came peeping in at morn;
He never came a wink too soon
Nor brought too long a day;
But now, I often wish the night
Had borne my breath away.

I remember, I remember
The roses, red and white,
The violets, and the lily-cups—
Those flowers made of light!
The lilacs where the robin built,
And where my brother set
The laburnum on his birth-day,—
The tree is living yet!

I remember, I remember
Where I was used to swing,
And thought the air must rush as fresh
To swallows on the wing;
My spirit flew in feathers then
That is so heavy now,
And summer pools could hardly cool
The fever on my brow.

I remember, I remember
The fir trees dark and high;
I used to think their slender tops
Were close against the sky:
It was a childish ignorance,
But now 'tis little joy
To know I'm farther off from Heaven
Than when I was a boy.

T. Hood

CCLXIX

THE LIGHT OF OTHER DAYS

Oft in the stilly night
  Ere slumber's chain has bound me,
Fond Memory brings the light
  Of other days around me:
    The smiles, the tears
    Of boyhood's years,
  The words of love then spoken;
    The eyes that shone,
    Now dimm'd and gone,
  The cheerful hearts now broken!
Thus in the stilly night
  Ere slumber's chain has bound me,
Sad Memory brings the light
  Of other days around me.

When I remember all
  The friends so link'd together
I've seen around me fall
  Like leaves in wintry weather,
    I feel like one
    Who treads alone
  Some banquet-hall deserted,
    Whose lights are fled,
    Whose garlands dead,
  And all but he departed!
Thus in the stilly night
  Ere slumber's chain has bound me,
Sad Memory brings the light
  Of other days around me.

T. Moore

CCLXX

STANZAS WRITTEN IN DEJECTION
NEAR NAPLES

The sun is warm, the sky is clear,
The waves are dancing fast and bright,
Blue isles and snowy mountains wear
The purple noon's transparent might :
The breath of the moist earth is light
Around its unexpanded buds;
Like many a voice of one delight—
The winds', the birds', the ocean-floods'—
The city's voice itself is soft like Solitude's.

I see the deep's untrampled floor
With green and purple sea-weeds strown ;
I see the waves upon the shore
Like light dissolved in star-showers thrown :
I sit upon the sands alone ;
The lightning of the noon-tide ocean
Is flashing round me, and a tone
Arises from its measured motion—
How sweet ! did any heart now share in my emotion.

Alas ! I have nor hope nor health,
Nor peace within nor calm around,
Nor that content, surpassing wealth,
The sage in meditation found,
And walk'd with inward glory crown'd—
Nor fame, nor power, nor love, nor leisure;
Others I see whom these surround—
Smiling they live, and call life pleasure;
To me that cup has been dealt in another measure.

Yet now despair itself is mild
Even as the winds and waters are;
I could lie down like a tired child,
And weep away the life of care
Which I have borne, and yet must bear,—
Till death like sleep might steal on me,
And I might feel in the warm air
My cheek grow cold, and hear the sea
Breathe o'er my dying brain its last monotony.

P. B. Shelley

CCLXXI

THE SCHOLAR

My days among the Dead are past;
Around me I behold,
Where'er these casual eyes are cast,
The mighty minds of old:
My never-failing friends are they,
With whom I converse day by day.

With them I take delight in weal
And seek relief in woe;
And while I understand and feel
How much to them I owe,
My cheeks have often been bedew'd
With tears of thoughtful gratitude.

My thoughts are with the Dead; with them
I live in long-past years,
Their virtues love, their faults condemn,
Partake their hopes and fears,
And from their lessons seek and find
Instruction with an humble mind.

My hopes are with the Dead; anon
My place with them will be,
And I with them shall travel on
Through all Futurity;
Yet leaving here a name, I trust,
That will not perish in the dust.

R. Southey

CCLXXII

THE MERMAID TAVERN

Souls of Poets dead and gone,
What Elysium have ye known,
Happy field or mossy cavern,
Choicer than the Mermaid Tavern?
Have ye tippled drink more fine
Than mine host's Canary wine?

Or are fruits of Paradise
Sweeter than those dainty pies
Of venison ? O generous food !
Drest as though bold Robin Hood
Would, with his Maid Marian,
Sup and bowse from horn and can.

I have heard that on a day
Mine host's sign-board flew away
Nobody knew whither, till
An astrologer's old quill
To a sheepskin gave the story,
Said he saw you in your glory,
Underneath a new-old sign
Sipping beverage divine,
And pledging with contented smack
The Mermaid in the Zodiac.

Souls of Poets dead and gone,
What Elysium have ye known,
Happy field or mossy cavern,
Choicer than the Mermaid Tavern ?

J. Keats

CCLXXIII

THE PRIDE OF YOUTH

Proud Maisie is in the wood,
   Walking so early ;
Sweet Robin sits on the bush,
   Singing so rarely.

' Tell me, thou bonny bird,
   When shall I marry me ? '
—' When six braw gentlemen
   Kirkward shall carry ye.'

' Who makes the bridal bed,
   Birdie, say truly ? '
—' The gray-headed sexton
   That delves the grave duly ;

' The glowworm o'er grave and stone
  Shall light thee steady;
The owl from the steeple sing
  Welcome, proud lady.'

Sir W. Scott

CCLXXIV

THE BRIDGE OF SIGHS

One more Unfortunate
Weary of breath
Rashly importunate,
Gone to her death!
Take her up tenderly,
Lift her with care;
Fashion'd so slenderly,
Young, and so fair!

Look at her garments
Clinging like cerements;
Whilst the wave constantly
Drips from her clothing;
Take her up instantly,
Loving, not loathing.

Touch her not scornfully;
Think of her mournfully,
Gently and humanly;
Not of the stains of her—
All that remains of her
Now is pure womanly.

Make no deep scrutiny
Into her mutiny
Rash and undutiful:
Past all dishonour,
Death has left on her
Only the beautiful.

Still, for all slips of hers,
One of Eve's family—
Wipe those poor lips of hers
Oozing so clammily.

Loop up her tresses
Escaped from the comb,
Her fair auburn tresses;
Whilst wonderment guesses
Where was her home?

Who was her father?
Who was her mother?
Had she a sister?
Had she a brother?
Or was there a dearer one
Still, and a nearer one
Yet, than all other?

Alas! for the rarity
Of Christian charity
Under the sun!
Oh! it was pitiful!
Near a whole city full,
Home she had none.

Sisterly, brotherly,
Fatherly, motherly
Feelings had changed:
Love, by harsh evidence,
Thrown from its eminence;
Even God's providence
Seeming estranged.

Where the lamps quiver
So far in the river,
With many a light
From window and casement,
From garret to basement,
She stood, with amazement,
Houseless by night.

The bleak wind of March
Made her tremble and shiver
But not the dark arch,
Or the black flowing river:
Mad from life's history,

Glad to death's mystery
Swift to be hurl'd—
Any where, any where
Out of the world !

In she plunged boldly,
No matter how coldly
The rough river ran,—
Over the brink of it,
Picture it—think of it,
Dissolute Man !
Lave in it, drink of it,
Then, if you can !

Take her up tenderly,
Lift her with care ;
Fashion'd so slenderly,
Young, and so fair !

Ere her limbs frigidly
Stiffen too rigidly,
Decently, kindly,
Smooth and compose them,
And her eyes, close them,
Staring so blindly !

Dreadfully staring
Thro' muddy impurity,
As when with the daring
Last look of despairing
Fix'd on futurity.

Perishing gloomily,
Spurr'd by contumely,
Cold inhumanity,
Burning insanity,
Into her rest.
—Cross her hands humbly
As if praying dumbly,
Over her breast !

Owning her weakness,
Her evil behaviour,
And leaving, with meekness,
Her sins to her Saviour.

                                    T. Hood

ELEGY

Oh snatch'd away in beauty's bloom !
On thee shall press no ponderous tomb;
But on thy turf shall roses rear
Their leaves, the earliest of the year,
And the wild cypress wave in tender gloom :

And oft by yon blue gushing stream
Shall Sorrow lean her drooping head,
And feed deep thought with many a dream,
And lingering pause and lightly tread;
Fond wretch ! as if her step disturb'd the dead !

Away ! we know that tears are vain,
That Death nor heeds nor hears distress :
Will this unteach us to complain ?
Or make one mourner weep the less ?
And thou, who tell'st me to forget,
Thy looks are wan, thine eyes are wet.

Lord Byron

HESTER

When maidens such as Hester die
Their place ye may not well supply,
Though ye among a thousand try
      With vain endeavour.
A month or more hath she been dead,
Yet cannot I by force be led
To think upon the wormy bed
      And her together.

A springy motion in her gait,
A rising step, did indicate
Of pride and joy no common rate
      That flush'd her spirit :
I know not by what name beside
I shall it call : if 'twas not pride,
It was a joy to that allied
      She did inherit.

Her parents held the Quaker rule,
Which doth the human feeling cool;
But she was train'd in Nature's school,
   Nature had blest her.
A waking eye, a prying mind,
A heart that stirs, is hard to bind;
A hawk's keen sight ye cannot blind,
   Ye could not Hester.

My sprightly neighbour! gone before
To that unknown and silent shore,
Shall we not meet, as heretofore
   Some summer morning—
When from thy cheerful eyes a ray
Hath struck a bliss upon the day,
A bliss that would not go away,
   A sweet fore-warning?

       C. Lamb

CCLXXVII

TO MARY

If I had thought thou couldst have died,
  I might not weep for thee;
But I forgot, when by thy side,
  That thou couldst mortal be:
It never through my mind had past
  The time would e'er be o'er,
And I on thee should look my last,
  And thou shouldst smile no more!

And still upon that face I look,
  And think 'twill smile again;
And still the thought I will not brook
  That I must look in vain!
But when I speak—thou dost not say
  What thou ne'er left'st unsaid;
And now I feel, as well I may,
  Sweet Mary! thou art dead!

If thou wouldst stay, e'en as thou art,
    All cold and all serene—
I still might press thy silent heart,
    And where thy smiles have been.
While e'en thy chill, bleak corse I have.
    Thou seemest still mine own;
But there I lay thee in thy grave—
    And I am now alone!

I do not think, where'er thou art,
    Thou hast forgotten me;
And I, perhaps, may soothe this heart,
    In thinking too of thee:
Yet there was round thee such a dawn
    Of light ne'er seen before,
As fancy never could have drawn,
    And never can restore!

                                    C. Wolfe

CCLXXVIII

CORONACH

He is gone on the mountain,
    He is lost to the forest,
Like a summer-dried fountain,
    When our need was the sorest.
The font reappearing
    From the raindrops shall borrow,
But to us comes no cheering,
    To Duncan no morrow!

The hand of the reaper
    Takes the ears that are hoary,
But the voice of the weeper
    Wails manhood in glory.
The autumn winds rushing
    Waft the leaves that are searest,
But our flower was in flushing
    When blighting was nearest.

Fleet foot on the correi,
    Sage counsel in cumber,
Red hand in the foray,
    How sound is thy slumber!

Like the dew on the mountain,
   Like the foam on the river,
Like the bubble on the fountain,
   Thou art gone; and for ever!

Sir W. Scott

CCLXXIX

THE DEATH BED

We watch'd her breathing thro' the night,
   Her breathing soft and low,
As in her breast the wave of life
   Kept heaving to and fro.

So silently we seem'd to speak,
   So slowly moved about,
As we had lent her half our powers
   To eke her living out.

Our very hopes belied our fears,
   Our fears our hopes belied—
We thought her dying when she slept,
   And sleeping when she died.

For when the morn came dim and sad
   And chill with early showers,
Her quiet eyelids closed—she had
   Another morn than ours.

T. Hood

CCLXXX

AGNES

I saw her in childhood—
   A bright, gentle thing,
Like the dawn of the morn,
   Or the dews of the spring:
The daisies and hare-bells
   Her playmates all day;
Herself as light-hearted
   And artless as they.

I saw her again—
  A fair girl of eighteen,
Fresh glittering with graces
  Of mind and of mien.
Her speech was all music;
  Like moonlight she shone;
The envy of many,
  The glory of one.

Years, years fleeted over—
  I stood at her foot:
The bud had grown blossom,
  The blossom was fruit.
A dignified mother,
  Her infant she bore;
And look'd, I thought, fairer
  Then ever before.

I saw her once more—
  'Twas the day that she died;
Heaven's light was around her,
  And God at her side;
No wants to distress her,
  No fears to appal—
O then, I felt, then
  She was fairest of all!

H. F. Lyte

CCLXXXI

ROSABELLE

O listen, listen, ladies gay!
  No haughty feat of arms I tell;
Soft is the note, and sad the lay
  That mourns the lovely Rosabelle.

'Moor, moor the barge, ye gallant crew!
  And, gentle ladye, deign to stay!
Rest thee in Castle Ravensheuch,
  Nor tempt the stormy firth to-day.

' The blackening wave is edged with white;
  To inch and rock the sea-mews fly;
The fishers have heard the Water-Sprite,
  Whose screams forebode that wreck is nigh.

' Last night the gifted Seer did view
  A wet shroud swathed round ladye gay;
Then stay thee, Fair, in Ravensheuch;
  Why cross the gloomy firth to-day?'

' 'Tis not because Lord Lindesay's heir
  To-night at Roslin leads the ball,
But that my ladye-mother there
  Sits lonely in her castle-hall.

' 'Tis not because the ring they ride,
  And Lindesay at the ring rides well,
But that my sire the wine will chide
  If 'tis not fill'd by Rosabelle.'

—O'er Roslin all that dreary night
  A wondrous blaze was seen to gleam;
'Twas broader than the watch-fire's light,
  And redder than the bright moonbeam.

It glared on Roslin's castled rock,
  It ruddied all the copse-wood glen;
'Twas seen from Dryden's groves of oak,
  And seen from cavern'd Hawthornden.

Seem'd all on fire that chapel proud
  Where Roslin's chiefs uncoffin'd lie,
Each Baron, for a sable shroud,
  Sheathed in his iron panoply.

Seem'd all on fire within, around,
  Deep sacristy and altar's pale;
Shone every pillar foliage-bound,
  And glimmer'd all the dead men's mail.

Blazed battlement and pinnet high,
  Blazed every rose-carved buttress fair—
So still they blaze, when fate is nigh
  The lordly line of high Saint Clair.

There are twenty of Roslin's barons bold—
    Lie buried within that proud chapelle;
Each one the holy vault doth hold—
    But the sea holds lovely Rosabelle.

And each Saint Clair was buried there,
    With candle, with book, and with knell;
But the sea-caves rung, and the wild winds sung
    The dirge of lovely Rosabelle.

               Sir W. Scott

CCLXXXII

ON AN INFANT DYING AS SOON AS BORN

I saw where in the shroud did lurk
A curious frame of Nature's work;
A flow'ret crushéd in the bud,
A nameless piece of Babyhood,
Was in her cradle-coffin lying;
Extinct, with scarce the sense of dying:
So soon to exchange the imprisoning womb
For darker closets of the tomb!
She did but ope an eye, and put
A clear beam forth, then straight up shut
For the long dark : ne'er more to see
Through glasses of mortality.
Riddle of destiny, who can show
What thy short visit meant, or know
What thy errand here below?
Shall we say, that Nature blind
Check'd her hand, and changed her mind
Just when she had exactly wrought
A finish'd pattern without fault?
Could she flag, or could she tire,
Or lack'd she the Promethean fire
(With her nine moons' long workings sicken'd)
That should thy little limbs have quicken'd?
Limbs so firm, they seem'd to assure
Life of health, and days mature :
Woman's self in miniature!

Limbs so fair, they might supply
(Themselves now but cold imagery)
The sculptor to make Beauty by.
Or did the stern-eyed Fate descry
That babe or mother, one must die;
So in mercy left the stock
And cut the branch; to save the shock
Of young years widow'd, and the pain
When Single State comes back again
To the lone man who, reft of wife,
Thenceforward drags a maiméd life?
The economy of Heaven is dark,
And wisest clerks have miss'd the mark
Why human buds, like this, should fall,
More brief than fly ephemeral
That has his day; while shrivell'd crones
Stiffen with age to stocks and stones;
And crabbéd use the conscience sears
In sinners of an hundred years.
—Mother's prattle, mother's kiss,
Baby fond, thou ne'er wilt miss:
Rites, which custom does impose,
Silver bells, and baby clothes;
Coral redder than those lips
Which pale death did late eclipse;
Music framed for infants' glee,
Whistle never tuned for thee;
Though thou want'st not, thou shalt have them.
Loving hearts were they which gave them.
Let not one be missing; nurse,
See them laid upon the hearse
Of infant slain by doom perverse.
Why should kings and nobles have
Pictured trophies to their grave,
And we, churls, to thee deny
Thy pretty toys with thee to lie—
A more harmless vanity?

                                    C. Lamb

IN MEMORIAM

A child's a plaything for an hour;
  Its pretty tricks we try
For that or for a longer space,—
  Then tire, and lay it by.

But I knew one that to itself
  All seasons could control;
That would have mock'd the sense of pain
  Out of a grievéd soul.

Thou straggler into loving arms,
  Young climber up of knees,
When I forget thy thousand ways
  Then life and all shall cease!

M. Lamb

THE AFFLICTION OF MARGARET

Where art thou, my beloved Son,
Where art thou, worse to me than dead?
Oh find me, prosperous or undone!
Or if the grave be now thy bed,
Why am I ignorant of the same
That I may rest; and neither blame
Nor sorrow may attend thy name?

Seven years, alas! to have received
No tidings of an only child—
To have despair'd, have hoped, believed,
And been for evermore beguiled,—
Sometimes with thoughts of very bliss!
I catch at them, and then I miss;
Was ever darkness like to this?

He was among the prime in worth,
An object beauteous to behold;
Well born, well bred; I sent him forth
Ingenuous, innocent, and bold:
If things ensued that wanted grace
As hath been said, they were not base;
And never blush was on my face.

Ah ! little doth the young-one dream
When full of play and childish cares,
What power is in his wildest scream
Heard by his mother unawares !
He knows it not, he cannot guess ;
Years to a mother bring distress ;
But do not make her love the less.

Neglect me ! no, I suffer'd long
From that ill thought ; and being blind
Said ' Pride shall help me in my wrong :
Kind mother have I been, as kind
As ever breathed : ' and that is true ;
I've wet my path with tears like dew,
Weeping for him when no one knew.

My Son, if thou be humbled, poor,
Hopeless of honour and of gain,
Oh ! do not dread thy mother's door ;
Think not of me with grief and pain :
I now can see with better eyes ;
And worldly grandeur I despise
And fortune with her gifts and lies.

Alas ! the fowls of heaven have wings,
And blasts of heaven will aid their flight ;
They mount—how short a voyage brings
The wanderers back to their delight !
Chains tie us down by land and sea ;
And wishes, vain as mine, may be
All that is left to comfort thee.

Perhaps some dungeon hears thee groan
Maim'd, mangled by inhuman men ;
Or thou upon a desert thrown
Inheritest the lion's den ;
Or hast been summon'd to the deep
Thou, thou, and all thy mates, to keep
An incommunicable sleep.

I look for ghosts : but none will force
Their way to me ; 'tis falsely said
That there was ever intercourse
Between the living and the dead ;

For surely then I should have sight
Of him I wait for day and night
With love and longings infinite.

My apprehensions come in crowds;
I dread the rustling of the grass;
The very shadows of the clouds
Have power to shake me as they pass:
I question things, and do not find
One that will answer to my mind;
And all the world appears unkind.

Beyond participation lie
My troubles, and beyond relief:
If any chance to heave a sigh
They pity me, and not my grief.
Then come to me, my Son, or send
Some tidings that my woes may end!
I have no other earthly friend.

W. Wordsworth

CCLXXXV

HUNTING SONG

Waken, lords and ladies gay,
On the mountain dawns the day;
All the jolly chase is here
With hawk and horse and hunting-spear;
Hounds are in their couples yelling,
Hawks are whistling, horns are knelling,
Merrily merrily mingle they,
' Waken, lords and ladies gay.'

Waken, lords and ladies gay,
The mist has left the mountain gray,
Springlets in the dawn are steaming,
Diamonds on the brake are gleaming;
And foresters have busy been
To track the buck in thicket green;
Now we come to chant our lay
' Waken, lords and ladies gay.'

Waken, lords and ladies gay,
To the greenwood haste away;
We can show you where he lies,
Fleet of foot and tall of size;
We can show the marks he made
When 'gainst the oak his antlers fray'd;
You shall see him brought to bay;
' Waken, lords and ladies gay.'

Louder, louder chant the lay
Waken, lords and ladies gay!
Tell them youth and mirth and glee
Run a course as well as we;
Time, stern huntsman! who can baulk,
Stanch as hound and fleet as hawk;
Think of this, and rise with day,
Gentle lords and ladies gay!

Sir W. Scott

CCLXXXVI

TO THE SKYLARK

Ethereal minstrel! pilgrim of the sky!
Dost thou despise the earth where cares abound?
Or while the wings aspire, are heart and eye
Both with thy nest upon the dewy ground?
Thy nest which thou canst drop into at will,
Those quivering wings composed, that music still!

To the last point of vision, and beyond
Mount, daring warbler!—that love-prompted strain
—'Twixt thee and thine a never-failing bond—
Thrills not the less the bosom of the plain:
Yet might'st thou seem, proud privilege! to sing
All independent of the leafy Spring.

Leave to the nightingale her shady wood;
A privacy of glorious light is thine,
Whence thou dost pour upon the world a flood
Of harmony, with instinct more divine;
Type of the wise, who soar, but never roam—
True to the kindred points of Heaven and Home.

W. Wordsworth

CCLXXXVII

TO A SKYLARK

Hail to thee, blithe Spirit!
   Bird thou never wert,
That from heaven, or near it
   Pourest thy full heart
In profuse strains of unpremeditated art.

   Higher still and higher
      From the earth thou springest,
   Like a cloud of fire,
      The blue deep thou wingest,
And singing still dost soar, and soaring ever singest.

   In the golden lightning
      Of the sunken sun
   O'er which clouds are brightening,
      Thou dost float and run,
Like an unbodied joy whose race is just begun.

   The pale purple even
      Melts around thy flight;
   Like a star of heaven
      In the broad daylight
Thou art unseen, but yet I hear thy shrill delight:

   Keen as are the arrows
      Of that silver sphere,
   Whose intense lamp narrows
      In the white dawn clear
Until we hardly see, we feel that it is there.

   All the earth and air
      With thy voice is loud,
   As, when night is bare,
      From one lonely cloud
The moon rains out her beams, and heaven is over-
      flow'd.

   What thou art we know not;
      What is most like thee?
   From rainbow clouds there flow not
      Drops so bright to see
As from thy presence showers a rain of melody;—

Like a poet hidden
  In the light of thought,
Singing hymns unbidden,
  Till the world is wrought
To sympathy with hopes and fears it heeded not:

Like a high-born maiden
  In a palace tower,
Soothing her love-laden
  Soul in secret hour
With music sweet as love, which overflows her
    bower:

Like a glow-worm golden
  In a dell of dew,
Scattering unbeholden
  Its aerial hue
Among the flowers and grass, which screen it from
    the view:

Like a rose embower'd
  In its own green leaves,
By warm winds deflower'd,
  Till the scent it gives
Makes faint with too much sweet these heavy
    wingéd thieves.

Sound of vernal showers
  On the twinkling grass,
Rain-awaken'd flowers,
  All that ever was
Joyous, and clear, and fresh, thy music doth surpass.

Teach us, sprite or bird,
  What sweet thoughts are thine:
I have never heard
  Praise of love or wine
That panted forth a flood of rapture so divine.

Chorus hymeneal
  Or triumphal chaunt
Match'd with thine, would be all
  But an empty vaunt—
A thing wherein we feel there is some hidden want.

What objects are the fountains
   Of thy happy strain?
What fields, or waves, or mountains?
   What shapes of sky or plain?
What love of thine own kind? what ignorance of
    pain?

With thy clear keen joyance
   Languor cannot be:
Shadow of annoyance
   Never came near thee:
Thou lovest; but ne'er knew love's sad satiety.

Waking or asleep
   Thou of death must deem
Things more true and deep
   Than we mortals dream,
Or how could thy notes flow in such a crystal
    stream?

We look before and after,
   And pine for what is not:
Our sincerest laughter
   With some pain is fraught;
Our sweetest songs are those that tell of saddest
    thought.

Yet if we could scorn
   Hate, and pride, and fear;
If we were things born
   Not to shed a tear,
I know not how thy joy we ever should come near.

Better than all measures
   Of delightful sound,
Better than all treasures
   That in books are found,
Thy skill to poet were, thou scorner of the ground!

Teach me half the gladness
   That thy brain must know,
Such harmonious madness
   From my lips would flow,
The world should listen then, as I am listening now!

                  P. B. Shelley

THE GREEN LINNET

Beneath these fruit-tree boughs that shed
Their snow-white blossoms on my head,
With brightest sunshine round me spread
  Of Spring's unclouded weather,
In this sequester'd nook how sweet
To sit upon my orchard-seat !
And flowers and birds once more to greet,
  My last year's friends together.

One have I mark'd, the happiest guest
In all this covert of the blest :
Hail to Thee, far above the rest
  In joy of voice and pinion !
Thou, Linnet ! in thy green array
Presiding Spirit here to-day
Dost lead the revels of the May ;
  And this is thy dominion.

While birds, and butterflies, and flowers,
Make all one band of paramours,
Thou, ranging up and down the bowers,
  Art sole in thy employment ;
A Life, a Presence like the air,
Scattering thy gladness without care,
Too blest with any one to pair ;
  Thyself thy own enjoyment.

Amid yon tuft of hazel trees
That twinkle to the gusty breeze,
Behold him perch'd in ecstasies
  Yet seeming still to hover ;
There ! where the flutter of his wings
Upon his back and body flings
Shadows and sunny glimmerings,
  That cover him all over.

My dazzled sight he oft deceives—
A brother of the dancing leaves ;
Then flits, and from the cottage-eaves
  Pours forth his song in gushes ;

As if by that exulting strain
He mock'd and treated with disdain
The voiceless Form he chose to feign,
While fluttering in the bushes.

W. Wordsworth

CCLXXXIX

TO THE CUCKOO

O blithe new-comer! I have heard,
I hear thee and rejoice:
O Cuckoo! shall I call thee Bird,
Or but a wandering Voice?

While I am lying on the grass
Thy twofold shout I hear;
From hill to hill it seems to pass,
At once far off and near.

Though babbling only to the vale
Of sunshine and of flowers,
Thou bringest unto me a tale
Of visionary hours.

Thrice welcome, darling of the Spring!
Even yet thou art to me
No bird, but an invisible thing,
A voice, a mystery;

The same whom in my school-boy days
I listen'd to; that Cry
Which made me look a thousand ways
In bush, and tree, and sky.

To seek thee did I often rove
Through woods and on the green;
And thou wert still a hope, a love;
Still long'd for, never seen!

And I can listen to thee yet;
Can lie upon the plain
And listen, till I do beget
That golden time again.

O blessèd Bird ! the earth we pace
   Again appears to be
An unsubstantial, faery place,
   That is fit home for thee !

                    W. Wordsworth

CCXC

ODE TO A NIGHTINGALE

My heart aches, and a drowsy numbness pains
   My sense, as though of hemlock I had drunk,
Or emptied some dull opiate to the drains
   One minute past, and Lethe-wards had sunk :
'Tis not through envy of thy happy lot,
   But being too happy in thine happiness,—
      That thou, light-wingèd Dryad of the trees,
         In some melodious plot
Of beechen green, and shadows numberless,
   Singest of summer in full-throated ease.

O, for a draught of vintage ! that hath been
   Cool'd a long age in the deep-delvèd earth,
Tasting of Flora and the country green,
   Dance, and Provençal song, and sunburnt mirth !
O for a beaker full of the warm South,
   Full of the true, the blushful Hippocrene,
      With beaded bubbles winking at the brim,
         And purple-stainèd mouth ;
That I might drink, and leave the world unseen,
   And with thee fade away into the forest dim :

Fade far away, dissolve, and quite forget
   What thou among the leaves hast never known,
The weariness, the fever, and the fret
   Here, where men sit and hear each other groan ;
Where palsy shakes a few, sad, last gray hairs,
   Where youth grows pale, and spectre-thin, and
      dies ;
      Where but to think is to be full of sorrow
         And leaden-eyed despairs ;
Where Beauty cannot keep her lustrous eyes,
   Or new Love pine at them beyond to-morrow :

Away! away! for I will fly to thee,
  Not charioted by Bacchus and his pards,
But on the viewless wings of Poesy,
  Though the dull brain perplexes and retards:
Already with thee! tender is the night,
  And haply the Queen-Moon is on her throne,
    Cluster'd around by all her starry Fays;
      But here there is no light,
  Save what from heaven is with the breezes blown
    Through verdurous glooms and winding mossy
      ways.

I cannot see what flowers are at my feet,
  Nor what soft incense hangs upon the boughs,
But, in embalméd darkness, guess each sweet
  Wherewith the seasonable month endows
The grass, the thicket, and the fruit-tree wild;
  White hawthorn, and the pastoral eglantine;
    Fast fading violets cover'd up in leaves;
      And mid-May's eldest child,
  The coming musk-rose, full of dewy wine,
    The murmurous haunt of flies on summer eves.

Darkling I listen; and for many a time
  I have been half in love with easeful Death,
Call'd him soft names in many a muséd rhyme,
  To take into the air my quiet breath;
Now more than ever seems it rich to die,
  To cease upon the midnight with no pain,
    While thou art pouring forth thy soul abroad
      In such an ecstasy!
  Still wouldst thou sing, and I have ears in vain—
    To thy high requiem become a sod.

Thou wast not born for death, immortal Bird!
  No hungry generations tread thee down;
The voice I hear this passing night was heard
  In ancient days by emperor and clown:
Perhaps the self-same song that found a path
  Through the sad heart of Ruth, when, sick for
    home,

She stood in tears amid the alien corn;
    The same that oft-times hath
Charm'd magic casements, opening on the foam
  Of perilous seas, in faery lands forlorn.

Forlorn! the very word is like a bell
  To toll me back from thee to my sole self!
Adieu! the fancy cannot cheat so well
  As she is famed to do, deceiving elf.
Adieu! adieu! thy plaintive anthem fades
    Past the near meadows, over the still stream,
      Up the hill-side; and now 'tis buried deep
        In the next valley-glades:
  Was it a vision, or a waking dream?
    Fled is that music:—Do I wake or sleep?

                    J. Keats

CCXCI

UPON WESTMINSTER BRIDGE,
SEPT. 3, 1802

Earth has not anything to show more fair:
Dull would he be of soul who could pass by
A sight so touching in its majesty:
This City now doth like a garment wear

The beauty of the morning: silent, bare,
Ships, towers, domes, theatres, and temples lie
Open unto the fields, and to the sky,—
All bright and glittering in the smokeless air.

Never did sun more beautifully steep
In his first splendour valley, rock, or hill;
Ne'er saw I, never felt, a calm so deep!

The river glideth at his own sweet will:
Dear God! the very houses seem asleep;
And all that mighty heart is lying still!

                    W. Wordsworth

CCXCII

To one who has been long in city pent,
'Tis very sweet to look into the fair
And open face of heaven,—to breathe a prayer
Full in the smile of the blue firmament.

Who is more happy, when, with heart's content,
Fatigued he sinks into some pleasant lair
Of wavy grass, and reads a debonair
And gentle tale of love and languishment?

Returning home at evening, with an ear
Catching the notes of Philomel,—an eye
Watching the sailing cloudlet's bright career,

He mourns that day so soon has glided by:
E'en like the passage of an angel's tear
That falls through the clear ether silently.

J. Keats

CCXCIII

OZYMANDIAS OF EGYPT

I met a traveller from an antique land
Who said: Two vast and trunkless legs of stone
Stand in the desert.   Near them on the sand,
Half sunk, a shatter'd visage lies, whose frown
And wrinkled lip and sneer of cold command
Tell that its sculptor well those passions read
Which yet survive, stamp'd on these lifeless things,
The hand that mock'd them and the heart that fed;
And on the pedestal these words appear:
' My name is Ozymandias, king of kings:
Look on my works, ye Mighty, and despair!'
Nothing beside remains.   Round the decay
Of that colossal wreck, boundless and bare,
The lone and level sands stretch far away.

P. B. Shelley

CCXCIV

COMPOSED AT NEIDPATH CASTLE, THE PROPERTY OF LORD QUEENSBERRY,
1803

Degenerate Douglas ! oh, the unworthy lord !
Whom mere despite of heart could so far please
And love of havoc, (for with such disease
Fame taxes him,) that he could send forth word

To level with the dust a noble horde,
A brotherhood of venerable trees,
Leaving an ancient dome, and towers like these,
Beggar'd and outraged !—Many hearts deplored

The fate of those old trees ; and oft with pain
The traveller at this day will stop and gaze
On wrongs, which Nature scarcely seems to heed :

For shelter'd places, bosoms, nooks, and bays,
And the pure mountains, and the gentle Tweed,
And the green silent pastures, yet remain.

W. Wordsworth

CCXCV

THE BEECH TREE'S PETITION

O leave this barren spot to me !
Spare, woodman, spare the beechen tree !
Though bush or floweret never grow
My dark unwarming shade below ;
Nor summer bud perfume the dew
Of rosy blush, or yellow hue ;
Nor fruits of autumn, blossom-born,
My green and glossy leaves adorn ;
Nor murmuring tribes from me derive
Th' ambrosial amber of the hive ;
Yet leave this barren spot to me :
Spare, woodman, spare the beechen tree !

Thrice twenty summers I have seen
The sky grow bright, the forest green;
And many a wintry wind have stood
In bloomless, fruitless solitude,
Since childhood in my pleasant bower
First spent its sweet and sportive hour;
Since youthful lovers in my shade
Their vows of truth and rapture made,
And on my trunk's surviving frame
Carved many a long-forgotten name.
Oh! by the sighs of gentle sound,
First breathed upon this sacred ground;
By all that Love has whisper'd here,
Or Beauty heard with ravish'd ear;
As Love's own altar honour me:
Spare, woodman, spare the beechen tree!

T. Campbell

CCXCVI

ADMONITION TO A TRAVELLER

Yes, there is holy pleasure in thine eye!
—The lovely Cottage in the guardian nook
Hath stirr'd thee deeply; with its own dear brook,
Its own small pasture, almost its own sky!

But covet not the abode; forbear to sigh
As many do, repining while they look;
Intruders—who would tear from Nature's book
This precious leaf with harsh impiety.

—Think what the home must be if it were thine,
Even thine, though few thy wants!—Roof, window,
    door,
The very flowers are sacred to the Poor,

The roses to the porch which they entwine:
Yea, all that now enchants thee, from the day
On which it should be touch'd, would melt away!

W. Wordsworth

CCXCVII

TO THE HIGHLAND GIRL OF INVERSNEYDE

Sweet Highland Girl, a very shower
Of beauty is thy earthly dower !
Twice seven consenting years have shed
Their utmost bounty on thy head :
And these gray rocks, that household lawn,
Those trees—a veil just half withdrawn,
This fall of water that doth make
A murmur near the silent lake,
This little bay, a quiet road
That holds in shelter thy abode ;
In truth together ye do seem
Like something fashion'd in a dream ;
Such forms as from their covert peep
When earthly cares are laid asleep !
But O fair Creature ! in the light
Of common day, so heavenly bright
I bless Thee, Vision as thou art,
I bless thee with a human heart :
God shield thee to thy latest years !
Thee neither know I nor thy peers :
And yet my eyes are fill'd with tears.

With earnest feeling I shall pray
For thee when I am far away ;
For never saw I mien or face
In which more plainly I could trace
Benignity and home-bred sense
Ripening in perfect innocence.
Here scatter'd, like a random seed,
Remote from men, Thou dost not need
The embarrass'd look of shy distress,
And maidenly shamefacédness :
Thou wear'st upon thy forehead clear
The freedom of a Mountaineer :
A face with gladness overspread ;
Soft smiles, by human kindness bred ;

And seemliness complete, that sways
Thy courtesies, about thee plays;
With no restraint, but such as springs
From quick and eager visitings
Of thoughts that lie beyond the reach
Of thy few words of English speech :
A bondage sweetly brook'd, a strife
That gives thy gestures grace and life !
So have I, not unmoved in mind,
Seen birds of tempest-loving kind—
Thus beating up against the wind.

What hand but would a garland cull
For thee who art so beautiful ?
O happy pleasure ! here to dwell
Beside thee in some heathy dell;
Adopt your homely ways, and dress,
A shepherd, thou a shepherdess !
But I could frame a wish for thee
More like a grave reality :
Thou art to me but as a wave
Of the wild sea : and I would have
Some claim upon thee, if I could,
Though but of common neighbourhood.
What joy to hear thee, and to see !
Thy elder brother I would be,
Thy father—anything to thee.

Now thanks to Heaven ! that of its grace
Hath led me to this lonely place :
Joy have I had ; and going hence
I bear away my recompence.
In spots like these it is we prize
Our Memory, feel that she hath eyes :
Then why should I be loth to stir ?
I feel this place was made for her;
To give new pleasure like the past,
Continued long as life shall last.
Nor am I loth, though pleased at heart,
Sweet Highland Girl ! from thee to part;
For I, methinks, till I grow old

As fair before me shall behold
As I do now, the cabin small,
The lake, the bay, the waterfall;
And Thee, the Spirit of them all!

W. Wordsworth

CCXCVIII

THE REAPER

Behold her, single in the field,
Yon solitary Highland Lass!
Reaping and singing by herself;
Stop here, or gently pass!
Alone she cuts and binds the grain,
And sings a melancholy strain;
O listen! for the vale profound
Is overflowing with the sound.

No nightingale did ever chaunt
More welcome notes to weary bands
Of travellers in some shady haunt,
Among Arabian sands:
A voice so thrilling ne'er was heard
In spring-time from the cuckoo-bird,
Breaking the silence of the seas
Among the farthest Hebrides.

Will no one tell me what she sings?
Perhaps the plaintive numbers flow
For old, unhappy, far-off things,
And battles long ago:
Or is it some more humble lay,
Familiar matter of to-day?
Some natural sorrow, loss, or pain,
That has been, and may be again!

Whate'er the theme, the maiden sang
As if her song could have no ending;
I saw her singing at her work,
And o'er the sickle bending;—
I listen'd, motionless and still;

And, as I mounted up the hill,
The music in my heart I bore
Long after it was heard no more.

W. Wordsworth

CCXCIX

THE REVERIE OF POOR SUSAN

At the corner of Wood Street, when daylight appears,
Hangs a Thrush that sings loud, it has sung for three years:
Poor Susan has pass'd by the spot, and has heard
In the silence of morning the song of the bird.

'Tis a note of enchantment; what ails her? She sees
A mountain ascending, a vision of trees;
Bright volumes of vapour through Lothbury glide,
And a river flows on through the vale of Cheapside.

Green pastures she views in the midst of the dale
Down which she so often has tripp'd with her pail;
And a single small cottage, a nest like a dove's,
The one only dwelling on earth that she loves.

She looks, and her heart is in heaven: but they fade,
The mist and the river, the hill and the shade;
The stream will not flow, and the hill will not rise,
And the colours have all pass'd away from her eyes!

W. Wordsworth

CCC

TO A LADY, WITH A GUITAR

Ariel to Miranda:—Take
This slave of music, for the sake
Of him, who is the slave of thee;
And teach it all the harmony
In which thou canst, and only thou,
Make the delighted spirit glow,
Till joy denies itself again
And, too intense, is turn'd to pain.

For by permission and command
Of thine own Prince Ferdinand,
Poor Ariel sends this silent token
Of more than ever can be spoken;
Your guardian spirit, Ariel, who
From life to life must still pursue
Your happiness, for thus alone
Can Ariel ever find his own.
From Prospero's enchanted cell,
As the mighty verses tell,
To the throne of Naples he
Lit you o'er the trackless sea,
Flitting on, your prow before,
Like a living meteor.
When you die, the silent Moon
In her interlunar swoon
Is not sadder in her cell
Then deserted Ariel :—
When you live again on earth,
Like an unseen Star of birth
Ariel guides you o'er the sea
Of life from your nativity :—
Many changes have been run
Since Ferdinand and you begun
Your course of love, and Ariel still
Has track'd your steps and served your will.
Now in humbler, happier lot,
This is all remember'd not;
And now, alas ! the poor Sprite is
Imprison'd for some fault of his
In a body like a grave—
From you he only dares to crave,
For his service and his sorrow
A smile to day, a song to morrow.

The artist who this idol wrought
To echo all harmonious thought,
Fell'd a tree, while on the steep
The woods were in their winter sleep,
Rock'd in that repose divine
On the wind-swept Apennine;
And dreaming, some of Autumn past,

And some of Spring approaching fast,
And some of April buds and showers,
And some of songs in July bowers,
And all of love : And so this tree,—
Oh that such our death may be !—
Died in sleep, and felt no pain,
To live in happier form again :
From which, beneath heaven's fairest star,
The artist wrought this loved Guitar ;
And taught it justly to reply
To all who question skilfully
In language gentle as thine own ;
Whispering in enamour'd tone
Sweet oracles of woods and dells,
And summer winds in sylvan cells :
—For it had learnt all harmonies
Of the plains and of the skies,
Of the forests and the mountains,
And the many-voicéd fountains ;
The clearest echoes of the hills,
The softest notes of falling rills,
The melodies of birds and bees,
The murmurings of summer seas,
And pattering rain, and breathing dew,
And airs of evening ; and it knew
That seldom-heard mysterious sound
Which, driven on its diurnal round,
As it floats through boundless day,
Our world enkindles on its way :
—All this it knows, but will not tell
To those who cannot question well
The Spirit that inhabits it ;
It talks according to the wit
Of its companions ; and no more
Is heard than has been felt before
By those who tempt it to betray
These secrets of an elder day.
But, sweetly as its answers will
Flatter hands of perfect skill,
It keeps its highest holiest tone
For our beloved Friend alone.

                              P. B. Shelley

CCCI

THE DAFFODIL

I wander'd lonely as a cloud
That floats on high o'er vales and hills,
When all at once I saw a crowd,
A host of golden daffodils,
Beside the lake, beneath the trees,
Fluttering and dancing in the breeze

Continuous as the stars that shine
And twinkle on the milky way,
They stretch'd in never-ending line
Along the margin of a bay;
Ten thousand saw I at a glance
Tossing their heads in sprightly dance.

The waves beside them danced, but they
Out-did the sparkling waves in glee :—
A Poet could not but be gay
In such a jocund company !
I gazed—and gazed—but little thought
What wealth the show to me had brought;

For oft, when on my couch I lie
In vacant or in pensive mood,
They flash upon that inward eye
Which is the bliss of solitude;
And then my heart with pleasure fills,
And dances with the daffodils.

W. Wordsworth

CCCII

TO THE DAISY

With little here to do or see
Of things that in the great world be,
Sweet Daisy ! oft I talk to thee
    For thou art worthy,
Thou unassuming Common-place
Of Nature, with that homely face,
And yet with something of a grace
    Which Love makes for thee !

Oft on the dappled turf at ease
I sit and play with similes,
Loose types of things through all degrees,
            Thoughts of thy raising;
And many a fond and idle name
I give to thee, for praise or blame
As is the humour of the game,
            While I am gazing.

A nun demure, of lowly port;
Or sprightly maiden, of Love's court,
In thy simplicity the sport
            Of all temptations;
A queen in crown of rubies drest;
A starveling in a scanty vest;
Are all, as seems to suit thee best,
            Thy appellations.

A little Cyclops, with one eye
Staring to threaten and defy,
That thought comes next,—and instantly
            The freak is over,
The shape will vanish, and behold!
A silver shield with boss of gold
That spreads itself, some faery bold
            In fight to cover.

I see thee glittering from afar—
And then thou art a pretty star,
Not quite so fair as many are
            In heaven above thee!
Yet like a star, with glittering crest,
Self-poised in air thou seem'st to rest;—
May peace come never to his nest
            Who shall reprove thee!

Sweet Flower! for by that name at last
When all my reveries are past
I call thee, and to that cleave fast,
            Sweet silent Creature!
That breath'st with me in sun and air,
Do thou, as thou art wont, repair
My heart with gladness, and a share
            Of thy meek nature!

                                    W. Wordsworth

CCCIII

ODE TO AUTUMN

Season of mists and mellow fruitfulness,
Close bosom-friend of the maturing sun;
Conspiring with him how to load and bless
With fruit the vines that round the thatch-eaves run;
To bend with apples the moss'd cottage-trees,
And fill all fruit with ripeness to the core;
To swell the gourd, and plump the hazel shells
With a sweet kernel; to set budding more,
And still more, later flowers for the bees,
Until they think warm days will never cease;
For Summer has o'erbrimm'd their clammy cells.

Who hath not seen thee oft amid thy store?
Sometimes whoever seeks abroad may find
Thee sitting careless on a granary floor,
Thy hair soft-lifted by the winnowing wind;
Or in a half-reap'd furrow sound asleep,
Drowsed with the fume of poppies, while thy hook
Spares the next swath and all its twinéd flowers:
And sometimes like a gleaner thou dost keep
Steady thy laden head across a brook;
Or by a cyder-press, with patient look,
Thou watchest the last oozings, hours by hours.

Where are the songs of Spring? Ay, where are they?
Think not of them, thou hast thy music too,—
While barréd clouds bloom the soft-dying day
And touch the stubble-plains with rosy hue;
Then in a wailful choir the small gnats mourn
Among the river-sallows, borne aloft
Or sinking as the light wind lives or dies;
And full-grown lambs loud bleat from hilly bourn;
Hedge-crickets sing; and now with treble soft
The red-breast whistles from a garden-croft;
And gathering swallows twitter in the skies.

J. Keats

CCCIV

ODE TO WINTER

Germany, December, 1800

When first the fiery-mantled Sun
His heavenly race began to run,
Round the earth and ocean blue
His children four the Seasons flew.
    First, in green apparel dancing,
The young Spring smiled with angel-grace;
    Rosy Summer next advancing,
Rush'd into her sire's embrace—
Her bright-hair'd sire, who bade her keep
    For ever nearest to his smiles,
On Calpe's olive-shaded steep
    Or India's citron-cover'd isles:
More remote, and buxom-brown,
    The Queen of vintage bow'd before his throne;
A rich pomegranate gemm'd her crown,
    A ripe sheaf bound her zone.

But howling Winter fled afar
To hills that prop the polar star;
And loves on deer-borne car to ride
With barren darkness by his side,
Round the shore where loud Lofoden
    Whirls to death the roaring whale,
Round the hall where Runic Odin
    Howls his war-song to the gale;
Save when adown the ravaged globe
    He travels on his native storm,
Deflowering Nature's grassy robe
    And trampling on her faded form:—
Till light's returning Lord assume
    The shaft that drives him to his polar field,
Of power to pierce his raven plume
    And crystal-cover'd shield.

Oh, sire of storms! whose savage ear
The Lapland drum delights to hear,
When Frenzy with her blood-shot eye
Implores thy dreadful deity—

Archangel! Power of desolation!
  Fast descending as thou art,
Say, hath mortal invocation
  Spells to touch thy stony heart?
Then, sullen Winter! hear my prayer,
And gently rule the ruin'd year;
Nor chill the wanderer's bosom bare
Nor freeze the wretch's falling tear:
To shuddering Want's unmantled bed
  Thy horror-breathing agues cease to lend,
And gently on the orphan's head
  Of Innocence descend.

But chiefly spare, O king of clouds!
The sailor on his airy shrouds,
When wrecks and beacons strew the steep,
And spectres walk along the deep.
Milder yet thy snowy breezes
  Pour on yonder tented shores,
Where the Rhine's broad billow freezes,
  Or the dark-brown Danube roars.
Oh, winds of Winter! list ye there
  To many a deep and dying groan?
Or start, ye demons of the midnight air,
  At shrieks and thunders louder than your own?
Alas! ev'n your unhallow'd breath
  May spare the victim fallen low;
But Man will ask no truce to death,—
  No bounds to human woe.

T. Campbell

CCCV

YARROW UNVISITED

1803

From Stirling Castle we had seen
The mazy Forth unravell'd,
Had trod the banks of Clyde and Tay,
And with the Tweed had travell'd;
And when we came to Clovenford,
Then said my ' winsome Marrow,'
' Whate'er betide, we'll turn aside,
And see the Braes of Yarrow.'

' Let Yarrow folk, frae Selkirk town,
Who have been buying, selling,
Go back to Yarrow, 'tis their own,
Each maiden to her dwelling !
On Yarrow's banks let herons feed,
Hares couch, and rabbits burrow ;
But we will downward with the Tweed,
Nor turn aside to Yarrow.

' There's Gala Water, Leader Haughs,
Both lying right before us ;
And Dryburgh, where with chiming Tweed
The lintwhites sing in chorus ;
There's pleasant Tiviot-dale, a land
Made blithe with plough and harrow :
Why throw away a needful day
To go in search of Yarrow ?

' What's Yarrow but a river bare
That glides the dark hills under ?
There are a thousand such elsewhere
As worthy of your wonder.'
—Strange words they seem'd of slight and scorn ;
My True-love sigh'd for sorrow,
And look'd me in the face, to think
I thus could speak of Yarrow !

' O green,' said I, ' are Yarrow's holms,
And sweet is Yarrow flowing !
Fair hangs the apple frae the rock,
But we will leave it growing.
O'er hilly path and open strath
We'll wander Scotland thorough ;
But, though so near, we will not turn
Into the dale of Yarrow.

' Let beeves and home-bred kine partake
The sweets of Burn-mill meadow ;
The swan on still Saint Mary's Lake
Float double, swan and shadow !
We will not see them ; will not go
To-day, nor yet to-morrow ;
Enough if in our hearts we know
There's such a place as Yarrow.

' Be Yarrow stream unseen, unknown !
It must, or we shall rue it :
We have a vision of our own,
Ah ! why should we undo it ?
The treasured dreams of times long past,
We'll keep them, winsome Marrow !
For when we're there, although 'tis fair,
'Twill be another Yarrow !

' If Care with freezing years should come
And wandering seem but folly,—
Should we be loth to stir from home,
And yet be melancholy;
Should life be dull, and spirits low,
'Twill soothe us in our sorrow
That earth has something yet to show,
The bonny holms of Yarrow ! '

W. Wordsworth

CCCVI

YARROW VISITED

September, 1814

And is this—Yarrow ?—This the stream
Of which my fancy cherish'd
So faithfully, a waking dream,
An image that hath perish'd ?
O that some minstrel's harp were near
To utter notes of gladness
And chase this silence from the air,
That fills my heart with sadness !

Yet why ?—a silvery current flows
With uncontroll'd meanderings;
Nor have these eyes by greener hills
Been soothed, in all my wanderings.
And, through her depths, Saint Mary's Lake
Is visibly delighted;
For not a feature of those hills
Is in the mirror slighted.

A blue sky bends o'er Yarrow Vale,
Save where that pearly whiteness
Is round the rising sun diffused,
A tender hazy brightness;
Mild dawn of promise! that excludes
All profitless dejection;
Though not unwilling here to admit
A pensive recollection.

Where was it that the famous Flower
Of Yarrow Vale lay bleeding?
His bed perchance was yon smooth mound
On which the herd is feeding:
And haply from this crystal pool,
Now peaceful as the morning,
The Water-wraith ascended thrice,
And gave his doleful warning.

Delicious is the lay that sings
The haunts of happy lovers,
The path that leads them to the grove,
The leafy grove that covers:
And pity sanctifies the verse
That paints, by strength of sorrow,
The unconquerable strength of love:
Bear witness, rueful Yarrow!

But thou that didst appear so fair
To fond imagination,
Dost rival in the light of day
Her delicate creation:
Meek loveliness is round thee spread,
A softness still and holy:
The grace of forest charms decay'd,
And pastoral melancholy.

That region left, the vale unfolds
Rich groves of lofty stature,
With Yarrow winding through the pomp
Of cultivated nature;
And rising from those lofty groves
Behold a ruin hoary,
The shatter'd front of Newark's towers,
Renown'd in Border story.

Fair scenes for childhood's opening bloom,
For sportive youth to stray in,
For manhood to enjoy his strength,
And age to wear away in!
Yon cottage seems a bower of bliss,
A covert for protection
Of tender thoughts that nestle there—
The brood of chaste affection.

How sweet on this autumnal day
The wild-wood fruits to gather,
And on my True-love's forehead plant
A crest of blooming heather!
And what if I enwreathed my own?
'Twere no offence to reason;
The sober hills thus deck their brows
To meet the wintry season.

I see—but not by sight alone,
Loved Yarrow, have I won thee;
A ray of Fancy still survives—
Her sunshine plays upon thee!
Thy ever-youthful waters keep
A course of lively pleasure;
And gladsome notes my lips can breathe
Accordant to the measure.

The vapours linger round the heights,
They melt, and soon must vanish;
One hour is theirs, nor more is mine—
Sad thought! which I would banish,
But that I know, where'er I go,
Thy genuine image, Yarrow!
Will dwell with me, to heighten joy,
And cheer my mind in sorrow.

W. Wordsworth

CCCVII

THE INVITATION

Best and brightest, come away,—
Fairer far than this fair Day,

Which, like thee, to those in sorrow
Comes to bid a sweet good-morrow
To the rough year just awake
In its cradle on the brake.
The brightest hour of unborn Spring
Through the winter wandering,
Found, it seems, the halcyon morn
To hoar February born;
Bending from heaven, in azure mirth,
It kiss'd the forehead of the earth,
And smiled upon the silent sea,
And bade the frozen streams be free,
And waked to music all their fountains,
And breathed upon the frozen mountains,
And like a prophetess of May
Strew'd flowers upon the barren way,
Making the wintry world appear
Like one on whom thou smilest, dear.

Away, away, from men and towns,
To the wild wood and the downs—
To the silent wilderness
Where the soul need not repress
Its music, lest it should not find
An echo in another's mind,
While the touch of Nature's art
Harmonizes heart to heart.

Radiant Sister of the Day
Awake! arise! and come away!
To the wild woods and the plains,
To the pools where winter rains
Image all their roof of leaves,
Where the pine its garland weaves
Of sapless green, and ivy dun,
Round stems that never kiss the sun;
Where the lawns and pastures be
And the sandhills of the sea;
Where the melting hoar-frost wets
The daisy-star that never sets,
And wind-flowers and violets
Which yet join not scent to hue
Crown the pale year weak and new;

When the night is left behind
In the deep east, dim and blind,
And the blue noon is over us,
And the multitudinous
Billows murmur at our feet,
Where the earth and ocean meet,
And all things seem only one
In the universal Sun.

P. B. Shelley

CCCVIII

THE RECOLLECTION

Now the last day of many days
All beautiful and bright as thou,
The loveliest and the last, is dead :
Rise, Memory, and write its praise !
Up—to thy wonted work ! come, trace
The epitaph of glory fled,
For now the earth has changed its face,
A frown is on the heaven's brow.

We wander'd to the Pine Forest
　　That skirts the Ocean's foam ;
The lightest wind was in its nest,
　　The tempest in its home.
The whispering waves were half asleep,
　　The clouds were gone to play,
And on the bosom of the deep
　　The smile of heaven lay ;
It seem'd as if the hour were one
　　Sent from beyond the skies
Which scatter'd from above the sun
　　A light of Paradise !

We paused amid the pines that stood
　　The giants of the waste,
Tortured by storms to shapes as rude
　　As serpents interlaced,—
And soothed by every azure breath
　　That under heaven is blown,

To harmonies and hues beneath,
  As tender as its own :
Now all the tree-tops lay asleep
  Like green waves on the sea,
As still as in the silent deep
  The ocean-woods may be.

How calm it was !—The silence there
  By such a chain was bound,
That even the busy woodpecker
  Made stiller with her sound
The inviolable quietness;
  The breath of peace we drew
With its soft motion made not less
  The calm that round us grew.
There seem'd, from the remotest seat
  Of the white mountain waste
To the soft flower beneath our feet,
  A magic circle traced,—
A spirit interfused around,
  A thrilling silent life;
To momentary peace it bound
  Our mortal nature's strife;—
And still I felt the centre of
  The magic circle there
Was one fair form that fill'd with love
  The lifeless atmosphere.

We paused beside the pools that lie
  Under the forest bough;
Each seem'd as 'twere a little sky
  Gulf'd in a world below;
A firmament of purple light
  Which in the dark earth lay,
More boundless than the depth of night
  And purer than the day—
In which the lovely forests grew
  As in the upper air,
More perfect both in shape and hue
  Than any spreading there.
There lay the glade and neighbouring lawn,
  And through the dark-green wood

The white sun twinkling like the dawn
    Out of a speckled cloud.
Sweet views which in our world above
    Can never well be seen
Were imaged in the water's love
    Of that fair forest green :
And all was interfused beneath
    With an Elysian glow,
An atmosphere without a breath,
    A softer day below.
Like one beloved, the scene had lent
    To the dark water's breast
Its every leaf and lineament
    With more than truth exprest;
Until an envious wind crept by,
    Like an unwelcome thought
Which from the mind's too faithful eye
    Blots one dear image out.
—Though thou art ever fair and kind,
    The forests ever green,
Less oft is peace in Shelley's mind
    Than calm in waters seen !

                P. B. Shelley

CCCIX

BY THE SEA

It is a beauteous evening, calm and free;
The holy time is quiet as a Nun
Breathless with adoration; the broad sun
Is sinking down in its tranquillity;

The gentleness of heaven is on the Sea :
Listen ! the mighty Being is awake,
And doth with his eternal motion make
A sound like thunder—everlastingly.

Dear child ! dear girl ! that walkest with me here,
If thou appear untouch'd by solemn thought
Thy nature is not therefore less divine :

Thou liest in Abraham's bosom all the year,
And worshipp'st at the Temple's inner shrine,
God being with thee when we know it not.

W. Wordsworth

CCCX

SONG TO THE EVENING STAR

Star that bringest home the bee,
And sett'st the weary labourer free !
If any star shed peace, 'tis Thou
  That send'st it from above,
Appearing when Heaven's breath and brow
  Are sweet as hers we love.

Come to the luxuriant skies,
Whilst the landscape's odours rise,
Whilst far-off lowing herds are heard
  And songs when toil is done,
From cottages whose smoke unstirr'd
  Curls yellow in the sun.

Star of love's soft interviews,
Parted lovers on thee muse;
Their remembrancer in Heaven
  Of thrilling vows thou art,
Too delicious to be riven
  By absence from the heart.

T. Campbell

CCCXI

DATUR HORA QUIETI

The sun upon the lake is low,
  The wild birds hush their song,
The hills have evening's deepest glow,
  Yet Leonard tarries long.
Now all whom varied toil and care
  From home and love divide,
In the calm sunset may repair
  Each to the loved one's side.

The noble dame, on turret high,
  Who waits her gallant knight,
Looks to the western beam to spy
  The flash of armour bright.
The village maid, with hand on brow
  The level ray to shade,
Upon the footpath watches now
  For Colin's darkening plaid.

Now to their mates the wild swans row,
  By day they swam apart,
And to the thicket wanders slow
  The hind beside the hart.
The woodlark at his partner's side
  Twitters his closing song—
All meet whom day and care divide,
  But Leonard tarries long !

             Sir W. Scott

CCCXII

TO THE MOON

Art thou pale for weariness
Of climbing heaven, and gazing on the earth,
  Wandering companionless
Among the stars that have a different birth,—
And ever-changing, like a joyless eye
That finds no object worth its constancy ?

             P. B. Shelley

CCCXIII

TO SLEEP

A flock of sheep that leisurely pass by
One after one; the sound of rain, and bees
Murmuring; the fall of rivers, winds and seas,
Smooth fields, white sheets of water, and pure sky;

I've thought of all by turns, and yet do lie
Sleepless; and soon the small birds' melodies
Must hear, first utter'd from my orchard trees,
And the first cuckoo's melancholy cry.

Even thus last night, and two nights more I lay,
　And could not win thee, Sleep ! by any stealth :
So do not let me wear to-night away :

Without Thee what is all the morning's wealth ?
Come, blesséd barrier between day and day,
　Dear mother of fresh thoughts and joyous health !

　　　　　　　　　　　　　　W. Wordsworth

CCCXIV

THE SOLDIER'S DREAM

Our bugles sang truce, for the night-cloud had lower'd,
　And the sentinel stars set their watch in the sky ;
And thousands had sunk on the ground overpower'd,
　The weary to sleep, and the wounded to die.

When reposing that night on my pallet of straw
　By the wolf-scaring faggot that guarded the slain,
At the dead of the night a sweet Vision I saw ;
　And thrice ere the morning I dreamt it again.

Methought from the battle-field's dreadful array
　Far, far, I had roam'd on a desolate track :
'Twas Autumn,—and sunshine arose on the way
　To the home of my fathers, that welcomed me back.

I flew to the pleasant fields traversed so oft
　In life's morning march, when my bosom was young ;
I heard my own mountain-goats bleating aloft,
　And knew the sweet strain that the corn-reapers
　　　　sung.

Then pledged we the wine-cup, and fondly I swore
　From my home and my weeping friends never to
　　　part ;
My little ones kiss'd me a thousand times o'er,
　And my wife sobb'd aloud in her fulness of heart.

' Stay—stay with us !—rest !—thou art weary and
　　worn ! '—
　And fain was their war-broken soldier to stay ;—
But sorrow return'd with the dawning of morn,
　And the voice in my dreaming ear melted away.

　　　　　　　　　　　　　　T. Campbell

CCCXV

A DREAM OF THE UNKNOWN

I dream'd that as I wander'd by the way
  Bare Winter suddenly was changed to Spring,
And gentle odours led my steps astray,
  Mix'd with a sound of waters murmuring
Along a shelving bank of turf, which lay
  Under a copse, and hardly dared to fling
Its green arms round the bosom of the stream,
But kiss'd it and then fled, as Thou mightest in
      dream.

There grew pied wind-flowers and violets,
  Daisies, those pearl'd Arcturi of the earth,
The constellated flower that never sets;
  Faint oxlips; tender blue-bells, at whose birth
The sod scarce heaved; and that tall flower that wets
  Its mother's face with heaven-collected tears,
When the low wind, its playmate's voice, it hears.

And in the warm hedge grew lush eglantine,
  Green cow-bind and the moonlight-colour'd May,
And cherry-blossoms, and white cups, whose wine
  Was the bright dew yet drain'd not by the day;
And wild roses, and ivy serpentine
  With its dark buds and leaves, wandering astray;
And flowers azure, black, and streak'd with gold,
Fairer than any waken'd eyes behold.

And nearer to the river's trembling edge
  There grew broad flag-flowers, purple prank'd with
     white,
And starry river-buds among the sedge,
  And floating water-lilies, broad and bright,
Which lit the oak that overhung the hedge
  With moonlight beams of their own watery light;
And bulrushes, and reeds of such deep green
As soothed the dazzled eye with sober sheen.

Methought that of these visionary flowers
  I made a nosegay, bound in such a way

That the same hues, which in their natural bower
  Were mingled or opposed, the like array
Kept these imprison'd children of the Hours
  Within my hand,—and then, elate and gay,
I hasten'd to the spot whence I had come
That I might there present it—O ! to Whom ?

P. B. Shelley

CCCXVI

KUBLA KHAN

In Xanadu did Kubla Khan
A stately pleasure-dome decree :
Where Alph, the sacred river, ran
Through caverns measureless to man
  Down to a sunless sea.
So twice five miles of fertile ground
With walls and towers were girdled round :
And there were gardens bright with sinuous rills
Where blossom'd many an incense-bearing tree;
And here were forests ancient as the hills,
Enfolding sunny spots of greenery.

  But oh ! that deep romantic chasm which slanted
Down the green hill athwart a cedarn cover !
A savage place ! as holy and enchanted
As e'er beneath a waning moon was haunted
By woman wailing for her demon-lover !
And from this chasm, with ceaseless turmoil seething,
As if this earth in fast thick pants were breathing,
A mighty fountain momently was forced :
Amid whose swift half-intermitted burst
Huge fragments vaulted like rebounding hail,
Or chaffy grain beneath the thresher's flail :
And 'mid these dancing rocks at once and ever
It flung up momently the sacred river.
Five miles meandering with a mazy motion
Through wood and dale the sacred river ran,
Then reach'd the caverns measureless to man,
And sank in tumult to a lifeless ocean :
And 'mid this tumult Kubla heard from far
Ancestral voices prophesying war !

    The shadow of the dome of pleasure
    Floated midway on the waves;
    Where was heard the mingled measure
    From the fountain and the caves.
It was a miracle of rare device,
A sunny pleasure-dome with caves of ice!
    A damsel with a dulcimer
    In a vision once I saw:
    It was an Abyssinian maid,
    And on her dulcimer she play'd,
    Singing of Mount Abora.
    Could I revive within me
    Her symphony and song,
To such a deep delight 'twould win me
That with music loud and long,
I would build that dome in air,
That sunny dome! those caves of ice!
And all who heard should see them there,
And all should cry, Beware! Beware!
His flashing eyes, his floating hair!
Weave a circle round him thrice,
And close your eyes with holy dread,
For he on honey-dew hath fed,
And drunk the milk of Paradise.

                              S. T. Coleridge

                    CCCXVII

              THE INNER VISION

Most sweet it is with unuplifted eyes
To pace the ground, if path be there or none,
While a fair region round the traveller lies
Which he forbears again to look upon;

Pleased rather with some soft ideal scene,
The work of Fancy, or some happy tone
Of meditation, slipping in between
The beauty coming and the beauty gone.

—If Thought and Love desert us, from that day
Let us break off all commerce with the Muse:
With Thought and Love companions of our way—

Whate'er the senses take or may refuse,—
The Mind's internal heaven shall shed her dews
Of inspiration on the humblest lay.

W. Wordsworth

CCCXVIII

THE REALM OF FANCY

Ever let the Fancy roam;
Pleasure never is at home:
At a touch sweet Pleasure melteth,
Like to bubbles when rain pelteth;
Then let wingéd Fancy wander
Through the thought still spread beyond her:
Open wide the mind's cage-door,
She'll dart forth, and cloudward soar.
O sweet Fancy! let her loose;
Summer's joys are spoilt by use,
And the enjoying of the Spring
Fades as does its blossoming;
Autumn's red-lipp'd fruitage too,
Blushing through the mist and dew,
Cloys with tasting: What do then?
Sit thee by the ingle, when
The sear faggot blazes bright,
Spirit of a winter's night;
When the soundless earth is muffled,
And the cakéd snow is shuffled
From the ploughboy's heavy shoon;
When the Night doth meet the Noon
In a dark conspiracy
To banish Even from her sky.
Sit thee there, and send abroad,
With a mind self-overaw'd,
Fancy, high-commission'd:—send her!
She has vassals to attend her:
She will bring, in spite of frost,
Beauties that the earth hath lost;
She will bring thee, all together,
All delights of summer weather;
All the buds and bells of May,

From dewy sward or thorny spray;
All the heapéd Autumn's wealth,
With a still, mysterious stealth:
She will mix these pleasures up
Like three fit wines in a cup,
And thou shalt quaff it:—thou shalt hear
Distant harvest-carols clear;
Rustle of the reapéd corn;
Sweet birds antheming the morn:
And, in the same moment—hark!
'Tis the early April lark,
Or the rooks, with busy caw,
Foraging for sticks and straw.
Thou shalt, at one glance, behold
The daisy and the marigold;
White-plumed lilies, and the first
Hedge-grown primrose that hath burst;
Shaded hyacinth, alway
Sapphire queen of the mid-May;
And every leaf, and every flower
Pearléd with the self-same shower.
Thou shalt see the field-mouse peep
Meagre from its celléd sleep;
And the snake all winter-thin
Cast on sunny bank its skin;
Freckled nest-eggs thou shalt see
Hatching in the hawthorn-tree,
When the hen-bird's wing doth rest
Quiet on her mossy nest;
Then the hurry and alarm
When the bee-hive casts its swarm;
Acorns ripe down-pattering,
While the autumn breezes sing.

Oh, sweet Fancy! let her loose;
Everything is spoilt by use:
Where's the cheek that doth not fade,
Too much gazed at? Where's the maid
Whose lip mature is ever new?
Where's the eye, however blue,
Doth not weary? Where's the face
One would meet in every place?
Where's the voice, however soft,

One would hear so very oft?
At a touch sweet Pleasure melteth
Like to bubbles when rain pelteth.
Let then wingéd Fancy find
Thee a mistress to thy mind :
Dulcet-eyed as Ceres' daughter,
Ere the God of Torment taught her
How to frown and how to chide;
With a waist and with a side
White as Hebe's, when her zone
Slipt its golden clasp, and down
Fell her kirtle to her feet,
While she held the goblet sweet,
And Jove grew languid.—Break the mesh
Of the Fancy's silken leash ;
Quickly break her prison-string,
And such joys as these she'll bring.
—Let the wingéd Fancy roam,
Pleasure never is at home.

                                      J. Keats

CCCXIX

WRITTEN IN EARLY SPRING

I heard a thousand blended notes
While in a grove I sate reclined,
In that sweet mood when pleasant thoughts
Bring sad thoughts to the mind.

To her fair works did Nature link
The human soul that through me ran ;
And much it grieved my heart to think
What Man has made of Man.

Through primrose tufts, in that sweet bower,
The periwinkle trail'd its wreaths ;
And 'tis my faith, that every flower
Enjoys the air it breathes.

The birds around me hopp'd and play'd,
Their thoughts I cannot measure,—
But the least motion which they made
It seem'd a thrill of pleasure.

The budding twigs spread out their fan
To catch the breezy air;
And I must think, do all I can,
That there was pleasure there.

If this belief from heaven be sent,
If such be Nature's holy plan,
Have I not reason to lament
What Man has made of Man?

W. Wordsworth

CCCXX

RUTH : OR THE INFLUENCES OF NATURE

When Ruth was left half desolate
Her father took another mate;
And Ruth, not seven years old,
A slighted child, at her own will
Went wandering over dale and hill,
In thoughtless freedom, bold.

And she had made a pipe of straw,
And music from that pipe could draw
Like sounds of winds and floods;
Had built a bower upon the green,
As if she from her birth had been
An infant of the woods.

Beneath her father's roof, alone
She seem'd to live; her thoughts her own;
Herself her own delight:
Pleased with herself, nor sad nor gay;
And passing thus the live-long day,
She grew to woman's height.

There came a youth from Georgia's shore—
A military casque he wore
With splendid feathers drest;
He brought them from the Cherokees;
The feathers nodded in the breeze
And made a gallant crest.

From Indian blood you deem him sprung:
But no! he spake the English tongue
And bore a soldier's name;
And, when America was free
From battle and from jeopardy,
He 'cross the ocean came.

With hues of genius on his cheek,
In finest tones the youth could speak:
—While he was yet a boy
The moon, the glory of the sun,
And streams that murmur as they run
Had been his dearest joy.

He was a lovely youth! I guess
The panther in the wilderness
Was not so fair as he;
And when he chose to sport and play,
No dolphin ever was so gay
Upon the tropic sea.

Among the Indians he had fought;
And with him many tales he brought
Of pleasure and of fear;
Such tales as, told to any maid
By such a youth, in the green shade,
Were perilous to hear.

He told of girls, a happy rout!
Who quit their fold with dance and shout,
Their pleasant Indian town,
To gather strawberries all day long;
Returning with a choral song
When daylight is gone down.

He spake of plants that hourly change
Their blossoms, through a boundless range
Of intermingling hues;
With budding, fading, faded flowers,
They stand the wonder of the bowers
From morn to evening dews.

He told of the magnolia, spread
High as a cloud, high over head!
The cypress and her spire;

—Of flowers that with one scarlet gleam
Cover a hundred leagues. and seem
To set the hills on fire.

The youth of green savannahs spake,
And many an endless, endless lake
With all its fairy crowds
Of islands, that together lie
As quietly as spots of sky
Among the evening clouds.

' How pleasant,' then he said, 'it were
A fisher or a hunter there,
In sunshine or in shade
To wander with an easy mind,
And build a household fire, and find
A home in every glade !

' What days and what bright years !   Ah me :
Our life were life indeed, with thee
So pass'd in quiet bliss ;
And all the while,' said he, ' to know
That we were in a world of woe,
On such an earth as this ! '

And then he sometimes interwove
Fond thoughts about a father's love,
' For there,' said he, ' are spun
Around the heart such tender ties,
That our own children to our eyes
Are dearer than the sun.

' Sweet Ruth ! and could you go with me
My helpmate in the woods to be,
Our shed at night to rear ;
Or run, my own adopted bride,
A sylvan huntress at my side,
And drive the flying deer !

' Beloved Ruth ! '—No more he said.
The wakeful Ruth at midnight shed
A solitary tear :
She thought again—and did agree
With him to sail across the sea,
And drive the flying deer.

' And now, as fitting is and right,
We in the church our faith will plight,
A husband and a wife.'
Even so they did; and I may say
That to sweet Ruth that happy day
Was more than human life.

Through dream and vision did she sink,
Delighted all the while to think
That, on those lonesome floods
And green savannahs, she should share
His board with lawful joy, and bear
His name in the wild woods.

But, as you have before been told,
This Stripling, sportive, gay, and bold,
And with his dancing crest
So beautiful, through savage lands
Had roam'd about, with vagrant bands
Of Indians in the West.

The wind, the tempest roaring high,
The tumult of a tropic sky
Might well be dangerous food
For him, a youth to whom was given
So much of earth—so much of heaven,
And such impetuous blood.

Whatever in those climes he found
Irregular in sight or sound
Did to his mind impart
A kindred impulse, seem'd allied
To his own powers, and justified
The workings of his heart.

Nor less, to feed voluptuous thought,
The beauteous forms of Nature wrought,—
Fair trees and gorgeous flowers;
The breezes their own languor lent;
The stars had feelings, which they sent
Into those favour'd bowers.

Yet, in his worst pursuits, I ween
That sometimes there did intervene
Pure hopes of high intent:

For passions link'd to forms so fair
And stately, needs must have their share
Of noble sentiment.

But ill he lived, much evil saw,
With men to whom no better law
Nor better life was known;
Deliberately and undeceived
Those wild men's vices he received,
And gave them back his own.

His genius and his moral frame
Were thus impair'd, and he became
The slave of low desires:
A man who without self-control
Would seek what the degraded soul
Unworthily admires.

And yet he with no feign'd delight
Had woo'd the maiden, day and night
Had loved her, night and morn:
What could he less than love a maid
Whose heart with so much nature play'd—
So kind and so forlorn?

Sometimes most earnestly he said,
' O Ruth! I have been worse than dead;
False thoughts, thoughts bold and vain
Encompass'd me on every side
When I, in confidence and pride,
Had cross'd the Atlantic main.

' Before me shone a glorious world
Fresh as a banner bright, unfurl'd
To music suddenly:
I look'd upon those hills and plains,
And seem'd as if let loose from chains
To live at liberty!

' No more of this—for now, by thee,
Dear Ruth! more happily set free,
With nobler zeal I burn;
My soul from darkness is released
Like the whole sky when to the east
The morning doth return.'

Full soon that better mind was gone;
No hope, no wish remain'd, not one,—
They stirr'd him now no more;
New objects did new pleasure give,
And once again he wish'd to live
As lawless as before.

Meanwhile, as thus with him it fared,
They for the voyage were prepared,
And went to the sea-shore:
But, when they thither came, the youth
Deserted his poor bride, and Ruth
Could never find him more.

God help thee, Ruth!—Such pains she had
That she in half a year was mad
And in a prison housed;
And there, with many a doleful song
Made of wild words, her cup of wrong
She fearfully caroused.

Yet sometimes milder hours she knew,
Nor wanted sun, nor rain, nor dew,
Nor pastimes of the May,
—They all were with her in her cell;
And a clear brook with cheerful knell
Did o'er the pebbles play.

When Ruth three seasons thus had lain,
There came a respite to her pain;
She from her prison fled;
But of the Vagrant none took thought;
And where it liked her best she sought
Her shelter and her bread.

Among the fields she breathed again:
The master-current of her brain
Ran permanent and free;
And, coming to the banks of Tone,
There did she rest; and dwell alone
Under the greenwood tree.

The engines of her pain, the tools
That shaped her sorrow, rocks and pools,
And airs that gently stir

The vernal leaves—she loved them still,
Nor ever tax'd them with the ill
Which had been done to her.

A barn her Winter bed supplies;
But, till the warmth of Summer skies
And Summer days is gone,
(And all do in this tale agree)
She sleeps beneath the greenwood tree,
And other home hath none.

An innocent life, yet far astray!
And Ruth will, long before her day,
Be broken down and old.
Sore aches she needs must have! but less
Of mind, than body's wretchedness,
From damp, and rain, and cold.

If she is prest by want of food
She from her dwelling in the wood
Repairs to a road-side;
And there she begs at one steep place,
Where up and down with easy pace
The horsemen-travellers ride.

That oaten pipe of hers is mute
Or thrown away: but with a flute
Her loneliness she cheers;
This flute, made of a hemlock stalk,
At evening in his homeward walk
The Quantock woodman hears.

I, too, have pass'd her on the hills
Setting her little water-mills
By spouts and fountains wild—
Such small machinery as she turn'd
Ere she had wept, ere she had mourn'd,—
A young and happy child!

Farewell! and when thy days are told,
Ill-fated Ruth! in hallow'd mould
Thy corpse shall buried be;
For thee a funeral bell shall ring,
And all the congregation sing
A Christian psalm for thee.

W. Wordsworth

CCCXXI

WRITTEN AMONG THE
EUGANEAN HILLS

Many a green isle needs must be
In the deep wide sea of Misery,
Or the mariner, worn and wan,
Never thus could voyage on
Day and night, and night and day,
Drifting on his dreary way,
With the solid darkness black
Closing round his vessel's track;
Whilst above, the sunless sky
Big with clouds, hangs heavily,
And behind the tempest fleet
Hurries on with lightning feet,
Riving sail, and cord, and plank,
Till the ship has almost drank
Death from the o'er-brimming deep;
And sinks down, down, like that sleep
When the dreamer seems to be
Weltering through eternity;
And the dim low line before
Of a dark and distant shore
Still recedes, as ever still
Longing with divided will,
But no power to seek or shun,
He is ever drifted on
O'er the unreposing wave,
To the haven of the grave.

Ah, many flowering islands lie
In the waters of wide Agony:
To such a one this morn was led
My bark, by soft winds piloted.
—'Mid the mountains Euganean
I stood listening to the paean
With which the legion'd rooks did hail
The Sun's uprise majestical:
Gathering round with wings all hoar,

Through the dewy mist they soar
Like gray shades, till the eastern heaven
Bursts; and then,—as clouds of even
Fleck'd with fire and azure, lie
In the unfathomable sky,—
So their plumes of purple grain
Starr'd with drops of golden rain
Gleam above the sunlight woods,
As in silent multitudes
On the morning's fitful gale
Through the broken mist they sail;
And the vapours cloven and gleaming
Follow down the dark steep streaming,
Till all is bright, and clear, and still
Round the solitary hill.

Beneath is spread like a green sea
The waveless plain of Lombardy,
Bounded by the vaporous air,
Islanded by cities fair;
Underneath Day's azure eyes,
Ocean's nursling, Venice lies,—
A peopled labyrinth of walls,
Amphitrite's destined halls,
Which her hoary sire now paves
With his blue and beaming waves.
Lo! the sun upsprings behind,
Broad, red, radiant, half-reclined
On the level quivering line
Of the waters crystalline;
And before that chasm of light,
As within a furnace bright,
Column, tower, and dome, and spire,
Shine like obelisks of fire,
Pointing with inconstant motion
From the altar of dark ocean
To the sapphire-tinted skies;
As the flames of sacrifice
From the marble shrines did rise
As to pierce the dome of gold
Where Apollo spoke of old.

Sun-girt City! thou hast been

Ocean's child, and then his queen;
Now is come a darker day,
And thou soon must be his prey,
If the power that raised thee here
Hallow so thy watery bier.
A less drear ruin then than now,
With thy conquest-branded brow
Stooping to the slave of slaves
From thy throne among the waves
Wilt thou be,—when the sea-mew
Flies, as once before it flew,
O'er thine isles depopulate,
And all is in its ancient state,
Save where many a palace-gate
With green sea-flowers overgrown
Like a rock of ocean's own,
Topples o'er the abandon'd sea
As the tides change sullenly.
The fisher on his watery way
Wandering at the close of day,
Will spread his sail and seize his oar
Till he pass the gloomy shore,
Lest thy dead should, from their sleep,
Bursting o'er the starlight deep,
Lead a rapid masque of death
O'er the waters of his path.

Noon descends around me now:
'Tis the noon of autumn's glow,
When a soft and purple mist
Like a vaporous amethyst,
Or an air-dissolvéd star
Mingling light and fragrance, far
From the curved horizon's bound
To the point of heaven's profound,
Fills the overflowing sky;
And the plains that silent lie
Underneath; the leaves unsodden
Where the infant Frost has trodden
With his morning-wingéd feet
Whose bright print is gleaming yet;
And the red and golden vines

Piercing with their trellised lines
The rough, dark-skirted wilderness;
The dun and bladed grass no less,
Pointing from this hoary tower
In the windless air; the flower
Glimmering at my feet; the line
Of the olive-sandall'd Apennine
In the south dimly islanded;
And the Alps, whose snows are spread
High between the clouds and sun;
And of living things each one;
And my spirit, which so long
Darken'd this swift stream of song,—
Interpenetrated lie
By the glory of the sky;
Be it love, light, harmony,
Odour, or the soul of all
Which from heaven like dew doth fall,
Or the mind which feeds this verse,
Peopling the lone universe.

Noon descends, and after noon
Autumn's evening meets me soon,
Leading the infantine moon
And that one star, which to her
Almost seems to minister
Half the crimson light she brings
From the sunset's radiant springs:
And the soft dreams of the morn
(Which like wingéd winds had borne
To that silent isle, which lies
'Mid remember'd agonies,
The frail bark of this lone being),
Pass, to other sufferers fleeing,
And its ancient pilot, Pain,
Sits beside the helm again.

Other flowering isles must be
In the sea of Life and Agony:
Other spirits float and flee
O'er that gulf: Ev'n now, perhaps,
On some rock the wild wave wraps,

With folded wings they waiting sit
For my bark, to pilot it
To some calm and blooming cove;
Where for me, and those I love,
May a windless bower be built,
Far from passion, pain, and guilt,
In a dell 'mid lawny hills
Which the wild sea-murmur fills,
And soft sunshine, and the sound
Of old forests echoing round,
And the light and smell divine
Of all flowers that breathe and shine.
—We may live so happy there,
That the Spirits of the Air
Envying us, may ev'n entice
To our healing paradise
The polluting multitude:
But their rage would be subdued
By that clime divine and calm,
And the winds whose wings rain balm
On the uplifted soul, and leaves
Under which the bright sea heaves;
While each breathless interval
In their whisperings musical
The inspired soul supplies
With its own deep melodies;
And the Love which heals all strife
Circling, like the breath of life,
All things in that sweet abode
With its own mild brotherhood:—
They, not it, would change; and soon
Every sprite beneath the moon
Would repent its envy vain,
And the Earth grow young again.

P. B. Shelley

ODE TO THE WEST WIND

O wild West Wind, thou breath of Autumn's being,
Thou, from whose unseen presence the leaves dead
Are driven, like ghosts from an enchanter fleeing,
Yellow, and black, and pale, and hectic red,
Pestilence-stricken multitudes ! O thou
Who chariotest to their dark wintry bed
The wingèd seeds, where they lie cold and low,
Each like a corpse within its grave, until
Thine azure sister of the Spring shall blow
Her clarion o'er the dreaming earth, and fill
(Driving sweet buds like flocks to feed in air)
With living hues and odours plain and hill :
Wild Spirit, which art moving everywhere ;
Destroyer and Preserver ; Hear, oh hear !

Thou on whose stream, 'mid the steep sky's com-
        motion,
Loose clouds like earth's decaying leaves are shed,
Shook from the tangled boughs of heaven and ocean,
Angels of rain and lightning ! there are spread
On the blue surface of thine airy surge,
Like the bright hair uplifted from the head
Of some fierce Maenad, ev'n from the dim verge
Of the horizon to the zenith's height—
The locks of the approaching storm.   Thou dirge
Of the dying year, to which this closing night
Will be the dome of a vast sepulchre,
Vaulted with all thy congregated might
Of vapours, from whose solid atmosphere
Black rain, and fire, and hail, will burst : Oh hear !

Thou who didst waken from his summer-dreams
The blue Mediterranean, where he lay,
Lull'd by the coil of his crystalline streams,
Beside a pumice isle in Baiae's bay,
And saw in sleep old palaces and towers
Quivering within the wave's intenser day,

All overgrown with azure moss, and flowers
So sweet, the sense faints picturing them !   Thou
For whose path the Atlantic's level powers
Cleave themselves into chasms, while far below
The sea-blooms and the oozy woods which wear
The sapless foliage of the ocean, know
Thy voice, and suddenly grow gray with fear
And tremble and despoil themselves : Oh hear !

If I were a dead leaf thou mightest bear ;
If I were a swift-cloud to fly with thee ;
A wave to pant beneath thy power, and share
The impulse of thy strength, only less free
Than Thou, O uncontrollable !   If even
I were as in my boyhood, and could be
The comrade of thy wanderings over heaven,
As then, when to outstrip thy skiey speed
Scarce seem'd a vision,—I would ne'er have striven
As thus with thee in prayer in my sore need.
Oh ! lift me as a wave, a leaf, a cloud !
I fall upon the thorns of life ! I bleed !
A heavy weight of hours has chain'd and bow'd
One too like thee—tameless, and swift, and proud.

Make me thy lyre, ev'n as the forest is :
What if my leaves are falling like its own !
The tumult of thy mighty harmonies
Will take from both a deep autumnal tone,
Sweet though in sadness.   Be thou, Spirit fierce,
My spirit ! be thou me, impetuous one !
Drive my dead thoughts over the universe,
Like wither'd leaves, to quicken a new birth ;
And, by the incantation of this verse,
Scatter, as from an unextinguish'd hearth
Ashes and sparks, my words among mankind !
Be through my lips to unawaken'd earth
The trumpet of a prophecy ! O Wind,
If Winter comes, can Spring be far behind ?

                                        P. B. Shelley

CCCXXIII

NATURE AND THE POET

Suggested by a Picture of Peele Castle in a Storm, painted by Sir George Beaumont

I was thy neighbour once, thou rugged Pile !
Four summer weeks I dwelt in sight of thee :
I saw thee every day ; and all the while
Thy Form was sleeping on a glassy sea.

So pure the sky, so quiet was the air !
So like, so very like, was day to day !
Whene'er I look'd, thy image still was there ;
It trembled, but it never pass'd away.

How perfect was the calm ! It seem'd no sleep,
No mood, which season takes away, or brings :
I could have fancied that the mighty Deep
Was even the gentlest of all gentle things.

Ah ! then—if mine had been the painter's hand
To express what then I saw ; and add the gleam,
The light that never was on sea or land,
The consecration, and the Poet's dream,—

I would have planted thee, thou hoary pile,
Amid a world how different from this !
Beside a sea that could not cease to smile ;
On tranquil land, beneath a sky of bliss.

Thou shouldst have seem'd a treasure-house divine
Of peaceful years ; a chronicle of heaven ;—
Of all the sunbeams that did ever shine
The very sweetest had to thee been given.

A picture had it been of lasting ease,
Elysian quiet, without toil or strife ;
No motion but the moving tide ; a breeze ;
Or merely silent Nature's breathing life.

Such, in the fond illusion of my heart,
Such picture would I at that time have made;
And seen the soul of truth in every part,
A steadfast peace that might not be betray'd.

So once it would have been,—it's so no more;
I have submitted to a new control;
A power is gone, which nothing can restore;
A deep distress hath humanized my soul.

Not for a moment could I now behold
A smiling sea, and be what I have been:
The feeling of my loss will ne'er be old;
This, which I know, I speak with mind serene.

Then, Beaumont, Friend! who would have been the
        friend
If he had lived, of Him whom I deplore,
This work of thine I blame not, but commend;
This sea in anger, and that dismal shore.

O 'tis a passionate work!—yet wise and well,
Well chosen is the spirit that is here;
That hulk which labours in the deadly swell,
This rueful sky, this pageantry of fear!

And this huge Castle, standing here sublime,
I love to see the look with which it braves,
—Cased in the unfeeling armour of old time—
The lightning, the fierce wind, and trampling waves.

—Farewell, farewell the heart that lives alone,
Housed in a dream, at distance from the Kind!
Such happiness, wherever it be known,
Is to be pitied; for 'tis surely blind.

But welcome fortitude, and patient cheer,
And frequent sights of what is to be borne!
Such sights, or worse, as are before me here:—
Not without hope we suffer and we mourn.

                                        W. Wordsworth

CCCXXIV

THE POET'S DREAM

On a Poet's lips I slept
Dreaming like a love-adept
In the sound his breathing kept;
Nor seeks nor finds he mortal blisses,
But feeds on the aërial kisses
Of shapes that haunt Thought's wildernesses.
He will watch from dawn to gloom
The lake-reflected sun illume
The yellow bees in the ivy-bloom,
    Nor heed nor see what things they be—
But from these create he can
Forms more real than living Man,
    Nurslings of Immortality!

P. B. Shelley

CCCXXV

GLEN-ALMAIN, THE NARROW GLEN

In this still place, remote from men,
Sleeps Ossian, in the Narrow Glen;
In this still place, where murmurs on
But one meek streamlet, only one:
He sang of battles, and the breath
Of stormy war, and violent death;
And should, methinks, when all was past,
Have rightfully been laid at last
Where rocks were rudely heap'd, and rent
As by a spirit turbulent;
Where sights were rough, and sounds were wild,
And everything unreconciled;
In some complaining, dim retreat,
For fear and melancholy meet;
But this is calm; there cannot be
A more entire tranquillity.

Does then the Bard sleep here indeed?
Or is it but a groundless creed?
What matters it?—I blame them not
Whose fancy in this lonely spot
Was moved; and in such way express'd
Their notion of its perfect rest.
A convent, even a hermit's cell,
Would break the silence of this Dell:
It is not quiet, is not ease;
But something deeper far than these:
The separation that is here
Is of the grave; and of austere
Yet happy feelings of the dead:
And, therefore, was it rightly said
That Ossian, last of all his race!
Lies buried in this lonely place.

W. Wordsworth

CCCXXVI

The World is too much with us; late and soon,
Getting and spending, we lay waste our powers;
Little we see in Nature that is ours;
We have given our hearts away, a sordid boon!

This Sea that bares her bosom to the moon,
The winds that will be howling at all hours
And are up-gather'd now like sleeping flowers,
For this, for every thing, we are out of tune;

It moves us not.—Great God! I'd rather be
A Pagan suckled in a creed outworn,—
So might I, standing on this pleasant lea,

Have glimpses that would make me less forlorn;
Have sight of Proteus rising from the sea;
Or hear old Triton blow his wreathéd horn.

W. Wordsworth.

CCCXXVII

WITHIN KING'S COLLEGE CHAPEL,
CAMBRIDGE

Tax not the royal Saint with vain expense,
With ill-match'd aims the Architect who plann'd
(Albeit labouring for a scanty band
Of white-robed Scholars only) this immense

And glorious work of fine intelligence !
—Give all thou canst; high Heaven rejects the lore
Of nicely-calculated less or more :—
So deem'd the man who fashion'd for the sense

These lofty pillars, spread that branching roof
Self-poised, and scoop'd into ten thousand cells
Where light and shade repose, where music dwells

Lingering—and wandering on as loth to die;
Like thoughts whose very sweetness yieldeth proof
That they were born for immortality.

W. Wordsworth

CCCXXVIII

ODE ON A GRECIAN URN

Thou still unravish'd bride of quietness,
  Thou foster-child of silence and slow time,
Sylvan historian, who canst thus express
  A flowery tale more sweetly than our rhyme :
What leaf-fringed legend haunts about thy shape
    Of deities or mortals, or of both,
      In Tempé or the dales of Arcady ?
What men or gods are these ? What maidens loth ?
    What mad pursuit ? What struggle to escape ?
      What pipes and timbrels ? What wild ecstasy ?

Heard melodies are sweet, but those unheard
  Are sweeter ; therefore, ye soft pipes, play on ;
Not to the sensual ear, but, more endear'd,
  Pipe to the spirit ditties of no tone :

Fair youth, beneath the trees, thou canst not leave
   Thy song, nor ever can those trees be bare;
     Bold Lover, never, never canst thou kiss,
Though winning near the goal—yet, do not grieve;
   She cannot fade, though thou hast not thy bliss,
     For ever wilt thou love, and she be fair!

Ah, happy, happy boughs! that cannot shed
   Your leaves, nor ever bid the Spring adieu;
And, happy melodist, unwearièd,
   For ever piping songs for ever new;
More happy love! more happy, happy love!
   For ever warm and still to be enjoy'd,
     For ever panting, and for ever young;
All breathing human passion far above,
   That leaves a heart high-sorrowful and cloy'd,
     A burning forehead, and a parching tongue.

Who are these coming to the sacrifice?
   To what green altar, O mysterious priest,
Lead'st thou that heifer lowing at the skies,
   And all her silken flanks with garlands drest?
What little town by river or sea shore,
   Or mountain-built with peaceful citadel,
     Is emptied of this folk, this pious morn?
And, little town, thy streets for evermore
   Will silent be; and not a soul to tell
     Why thou art desolate, can e'er return.

O Attic shape! Fair attitude! with brede
   Of marble men and maidens overwrought,
With forest branches and the trodden weed;
   Thou, silent form, dost tease us out of thought
As doth eternity: Cold Pastoral!
   When old age shall this generation waste,
     Thou shalt remain, in midst of other woe
Than ours, a friend to man, to whom thou say'st,
   ' Beauty is truth, truth beauty,'—that is all
     Ye know on earth, and all ye need to know.

J. Keats

CCCXXIX

YOUTH AND AGE

Verse, a breeze 'mid blossoms straying,
Where Hope clung feeding, like a bee—
Both were mine !   Life went a-maying
    With Nature, Hope, and Poesy,
        When I was young !
When I was young ?—Ah, woful when !
Ah ! for the change 'twixt Now and Then !
This breathing house not built with hands,
This body that does me grievous wrong,
O'er aery cliffs and glittering sands
How lightly then it flash'd along :
Like those trim skiffs, unknown of yore,
On winding lakes and rivers wide,
That ask no aid of sail or oar,
That fear no spite of wind or tide !
Nought cared this body for wind or weather
When Youth and I lived in't together.

Flowers are lovely ; Love is flower-like ;
Friendship is a sheltering tree ;
O ! the joys, that came down shower-like,
Of Friendship, Love, and Liberty,
        Ere I was old !
Ere I was old ? Ah woful Ere,
Which tells me, Youth's no longer here !
O Youth ! for years so many and sweet,
'Tis known that Thou and I were one,
I'll think it but a fond conceit—
It cannot be, that Thou art gone !
Thy vesper-bell hath not yet toll'd :—
And thou wert aye a masker bold !
What strange disguise hast now put on
To make believe that Thou art gone ?
I see these locks in silvery slips,
This drooping gait, this alter'd size :
But Springtide blossoms on thy lips,
And tears take sunshine from thine eyes !
Life is but Thought : so think I will
That Youth and I are house-mates still.

Dew-drops are the gems of morning,
But the tears of mournful eve !
Where no hope is, life's a warning
That only serves to make us grieve
          When we are old :
—That only serves to make us grieve
With oft and tedious taking-leave,
Like some poor nigh-related guest
That may not rudely be dismist,
Yet hath out-stay'd his welcome while,
And tells the jest without the smile.

                              S. T. Coleridge

CCCXXX

THE TWO APRIL MORNINGS

We walk'd along, while bright and red
Uprose the morning sun;
And Matthew stopp'd, he look'd, and said
' The will of God be done ! '

A village schoolmaster was he,
With hair of glittering gray;
As blithe a man as you could see
On a spring holiday.

And on that morning, through the grass
And by the steaming rills
We travell'd merrily, to pass
A day among the hills.

' Our work,' said I, ' was well begun;
Then, from thy breast what thought,
Beneath so beautiful a sun,
So sad a sigh has brought ? '

A second time did Matthew stop;
And fixing still his eye
Upon the eastern mountain-top,
To me he made reply :

' Yon cloud with that long purple cleft
Brings fresh into my mind
A day like this, which I have left
Full thirty years behind.

' And just above yon slope of corn
Such colours, and no other,
Were in the sky that April morn,
Of this the very brother.

' With rod and line I sued the sport
Which that sweet season gave,
And to the church-yard come, stopp'd short
Beside my daughter's grave.

' Nine summers had she scarcely seen,
The pride of all the vale;
And then she sang,—she would have been
A very nightingale.

' Six feet in earth my Emma lay,
And yet I loved her more—
For so it seem'd,—than till that day
I e'er had loved before.

' And turning from her grave, I met,
Beside the churchyard yew,
A blooming Girl, whose hair was wet
With points of morning dew.

' A basket on her head she bare;
Her brow was smooth and white:
To see a child so very fair,
It was a pure delight!

' No fountain from its rocky cave
E'er tripp'd with foot so free;
She seem'd as happy as a wave
That dances on the sea.

' There came from me a sigh of pain
Which I could ill confine;
I look'd at her, and look'd again:
And did not wish her mine! '

—Matthew is in his grave, yet now
Methinks I see him stand
As at that moment, with a bough
Of wilding in his hand.

W. Wordsworth

CCCXXXI

THE FOUNTAIN

A Conversation

We talk'd with open heart, and tongue
Affectionate and true,
A pair of friends, though I was young,
And Matthew seventy-two.

We lay beneath a spreading oak,
Beside a mossy seat;
And from the turf a fountain broke
And gurgled at our feet.

' Now, Matthew ! ' said I, ' let us match
This water's pleasant tune
With some old border-song, or catch
That suits a summer's noon;

' Or of the church-clock and the chimes
Sing here beneath the shade
That half-mad thing of witty rhymes
Which you last April made ! '

In silence Matthew lay, and eyed
The spring beneath the tree;
And thus the dear old man replied,
The gray-hair'd man of glee :

' No check, no stay, this Streamlet fears,
How merrily it goes !
'Twill murmur on a thousand years
And flow as now it flows.

' And here, on this delightful day,
I cannot choose but think
How oft, a vigorous man, I lay
Beside this fountain's brink.

' My eyes are dim with childish tears,
My heart is idly stirr'd,
For the same sound is in my ears
Which in those days I heard.

' Thus fares it still in our decay :
And yet the wiser mind
Mourns less for what Age takes away,
Than what it leaves behind.

' The blackbird amid leafy trees,
The lark above the hill,
Let loose their carols when they please,
Are quiet when they will.

' With Nature never do they wage
A foolish strife ; they see
A happy youth, and their old age
Is beautiful and free :

' But we are press'd by heavy laws ;
And often, glad no more,
We wear a face of joy, because
We have been glad of yore.

' If there be one who need bemoan
His kindred laid in earth,
The household hearts that were his own,—
It is the man of mirth.

' My days, my friend, are almost gone,
My life has been approved,
And many love me ; but by none
Am I enough beloved.'

' Now both himself and me he wrongs,
The man who thus complains !
I live and sing my idle songs
Upon these happy plains :

'And Matthew, for thy children dead
I'll be a son to thee!'
At this he grasp'd my hand and said,
'Alas! that cannot be.'

—We rose up from the fountain-side;
And down the smooth descent
Of the green sheep-track did we glide;
And through the wood we went;

And ere we came to Leonard's rock
He sang those witty rhymes
About the crazy old church-clock,
And the bewilder'd chimes.

                              W. Wordsworth

CCCXXXII

THE RIVER OF LIFE

The more we live, more brief appear
    Our life's succeeding stages:
A day to childhood seems a year,
    And years like passing ages.

The gladsome current of our youth,
    Ere passion yet disorders,
Steals lingering like a river smooth
    Along its grassy borders.

But as the care-worn cheek grows wan,
    And sorrow's shafts fly thicker,
Ye Stars, that measure life to man,
    Why seem your courses quicker?

When joys have lost their bloom and breath
    And life itself is vapid,
Why, as we reach the Falls of Death,
    Feel we its tide more rapid?

It may be strange—yet who would change
    Time's course to slower speeding,
When one by one our friends have gone
    And left our bosoms bleeding?

Heaven gives our years of fading strength
   Indemnifying fleetness;
And those of youth, a seeming length,
Proportion'd to their sweetness.

T. Campbell

CCCXXXIII

THE HUMAN SEASONS

Four Seasons fill the measure of the year;
There are four seasons in the mind of man:
He has his lusty Spring, when fancy clear
Takes in all beauty with an easy span:

He has his Summer, when luxuriously
Spring's honey'd cud of youthful thought he loves
To ruminate, and by such dreaming high
Is nearest unto heaven: quiet coves

His soul has in its Autumn, when his wings
He furleth close; contented so to look
On mists in idleness—to let fair things
Pass by unheeded as a threshold brook.

He has his Winter too of pale misfeature,
Or else he would forego his mortal nature.

J. Keats

CCCXXXIV

A DIRGE

Rough wind, that moanest loud
   Grief too sad for song;
Wild wind, when sullen cloud
   Knells all the night long;
Sad storm whose tears are vain,
Bare woods whose branches stain,
Deep caves and dreary main,—
   Wail for the world's wrong!

P. B. Shelley

CCCXXXV

THRENOS

O World ! O Life ! O Time !
On whose last steps I climb,
　　Trembling at that where I had stood before;
When will return the glory of your prime ?
　　　No more—Oh, never more !

Out of the day and night
A joy has taken flight :
　　Fresh spring, and summer, and winter hoar
Move my faint heart with grief, but with delight
　　　No more—Oh, never more !

P. B. Shelley

CCCXXXVI

THE TROSSACHS

There's not a nook within this solemn Pass,
But were an apt confessional for One
Taught by his summer spent, his autumn gone,
That Life is but a tale of morning grass

Wither'd at eve.　From scenes of art which chase
That thought away, turn, and with watchful eyes
Feed it 'mid Nature's old felicities,
Rocks, rivers, and smooth lakes more clear than glass

Untouch'd, unbreathed upon :—Thrice happy quest,
If from a golden perch of aspen spray
(October's workmanship to rival May),

The pensive warbler of the ruddy breast
That moral sweeten by a heaven-taught lay,
Lulling the year, with all its cares, to rest !

W. Wordsworth

CCCXXXVII

My heart leaps up when I behold
    A rainbow in the sky:
So was it when my life began,
So is it now I am a man,
So be it when I shall grow old
        Or let me die!
The Child is father of the Man:
And I could wish my days to be
Bound each to each by natural piety.

W. Wordsworth

CCCXXXVIII

ODE ON INTIMATIONS OF IMMORTALITY FROM RECOLLECTIONS OF EARLY CHILDHOOD

There was a time when meadow, grove, and stream,
The earth, and every common sight
        To me did seem
        Apparell'd in celestial light,
The glory and the freshness of a dream.
It is not now as it hath been of yore;—
        Turn wheresoe'er I may,
            By night or day,
The things which I have seen I now can see no more.

        The rainbow comes and goes,
        And lovely is the rose;
        The moon doth with delight
Look round her when the heavens are bare;
        Waters on a starry night
        Are beautiful and fair;
    The sunshine is a glorious birth;
    But yet I know, where'er I go,
That there hath past away a glory from the earth.

Now, while the birds thus sing a joyous song,
        And while the young lambs bound
            As to the tabor's sound,

To me alone there came a thought of grief :
A timely utterance gave that thought relief,
  And I again am strong.
The cataracts blow their trumpets from the steep ;—
No more shall grief of mine the season wrong :
I hear the echoes through the mountains throng,
The winds come to me from the fields of sleep,
    And all the earth is gay ;
    Land and sea
  Give themselves up to jollity
    And with the heart of May
Doth every beast keep holiday ;—
    Thou child of joy
Shout round me, let me hear thy shouts, thou happy
  Shepherd-boy !

Ye blessèd Creatures, I have heard the call
  Ye to each other make ; I see
The heavens laugh with you in your jubilee ;
  My heart is at your festival,
  My head hath its coronal,
The fulness of your bliss, I feel—I feel it all.
    Oh evil day ! if I were sullen
   While Earth herself is adorning
    This sweet May-morning ;
   And the children are culling
    On every side
  In a thousand valleys far and wide,
  Fresh flowers ; while the sun shines warm
And the babe leaps up on his mother's arm :—
   I hear, I hear, with joy I hear !
  —But there's a tree, of many, one,
A single field which I have look'd upon,
Both of them speak of something that is gone :
   The pansy at my feet
   Doth the same tale repeat :
Whither is fled the visionary gleam ?
Where is it now, the glory and the dream ?

Our birth is but a sleep and a forgetting ;
The Soul that rises with us, our life's Star,
   Hath had elsewhere its setting
    And cometh from afar ;

Not in entire forgetfulness,
And not in utter nakedness,
But trailing clouds of glory do we come
        From God, who is our home :
Heaven lies about us in our infancy !
Shades of the prison-house begin to close
        Upon the growing Boy,
But he beholds the light, and whence it flows,
        He sees it in his joy;
The Youth, who daily farther from the east
        Must travel, still is Nature's priest,
        And by the vision splendid
        Is on his way attended ;
At length the Man perceives it die away,
And fade into the light of common day.

Earth fills her lap with pleasures of her own ;
Yearnings she hath in her own natural kind,
And, even with something of a mother's mind
        And no unworthy aim,
        The homely nurse doth all she can
To make her foster-child, her inmate, Man,
        Forget the glories he hath known,
And that imperial palace whence he came.

Behold the Child among his new-born blisses,
A six years' darling of a pigmy size !
See, where 'mid work of his own hand he lies,
Fretted by sallies of his mother's kisses,
With light upon him from his father's eyes !
See, at his feet, some little plan or chart,
Some fragment from his dream of human life,
Shaped by himself with newly-learnèd art ;
        A wedding or a festival,
        A mourning or a funeral ;
        And this hath now his heart,
        And unto this he frames his song :
        Then will he fit his tongue
To dialogues of business, love, or strife ;
        But it will not be long
        Ere this be thrown aside,
        And with new joy and pride

The little actor cons another part;
Filling from time to time his ' humorous stage '
With all the Persons, down to palsied Age,
That life brings with her in her equipage;
      As if his whole vocation
      Were endless imitation.

Thou, whose exterior semblance doth belie
      Thy soul's immensity;
Thou best philosopher, who yet dost keep
Thy heritage, thou eye among the blind,
That, deaf and silent, read'st the eternal deep,
Haunted for ever by the eternal Mind,—
      Mighty Prophet ! Seer blest !
      On whom those truths do rest
Which we are toiling all our lives to find,
In darkness lost, the darkness of the grave;
Thou, over whom thy Immortality
Broods like the day, a master o'er a slave,
A Presence which is not to be put by;
Thou little child, yet glorious in the might
Of heaven-born freedom on thy being's height,
Why with such earnest pains dost thou provoke
The years to bring the inevitable yoke,
Thus blindly with thy blessedness at strife ?
Full soon thy soul shall have her earthly freight,
And custom lie upon thee with a weight
Heavy as frost, and deep almost as life !

      O joy ! that in our embers
      Is something that doth live,
      That Nature yet remembers
      What was so fugitive !
The thought of our past years in me doth breed
Perpetual benediction : not indeed
For that which is most worthy to be blest,
Delight and liberty, the simple creed
Of Childhood, whether busy or at rest,
With new-fledged hope still fluttering in his breast:—
      —Not for these I raise
      The song of thanks and praise;
      But for those obstinate questionings

Of sense and outward things,
Fallings from us, vanishings;
Blank misgivings of a creature
Moving about in worlds not realized,
High instincts, before which our mortal nature
Did tremble like a guilty thing surprized :
But for those first affections,
Those shadowy recollections,
Which, be they what they may,
Are yet the fountain-light of all our day,
Are yet a master-light of all our seeing;
Uphold us, cherish, and have power to make
Our noisy years seem moments in the being
Of the eternal Silence : truths that wake,
To perish never;
Which neither listlessness, nor mad endeavour,
Nor man nor boy
Nor all that is at enmity with joy,
Can utterly abolish or destroy !
Hence, in a season of calm weather
Though inland far we be,
Our souls have sight of that immortal sea
Which brought us hither;
Can in a moment travel thither—
And see the children sport upon the shore,
And hear the mighty waters rolling evermore.

Then, sing ye birds, sing, sing a joyous song !
And let the young lambs bound
As to the tabor's sound !
We, in thought, will join your throng
Ye that pipe and ye that play,
Ye that through your hearts to-day
Feel the gladness of the May !
What though the radiance which was once so bright
Be now for ever taken from my sight,
Though nothing can bring back the hour
Of splendour in the grass, of glory in the flower;
We will grieve not, rather find
Strength in what remains behind;
In the primal sympathy
Which having been must ever be;

In the soothing thoughts that spring
Out of human suffering;
In the faith that looks through death,
In years that bring the philosophic mind.

And O, ye Fountains, Meadows, Hills, and Groves,
Forbode not any severing of our loves!
Yet in my heart of hearts I feel your might;
I only have relinquish'd one delight
To live beneath your more habitual sway:
I love the brooks which down their channels fret
Even more than when I tripp'd lightly as they ·
The innocent brightness of a new-born day
Is lovely yet;
The clouds that gather round the setting sun
Do take a sober colouring from an eye
That hath kept watch o'er man's mortality;
Another race hath been, and other palms are won.
Thanks to the human heart by which we live,
Thanks to its tenderness, its joys, and fears,
To me the meanest flower that blows can give
Thoughts that do often lie too deep for tears.

W. Wordsworth

CCCXXXIX

Music, when soft voices die,
Vibrates in the memory—
Odours, when sweet violets sicken,
Live within the sense they quicken.

Rose leaves, when the rose is dead,
Are heap'd for the beloved's bed;
And so thy thoughts, when Thou art gone,
Love itself shall slumber on.

P. B. Shelley

The Golden Treasury

Book Fifth

THE LOTOS-EATERS : CHORIC SONG

I

There is sweet music here that softer falls
Than petals from blown roses on the grass,
Or night-dews on still waters between walls
Of shadowy granite, in a gleaming pass;
Music that gentlier on the spirit lies,
Than tir'd eyelids upon tir'd eyes;
Music that brings sweet sleep down from the blissful
    skies.
Here are cool mosses deep,
And thro' the moss the ivies creep,
And in the stream the long-leaved flowers weep,
And from the craggy ledge the poppy hangs in sleep.

2

Why are we weigh'd upon with heaviness,
And utterly consumed with sharp distress,
While all things else have rest from weariness
All things have rest : why should we toil alone,
We only toil, who are the first of things,
And make perpetual moan,
Still from one sorrow to another thrown :
Nor ever fold our wings,
And cease from wanderings,

Nor steep our brows in slumber's holy balm;
Nor hearken what the inner spirit sings,
' There is no joy but calm ! '
Why should we only toil, the roof and crown of
    things?

3

Lo ! in the middle of the wood,
The folded leaf is woo'd from out the bud
With winds upon the branch, and there
Grows green and broad, and takes no care,
Sun-steep'd at noon, and in the moon
Nightly dew-fed; and turning yellow
Falls, and floats adown the air.
Lo ! sweeten'd with the summer light,
The full-juiced apple, waxing over-mellow,
Drops in a silent autumn night.
All its allotted length of days,
The flower ripens in its place,
Ripens and fades, and falls, and hath no toil,
Fast-rooted in the fruitful soil.

4

Hateful is the dark-blue sky,
Vaulted o'er the dark-blue sea.
Death is the end of life; ah, why
Should life all labour be?
Let us alone.   Time driveth onward fast,
And in a little while our lips are dumb.
Let us alone.   What is it that will last?
All things are taken from us, and become
Portions and parcels of the dreadful Past.
Let us alone.   What pleasure can we have
To war with evil?   Is there any peace
In ever climbing up the climbing wave?
All things have rest, and ripen toward the grave
In silence; ripen, fall and cease:
Give us long rest or death, dark death, or dreamful
    ease.

5

How sweet it were, hearing the downward stream,
With half-shut eyes ever to seem

Falling asleep in a half-dream !
To dream and dream, like yonder amber light,
Which will not leave the myrrh-bush on the height;
To hear each other's whisper'd speech;
Eating the Lotos day by day,
To watch the crisping ripples on the beach,
And tender curving lines of creamy spray;
To lend our hearts and spirits wholly
To the influence of mild-minded melancholy;
To muse and brood and live again in memory,
With those old faces of our infancy
Heap'd over with a mound of grass,
Two handfuls of white dust, shut in an urn of brass !

6

Dear is the memory of our wedded lives,
And dear the last embraces of our wives
And their warm tears : but all hath suffer'd change :
For surely now our household hearths are cold :
Our sons inherit us : our looks are strange :
And we should come like ghosts to trouble joy,
Or else the island princes over-bold
Have eat our substance, and the minstrel sings
Before them of the ten years' war in Troy,
And our great deeds, as half-forgotten things.
Is there confusion in the little isle ?
Let what is broken so remain.
The Gods are hard to reconcile :
'Tis hard to settle order once again.
There *is* confusion worse than death,
Trouble on trouble, pain on pain,
Long labour unto aged breath,
Sore task to hearts worn out by many wars
And eyes grown dim with gazing on the pilot-stars.

7

But, propt on beds of amaranth and moly,
How sweet (while warm airs lull us, blowing lowly)
With half-dropt eyelid still,
Beneath a heaven dark and holy,
To watch the long bright river drawing slowly
His waters from the purple hill—

To hear the dewy echoes calling
From cave to cave thro' the thick-twined vine—
To watch the emerald-colour'd water falling
Thro' many a wov'n acanthus-wreath divine !
Only to hear and see the far-off sparkling brine,
Only to hear were sweet, stretch'd out beneath the
    pine.

8

The Lotos blooms below the barren peak :
The Lotos blows by every winding creek :
All day the wind breathes low with mellower tone :
Thro' every hollow cave and alley lone
Round and round the spicy downs the yellow Lotos-
    dust is blown.
We have had enough of action, and of motion we,
Roll'd to starboard, roll'd to larboard, when the
    surge was seething free,
Where the wallowing monster spouted his foam-
    fountains in the sea.
Let us swear an oath, and keep it with an equal
    mind,
In the hollow Lotos-land to live and lie reclined
On the hills like Gods together, careless of man-
    kind.
For they lie beside their nectar, and the bolts are
    hurl'd
Far below them in the valleys, and the clouds are
    lightly curl'd
Round their golden houses, girdled with the gleam-
    ing world :
Where they smile in secret, looking over wasted lands,
Blight and famine, plague and earthquake, roaring
    deeps and fiery sands,
Clanging fights, and flaming towns, and sinking
    ships, and praying hands.
But they smile, they find a music centred in a doleful
    song
Steaming up, a lamentation and an ancient tale of
    wrong,
Like a tale of little meaning tho' the words are
    strong ;

Chanted from an ill-used race of men that cleave the
  soil,
Sow the seed, and reap the harvest with enduring
  toil,
Storing yearly little dues of wheat, and wine and oil;
Till they perish and they suffer—some, 'tis whisper'd
  —down in hell
Suffer endless anguish, others in Elysian valleys
  dwell,
Resting weary limbs at last on beds of asphodel.
Surely, surely, slumber is more sweet than toil, the
  shore
Than labour in the deep mid-ocean, wind and wave
  and oar;
Oh rest ye, brother mariners, we will not wander
  more.

Lord Tennyson

CCCXLI

THE VISION OF THE STRAYED REVELLER

The Gods are happy.
They turn on all sides
Their shining eyes,
And see below them
The earth and men.

They see Tiresias
Sitting, staff in hand,
On the warm, grassy
Asopus bank,
His robe drawn over
His old, sightless head,
Revolving inly
The doom of Thebes.

They see the Centaurs
In the upper glens
Of Pelion, in the streams,
Where red-berried ashes fringe

The clear-brown shallow pools,
With streaming flanks, and heads
Rear'd proudly, snuffing
The mountain wind.

They see the Indian
Drifting, knife in hand,
His frail boat moor'd to
A floating isle thick-matted
With large-leaved, low-creeping melon-plants
And the dark cucumber.
He reaps, and stows them,
Drifting—drifting;—round him,
Round his green harvest-plot,
Flow the cool lake-waves,
The mountains ring them.

They see the Scythian
On the wide stepp, unharnessing
His wheel'd house at noon.
He tethers his beast down, and makes his meal—
Mares' milk, and bread
Baked on the embers;—all around
The boundless, waving grass-plains stretch, thick-
        starr'd
With saffron and the yellow hollyhock
And flag-leaved iris-flowers.
Sitting in his cart
He makes his meal; before him, for long miles,
Alive with bright green lizards,
And the springing bustard-fowl,
The track, a straight black line,
Furrows the rich soil; here and there
Clusters of lonely mounds
Topp'd with rough-hewn,
Grey, rain-blear'd statues, overpeer
The sunny waste.

They see the ferry
On the broad, clay-laden
Lone Chorasmian stream;—thereon,
With snort and strain,

Two horses, strongly swimming, tow
The ferry-boat, with woven ropes
To either bow
Firm-harness'd by the mane; a chief
With shout and shaken spear,
Stands at the prow, and guides them; but astern
The cowering merchants, in long robes,
Sit pale beside their wealth
Of silk-bales and of balsam-drops,
Of gold and ivory,
Of turquoise-earth and amethyst,
Jasper and chalcedony,
And milk-barr'd onyx-stones.
The loaded boat swings groaning
In the yellow eddies;
The Gods behold them.

They see the Heroes
Sitting in the dark ship
On the foamless, long-heaving,
Violet sea,
At sunset nearing
The Happy Islands.

These things, Ulysses,
The wise bards also
Behold and sing.
But oh, what labour!
O prince, what pain!

They too can see
Tiresias;—but the Gods,
Who give them vision,
Added this law:
That they should bear too
His groping blindness,
His dark foreboding,
His scorn'd white hairs;
Bear Hera's anger
Through a life lengthen'd
To seven ages.

They see the Centaurs
On Pelion;—then they feel,

They too, the maddening wine
Swell their large veins to bursting; in wild pain
They feel the biting spears
Of the grim Lapithæ, and Theseus, drive,
Drive crashing through their bones; they feel
High on a jutting rock in the red stream
Alcmena's dreadful son
Ply his bow;—such a price
The Gods exact for song:
To become what we sing.

They see the Indian
On his mountain lake; but squalls
Make their skiff reel, and worms
In the unkind spring have gnawn
Their melon-harvest to the heart—They see
The Scythian; but long frosts
Parch them in winter-time on the bare stepp,
Till they fade like grass; they crawl
Like shadows forth in spring.

They see the merchants
On the Oxus stream;—but care
Must visit first them too, and make them pale.
Whether, through whirling sand,
A cloud of desert robber-horse have burst
Upon their caravan; or greedy kings,
In the wall'd cities the way passes through,
Crush'd them with tolls; or fever-airs,
On some great river's marge,
Mown them down, far from home.

They see the Heroes
Near harbour;—but they share
Their lives, and former violent toil in Thebes,
Seven-gated Thebes, or Troy;
Or where the echoing oars
Of Argo first
Startled the unknown sea.

The old Silenus
Came, lolling in the sunshine.
From the dewy forest-coverts,

This way, at noon.
Sitting by me, while his Fauns
Down at the water-side
Sprinkled and smoothed
His drooping garland,
He told me these things.

M. Arnold

A MUSICAL INSTRUMENT

What was he doing, the great god Pan,
  Down in the reeds by the river?
Spreading ruin and scattering ban,
Splashing and paddling with hoofs of a goat,
And breaking the golden lilies afloat
  With the dragon-fly on the river.

He tore out a reed, the great god Pan,
  From the deep cool bed of the river:
The limpid water turbidly ran,
And the broken lilies a-dying lay,
And the dragon-fly had fled away,
  Ere he brought it out of the river.

High on the shore sate the great god Pan,
  While turbidly flowed the river;
And hacked and hewed as a great god can,
With his hard bleak steel at the patient reed,
Till there was not a sign of a leaf indeed
  To prove it fresh from the river.

He cut it short, did the great god Pan
  (How tall it stood in the river!),
Then drew the pith, like the heart of a man,
Steadily from the outside ring,
And notched the poor dry empty thing
  In holes, as he sate by the river.

' This is the way,' laughed the great god Pan
  (Laughed while he sate by the river),
' The only way, since gods began

To make sweet music, they could succeed.'
Then, dropping his mouth to a hole in the reed,
   He blew in power by the river.

Sweet, sweet, sweet, O Pan !
   Piercing sweet by the river !
Blinding sweet, O great god Pan !
The sun on the hill forgot to die,
And the lilies revived, and the dragon-fly
   Came back to dream on the river.

Yet half a beast is the great god Pan,
   To laugh as he sits by the river,
Making a poet out of a man :
The true gods sigh for the cost and pain—
For the reed which grows nevermore again
   As a reed with the reeds in the river.
              E. B. Browning

CCCXLIII

SONG IN THE SONGLESS

They have no song, the sedges dry,
   And still they sing.
It is within my breast they sing,
   As I pass by.
Within my breast they touch a string,
   They wake a sigh.
There is but sound of sedges dry;
   In me they sing.
     G. Meredith

CCCXLIV

SIBYLLA PALMIFERA

Under the arch of Life, where love and death,
Terror and mystery, guard her shrine, I saw
Beauty enthroned ; and though her gaze struck awe,
I drew it in as simply as my breath.

Hers are the eyes which, over and beneath,
The sky and sea bend on thee,—which can draw,
By sea or sky or woman, to one law,
The allotted bondman of her palm and wreath.

This is that Lady Beauty, in whose praise
Thy voice and hand shake still,—long known to thee
By flying hair and fluttering hem,—the beat
Following her daily of thy heart and feet,
How passionately and irretrievably,
In what fond flight, how many ways and days !

D. G. Rossetti

CCCXLV

EARLY SPRING

Once more the Heavenly Power
    Makes all things new,
And domes the red-plow'd hills
    With loving blue;
The blackbirds have their wills,
    The throstles too.

Opens a door in Heaven;
    From skies of glass
A Jacob's ladder falls
    On greening grass,
And o'er the mountain-walls
    Young angels pass.

Before them fleets the shower,
    And burst the buds,
And shine the level lands,
    And flash the floods;
The stars are from their hands
    Flung thro' the woods,

The woods with living airs
    How softly fann'd,
Light airs from where the deep,
    All down the sand,
Is breathing in his sleep,
    Heard by the land.

O follow, leaping blood,
   The season's lure !
O heart, look down and up
   Serene, secure,
Warm as the crocus cup,
   Like snowdrops, pure !

Past, Future glimpse and fade
   Thro' some slight spell,
A gleam from yonder vale,
   Some far blue fell,
And sympathies, how frail,
   In sound and smell !

Till at thy chuckled note,
   Thou twinkling bird,
The fairy fancies range,
   And, lightly stirr'd,
Ring little bells of change
   From word to word.

For now the Heavenly Power
   Makes all things new,
And thaws the cold, and fills
   The flower with dew;
The blackbirds have their wills,
   The poets too.

               Lord Tennyson

CCCXLVI

ST. VALENTINE'S DAY

Well dost thou, Love, thy solemn Feast to hold
In vestal February ;
Not rather choosing out some rosy day
From the rich coronet of the coming May,
When all things meet to marry !
  O quick, prævernal Power
That signall'st punctual through the sleepy mould
The Snowdrop's time to flower,

Fair as the rash oath of virginity
Which is first-love's first cry;
O, Baby spring,
That flutter'st sudden 'neath the breast of Earth
A month before the birth;
Whence is the peaceful poignancy,
The joy contrite,
Sadder than sorrow, sweeter than delight,
That burthens now the breath of everything,
Though each one sighs as if to each alone
The cherish'd pang were known?
At dusk of dawn, on his dark spray apart,
With it the Blackbird breaks the young Day's heart;
In evening's hush
About it talks the heavenly-minded Thrush;
The hill with like remorse
Smiles to the Sun's smile in his westering course;
The fisher's drooping skiff
In yonder sheltering bay;
The choughs that call about the shining cliff;
The children, noisy in the setting ray;
Own the sweet season, each thing as it may;
Thoughts of strange kindness and forgotten peace
In me increase;
And tears arise
Within my happy, happy Mistress' eyes,
And, lo, her lips, averted from my kiss,
Ask from Love's bounty, ah, much more than bliss!
    Is't the sequester'd and exceeding sweet
Of dear Desire electing his defeat?
Is't the waked Earth now to yon purpling cope
Uttering first-love's first cry,
Vainly renouncing, with a seraph's sigh,
Love's natural hope?
Fair-meaning Earth, foredoom'd to perjury!
Behold, all amorous May,
With roses heap'd upon her laughing brows,
Avoids thee of thy vows!
Were it for thee, with her warm bosom near,
To abide the sharpness of the Seraph's sphere?
Forget thy foolish words;
Go to her summons gay,

Thy heart with dead, wing'd Innocencies fill'd,
  Ev'n as a nest with birds
After the old ones by the hawk are kill'd.
  Well dost thou, Love, to celebrate
The noon of thy soft ecstasy,
  Or e'er it be too late,
Or e'er the Snowdrop die !

C. Patmore

CCCXLVII

DREAM-LOVE

Young Love lies sleeping
  In May-time of the year,
Among the lilies,
  Lapped in the tender light :
White lambs come grazing,
  White doves come building there;
And round about him
  The May-bushes are white.

Soft moss the pillow
  For oh, a softer cheek;
Broad leaves cast shadow
  Upon the heavy eyes :
There wind and waters
  Grow lulled and scarcely speak,
There twilight lingers
  The longest in the skies.

Young Love lies dreaming;
  But who shall tell the dream ?
A perfect sunlight
  On rustling forest tips;
Or perfect moonlight
  Upon a rippling stream;
Or perfect silence,
  Or song of cherished lips.

Burn odours round him
　To fill the drowsy air;
Weave silent dances
　Around him to and fro;
For oh, in waking
　The sights are not so fair,
And song and silence,
　Are not like these below.

Young Love lies dreaming
　Till summer days are gone,—
Dreaming and drowsing
　Away to perfect sleep:
He sees the beauty
　Sun hath not looked upon,
And tastes the fountain
　Unutterably deep.

Him perfect music
　Doth hush unto his rest,
And through the pauses
　The perfect silence calms:
Oh, poor the voices
　Of earth from east to west,
And poor earth's stillness
　Between her stately palms.

Young Love lies drowsing
　Away to poppied death;
Cool shadows deepen
　Across the sleeping face:
So fails the summer
　With warm, delicious breath;
And what hath autumn
　To give us in its place?

Draw close the curtains
　Of branched evergreen;
Change cannot touch them
　With fading fingers sere:
Here first the violets
　Perhaps will bud unseen,
And a dove, may be,
　Return to nestle here.

C. G. Rossetti

DAISY

Where the thistle lifts a purple crown
    Six foot out of the turf,
And the harebell shakes on the windy hill—
    O the breath of the distant surf !—

The hills look over on the South,
    And southward dreams the sea ;
And, with the sea-breeze hand in hand,
    Came innocence and she.

Where 'mid the gorse the raspberry
    Red for the gatherer springs,
Two children did we stray and talk
    Wise, idle, childish things.

She listened with big-lipped surprise,
    Breast-deep 'mid flower and spine :
Her skin was like a grape, whose veins
    Run snow instead of wine.

She knew not those sweet words she spake,
    Nor knew her own sweet way ;
But there's never a bird, so sweet a song
    Thronged in whose throat that day !

Oh, there were flowers in Storrington
    On the turf and on the spray ;
But the sweetest flower on Sussex hills
    Was the Daisy-flower that day !

Her beauty smoothed earth's furrowed face !
    She gave me tokens three :—
A look, a word of her winsome mouth,
    And a wild raspberry.

A berry red, a guileless look,
    A still word,—strings of sand !
And yet they made my wild, wild heart
    Fly down to her little hand.

For, standing artless as the air,
   And candid as the skies,
She took the berries with her hand,
   And the love with her sweet eyes.

The fairest things have fleetest end :
   Their scent survives their close,
But the rose's scent is bitterness
   To him that loved the rose !

She looked a little wistfully,
   Then went her sunshine way :—
The sea's eye had a mist on it,
   And the leaves fell from the day.

She went her unremembering way ;
   She went, and left in me
The pang of all the partings gone,
   And the partings yet to be.

She left me marvelling why my soul
   Was sad that she was glad ;
At all the sadness in the sweet,
   The sweetness in the sad.

Still, still I seemed to see her, still
   Look up with soft replies,
And take the berries with her hand,
   And the love with her lovely eyes.

Nothing begins, and nothing ends,
   That is not paid with moan ;
For we are born in other's pain,
   And perish in our own.

             F. Thompson

CCCXLIX

HOME THOUGHTS, FROM ABROAD

   Oh, to be in England,
   Now that April's there,
   And whoever wakes in England
   Sees, some morning, unaware,

That the lowest boughs and the brushwood sheaf
Round the elm-tree bole are in tiny leaf,
While the chaffinch sings on the orchard bough
In England—now !

And after April, when May follows,
And the whitethroat builds, and all the swallows !
Hark, where my blossomed pear-tree in the hedge
Leans to the field and scatters on the clover
Blossoms and dewdrops—at the bent spray's edge—
That's the wise thrush; he sings each song twice
　　　over,
Lest you should think he never could recapture
The first fine careless rapture !
And though the fields look rough with hoary dew,
All will be gay when noontide wakes anew
The buttercups, the little children's dower—
Far brighter than this gaudy melon-flower.

　　　　　　　　　　　　　　　　R. B. owning

CCCL

WEATHERS

This is the weather the cuckoo likes,
　　　　　And so do I ;
When showers betumble the chestnut spikes,
　　　　　And nestlings fly :
And the little brown nightingale bills his best.
And they sit outside at " The Travellers' Rest,"
And maids come forth sprig-muslin drest,
And citizens dream of the south and west,
　　　　　And so do I.

This is the weather the shepherd shuns,
　　　　　And so do I ;
When beeches drip in browns and duns,
　　　　　And thresh, and ply ;
　And hill-hid tides throb, throe on throe,
And meadow rivulets overflow,
And drops on gate-bars hang in a row,
And rooks in families homeward go,
　　　　　And so do I.
　　　　　　　　T. Hardy

CCCLI

SUMMER EVENING

The frog half-fearful jumps across the path,
And little mouse that leaves its hole at eve
Nimbles with timid dread beneath the swath;
My rustling steps awhile their joys deceive,
Till past,—and then the cricket sings more strong,
And grasshoppers in merry mood still wear
The short night weary with their fretting song.
Up from behind the molehill jumps the hare,
Cheat of his chosen bed, and from the bank
The yellowhammer flutters in short fears
From off its nest hid in the grasses rank,
And drops again when no more noise it hears.
Thus nature's human link and endless thrall,
Proud man, still seems the enemy of all.

J. Clare

CCCLII

A GARDEN BY THE SEA

I know a little garden-close,
Set thick with lily and red rose,
Where I would wander if I might
From dewy morn to dewy night,
And have one with me wandering.

And though within it no birds sing,
And though no pillared house is there,
And though the apple-boughs are bare
Of fruit and blossom, would to God
Her feet upon the green grass trod,
And I beheld them as before.

There comes a murmur from the shore,
And in the close two fair streams are,
Drawn from the purple hills afar,

Drawn down unto the restless sea .
Dark hills whose heath-bloom feeds no bee,
Dark shore no ship has ever seen,
Tormented by the billows green
Whose murmur comes unceasingly
Unto the place for which I cry.
For which I cry both day and night,
For which I let slip all delight,
Whereby I grow both deaf and blind,
Careless to win, unskilled to find,
And quick to lose what all men seek.
Yet tottering as I am and weak,
Still have I left a little breath
To seek within the jaws of death
An entrance to that happy place,
To seek the unforgotten face,
Once seen, once kissed, once reft from me
Anigh the murmuring of the sea.

W. Morris

CCCLIII

THE LAKE ISLE OF INNISFREE

1 will arise and go now, and go to Innisfree,
And a small cabin build there, of clay and wattles
made :
Nine bean rows will I have there, a hive for the
honey-bee,
And live alone in the bee-loud glade.

And I shall have some peace there, for peace comes
dropping slow,
Dropping from the veils of the morning to where the
cricket sings;
There midnight's all a glimmer, and noon a purple
glow
And evening full of the linnet's wings.

I will arise and go now, for always night and day
I hear lake water lapping with low sounds by the
    shore;
While I stand on the roadway, or on the pavements
    gray,
  I hear it in the deep heart's core.

W. B. Yeats

CCCLIV

Often rebuked, yet always back returning
  To those first feelings that were born with me,
And leaving busy chase of wealth and learning
  For idle dreams of things which cannot be;

To-day, I will not seek the shadowy region;
  Its unsustaining vastness waxes drear;
And visions rising, legion after legion,
  Bring the unreal world too strangely near.

I'll walk, but not in old heroic traces,
  And not in paths of high morality,
And not among the half-distinguished faces,
  The clouded forms of long-past history.

I'll walk where my own nature would be leading:
  It vexes me to choose another guide:
Where the gray flocks in ferny glens are feeding;
  Where the wild wind blows on the mountain side.

What have those lonely mountains worth revealing?
  More glory and more grief than I can tell:
The earth that wakes one human heart to feeling
  Can centre both the worlds of Heaven and Hell.

E. Brontë

CCCLV

NIGHTINGALES

Beautiful must be the mountains whence ye come,
And bright in the fruitful valleys the streams,
    wherefrom
      Ye learn your song:

Where are those starry woods? O might I wander
    there,
   Among the flowers, which in that heavenly air
      Bloom the year long!

Nay, barren are those mountains and spent the
    streams:
   Our song is the voice of desire, that haunts our
    dreams,
      A throe of the heart,
Whose pining visions dim, forbidden hopes profound,
   No dying cadence nor long sigh can sound,
      For all our art.

Alone, aloud in the raptured ear of men
   We pour our dark nocturnal secret; and then,
      As night is withdrawn
From these sweet-springing meads and bursting
    boughs of May,
   Dream, while the innumerable choir of day
      Welcome the dawn.
                R. Bridges

CCCLVI

TEARS, IDLE TEARS

Tears, idle tears, I know not what they mean,
Tears from the depth of some divine despair
Rise in the heart, and gather to the eyes,
In looking on the happy Autumn-fields,
And thinking of the days that are no more.

Fresh as the first beam glittering on a sail,
That brings our friends up from the underworld,
Sad as the last which reddens over one
That sinks with all we love below the verge;
So sad, so fresh, the days that are no more.

Ah, sad and strange as in dark, summer dawns
The earliest pipe of half-awaken'd birds
To dying ears, when unto dying eyes
The casement slowly grows a glimmering square;
So sad, so strange, the days that are no more.

Dear as remember'd kisses after death,
And sweet as those by hopeless fancy feign'd
On lips that are for others; deep as love,
Deep as first love, and wild with all regret;
O Death in Life, the days that are no more.

Lord Tennyson

CCCLVII

LAMENT FOR VANISHED BEAUTY

Heap cassia, sandal-buds and stripes
   Of labdanum, and aloe-balls,
Smeared with dull nard an Indian wipes
   From out her hair; such balsam falls
   Down seaside mountain pedestals,
From tree-tops where tired winds are fain,
Spent with the vast and howling main,
To treasure half their island-gain.

And strew faint sweetness from some old
   Egyptian's fine worm-eaten shroud
Which breaks to dust when once unrolled;
   Or shredded perfume, like a cloud
   From closet long to quiet vowed,
With mothed and dropping arras hung,
Mouldering her lute and books among,
As when a queen, long dead, was young.

R. Browning

CCCLVIII

They say the Lion and the Lizard keep
The Courts where Jamshyd gloried and drank deep,
   And Bahram, that great Hunter—the Wild Ass
Stamps o'er his Head, and he lies fast asleep.

I sometimes think that never blows so red
The Rose as where some buried Caesar bled;
   That every Hyacinth the Garden wears
Dropt in its Lap from some once lovely Head.

And this delightful Herb whose tender Green
Fledges the River's Lip on which we lean—
   Ah, lean upon it lightly ! for who knows
From what once lovely Lip it springs unseen !

E. FitzGerald

CCCLIX

THE PHOENIX

O blest unfabled Incense Tree,
That burns in glorious Araby,
With red scent chalicing the air,
Till earth-life grow Elysian there !

Half buried to her flaming breast
In this bright tree, she makes her nest,
Hundred-sunned Phoenix ! when she must
Crumble at length to hoary dust ¡

Her gorgeous death-bed ! her rich pyre
Burnt up with aromatic fire !
Her urn, sight-high from spoiler men !
Her birthplace when self-born again !

The mountainless green wilds among,
Here ends she her unechoing song !
With amber tears and odorous sighs
Mourned by the desert where she dies !

G. Darley

CCCLX

THE LADY OF SHALOTT

Part I

On either side the river lie
Long fields of barley and of rye,
That clothe the wold and meet the sky ;
And thro' the field the road runs by
    To many-tower'd Camelot ·

And up and down the people go,
Gazing where the lilies blow
Round an island there below,
    The island of Shalott.

Willows whiten, aspens quiver,
Little breezes dusk and shiver
Thro' the wave that runs for ever
By the island in the river
    Flowing down to Camelot.
Four gray walls, and four gray towers,
Overlook a space of flowers,
And the silent isle imbowers
    The Lady of Shalott.

By the margin, willow-veil'd,
Slide the heavy barges trail'd
By slow horses; and unhail'd
The shallop flitteth silken-sail'd
    Skimming down to Camelot:
But who hath seen her wave her hand?
Or at the casement seen her stand?
Or is she known in all the land,
    The Lady of Shalott?

Only reapers, reaping early
In among the bearded barley,
Hear a song that echoes cheerly
From the river winding clearly,
    Down to tower'd Camelot:
And by the moon the reaper weary,
Piling sheaves in uplands airy,
Listening, whispers ' 'Tis the fairy
    Lady of Shalott.'

Part II

There she weaves by night and day
A magic web with colours gay.
She has heard a whisper say,
A curse is on her if she stay
    To look down to Camelot.

She knows not what the curse may be,
And so she weaveth steadily,
And little other care hath she,
    The Lady of Shalott.

And moving thro' a mirror clear
That hangs before her all the year,
Shadows of the world appear.
There she sees the highway near
    Winding down to Camelot:
There the river eddy whirls,
And there the surly village-churls,
And the red cloaks of market girls,
    Pass onward from Shalott.

Sometimes a troop of damsels glad,
An abbot on an ambling pad,
Sometimes a curly shepherd-lad,
Or long-hair'd page in crimson clad,
    Goes by to tower'd Camelot;
And sometimes thro' the mirror blue
The knights come riding two and two:
She hath no loyal knight and true,
    The Lady of Shalott.

But in her web she still delights
To weave the mirror's magic sights,
For often thro' the silent nights
A funeral, with plumes and lights
    And music, went to Camelot:
Or when the moon was overhead,
Came two young lovers lately wed;
' I am half sick of shadows,' said
    The Lady of Shalott.

Part III

A bow-shot from her bower-eaves,
He rode between the barley-sheaves,
The sun came dazzling thro' the leaves,
And flamed upon the brazen greaves
    Of bold Sir Lancelot.

A red-cross knight for ever kneel'd
To a lady in his shield,
That sparkled on the yellow field
        Beside remote Shalott.

The gemmy bridle glitter'd free,
Like to some branch of stars we see
Hung in the golden Galaxy.
The bridle bells rang merrily
        As he rode down to Camelot:
And from his blazon'd baldric slung
A mighty silver bugle hung,
And as he rode his armour rung,
        Beside remote Shalott.

All in the blue unclouded weather
Thick-jewell'd shone the saddle-leather,
The helmet and the helmet-feather
Burn'd like one burning flame together,
        As he rode down to Camelot.
As often thro' the purple night,
Below the starry clusters bright,
Some bearded meteor, trailing light,
        Moves over still Shalott.

His broad clear brow in sunlight glow'd;
On burnish'd hooves his war-horse trode;
From underneath his helmet flow'd
His coal-black curls as on he rode,
        As he rode down to Camelot.
From the bank and from the river
He flash'd into the crystal mirror,
'Tirra lirra,' by the river
        Sang Sir Lancelot.

She left the web, she left the loom,
She made three paces thro' the room,
She saw the water-lily bloom,
She saw the helmet and the plume,
        She look'd down to Camelot.
Out flew the web and floated wide;
The mirror crack'd from side to side;
'The curse is come upon me,' cried
        The Lady of Shalott.

Part IV

In the stormy east-wind straining,
The pale yellow woods were waning,
The broad stream in his banks complaining,
Heavily the low sky raining
     Over tower'd Camelot;
Down she came and found a boat
Beneath a willow left afloat,
And round about the prow she wrote
    The Lady of Shalott.

And down the river's dim expanse
Like some bold seër in a trance,
Seeing all his own mischance—
With a glassy countenance
     Did she look to Camelot.
And at the closing of the day
She loosed the chain, and down she lay;
The broad stream bore her far away,
     The Lady of Shalott.

Lying, robed in snowy white
That loosely flew to left and right—
The leaves upon her falling light—
Thro' the noises of the night
     She floated down to Camelot:
And as the boat-head wound along
The willowy hills and fields among,
They heard her singing her last song,
     The Lady of Shalott.

Heard a carol, mournful, holy,
Chanted loudly, chanted lowly,
Till her blood was frozen slowly,
And her eyes were darken'd wholly,
     Turn'd to tower'd Camelot.
For ere she reach'd upon the tide
The first house by the water-side,
Singing in her song she died,
     The Lady of Shalott.

Under tower and balcony,
By garden-wall and gallery,
A gleaming shape she floated by,
Dead-pale between the houses high,
    Silent into Camelot.
Out upon the wharfs they came,
Knight and burgher, lord and dame,
And round the prow they read her name,
    The Lady of Shalott.

Who is this? and what is here?
And in the lighted palace near
Died the sound of royal cheer;
And they cross'd themselves for fear,
    All the knights at Camelot:
But Lancelot mused a little space;
He said, ' She has a lovely face;
God in his mercy lend her grace,
    The Lady of Shalott.'

                Lord Tennyson

CCCLXI

THE STOLEN CHILD

Where dips the rocky highland
Of Sleuth Wood in the lake,
There lies a leafy island
Where flapping herons wake
The drowsy water rats;
There we've hid our faery vats,
Full of berries,
And of reddest stolen cherries.
Come away, O human child!
To the waters and the wild
With a faery, hand in hand,
For the world's more full of weeping than you can
    understand.

Where the wave of moonlight glosses
The dim gray sands with light,
Far off by furthest Rosses
We foot it all the night,

Weaving olden dances,
Mingling hands and mingling glances
Till the moon has taken flight;
To and fro we leap
And chase the frothy bubbles,
While the world is full of troubles
And is anxious in its sleep.
Come away, O human child!
To the waters and the wild
With a faery, hand in hand,
For the world's more full of weeping than you can
understand.

Where the wandering water gushes
From the hills above Glen-Car,
In pools among the rushes
That scarce could bathe a star,
We seek for slumbering trout,
And whispering in their ears
Give them unquiet dreams;
Leaning softly out
From ferns that drop their tears
Over the young streams.
Come away, O human child!
To the waters and the wild
With a faery, hand in hand,
For the world's more full of weeping than you can
understand.

Away with us he's going,
The solemn-eyed;
He'll hear no more the lowing
Of the calves on the warm hillside;
Or the kettle on the hob
Sing peace into his breast,
Or see the brown mice bob
Round and round the oatmeal-chest.
For he comes, the human child,
To the waters and the wild
With a faery, hand in hand,
From a world more full of weeping than he can
understand.

W. B. Yeats

CCCLXII

A PASSER-BY

Whither, O splendid ship, thy white sails crowding,
  Leaning across the bosom of the urgent West,
That fearest nor sea rising, nor sky clouding,
  Whither away, fair rover, and what thy quest?
  Ah! soon, when Winter has all our vales opprest,
When skies are cold and misty, and hail is hurling,
  Wilt thou glide on the blue Pacific, or rest
In a summer haven asleep, thy white sails furling.

I there before thee, in the country that well thou
    knowest,
  Already arrived am inhaling the odorous air:
I watch thee enter unerringly where thou goest,
  And anchor queen of the strange shipping there,
  Thy sails for awnings spread, thy masts bare:
Nor is aught from the foaming reef to the snow-
    capped, grandest
  Peak, that is over the feathery palms more fair
Than thou, so upright, so stately, and still thou
    standest.

And yet, O splendid ship, unhailed and nameless,
  I know not if, aiming a fancy, I rightly divine
That thou hast a purpose joyful, a courage blameless,
  Thy port assured in a happier land than mine.
  But for all I have given thee, beauty enough is
    thine,
As thou, aslant with trim tackle and shrouding,
  From the proud nostril curve of a prow's line
In the offing scatterest foam, thy white sails
    crowding.

                                        R. Bridges

CCCLXIII

THE EAGLE

  He clasps the crag with crooked hands;
  Close to the sun in lonely lands,
  Ring'd with the azure world, he stands.

The wrinkled sea beneath him crawls;
He watches from his mountain walls,
And like a thunderbolt he falls.

Lord Tennyson

CCCLXIV

WAR SONG OF THE SARACENS

We are they who come faster than fate : we are they
    who ride early or late :
We storm at your ivory gate : Pale Kings of the
    Sunset, beware :
Not on silk nor in samet we lie, not in curtained
    solemnity die
Among women who chatter and cry, and children
    who mumble a prayer.
But we sleep by the ropes of the camp, and we rise
    with a shout, and we tramp
With the sun or the moon for a lamp, and the spray
    of the wind in our hair.

From the lands, where the elephants are, to the forts
    of Merou and Balghar,
Our steel we have brought and our star to shine on
    the ruins of Rum.
We have marched from the Indus to Spain, and by
    God we will go there again;
We have stood on the shore of the plain where the
    Waters of Destiny boom.
A mart of destruction we made at Jalula where men
    were afraid,
For death was a difficult trade, and the sword was
    a broker of doom;

And the Spear was a Desert Physician who cured not
    a few of ambition,
And drave not a few to perdition with medicine
    bitter and strong :
And the shield was a grief to the fool and as bright
    as a desolate pool,

And as straight as the rock of Stamboul when their
    cavalry thundered along :
For the coward was drowned with the brave when
    our battle sheered up like a wave,
And the dead to the desert we gave, and the glory to
    God in our song.

J. E. Flecker

CCCLXV

THE HOUNDS OF SPRING

When the hounds of spring are on winter's traces,
    The mother of months in meadow or plain
Fills the shadows and windy places
    With lisp of leaves and ripple of rain ;
And the brown bright nightingale amorous
Is half assuaged for Itylus,
For the Thracian ships and the foreign faces,
    The tongueless vigil, and all the pain.

Come with bows bent and with emptying of quivers,
    Maiden most perfect, lady of light,
With a noise of winds and many rivers,
    With a clamour of waters, and with might ;
Bind on thy sandals, O thou most fleet,
Over the splendour and speed of thy feet ;
For the faint east quickens, the wan west shivers,
    Round the feet of the day and the feet of the night.

Where shall we find her, how shall we sing to her,
    Fold our hands round her knees, and cling ?
O that man's heart were as fire and could spring
    to her,
    Fire, or the strength of the streams that spring !
For the stars and the winds are unto her
As raiment, as songs of the harp-player ;
For the risen stars and the fallen cling to her,
    And the south-west wind and the west wind sing.

For winter's rains and ruins are over,
    And all the season of snows and sins ;
The days dividing lover and lover,
    The light that loses, the night that wins ;

And time remembered is grief forgotten,
And frosts are slain and flowers begotten,
And in green underwood and cover
    Blossom by blossom the spring begins.

The full streams feed on flower of rushes,
    Ripe grasses trammel a travelling foot,
The faint fresh flame of the young year flushes
    From leaf to flower and flower to fruit;
And fruit and leaf are as gold and fire,
And the oat is heard above the lyre,
And the hoofèd heel of a satyr crushes
    The chestnut-husk at the chestnut-root.

And Pan by noon and Bacchus by night,
    Fleeter of foot than the fleet-foot kid,
Follows with dancing and fills with delight
    The Mænad and the Bassarid;
And soft as lips that laugh and hide
The laughing leaves of the trees divide,
And screen from seeing and leave in sight
    The god pursuing, the maiden hid.

The ivy falls with the Bacchanal's hair
    Over her eyebrows hiding her eyes;
The wild vine slipping down leaves bare
    Her bright breast shortening into sighs;
The wild vine slips with the weight of its leaves,
But the berried ivy catches and cleaves
To the limbs that glitter, the feet that scare
    The wolf that follows, the fawn that flies.

A. C. Swinburne

CCCLXVI

LOVE IN THE VALLEY

Shy as the squirrel and wayward as the swallow,
    Swift as the swallow along the river's light
Circleting the surface to meet his mirror'd winglets,
    Fleeter she seems in her stay than in her flight.

Shy as the squirrel that leaps among the pine-tops,
    Wayward as the swallow overhead at set of sun,
She whom I love is hard to catch and conquer,
    Hard, but O the glory of the winning were she won!

When her mother tends her before the laughing
        mirror,
    Tying up her laces, looping up her hair,
Often she thinks, were this wild thing wedded,
    More love should I have, and much less care.
When her mother tends her before the lighted mirror,
    Loosening her laces, combing down her curls,
Often she thinks, were this wild thing wedded
    I should miss but one for many boys and girls.

Heartless she is as the shadow in the meadows
    Flying to the hills on a blue and breezy noon.
No, she is athirst and drinking up her wonder:
    Earth to her is young as the slip of the new moon.
Deals she an unkindness, 'tis but her rapid measure,
    Even as in a dance; and her smile can heal no less:
Like the swinging May-cloud that pelts the flowers
        with hailstones
    Off a sunny border, she was made to bruise and
        bless.

Stepping down the hill with her fair companions,
    Arm in arm, all against the raying West,
Boldly she sings, to the merry tune she marches,
    Brave in her shape, and sweeter unpossess'd.
Sweeter, for she is what my heart first awaking
    Whisper'd the world was; morning light is she.
Love that so desires would fain keep her changeless;
    Fain would fling the net, and fain have her free.

                                            G. Meredith

CCCLXVII

A BIRTHDAY

My heart is like a singing bird
    Whose nest is in a watered shoot:
My heart is like an apple-tree
    Whose boughs are bent with thickset fruit;

My heart is like a rainbow shell
    That paddles in a halcyon sea;
My heart is gladder than all these
    Because my love is come to me.

Raise me a dais of silk and down;
    Hang it with vair and purple dyes;
Carve it in doves and pomegranates,
    And peacocks with a hundred eyes.
Work it in gold and silver grapes,
    In leaves and silver fleurs-de-lys;
Because the birthday of my life
    Is come, my love is come to me.

C. G. Rossetti

CCCLXVIII

COME INTO THE GARDEN, MAUD

Come into the garden, Maud,
    For the black bat, night, has flown,
Come into the garden, Maud,
    I am here at the gate alone;
And the woodbine spices are wafted abroad,
    And the musk of the rose is blown.

For a breeze of morning moves,
    And the planet of Love is on high,
Beginning to faint in the light that she loves
    On a bed of daffodil sky,
To faint in the light of the sun she loves,
    To faint in his light, and to die.

All night have the roses heard
    The flute, violin, bassoon;
All night has the casement jessamine stirr'd
    To the dancers dancing in tune;
Till a silence fell with the waking bird,
    And a hush with the setting moon.

I said to the lily, ' There is but one
    With whom she has heart to be gay.
When will the dancers leave her alone?
    She is weary of dance and play.'

Now half to the setting moon are gone,
 And half to the rising day;
Low on the sand and loud on the stone
 The last wheel echoes away.

I said to the rose, ' The brief night goes
 In babble and revel and wine.
O young lord-lover, what sighs are those
 For one that will never be thine?
But mine, but mine,' so I sware to the rose,
 ' For ever and ever, mine.'

And the soul of the rose went into my blood,
 As the music clash'd in the hall;
And long by the garden lake I stood,
 For I heard your rivulet fall
From the lake to the meadow and on to the wood,
 Our wood, that is dearer than all;

From the meadow your walks have left so sweet
 That whenever a March-wind sighs
He sets the jewel-print of your feet
 In violets blue as your eyes,
To the woody hollows in which we meet
 And the valleys of Paradise.

The slender acacia would not shake
 One long milk-bloom on the tree;
The white lake-blossom fell into the lake,
 As the pimpernel dozed on the lea;
But the rose was awake all night for your sake,
 Knowing your promise to me;
The lilies and roses were all awake,
 They sigh'd for the dawn and thee.

Queen rose of the rosebud garden of girls,
 Come hither, the dances are done,
In gloss of satin and glimmer of pearls,
 Queen lily and rose in one;
Shine out, little head, sunning over with curls,
 To the flowers, and be their sun.

There has fallen a splendid tear
　　From the passion-flower at the gate.
She is coming, my dove, my dear;
　　She is coming, my life, my fate;
The red rose cries, ' She is near, she is near; '
　　And the white rose weeps, ' She is late; '
The larkspur listens, ' I hear, I hear; '
　　And the lily whispers, ' I wait.'

She is coming, my own, my sweet;
　　Were it ever so airy a tread,
My heart would hear her and beat,
　　Were it earth in an earthy bed;
My dust would hear her and beat,
　　Had I lain for a century dead;
Would start and tremble under her feet,
　　And blossom in purple and red.

Lord Tennyson

CCCLXIX

PORPHYRIA'S LOVER

The rain set early in to-night,
　　The sullen wind was soon awake,
It tore the elm-tops down for spite,
　　And did its worst to vex the lake:
I listened with heart fit to break.
When glided in Porphyria; straight
　　She shut the cold out and the storm,
And kneeled and made the cheerless grate
　　Blaze up, and all the cottage warm;
　　Which done, she rose, and from her form
Withdrew the dripping cloak and shawl,
　　And laid her soiled gloves by, untied
Her hat and let the damp hair fall,
　　And, last, she sat down by my side
And called me.　When no voice replied,
She put my arm about her waist,
　　And made her smooth white shoulder bare,
And all her yellow hair displaced,
　　And stooping, made my cheek lie there,
　　And spread, o'er all, her yellow hair,

Murmuring how she loved me—she
 Too weak, for all her heart's endeavour,
To set its struggling passion free
 From pride, and vainer ties dissever,
 And give herself to me for ever.
But passion sometimes would prevail,
 Nor could to-night's gay feast restrain
A sudden thought of one so pale
 For love of her, and all in vain :
 So, she was come through wind and rain,
Be sure I looked up at her eyes
 Happy and proud ; at last I knew
Porphyria worshipped me; surprise
 Made my heart swell, and still it grew
 While I debated what to do.
That moment she was mine, mine, fair,
 Perfectly pure and good : I found
A thing to do, and all her hair
 In one long yellow string I wound
 Three times her little throat around,
And strangled her. No pain felt she;
 I am quite sure she felt no pain.
As a shut bud that holds the bee,
 I warily oped her lids : again
 Laughed the blue eyes without a stain.
And I untightened next the tress
 About her neck; her cheek once more
Blushed bright beneath my burning kiss .
 I propped her head up as before,
 Only, this time my shoulder bore
Her head, which droops upon it still :
 The smiling rosy little head,
So glad it has its utmost will,
 That all it scorned at once is fled,
 And I, its love, am gained instead !
Porphyria's love : she guessed not how
 Her darling one wish would be heard.
And thus we sit together now,
 And all night long we have not stirred,
 And yet God has not said a word !

        R. Browning

CCCLXX

THE LABORATORY : ANCIEN RÉGIME

Now that I, tying thy glass mask tightly,
May gaze thro' these faint smokes curling whitely,
As thou pliest thy trade in this devil's-smithy—
Which is the poison to poison her, prithee ?

He is with her, and they know that I know
Where they are, what they do : they believe my
    tears flow
While they laugh, laugh at me, at me fled to the
    drear
Empty church, to pray God in, for them !—I am
    here.

Grind away, moisten and mash up thy paste,
Pound at thy powder,—I am not in haste !
Better sit thus, and observe thy strange things
Than go where men wait me and dance at the King's.

That in the mortar—you call it a gum ?
Ah, the brave tree whence such gold oozings come
And yonder soft phial, the exquisite blue,
Sure to taste sweetly,—is that poison too ?

Had I but all of them, thee and thy treasures,
What a wild crowd of invisible pleasures !
To carry pure death in an ear-ring, a casket,
A signet, a fan-mount, a filigree basket !

Soon, at the King's, a mere lozenge to give,
And Pauline should have just thirty minutes to live !
But to light a pastille, and Elise, with her head
And her breast and her arms and her hands, should
    drop dead !

Quick—is it finished ? The colour's too grim !
Why not soft like the phial's, enticing and dim ?
Let it brighten her drink, let her turn it and stir,
And try it and taste, ere she fix and prefer !

What a drop! She's not little, no minion like me!
That's why she ensnared him: this never will free
The soul from those masculine eyes,—say, ' No ! '
To that pulse's magnificent come-and-go.

For only last night, as they whispered, I brought
My own eyes to bear on her so, that I thought
Could I keep them one half-minute fixed, she would
    fall
Shrivelled; she fell not; yet this does it all !

Not that I bid you spare her the pain;
Let death be felt and the proof remain;
Brand, burn up, bite into its grace—
He is sure to remember her dying face !

Is it done? Take my mask off! Nay, be not
    morose;
It kills her, and this prevents seeing it close :
The delicate droplet, my whole fortune's fee !
If it hurts her, beside, can it ever hurt me ?

Now, take all my jewels, gorge gold to your fill,
You may kiss me, old man, on my mouth, if you
    will !
But brush this dust off me, lest horror it brings
Ere I know it—next moment I dance at the King's !

R. Browning

RENOUNCEMENT

I must not think of thee; and, tired yet strong,
I shun the thought that lurks in all delight—
The thought of thee—and in the blue Heaven's
    height,
And in the sweetest passage of a song.
Oh, just beyond the fairest thoughts that throng
This breast, the thought of thee waits, hidden yet
    bright;
But it must never, never come in sight;
I must stop short of thee the whole day long.

But when sleep comes to close each difficult day,
When night gives pause to the long watch I keep,
And all my bonds I needs must loose apart,
Must doff my will as raiment laid away,—
With the first dream that comes with the first sleep
I run, I run, I am gathered to thy heart.

A. Meynell

CCCLXXII

We were not made for refuges of lies :
    And false embattled bulwarks will not screen us :
We mocked the careful shieldings of the wise,
    And only utter truth can be between us.

Long suns and moons have wrought this day at
    length,
    The heavens in naked majesty have told thee.
To see me as I am have thou the strength ;
    And, even as thou art, I dare behold thee.

M. E. Coleridge

CCCLXXIII

THE LAST RIDE TOGETHER

    I said—Then, dearest, since 'tis so,
    Since now at length my fate I know,
    Since nothing all my love avails,
    Since all, my life seemed meant for, fails,
        Since this was written and needs must be—
    My whole heart rises up to bless
    Your name in pride and thankfulness !
    Take back the hope you gave,—I claim
    Only a memory of the same,
    —And this beside, if you will not blame,
        Your leave for one more last ride with me.

    My mistress bent that brow of hers;
    Those deep dark eyes where pride demurs
    When pity would be softening through,
    Fixed me a breathing-while or two

With life or death in the balance : right !
The blood replenished me again ;
My last thought was at least not vain :
I, and my mistress, side by side,
Shall be together, breathe and ride,
So, one day more am I deified.
    Who knows but the world may end to-night ?

Hush ! if you saw some western cloud
All billowy-bosomed, over-bowed
By many benedictions—sun's
And moon's and evening-star's at once—
    And so, you, looking and loving best,
Conscious grew, your passion drew
Cloud, sunset, moonrise, star-shine too,
Down on you, near and yet more near,
Till flesh must fade for heaven was here !—
Thus leant she and lingered—joy and fear !
    Thus lay she a moment on my breast.

Then we began to ride. My soul
Smoothed itself out, a long-cramped scroll
Freshening and fluttering in the wind.
Past hopes already lay behind.
    What need to strive with a life awry ?
Had I said that, had I done this,
So might I gain, so might I miss.
Might she have loved me ? just as well
She might have hated, who can tell !
Where had I been now if the worst befell ?
    And here we are riding, she and I.

Fail I alone, in words and deeds ?
Why, all men strive and who succeeds ?
We rode ; it seemed my spirit flew,
Saw other regions, cities new,
    As the world rushed by on either side.
I thought,—All labour, yet no less
Bear up beneath their unsuccess.
Look at the end of work, contrast
The petty done, the undone vast,
This present of theirs with the hopeful past !
    I hoped she would love me ; here we ride.

What hand and brain went ever paired?
What heart alike conceived and dared?
What act proved all its thought had been?
What will but felt the fleshly screen?
　　We ride and I see her bosom heave.
There's many a crown for who can reach.
Ten lines, a statesman's life in each!
The flag stuck on a heap of bones,
A soldier's doing! what atones?
They scratch his name on the Abbey-stones.
　　My riding is better, by their leave.

What does it all mean, poet? Well,
Your brains beat into rhythm, you tell
What we felt only; you expressed
You hold things beautiful the best,
　　And pace them in rhyme so, side by side.
'Tis something, nay 'tis much: but then,
Have you yourself what's best for men?
Are you—poor, sick, old ere your time—
Nearer one whit your own sublime
Than we who never have turned a rhyme?
　　Sing, riding's a joy! For me, I ride.

And you, great sculptor—so, you gave
A score of years to Art, her slave,
And that's your Venus, whence we turn
To yonder girl that fords the burn!
　　You acquiesce, and shall I repine?
What, man of music, you grown grey
With notes and nothing else to say,
Is this your sole praise from a friend,
'Greatly his opera strains intend,
But in music we know how fashions end!'
　　I gave my youth; but we ride, in fine.

Who knows what's fit for us? Had fate
Proposed bliss here should sublimate
My being—had I signed the bond—
Still one must lead some life beyond,
　　Have a bliss to die with, dim-descried.
This foot once planted on the goal,
This glory-garland round my soul,

Could I descry such?   Try and test !
I sink back shuddering from the quest.
Earth being so good, would heaven seem best ?
    Now, heaven and she are beyond this ride.

And yet—she has not spoke so long !
What if heaven be that, fair and strong
At life's best, with our eyes upturned
Whither life's flower is first discerned,
    We, fixed so, ever should so abide?
What if we still ride on, we two
With life for ever old yet new,
Changed not in kind but in degree,
The instant made eternity,—
And·heaven just prove that I and she
    Ride, ride together, for ever ride?

                                    R. Browning.

CCCLXXIV

A FAREWELL

There lived a singer in France of old
    By the tideless dolorous midland sea.
In a land of sand and ruin and gold
    There shone one woman, and none but she.
And finding life for her love's sake fail,
Being fain to see her, he bade set sail,
Touched land, and saw her as life grew cold,
    And praised God, seeing; and so died he.

Died, praising God for his gift and grace :
    For she bowed down to him weeping, and said
' Live; ' and her tears were shed on his face
    Or ever the life in his face was shed.
The sharp tears fell through her hair, and stung
Once, and her close lips touched him and clung
Once, and grew one with his lips for a space;
    And so drew back, and the man was dead.

O brother, the gods were good to you.
    Sleep, and be glad while the world endures.
Be well content as the years wear through;
    Give thanks for life, and the loves and lures;

Give thanks for life, O brother, and death,
For the sweet last sound of her feet, her breath,
For gifts she gave you, gracious and few,
   Tears and kisses, that lady of yours.

Rest, and be glad of the gods; but I,
   How shall I praise them, or how take rest?
There is not room under all the sky
   For me that know not of worst or best,
Dream or desire of the days before,
Sweet things or bitterness, any more.
Love will not come to me now though I die,
   As love came close to you, breast to breast.

I shall never be friends again with roses;
   I shall loathe sweet tunes, where a note grown strong
Relents and recoils, and climbs and closes,
   As a wave of the sea turned back by song.
There are sounds where the soul's delight takes fire.
Face to face with its own desire:
A delight that rebels, a desire that reposes;
   I shall hate sweet music my whole life long.

The pulse of war and passion of wonder,
   The heavens that murmur, the sounds that shine
The stars that sing and the loves that thunder
   The music burning at heart like wine,
An armed archangel whose hands raise up
All senses mixed in the spirit's cup
Till flesh and spirit are molten in sunder—
   These things are over, and no more mine.

These were a part of the playing I heard
   Once, ere my love and my heart were at strife;
Love that sings and hath wings as a bird,
   Balm of the wound and heft of the knife.
Fairer than earth is the sea, and sleep
Than overwatching of eyes that weep,
Now time has done with his one sweet word,
   The wine and leaven of lovely life.

I shall go my ways, tread out my measure,
   Fill the days of my daily breath
With fugitive things not good to treasure,
   Do as the world doth, say as it saith;
But if we had loved each other—O sweet,
Had you felt, lying under the palms of your feet,
The heart of my heart, beating harder with pleasure
   To feel you tread it to dust and death—

Ah, had I not taken my life up and given
   All that life gives and the years let go,
The wine and honey, the balm and leaven,
   The dreams reared high and the hopes brought
      low?
Come life, come death, not a word be said;
Should I lose you living, and vex you dead?
I never shall tell you on earth; and in heaven,
   If I cry to you then, will you hear or know?

                       A. C. Swinburne

CCCLXXV

LOVESIGHT

When do I see thee most, beloved one?
When in the light the spirits of mine eyes
Before thy face, their altar, solemnise
The worship of that Love through thee made known?
Or when in the dusk hours (we two alone),
Close-kissed and eloquent of still replies
Thy twilight-hidden glimmering visage lies,
And my soul only sees thy soul its own?

O love, my love! if I no more should see
Thyself, nor on the earth the shadow of thee,
Nor image of thine eyes in any spring,—
How then should sound upon Life's darkening slope
The ground-whirl of the perished leaves of Hope,
The wind of Death's imperishable wing?

                       D. G. Rossetti

THE WAYS OF LOVE

How do I love thee ?   Let me count the ways.
I love thee to the depth and breadth and height
My soul can reach, when feeling out of sight
For the ends of Being and ideal Grace.
I love thee to the level of every day's
Most quiet need, by sun and candlelight.
I love thee freely, as men strive for Right:
I love thee purely, as they turn from Praise.

I love thee with the passion put to use
In my old griefs, and with my childhood's faith.
I love thee with a love I seemed to lose
With my lost saints,—I love thee with the breath,
Smiles, tears, of all my life !—and, if God choose,
I shall but love thee better after death.

E. B. Browning

THE OBLATION

Ask nothing more of me, sweet ;
    All I can give you I give.
        Heart of my heart, were it more,
More would be laid at your feet :
    Love that should help you to live,
        Song that should spur you to soar.

All things were nothing to give
    Once to have sense of you more,
        Touch you and taste of you, sweet.
Think you and breathe you and live,
    Swept of your wings as they soar,
        Trodden by chance of your feet.

.I that have love and no more
　Give you but love of you, sweet :
　　He that hath more, let him give ;
He that hath wings, let him soar ;
　Mine is the heart at your feet
　　Here, that must love you to live.

A. C. Swinburne

TWO IN THE CAMPAGNA

I wonder do you feel to-day
　As I have felt since, hand in hand,
We sat down on the grass, to stray
　In spirit better through the land,
This morn of Rome and May ?

For me, I touched a thought, I know,
　Has tantalized me many times,
(Like turns of thread the spiders throw
　Mocking across our path) for rhymes
To catch at and let go.

Help me to hold it !   First it left
　The yellowing fennel, run to seed
There, branching from the brickwork's cleft,
　Some old tomb's ruin : yonder weed
Took up the floating weft,

Where one small orange cup amassed
　Five beetles,—blind and green they grope
Among the honey-meal : and last,
　Everywhere on the grassy slope
I traced it.   Hold it fast !

The champaign with its endless fleece
　Of feathery grasses everywhere !
Silence and passion, joy and peace,
　An everlasting wash of air—
Rome's ghost since her decease.

Such life here, through such lengths of hours,
  Such miracles performed in play,
Such primal naked forms of flowers,
  Such letting nature have her way
While heaven looks from its towers!

How say you? Let us, O my dove,
  Let us be unashamed of soul,
As earth lies bare to heaven above!
  How is it under our control
To love or not to love?

I would that you were all to me,
  You that are just so much, no more.
Nor yours nor mine, nor slave nor free!
  Where does the fault lie? What the core
O' the wound, since wound must be?

I would I could adopt your will,
  See with your eyes, and set my heart
Beating by yours, and drink my fill
  At your soul's springs,—your part my part
In life, for good and ill.

No. I yearn upward, touch you close,
  Then stand away. I kiss your cheek,
Catch your soul's warmth—I pluck the rose
  And love it more than tongue can speak—
Then the good minute goes.

Already how am I so far
  Out of that minute? Must I go
Still like the thistle-ball, no bar,
  Onward, whenever light winds blow,
Fixed by no friendly star?

Just when I seemed about to learn!
  Where is the thread now? Off again?
The old trick! Only I discern—
  Infinite passion, and the pain
Of finite hearts that yearn.

                              R. Browning

CCCLXXIX

O let me be in loving nice,
Dainty, fine, and o'er-precise,
That I may charm my charmèd dear
As though I felt a secret fear
To lose what never can be lost,—
Her faith who still delights me most !
So shall I be more than true,
Ever in my ageing new ;
So dull habit shall not be
Wrongly called Fidelity.

M. E. Coleridge

CCCLXXX

FAME AND FRIENDSHIP

Fame is a food that dead men eat,—
I have no stomach for such meat.
In little light and narrow room,
They eat it in the silent tomb,
With no kind voice of comrade near
To bid the feaster be of cheer.

But friendship is a nobler thing,—
Of Friendship it is good to sing.
For truly, when a man shall end,
He lives in memory of his friend,
Who doth his better part recall
And of his fault make funeral.

A. Dobson

CCCLXXXI

PARTING AT MORNING

Round the cape of a sudden came the sea,
And the sun looked over the mountain's rim :
And straight was a path of gold for him,
And the need of a world of men for me.

R. Browning

CCCLXXXII

QUA CURSUM VENTUS

As ships, becalmed at eve, that lay
  With canvas drooping, side by side,
Two towers of sail at dawn of day
  Are scarce long leagues apart descried;

When fell the night, up sprung the breeze,
  And all the darkling hours they plied,
Nor dreamt but each the self-same seas
  By each was cleaving, side by side:

E'en so—but why the tale reveal
  Of those, whom year by year unchanged,
Brief absence joined anew to feel,
  Astounded, soul from soul estranged?

At dead of night their sails were filled,
  And onward each rejoicing steered—
Ah, neither blame, for neither willed,
  Or wist, what first with dawn appeared!

To veer, how vain! On, onward strain,
  Brave barks! In light, in darkness too,
Through winds and tides one compass guides—
  To that, and your own selves, be true.

But O blithe breeze! and O great seas,
  Though ne'er, that earliest parting past,
On your wide plain they join again
  Together lead them home at last.

One port, methought, alike they sought,
  One purpose hold where'er they fare,—
O bounding breeze, O rushing seas!
  At last, at last, unite them there!

A. H. Clough

CCCLXXXIII

HERACLITUS

They told me, Heraclitus, they told me you were
   dead,
They brought me bitter news to hear and bitter tears
   to shed.
I wept as I remembered how often you and I
Had tired the sun with talking and sent him down
   the sky.

And now that thou art lying, my dear old Carian
   guest,
A handful of grey ashes, long, long ago at rest,
Still are thy pleasant voices, thy nightingales,
   awake;
For Death, he taketh all away, but these he cannot
   take.

W. Cory

CCCLXXXIV

TO VIRGIL

Roman Virgil, thou that singest
   Ilion's lofty temples robed in fire,
Ilion falling, Rome arising,
   wars, and filial faith, and Dido's pyre;

Landscape-lover, lord of language
   more than he that sang the Works and Days,
All the chosen coin of fancy
   flashing out from many a golden phrase;

Thou that singest wheat and woodland,
   tilth and vineyard, hive and horse and herd;
All the charm of all the Muses
   often flowering in a lonely word;

Poet of the happy Tityrus
   piping underneath his beechen bowers;
Poet of the poet-satyr
   whom the laughing shepherd bound with
      flowers;

Chanter of the Pollio, glorying
    in the blissful years again to be,
Summers of the snakeless meadow,
    unlaborious earth and oarless sea;

Thou that seëst Universal
    Nature moved by Universal Mind;
Thou majestic in thy sadness
    at the doubtful doom of human kind;

Light among the vanish'd ages;
    star that gildest yet this phantom shore;
Golden branch amid the shadows,
    kings and realms that pass to rise no more;

Now thy Forum roars no longer,
    fallen every purple Caesar's dome—
Tho' thine ocean-roll of rhythm
    sound for ever of Imperial Rome—

Now the Rome of slaves hath perish'd,
    and the Rome of freemen holds her place,
I, from out the Northern Island
    sunder'd once from all the human race,

I salute thee, Mantovano,
    I that loved thee since my day began,
Wielder of the stateliest measure
    ever moulded by the lips of man.
                   Lord Tennyson

CCCLXXXV

THE SCHOLAR-GIPSY

Go, for they call you, shepherd, from the hill;
  Go, shepherd, and untie the wattled cotes!
    No longer leave thy wistful flock unfed,
  Nor let thy bawling fellows rack their throats,
    Nor the cropp'd herbage shoot another head.
      But when the fields are still,

And the tired men and dogs all gone to rest,
    And only the white sheep are sometimes seen
      Cross and recross the strips of moon-blanch'd
        green,
Come, shepherd, and again begin the quest!

Here, where the reaper was at work of late—
    In this high field's dark corner, where he leaves
      His coat, his basket, and his earthen cruse,
    And in the sun all morning binds the sheaves,
      Then here, at noon, comes back his stores to
        use—
      Here will I sit and wait,
    While to my ear from uplands far away
      The bleating of the folded flocks is borne,
      With distant cries of reapers in the corn—
All the live murmur of a summer's day.

Screen'd is this nook o'er the high, half-reap'd field,
    And here till sundown, shepherd! will I be.
      Through the thick corn the scarlet poppies peep,
    And round green roots and yellowing stalks I see
      Pale pink convolvulus in tendrils creep;
      And air-swept lindens yield
    Their scent, and rustle down their perfumed
        showers
      Of bloom on the bent grass where I am laid,
      And bower me from the August sun with shade;
And the eye travels down to Oxford's towers.

And near me on the grass lies Glanvil's book—
    Come, let me read the oft-read tale again!
      The story of the Oxford scholar poor,
    Of pregnant parts and quick inventive brain,
      Who, tired of knocking at preferment's door,
      One summer-morn forsook
    His friends, and went to learn the gipsy-lore,
      And roam'd the world with that wild brother-
        hood,
      And came, as most men deem'd, to little good,
But came to Oxford and his friends no more.

But once, years after, in the country-lanes,
 Two scholars, whom at college erst he knew,
  Met him, and of his way of life enquired;
 Whereat he answer'd, that the gipsy-crew,
  His mates, had arts to rule as they desired
   The workings of men's brains,
 And they can bind them to what thoughts they
    will.
  ' And I,' he said, ' the secret of their art,
   When fully learn'd, will to the world impart;
 But it needs heaven-sent moments for this skill.'

This said, he left them, and return'd no more.—
 But rumours hung about the country-side,
  That the lost Scholar long was seen to stray,
 Seen by rare glimpses, pensive and tongue-tied,
  In hat of antique shape, and cloak of grey,
   The same the gipsies wore.
 Shepherds had met him on the Hurst in spring;
  At some lone alehouse in the Berkshire moors,
  On the warm ingle-bench, the smock-frock'd
   boors
 Had found him seated at their entering.

But, 'mid their drink and clatter, he would fly.
 And I myself seem half to know thy looks,
  And put the shepherds, wanderer ! on thy trace;
 And boys who in lone wheatfields scare the rooks
  I ask if thou hast pass'd their quiet place;
   Or in my boat I lie
 Moor'd to the cool bank in the summer-heats,
  'Mid wide grass meadows which the sunshine
   fills,
  And watch the warm, green-muffled Cumner
   hills,
 And wonder if thou haunt'st their shy retreats.

For most, I know, thou lov'st retired ground !
 Thee at the ferry Oxford riders blithe,
  Returning home on summer-nights, have met
 Crossing the stripling Thames at Bab-lock-hithe,
  Trailing in the cool stream thy fingers wet,
   As the punt's rope chops round;

And leaning backward in a pensive dream,
    And fostering in thy lap a heap of flowers
    Pluck'd in shy fields and distant Wychwood
        bowers,
And thine eyes resting on the moonlit stream.

And then they land, and thou art seen no more !—
    Maidens, who from the distant hamlets come
      To dance around the Fyfield elm in May,
Oft through the darkening fields have seen thee
      roam,
      Or cross a stile into the public way.
        Oft thou hast given them store
Of flowers—the frail-leaf'd, white anemony,
    Dark bluebells drench'd with dews of summer
      eves,
    And purple orchises with spotted leaves—
But none hath words she can report of thee.

And, above Godstow Bridge, when hay-time's here
    In June, and many a scythe in sunshine flames,
    Men who through those wide fields of breezy
      grass
Where black-wing'd swallows haunt the glittering
      Thames,
      To bathe in the abandon'd lasher pass,
        Have often pass'd thee near
Sitting upon the river bank o'ergrown ;
    Mark'd thine outlandish garb, thy figure spare,
    Thy dark vague eyes, and soft abstracted air—
But, when they came from bathing, thou wast
      gone !

At some lone homestead in the Cumner hills,
    Where at her open door the housewife darns,
      Thou hast been seen, or hanging on a gate
To watch the threshers in the mossy barns.
      Children, who early range these slopes and late
        For cresses from the rills,
Have known thee eying, all an April-day,
    The springing pastures and the feeding kine ;
    And mark'd thee, when the stars come out and
      shine,
Through the long dewy grass move slow away.

In autumn, on the skirts of Bagley Wood—
  Where most the gipsies by the turf-edged way
    Pitch their smoked tents, and every bush you see
  With scarlet patches tagg'd and shreds of grey,
    Above the forest-ground called Thessaly—
      The blackbird, picking food,
  Sees thee, nor stops his meal, nor fears at all;
    So often has he known thee past him stray,
    Rapt, twirling in thy hand a wither'd spray,
And waiting for the spark from heaven to fall.

And once, in winter, on the causeway chill
  Where home through flooded fields foot-travellers
      go,
    Have I not pass'd thee on the wooden bridge,
  Wrapt in thy cloak and battling with the snow,
    Thy face tow'rd Hinksey and its wintry ridge?
      And thou hast climb'd the hill,
  And gain'd the white brow of the Cumner range;
    Turn'd once to watch, while thick the snow-
      flakes fall,
    The line of festal light in Christ-Church hall—
Then sought thy straw in some sequester'd
      grange.

But what—I dream! Two hundred years are flown
  Since first thy story ran through Oxford halls,
    And the grave Glanvil did the tale inscribe
  That whou wert wander'd from the studious walls
    To learn strange arts, and join a gipsy-tribe;
      And thou from earth art gone
  Long since, and in some quiet churchyard laid—
    Some country-nook, where o'er thy unknown
      grave
    Tall grasses and white flowering nettles wave,
Under a dark, red-fruited yew-tree's shade.

—No, no, thou hast not felt the lapse of hours!
  For what wears out the life of mortal men?
    'Tis that from change to change their being
      rolls;
    'Tis that repeated shocks, again, again,
      Exhaust the energy of strongest souls
        And numb the elastic powers.

Till having used our nerves with bliss and teen,
And tired upon a thousand schemes our wit,
To the just-pausing Genius we remit
Our worn-out life, and are—what we have been.

Thou hast not lived, why should'st thou perish,
   so ?
   Thou hadst *one* aim, *one* business, *one* desire ;
      Else wert thou long since number'd with the
         dead !
   Else hadst thou spent, like other men, thy fire !
      The generations of thy peers are fled,
         And we ourselves shall go ;
      But thou possessest an immortal lot,
         And we imagine thee exempt from age
         And living as thou liv'st on Glanvil's page,
   Because thou hadst—what we, alas ! have not.

For early didst thou leave the world, with powers
   Fresh, undiverted to the world without,
      Firm to their mark, not spent on other things ;
   Free from the sick fatigue, the languid doubt,
      Which much to have tried, in much been baffled,
         brings.
         O life unlike to ours !
   Who fluctuate idly without term or scope,
      Of whom each strives, nor knows for what he
         strives,
      And each half-lives a hundred different lives ;
   Who wait like thee, but not, like thee, in hope.

Thou waitest for the spark from heaven ! and we,
   Light half-believers of our casual creeds,
      Who never deeply felt, nor clearly will'd,
   Whose insight never has borne fruit in deeds,
      Whose vague resolves never have been fulfill'd ;
         For whom each year we see
   Breeds new beginnings, disappointments new ;
      Who hesitate and falter life away,
      And lose to-morrow, the ground won to-day—
Ah ! do not we, wanderer ! await it too ?

Yes, we await it!—but it still delays,
   And then we suffer! and amongst us one,
     Who most has suffer'd, takes dejectedly
   His seat upon the intellectual throne;
     And all his store of sad experience he
       Lays bare of wretched days:
   Tells us his misery's birth and growth and signs,
     And how the dying spark of hope was fed,
     And how the breast was soothed, and how the
       head,
And all his hourly varied anodynes.

This for our wisest! and we others pine,
   And wish the long unhappy dream would end,
     And waive all claim to bliss, and try to bear;
   With close-lipp'd patience for our only friend,
     Sad patience, too near neighbour to despair—
       But none has hope like thine!
   Thou through the fields and through the woods
       dost stray,
     Roaming the country-side, a truant boy,
     Nursing thy project in unclouded joy,
And every doubt long blown by time away.

O born in days when wits were fresh and clear,
   And life ran gaily as the sparkling Thames;
     Before this strange disease of modern life,
   With its sick hurry, its divided aims,
     Its heads o'ertax'd, its palsied hearts, was rife—
       Fly hence, our contact fear!
   Still fly, plunge deeper in the bowering wood!
     Averse, as Dido did with gesture stern
     From her false friend's approach in Hades
       turn,
Wave us away, and keep thy solitude!

Still nursing the unconquerable hope,
   Still clutching the inviolable shade,
     With a free, onward impulse brushing through
   By night, the silver'd branches of the glade—
     Far on the forest-skirts, where none pursue,
       On some mild pastoral slope

Emerge, and resting on the moonlit pales
  Freshen thy flowers as in former years
  With dew, or listen with enchanted ears,
From the dark dingles, to the nightingales!

But fly our paths, our feverish contact fly!
  For strong the infection of our mental strife,
    Which, though it gives no bliss, yet spoils for
      rest;
  And we should win thee from thy own fair life,
    Like us distracted, and like us unblest.
      Soon, soon thy cheer would die,
  Thy hopes grow timorous, and unfix'd thy powers,
    And thy clear aims be cross and shifting made;
  And then thy glad perennial youth would fade,
Fade, and grow old at last, and die like ours.

Then fly our greetings, fly our speech and smiles!
  —As some grave Tyrian trader, from the sea,
    Descried at sunrise an emerging prow
  Lifting the cool-hair'd creepers stealthily,
    The fringes of a southward-facing brow
      Among the Ægaean isles;
  And saw the merry Grecian coaster come,
    Freighted with amber grapes, and Chian wine,
    Green, bursting figs, and tunnies steep'd in
      brine—
  And knew the intruders on his ancient home,

The young light-hearted masters of the waves—
  And snatch'd his rudder, and shook out more sail;
    And day and night held on indignantly
  O'er the blue Midland waters with the gale,
    Betwixt the Syrtes and soft Sicily,
      To where the Atlantic raves
  Outside the western straits; and unbent sails
    There, where down cloudy cliffs, through sheets
      of foam,
    Shy traffickers, the dark Iberians come;
  And on the beach undid his corded bales.

                       M. Arnold

CCCLXXXVI

Break, break, break,
  On thy cold gray stones, O Sea !
And I would that my tongue could utter
  The thoughts that arise in me.

O well for the fisherman's boy,
  That he shouts with his sister at play !
O well for the sailor lad,
  That he sings in his boat on the bay '

And the stately ships go on
  To their haven under the hill ;
But O for the touch of a vanish'd hand,
  And the sound of a voice that is still !

Break, break, break,
  At the foot of thy crags, O Sea !
But the tender grace of a day that is dead
  Will never come back to me.

Lord Tennyson

CCCLXXXVII

THE NIGHT HAS A THOUSAND EYES

The night has a thousand eyes,
  And the day but one ;
Yet the light of the bright world dies
  With the dying sun.

The mind has a thousand eyes,
  And the heart but one ;
Yet the light of a whole life dies
  When love is done.

F. W. Bourdillon

CCCLXXXVIII

ROSE AYLMER

Ah, what avails the sceptred race !
  Ah, what the form divine !
What every virtue, every grace |
  Rose Aylmer, all were thine.

Rose Aylmer, whom these wakeful eyes
  May weep, but never see,
A night of memories and sighs
  I consecrate to thee.

W. S. Landor

CCCLXXXIX

THE NEW HOUSE

Now first, as I shut the door,
  I was alone
In the new house ; and the wind
  Began to moan.

Old at once was the house,
  And I was old ;
My ears were teased with the dread
  Of what was foretold ;

Nights of storm, days of mist, without end ;
  Sad days when the sun
Shone in vain : old griefs and griefs
  Not yet begun.

All was foretold me ; naught
  Could I foresee ;
But I learnt how the wind would sound
  After these things should be.

E. Thomas

CCCXC

SILENCE

There is a silence where hath been no sound;
There is a silence where no sound may be;
In the cold grave, under the deep, deep sea,
Or in wide desert, where no life is found,
Which hath been mute, and still must sleep profound.
No voice is hushed, no life treads silently;
But clouds and cloudy shadows wander free,
That never spoke, over the idle ground.

But in green ruins, in the desolate walls
Of antique palaces, where Man hath been,
Though the dun fox, or wild hyaena, calls,
And owls, that flit continually between,
Shriek to the echo, and the low winds moan,
There the true Silence is, self-conscious and alone.

T. Hood

CCCXCI

WRITTEN IN NORTHAMPTON
COUNTY ASYLUM

I am! yet what I am, who cares or knows?
My friends forsake me, like a memory lost.
I am the self-consumer of my woes;
They rise and vanish, an oblivious host,
Shadows of life, whose very soul is lost.
And yet I am,—I live,—though I am tossed

Into the nothingness of scorn and noise,
Into the living sea of waking dream,
Where there is neither sense of life, nor joys,
But the huge shipwreck of my own esteem
And all that's dear. Even those I loved the best
Are strange, nay, they are stranger than the rest.

I long for scenes where never man has trod,
For scenes where woman never smiled nor wept,
There to abide with my creator, God,
And sleep as I in childhood sweetly slept,
Full of high thoughts, unborn.   So let me die—
The grass below; above, the vaulted sky.

J. Clare

CCCXCII

GRIEF

I tell you, hopeless grief is passionless;
That only men incredulous of despair
Half-taught in anguish, through the midnight air
Beat upward to God's throne in loud access
Of shrieking and reproach.   Full desertness
In souls, as countries, lieth silent-bare
Under the blanching, vertical eye-glare
Of the absolute Heavens.   Deep-hearted man,
   express
Grief for thy Dead in silence like to death:
Most like a monumental statue set
In everlasting watch and moveless woe,
Till itself crumble to the dust beneath.
Touch it: the marble eyelids are not wet;
If it could weep, it could arise and go.

E. B. Browning

CCCXCIII

O DREAMY, GLOOMY, FRIENDLY TREES

O dreamy, gloomy, friendly Trees,
  I came along your narrow track
To bring my gifts unto your knees
  And gifts did you give back;
For when I brought this heart that burns—
  These thoughts that bitterly repine—
And laid them here among the ferns
  And the hum of boughs divine.

Ye, vastest breathers of the air,
    Shook down with slow and mighty poise
Your coolness on the human care,
    Your wonder on its toys,
Your greenness on the heart's despair,
    Your darkness on its noise.

H. F. Trench

CCCXCIV

DE GUSTIBUS——'

Your ghost will walk, you lover of trees,
        (If our loves remain)
        In an English lane,
By a cornfield-side a-flutter with poppies.
Hark, those two in the hazel coppice—
A boy and a girl, if the good fates please,
        Making love, say,—
        The happier they!
Draw yourself up from the light of the moon,
And let them pass, as they will too soon,
        With the bean-flowers' boon,
        And the blackbird's tune,
        And May, and June!

What I love best in all the world
Is a castle, precipice-encurled,
In a gash of the wind-grieved Apennine.
Or look for me, old fellow of mine,
(If I get my head from out the mouth
O' the grave, and loose my spirit's bands,
And come again to the land of lands)—
In a sea-side house to the farther south,
Where the baked cicala dies of drouth,
And one sharp tree—'tis a cypress—stands,
By the many hundred years red-rusted,
Rough iron-spiked, ripe fruit-o'er-crusted,
My sentinel to guard the sands
To the water's edge.   For what expands
Before the house, but the great opaque
Blue breadth of sea without a break?

While, in the house, for ever crumbles
Some fragment of the frescoed walls,
From blisters where a scorpion sprawls.
A girl bare-footed brings, and tumbles
Down on the pavement, green-flesh melons,
And says there's news to-day—the King
Was shot at, touched in the liver-wing,
Goes with his Bourbon arm in a sling :
—She hopes they have not caught the felons.
  Italy, my Italy !
Queen Mary's saying serves for me—
   (When fortune's malice
   Lost her, Calais)—
Open my heart, and you will see
Graved inside of it, ' Italy.'
Such lovers old are I and she :
So it always was, so shall ever be !
      R. Browning

CCCXCV

THE WOODCUTTER'S NIGHT-SONG

 Welcome, red and roundy sun,
  Dropping lowly in the west ;
Now my hard day's work is done,
  I'm as happy as the best.

 Joyful are the thoughts of home,
  Now I'm ready for my chair,
So, till morrow-morning's come,
  Bill and mittens, lie ye there !

 Though to leave your pretty song,
  Little birds, it gives me pain,
Yet to-morrow is not long,
  Then I'm with you all again.

 If I stop, and stand about,
  Well I know how things will be,
Judy will be looking out
  Every now-and-then for me.

So fare ye well! and hold your tongues,
  Sing no more until I come;
They're not worthy of your songs
  That never care to drop a crumb.

All day long I love the oaks,
  But, at nights, yon little cot,
Where I see the chimney smokes,
  Is by far the prettiest spot.

Wife and children all are there,
  To revive with pleasant looks,
Table ready set, and chair,
  Supper hanging on the hooks.

Soon as ever I get in,
  When my faggot down I fling,
Little prattlers they begin
  Teasing me to talk and sing.

Welcome, red and roundy sun,
  Dropping lowly in the west;
Now my hard day's work is done,
  I'm as happy as the best.

Joyful are the thoughts of home,
  Now, I'm ready for my chair,
So, till morrow-morning's come,
  Bill and mittens, lie ye there!

J. Clare

CCCXCVI

LONDON SNOW

When men were all asleep the snow came flying,
In large white flakes falling on the city brown,
Stealthily and perpetually settling and loosely lying,
  Hushing the latest traffic of the drowsy town;
Deadening, muffling, stifling its murmurs failing;
Lazily and incessantly floating down and down:
  Silently sifting and veiling road, roof and railing;
Hiding difference, making unevenness even,
Into angles and crevices softly drifting and sailing.
  All night it fell, and when full inches seven

It lay in the depth of its uncompacted lightness,
The clouds blew off from a high and frosty heaven;
   And all woke earlier for the unaccustomed
      brightness
Of the winter dawning, the strange unheavenly glare :
The eye marvelled—marvelled at the dazzling white-
      ness;
   The ear hearkened to the stillness of the solemn
      air ;
No sound of wheel rumbling nor of foot falling,
And the busy morning cries came thin and spare.
   Then boys I heard, as they went to school, calling,
They gathered up the crystal manna to freeze
Their tongues with tasting, their hands with snow-
      balling ;
   Or rioted in a drift, plunging up to the knees ;
Or peering up from under the white-mossed wonder,
' O look at the trees ! ' they cried, ' O look at the
      trees ! '
   With lessened load a few carts creak and blunder,
Following along the white deserted way,
A country company long dispersed asunder :
   When now already the sun, in pale display
Standing by Paul's high dome, spread forth below
His sparkling beams, and awoke the stir of the day.
   For now doors open, and war is waged with the
      snow ;
And trains of sombre men, past tale of number,
Tread long brown paths, as toward their toil they go ;
   But even for them awhile no cares encumber
Their minds diverted ; the daily word is unspoken,
The daily thoughts of labour and sorrow slumber
At the sight of the beauty that greets them, for the
      charm they have broken.

                      R. Bridges

CCCXCVII

THE LADY POVERTY

   The Lady Poverty was fair :
   But she has lost her looks of late,

With change of times and change of air.
Ah slattern! she neglects her hair,
Her gown, her shoes; she keeps no state
As once when her pure feet were bare.

Or—almost worse, if worse can be—
She scolds in parlours, dusts and trims,
Watches and counts. Oh, is this she
Whom Francis met, whose step was free,
Who with Obedience carolled hymns,
In Umbria walked with Chastity?

Where is her ladyhood? Not here,
Not among modern kinds of men;
But in the stony fields, where clear
Through the thin trees the skies appear,
In delicate spare soil and fen,
And slender landscape and austere.

A. Meynell

CCCXCVIII

THE VAGABOND

Give to me the life I love,
   Let the lave go by me,
Give the jolly heaven above
   And the by-way nigh me.
Bed in the bush with stars to see—
   Bread I dip in the river—
There's the life for a man like me,
    There's the life for ever.

Let the blow fall soon or late,
   Let what will be o'er me;
Give the face of earth around
   And the road before me.
Wealth I seek not, hope nor love,
   Nor a friend to know me;
All I seek, the heaven above
   And the road below me.

Or let autumn fall on me
　　Where afield I linger,
Silencing the bird on tree,
　　Biting the blue finger.
White as meal the frosty field—
　　Warm the fireside haven—
Not to autumn will I yield,
　　Not to winter even;

Let the blow fall soon or late,
　　Let what will be o'er me;
Give the face of earth around
　　And the road before me.
Wealth I ask not, hope nor love,
　　Not a friend to know me.
All I ask, the heaven **above**,
　　And the road below me.

　　　　　　　　　　R. L. Stevenson

CCCXCIX

THE SONG OF THE UNGIRT RUNNERS

We swing ungirded hips,
And lightened are our eyes,
The rain is on our lips,
We do not run for prize.
We know not whom we trust
Nor witherward we fare,
But we run because we must
　　Through the great wide air.

The waters of the seas
Are troubled as by storm.
The tempest strips the trees
And does not leave them warm.
Does the tearing tempest pause?
Do the tree-tops ask it why?
So we run without a cause
　　'Neath the big bare sky.

The rain is on our lips,
We do not run for prize.
But the storm the water whips
And the wave howls to the skies.
The winds arise and strike it
And scatter it like sand,
And we run because we like it
    Through the broad bright land.

                                        C. H. Sorley

CCCC

CARGOES

Quinquireme of Nineveh from distant Ophir
Rowing home to haven in sunny Palestine,
With a cargo of ivory
And apes and peacocks,
Sandalwood, cedarwood, and sweet white wine.

Stately Spanish galleon coming from the Isthmus,
Dipping through the Tropics by the palm-grove
    shores,
With a cargo of diamonds,
Emeralds, amethysts,
Topazes, and cinnamon, and gold moidores.

Dirty British coaster with a salt-caked smoke-stack,
Butting through the Channel in the mad March days,
With a cargo of Tyne coal,
Road-rails, pig-lead,
Fire-wood, iron-ware, and cheap tin trays.

                                        J. Masefield

CCCCI

THE OLD SHIPS

I have seen old ships sail like swans asleep
Beyond the village which men still call Tyre,
With leaden age o'ercargoed, dipping deep
For Famagusta and the hidden sun

That rings black Cyprus with a lake of fire;
And all those ships were certainly so old
Who knows how oft with squat and noisy gun,
Questing brown slaves or Syrian oranges,
The pirate Genoese
Hell-raked them till they rolled
Blood, water, fruit, and corpses up the hold?
But now through friendly seas they softly run,
Painted the mid-sea blue or shore-sea green,
Still patterned with the vine and grapes in gold.

But I have seen,
Pointing her shapely shadows from the dawn
An image tumbled on a rose-swept bay,
A drowsy ship of some yet older day;
And, wonder's breath indrawn,
Thought I—who knows—who knows—but in that
    same
(Fished up beyond Aeaea, patched up new
—Stern painted brighter blue—)
That talkative, bald-headed seaman came
(Twelve patient comrades sweating at the oar)
From Troy's doom-crimson shore,
And with great lies about his wooden horse
Set the crew laughing, and forgot his course.

It was so old a ship—who knows—who knows?
—And yet so beautiful, I watched in vain
To see the mast burst open with a rose,
And the whole deck put on its leaves again.

J. E. Flecker

INVERSNAID

This darksome burn, horseback brown,
His rollrock highroad roaring down,
In coop and in comb the fleece of his foam
Flutes and low to the lake falls home.

A windpuff-bonnet of fawn-froth
Turns and twindles over the broth
Of a pool so pitchblack, fell-frowning,
It rounds and rounds Despair to drowning.

Degged with dew, dappled with dew
Are the groins of the braes that the brook treads
      through,
Wiry heathpacks, flitches of fern,
And the beadbonny ash that sits over the burn.

What would the world be, once bereft
Of wet and of wildness? Let them be left,
O let them be left, wildness and wet;
Long live the weeds and the wilderness yet.

                        G. M. Hopkins

CCCCIII

A RUNNABLE STAG

When the pods went pop on the broom, green broom,
  And apples began to be golden-skinn'd,
We harbour'd a stag in the Priory coomb,
  And we feather'd his trail up-wind, up-wind,
  We feathered his trail up-wind—
    A stag of warrant, a stag, a stag,
    A runnable stag, a kingly crop,
    Brow, bay and tray and three on top,
    A stag, a runnable stag.

Then the hunstman's horn, rang yap, yap, yap,
  And " Forwards " we heard the harbourer shout;
But 'twas only a brocket that broke a gap
  In the beechen underwood, driven out,
  From the underwood antler'd out
    By warrant and might of the stag, the stag,
    The runnable stag, whose lordly mind
    Was bent on sleep, though beam'd and tined
    He stood, a runnable stag.

So we tufted the covert till afternoon
  With Tinkerman's Pup and Bell-of-the-North;
And hunters were sulky and hounds out of tune
  Before we tufted the right stag forth,
  Before we tufted him forth,
    The stag of warrant, the wily stag,
    The runnable stag with his kingly crop,
    Brow, bay and tray and three on top,
    The royal and runnable stag.

It was Bell-of-the-North and Tinkerman's Pup
  That stuck to the scent till the copse was drawn,
' Tally ho ! tally ho ! ' and the hunt was up,
  The tufters whipp'd and the pack laid on,
  The resolute pack laid on,
    And the stag of warrant away at last,
    The runnable stag, the same, the same,
    His hoofs on fire, his horns like flame,
    A stag, a runnable stag.

' Let your gelding be : if you check or chide
  He stumbles at once and you're out of the hunt;
For three hundred gentlemen, able to ride,
  On hunters accustom'd to bear the brunt,
  Accustom'd to bear the brunt,
    Are after the runnable stag, the stag,
    The runnable stag with his kingly crop,
    Brow, bay and tray and three on top,
    The right, the runnable stag.'

By perilous paths in coomb and dell,
  The heather, the rocks, and the river-bed,
The pace grew hot, for the scent lay well,
  And a runnable stag goes right ahead,
  The quarry went right ahead—
    Ahead, ahead, and fast and far;
    His antler'd crest, his cloven hoof,
    Brow, bay and tray and three aloof,
    The stag, the runnable stag.

For a matter of twenty miles and more,
  By the densest hedge and the highest wall,
Through herds of bullocks he baffled the lore
  Of habourer, huntsman, hounds and all,
  Of harbourer, hounds and all—

The stag of warrant, the wily stag,
  For twenty miles, and five and five,
  He ran, and he never was caught alive,
    This stag, this runnable stag.

When he turn'd at bay in the leafy gloom,
  In the emerald gloom where the brook ran deep
He heard in the distance the rollers boom,
  And he saw in a vision of peaceful sleep
  In a wonderful vision of sleep,
    A stag of warrant, a stag, a stag,
    A runnable stag in a jewell'd bed,
    Under the sheltering ocean dead,
      A stag, a runnable stag.

So a fateful hope lit up his eye,
  And he open'd his nostrils wide again,
And he toss'd his branching antlers high
  As he headed the hunt down the Charlock glen
  As he raced down the echoing glen—
    For five miles more, the stag, the stag,
    For twenty miles, and five and five,
    Not to be caught now, dead or alive,
      The stag, the runnable stag.

Three hundred gentlemen, able to ride,
  Three hundred horses as gallant and free,
Beheld him escape on the evening tide,
  Far out till he sank in the Severn Sea,
  Till he sank in the depths of the sea—
    The stag, the buoyant stag, the stag
    That slept at last in a jewell'd bed
    Under the sheltering ocean spread,
      The stag, the runnable stag.

                                        J. Davidson

CCCCIV

SUSSEX

God gave all men all earth to love,
  But since our hearts are small,
Ordained for each one spot should prove
  Beloved over all;

That, as He watched Creation's birth,
  So we, in god-like mood,
May of our love create our earth
  And see that it is good.

So one shall Baltic pines content,
  As one some Surrey glade,
Or one the palm-grove's droned lament
  Before Levuka's trade.
Each to his choice, and I rejoice
  The lot has fallen to me
In a fair ground—in a fair ground—
  Yea, Sussex by the sea!

No tender-hearted garden crowns,
  No bosomed woods adorn
Our blunt, bow-headed, whale-backed Downs,
  But gnarled and writhen thorn—
Bare slopes where chasing shadows skim,
  And through the gaps revealed
Belt upon belt, the wooded, dim
  Blue goodness of the Weald.

Clean of officious fence or hedge,
  Half-wild and wholly tame,
The wise turf cloaks the white cliff edge
  As when the Romans came.
What sign of those that fought and died
  At shift of sword and sword?
The barrow and the camp abide,
  The sunlight and the sward.

Here leaps ashore the full Sou'west
  All heavy-winged with brine,
Here lies above the folded crest
  The Channel's leaden line;
And here the sea-fogs lap and cling,
  And here, each warning each,
The sheep-bells and the ship-bells ring
  Along the hidden beach.

We have no waters to delight
  Our broad and brookless vales—
Only the dewpond on the height
  Unfed, that never fails,

Whereby no tattered herbage tells
    Which way the season flies—
Only our close-bit thyme that smells
    Like dawn in Paradise.

Here through the strong unhampered days
    The tinkling silence thrills;
Or little, lost, Down churches praise
    The Lord who made the hills;
But here the Old Gods guard their round,
    And, in her secret heart,
The heathen kingdom Wilfrid found
    Dreams, as she dwells, apart.

Though all the rest were all my share,
    With equal soul I'd see
Her nine-and-thirty sisters fair,
    Yet none more fair than she.
Choose ye your need from Thames to Tweed,
    And I will choose instead
Such lands as lie 'twixt Rake and Rye,
    Black Down and Beachy Head.

I will go out against the sun
    Where the rolled scarp retires,
And the Long Man of Wilmington
    Looks naked towards the shires;
And east till doubling Rother crawls
    To find the fickle tide,
By dry and sea-forgotten walls,
    Our ports of stranded pride.

I will go north about the shaws
    And the deep ghylls that breed
Huge oaks and old, the which we hold
    No more than ' Sussex weed ';
Or South where windy Piddinghoe's
    Begilded dolphin veers,
And black beside wide-bankèd Ouse
    Lie down our Sussex steers.

So to the land our hearts we give
    Till the sure magic strike,
And Memory, Use, and Love make live
    Us and our fields alike—

That deeper than our speech and thought,
　　Beyond our reason's sway,
Clay of the pit whence we were wrought
　　Yearns to its fellow-clay.

God gives all men all earth to love,
　　But since man's heart is small,
Ordains for each one spot shall prove
　　Beloved over all.
Each to his choice, and I rejoice
　　The lot has fallen to me
In a fair ground—in a fair ground—
　　Yea, Sussex by the sea !
　　　　　　　　　　R. Kipling

CCCCV

DRAKE'S DRUM

Drake he's in his hammock an' a thousand mile
　　away,
　　(Capten, art tha sleepin' there below ?)
Slung atween the round shot in Nombre Dios Bay,
　　An' dreamin' arl the time o' Plymouth Hoe.
Yarnder lumes the Island, yarnder lie the ships,
　　Wi' sailor lads a-dancin' heel-an'-toe,
An' the shore-lights flashin', an' the night-tide
　　dashin',
　　He sees et arl so plainly as he saw et long ago.

Drake he was a Devon man, an' rüled the Devon
　　seas,
　　(Capten, art tha sleepin' there below ?)
Rovin' tho' his death fell, he went wi' heart at ease.
　　An' dreamin' arl the time o' Plymouth Hoe.
' Take my drum to England, hang et by the shore,
　　Strike et when your powder's runnin' low;
If the Dons sight Devon, I'll quit the port o' Heaven,
　　An' drum them up the Channel as we drumm'd
　　them long ago.'

Drake he's in his hammock till the great Armadas
come,
   (Capten, art tha sleepin' there below?)
Slung atween the round shot, listenin' for the drum,
   An' dreamin' arl the time o' Plymouth Hoe.
Call him on the deep sea, call him up the Sound,
   Call him when ye sail to meet the foe;
Where the old trade's plyin' and the old flag flyin'
   They shall find him ware an' wakin', as they found
   him long ago!

Sir H. Newbolt

CCCCVI

THE REVENGE

A Ballad of the Fleet

I

At Flores in the Azores Sir Richard Grenville lay,
And a pinnace, like a flutter'd bird, came flying
   from far away:
'Spanish ships of war at sea! we have sighted
   fifty-three!'
Then sware Lord Thomas Howard: ''Fore God I
   am no coward;
But I cannot meet them here, for my ships are out of
   gear,
And the half my men are sick. I must fly, but follow
   quick.
We are six ships of the line; can we fight with fifty-
   three?'

2

Then spake Sir Richard Grenville: 'I know you
   are no coward;
You fly them for a moment to fight with them again.
But I've ninety men and more that are lying sick
   ashore.
I should count myself the coward if I left them, my
   Lord Howard,
To these Inquisition dogs and the devildoms of
   Spain.'

3

So Lord Howard past away with five ships of war
  that day,
Till he melted like a cloud in the silent summer
  heaven;
But Sir Richard bore in hand all his sick men from
  the land
Very carefully and slow,
Men of Bideford in Devon,
And we laid them on the ballast down below;
For we brought them all aboard,
And they blest him in their pain, that they were not
  left to Spain,
To the thumbscrew and the stake, for the glory of the
  Lord.

4

He had only a hundred seamen to work the ship and
  to fight,
And he sailed away from Flores till the Spaniard
  came in sight,
With his huge sea-castles heaving upon the weather
  bow.
' Shall we fight or shall we fly?
Good Sir Richard, tell us now,
For to fight is but to die!
There'll be little of us left by the time this sun be
  set.'
And Sir Richard said again: ' We be all good
  English men.
Let us bang these dogs of Seville, the children of the
  devil,
For I never turn'd my back upon Don or devil
  yet.'

5

Sir Richard spoke and he laugh'd, and we roar'd a
  hurrah, and so
The little *Revenge* ran on sheer into the heart of the
  foe,
With her hundred fighters on deck, and her ninety
  sick below;

For half of their fleet to the right and half to the left
        were seen,
And the little *Revenge* ran on thro' the long sea-lane
        between.

6

Thousands of their soldiers look'd down from their
        decks and laugh'd.
Thousands of their seamen made mock at the mad
        little craft
Running on and on, till delay'd
By their mountain-like *San Philip* that, of fifteen
        hundred tons,
And up-shadowing high above us with her yawning
        tier of guns,
Took the breath from our sails, and we stay'd.

7

And while now the great *San Philip* hung above us
        like a cloud
Whence the thunderbolt will fall
Long and loud,
Four galleons drew away
From the Spanish fleet that day,
And two upon the larboard and two upon the
        starboard lay,
And the battle-thunder broke from them all.

8

But anon the great *San Philip*, she bethought herself
        and went
Having that within her womb that had left her ill
        content;
And the rest they came aboard us, and they fought
        us hand to hand,
For a dozen times they came with their pikes and
        musqueteers,
And a dozen times we shook 'em off as a dog that
        shakes his ears
When he leaps from the water to the land.

9

And the sun went down, and the stars came out far
    over the summer sea,
But never a moment ceased the fight of the one and
    the fifty-three.
Ship after ship, the whole night long, their high-built
    galleons came,
Ship after ship, the whole night long, with her
    battle-thunder and flame;
Ship after ship, the whole night long, drew back with
    her dead and her shame.
For some were sunk and many were shatter'd, and
    so could fight us no more—
God of battles, was ever a battle like this in the
    world before?

10

For he said ' Fight on! fight on! '
Tho' his vessel was all but a wreck;
And it chanced that, when half of the short summer
    night was gone,
With a grisly wound to be drest he had left the
    deck,
But a bullet struck him that was dressing it suddenly
    dead,
And himself he was wounded again in the side and
    the head,
And he said ' Fight on! fight on! '

11

And the night went down, and the sun smiled out
    far over the summer sea,
And the Spanish fleet with broken sides lay round us
    all in a ring;
But they dared not touch us again, for they fear'd
    that we still could sting,
So they watch'd what the end would be.
And we had not fought them in vain,
But in perilous plight were we,
Seeing forty of our poor hundred were slain,

And half of the rest of us maim'd for life
In the crash of the cannonades and the desperate
strife ;
And the sick men down in the hold were most of
them stark and cold,
And the pikes were all broken or bent, and the
powder was all of it spent ;
And the masts and the rigging were lying over the
side ;
But Sir Richard cried in his English pride,
' We have fought such a fight for a day and a night
As may never be fought again !
We have won great glory, my men !
And a day less or more
At sea or ashore,
We die—does it matter when ?
Sink me the ship, Master Gunner—sink her, split
her in twain !
Fall into the hands of God, not into the hands of
Spain ! '

12

And the gunner said, ' Ay, ay,' but the seamen
made reply :
' We have children, we have wives,
And the Lord hath spared our lives.
We will make the Spaniard promise, if we yield, to
let us go ;
We shall live to fight again and to strike another
blow.'
And the lion there lay dying, and they yielded to the
foe.

13

And the stately Spanish men to their flagship bore
him then,
Where they laid him by the mast, old Sir Richard
caught at last,
And they praised him to his face with their courtly
foreign grace ;
But he rose upon their decks, and he cried :

'I have fought for Queen and Faith like a valiant
    man and true;
I have only done my duty as a man is bound to do;
With a joyful spirit I Sir Richard Grenville die!'
And he fell upon their decks, and he died.

14

And they stared at the dead that had been so valiant
    and true,
And had holden the power and glory of Spain so
    cheap
That he dared her with one little ship and his
    English few;
Was he devil or man? He was devil for aught they
    knew,
But they sank his body with honour down into the
    deep,
And they mann'd the *Revenge* with a swarthier alien
    crew,
And away she sail'd with her loss and long'd for her
    own;
When a wind from the lands they had ruin'd awoke
    from sleep,
And the water began to heave and the weather to
    moan,
And or ever that evening ended a great gale blew,
And a wave like the wave that is raised by an earth-
    quake grew,
Till it smote on their hulls and their sails and their
    masts and their flags,
And the whole sea plunged and fell on the shot-
    shattered navy of Spain,
And the little *Revenge* herself went down by the
    island crags
To be lost evermore in the main.

                      Lord Tennyson.

CCCCVII

THE DEATH OF ADMIRAL BLAKE

Laden with spoil of the South, fulfilled with the glory
of achievement,
  And freshly crowned with never-dying fame,
Sweeping by shores where the names are the names
of the victories of England,
  Across the Bay the squadron homeward came.

Proudly they came, but their pride was the pomp of
a funeral at midnight,
  When dreader yet the lonely morrow looms;
Few are the words that are spoken, and faces are
gaunt beneath the torchlight
  That does but darken more the nodding plumes.

Low on the field of his fame, past hope lay the
Admiral triumphant,
  And fain to rest him after all his pain;
Yet for the love that he bore to his own land, ever
unforgotten,
  He prayed to see the western hills again.

Fainter than stars in a sky long gray with the coming
of the daybreak,
  Or sounds of night that fade when night is done,
So in the death-dawn faded the splendour and loud
renown of warfare,
  And life of all its longings kept but one.

' Oh ! to be there for an hour when the shade draws
in beside the hedgerows,
  And falling apples wake the drowsy noon :
Oh ! for the hour when the elms grow sombre and
human in the twilight,
  And gardens dream beneath the rising moon.

' Only to look once more on the land of the memories
of childhood,
  Forgetting weary winds and barren foam :
Only to bid farewell to the combe and the orchard
and the moorland,
  And sleep at last among the fields of home ! '

So he was silently praying, till now, when his
    strength was ebbing faster,
  The Lizard lay before them faintly blue ;
Now on the gleaming horizon the white cliffs laughed
    along the coast-line,
  And now the forelands took the shapes they knew.

There lay the Sound and the Island with green leaves
    down beside the water,
  The town, the Hoe, the masts with sunset fired—
Dreams ! ay, dreams of the dead ! for the great
    heart faltered on the threshold,
  And darkness took the land his soul desired.

Sir H. Newbolt

CCCCVIII

THE SOLDIER

If I should die, think only this of me :
That there's some corner of a foreign field
That is for ever England.   There shall be
In that rich earth a richer dust concealed ;
A dust whom England bore, shaped, made aware,
Gave, once, her flowers to love, her ways to roam,
A body of England's, breathing English air,
Washed by the rivers, blest by suns of home.

And think, this heart, all evil shed away,
A pulse in the eternal mind, no less
Gives somewhere back the thoughts by England
    given ;
Her sights and sounds ; dreams happy as her day ;
And laughter, learnt of friends ; and gentleness,
In hearts at peace, under an English heaven.

R. Brooke

CCCCIX

ANTHEM FOR DOOMED YOUTH

What passing-bells for these who die as cattle ?
Only the monstrous anger of the guns.
Only the stuttering rifles' rapid rattle
Can patter out their hasty orisons.

No mockeries for them; no prayers nor bells,
Nor any voice of mourning save the choirs,—
The shrill, demented choirs of wailing shells;
And bugles calling for them from sad shires.

What candles may be held to speed them all?
Not in the hands of boys, but in their eyes
Shall shine the holy glimmers of good-byes.
The pallor of girls' brows shall be their pall;
Their flowers the tenderness of patient minds,
And each slow dusk a drawing-down of blinds.

W. Owen

CCCCX

Say not the struggle nought availeth,
　　The labour and the wounds are vain,
The enemy faints not, nor faileth,
　　And as things have been they remain.

If hopes were dupes, fears may be liars;
　　It may be, in yon smoke concealed,
Your comrades chase e'en now the fliers,
　　And, but for you, possess the field.

For while the tired waves, vainly breaking,
　　Seem here no painful inch to gain,
Far back, through creeks and inlets making,
　　Comes silent, flooding in, the main.

And not by eastern windows only,
　　When daylight comes, comes in the light,
In front, the sun climbs slow, how slowly,
　　But westward, look, the land is bright!

A. H. Clough

CCCCXI

IN TIME OF 'THE BREAKING OF NATIONS'

Only a man harrowing clods
　　In a slow silent walk
With an old horse that stumbles and nods
　　Half asleep as they stalk.

Only thin smoke without flame
  From the heaps of couch-grass;
Yet this will go onward the same
  Though Dynasties pass.

Yonder a maid and her wight
  Come whispering by:
War's annals will cloud into night
  Ere their story die.
                              T. Hardy

CCCCXII

THE OLD STOIC

Riches I hold in light esteem,
  And Love I laugh to scorn;
And lust of fame was but a dream,
  That vanished with the morn:

And if I pray, the only prayer
  That moves my lips for me
Is, ' Leave the heart that now I bear,
  And give me liberty ! '

Yes, as my swift days near their goal,
  'Tis all that I implore;
In life and death a chainless soul,
  With courage to endure.
                              E. Brontë

CCCCXIII

BY THE STATUE OF KING CHARLES
AT CHARING CROSS

Sombre and rich, the skies;
Great glooms, and starry plains.
Gently the night wind sighs;
Else a vast silence reigns.

The splendid silence clings
Around me: and around
The saddest of all kings
Crowned, and again discrowned.

Comely and calm, he rides
Hard by his own Whitehall :
Only the night wind glides :
No crowds, nor rebels, brawl.

Gone, too, his Court; and yet,
The stars his courtiers are :
Stars in their stations set;
And every wandering star.

Alone he rides, alone,
The fair and fatal king :
Dark night is all his own,
That strange and solemn thing.

Which are more full of fate :
The stars; or those sad eyes ?
Which are more still and great :
Those brows; or the dark skies ?

Although his whole heart yearn
In passionate tragedy :
Never was face so stern
With sweet austerity.

Vanquished in life, his death
By beauty made amends :
The passing of his breath
Won his defeated ends.

Brief life, and hapless ? Nay :
Through death, life grew sublime.
Speak after sentence ? Yea :
And to the end of time.

Armoured he rides, his head
Bare to the stars of doom :
He triumphs now, the dead,
Beholding London's gloom.

Our wearier spirit faints,
Vexed in the world's employ :
His soul was of the saints;
And art to him was joy.

King, tried in fires of woe .
Men hunger for thy grace :
And through the night I go,
Loving thy mournful face.

Yet, when the city sleeps ;
When all the cries are still :
The stars and heavenly deeps
Work out a perfect will.

L. Johnson

CCCCXIV

AFTER AUGHRIM : IRELAND SPEAKS

She said, They gave me of their best,
They lived, they gave their lives for me ;
I tossed them to the howling waste,
And flung them to the foaming sea.

She said, I never gave them aught,
Not mine the power, if mine the will,
I let them starve, I let them bleed,—
They bled and starved, and loved me still.

She said, Ten times they fought for me,
Ten times they strove with might and main,
Ten times I saw them beaten down,
Ten times they rose, and fought again.

She said, I stayed alone at home,
A dreary woman, grey and cold ;
I never asked them how they fared,
Yet still they loved me as of old.

She said, I never called them sons,
I almost ceased to breathe their name,
Then caught it echoing down the wind,
Blown backwards from the lips of Fame.

She said, Not mine, not mine that fame.
Far over sea, far over land,
Cast forth like rubbish from my shores,
They won it yonder, sword in hand.

She said, God knows they owe me nought.
I tossed them to the foaming sea,
I tossed them to the howling waste,
Yet still their love comes home to me.

Hon. E. Lawless

CCCCXV

DARK ROSALEEN

O my Dark Rosaleen,
  Do not sigh, do not weep !
The priests are on the ocean green,
  They march along the deep.
There's wine from the royal Pope,
  Upon the ocean green ;
And Spanish ale shall give you hope,
  My Dark Rosaleen !
  My own Rosaleen !
Shall glad your heart, shall give you hope,
Shall give you health, and help, and hope,
  My Dark Rosaleen !

Over hills, and thro' dales,
  Have I roam'd for your sake ;
All yesterday I sail'd with sails
  On river and on lake.
The Erne, at its highest flood,
  I dash'd across unseen.
For there was lightning in my blood,
  My Dark Rosaleen !
  My own Rosaleen !
O, there was lightning in my blood,
Red lightning lighten'd thro' my blood,
  My Dark Rosaleen !

All day long, in unrest,
  To and fro do I move.
The very soul within my breast
  Is wasted for you, love !
The heart in my bosom faints
  To think of you, my Queen,

My life of life, my saint of saints,
   My Dark Rosaleen !
   My own Rosaleen !
To hear your sweet and sad complaints,
My life, my love, my saint of saints,
   My Dark Rosaleen !

Woe and pain, pain and woe,
   Are my lot, night and noon,
To see your bright face clouded so,
   Like to the mournful moon.
But yet will I rear your throne
   Again in golden sheen;
'Tis you shall reign, shall reign alone,
   My Dark Rosaleen !
   My own Rosaleen !
'Tis you shall have the golden throne,
'Tis you shall reign, and reign alone,
   My Dark Rosaleen !

Over dews, over sands,
   Will I fly, for your weal :
Your holy delicate white hands
   Shall girdle me with steel.
At home, in your emerald bowers,
   From morning's dawn till e'en,
You'll pray for me, my flower of flowers,
   My Dark Rosaleen !
   My fond Rosaleen !
You'll think of me thro' daylight hours,
My virgin flower, my flower of flowers,
   My Dark Rosaleen !

I could scale the blue air,
   I could plough the high hills,
O, I could kneel all night in prayer,
   To heal your many ills !
And one beamy smile from you
   Would float like light between
My toils and me, my own, my true,
   My Dark Rosaleen !
   My fond Rosaleen !

Would give me life and soul anew
A second life, a soul anew,
  My Dark Rosaleen !

O, the Erne shall run red,
  With redundance of blood,
The earth shall rock beneath our tread,
  And flames wrap hill and wood,
And gun-peal and slogan-cry
  Wake many a glen serene,
Ere you shall fade, ere you shall die,
  My Dark Rosaleen !
  My own Rosaleen !
The Judgment Hour must first be nigh,
Ere you can fade, ere you can die,
  My Dark Rosaleen !

                              J. C. Mangan

THE SHRINE

There is a shrine whose golden gate
  Was opened by the Hand of God ;
It stands serene, inviolate,
  Though millions have its pavement trod ;
As fresh, as when the first sunrise
Awoke the lark in Paradise

'Tis compassed with the dust and toil
  Of common days, yet should there fall
A single speck, a single soil
  Upon the whiteness of its wall,
The angels' tears in tender rain
Would make the temple theirs again.

Without, the world is tired and old,
  But, once within the enchanted door,
The mists of time are backward rolled,
  And creeds and ages are no more ;
But all the human-hearted meet
In one communion vast and sweet.

I enter—all is simply fair,
  Nor incense-clouds, nor carven throne;
But in the fragrant morning air
  A gentle lady sits alone;
My mother—ah! whom should I see
Within, save ever only thee?

                  D. M. Dolben

CCCCXVII

THE MORNING MOON

'Twas when the op'ning dawn was still,
I took my lonely road, uphill,
Toward the eastern sky, in gloom,
Or touch'd with palest primrose bloom;
And there the moon, at morning break,
Though yet unset, was gleaming weak,
And fresh'ning air began to pass,
All voiceless, over darksome grass,
      Before the sun
      Had yet begun
To dazzle down the morning moon.

By Maycreech hillock lay the cows,
Below the ash-trees' nodding boughs,
And water fell, from block to block
Of mossy stone, down Burncleeve rock,
By poplar-trees that stood, as slim
'S a feather, by the stream's green brim;
And down about the mill, that stood
Half darken'd off below the wood,
      The rambling brook,
      From nook to nook,
Flow'd on below the morning moon.

At mother's house I made a stand,
Where no one stirr'd with foot or hand;
No smoke above the chimney reek'd,
No winch above the well-mouth creak'd;
No casement open'd out, to catch
The air below the eaves of thatch;

Nor down before her cleanly floor
Had open'd back her heavy door;
    And there the catch,
    With fasten'd latch,
Stood close, below the morning moon.

And she, dear soul, so good and kind,
Had holden long, in my young mind,
Of holy thoughts the highest place
Of honour, for her love and grace.
But now my wife, to heart and sight,
May seem to shine a fuller light;
And as the sun may rise to view,
To dim the moon, from pale to blue,
    My comely bride
    May seem to hide
My mother, now my morning moon.

W. Barnes

CCCCXVIII

MOTHER AND SON

Now sleeps the land of houses,
And dead night holds the street,
And there thou liest, my baby,
And sleepest soft and sweet;
My man is away for awhile,
But safe and alone we lie,
And none heareth thy breath but thy mother,
And the moon looking down from the sky
On the weary waste of the town,
As it looked on the grass-edged road
Still warm with yesterday's sun,
When I left my old abode;
Hand in hand with my love,
That night of all night in the year;
When the river of love o'erflowed
And drowned all doubt and fear,
And we two were alone in the world,
And once if never again,
We knew of the secret of earth
And the tale of its labour and pain.

Lo amidst London I lift thee,
And how little and light thou art,
And thou without hope or fear
Thou fear and hope of my heart!
Lo there thy body beginning,
O son, and thy soul and thy life;
But how will it be if thou livest,
And enterest into the strife,
And in love we dwell together
When the man is grown in thee,
When thy sweet speech I shall hearken,
And yet 'twixt thee and me
Shall rise that wall of distance,
That round each one doth grow,
And maketh it hard and bitter
Each other's thought to know?
Now, therefore, while yet thou art little
And hast no thought of thine own,
I will tell thee a word of the world;
Of the hope whence thou hast grown;
Of the love that once begat thee,
Of the sorrow that hath made
Thy little heart of hunger,
And thy hands on my bosom laid,
Then mayst thou remember hereafter,
As whiles when people say
All this hath happened before
In the life of another day;
So mayest thou dimly remember
This tale of thy mother's voice,
As oft in the calm of dawning
I have heard the birds rejoice,
As oft I have heard the storm-wind
Go moaning through the wood;
And I knew that earth was speaking,
And the mother's voice was good.

Now, to thee alone will I tell it
That thy mother's body is fair,
In the guise of the country maidens
Who play with the sun and the air;
Who have stood in the row of the reapers

In the August afternoon,
Who have sat by the frozen water
In the high day of the moon,
When the lights of the Christmas feasting
Were dead in the house on the hill,
And the wild-geese gone to the salt-marsh
Had left the winter still.
Yea, I am fair, my firstling;
If thou couldst but remember me!
The hair that thy small hand clutcheth
Is a goodly sight to see;
I am true, but my face is a snare:
Soft and deep are my eyes,
And they seem for men's beguiling
Fulfilled with the dreams of the wise.
Kind are my lips, and they look
As though my soul had learned
Deep things I have never heard of.
My face and my hands are burned
By the lovely sun of the acres;
Three months of London town
And thy birth-bed have bleached them indeed,
' But lo, where the edge of the gown '
(So said thy father) ' is parting
The wrist that is white as the curd
From the brown of the hand that I love,
Bright as the wing of a bird.'

Such is thy mother, O firstling,
Yet strong as the maidens of old,
Whose spears and whose swords were the warders
Of homestead, of field and of fold.
Oft were my feet on the highway,
Often they wearied the grass;
From dusk unto dusk of the summer
Three times in a week would I pass
To the downs from the house on the river
Through the waves of the blossoming corn.
Fair then I lay down in the even,
And fresh I arose on the morn,
And scarce in the noon was I weary.
Ah, son, in the days of thy strife.

If thy soul could but harbour a dream
Of the blossom of my life !
It would be as the sunlit meadows
Beheld from a tossing sea,
And the soul should look on a vision
Of the peace that is to be.

Yet, yet the tears on my cheek !
And what is this doth move
My heart to thy heart, beloved,
Save the flood of yearning love ?
For fair and fierce is thy father,
And soft and strange are his eyes
That look on the days that shall be
With the hope of the brave and the wise.
It was many a day that we laughed,
As over the meadows we walked,
And many a day I hearkened
And the pictures came as he talked ;
It was many a day that we longed,
And we lingered late at eve
Ere speech from speech was sundered,
And my hand his hand could leave.
Then I wept when I was alone,
And I longed till the daylight came ;
And down the stairs I stole,
And there was our housekeeping dame
(No mother of me, the foundling)
Kindling the fire betimes
Ere the haymaking folk went forth
To the meadows down by the limes ;
All things I saw at a glance ;
The quickening fire-tongues leapt
Through the crackling heap of sticks,
And the sweet smoke up from it crept,
And close to the very hearth
The low sun flooded the floor,
And the cat and her kittens played
In the sun by the open door.
The garden was fair in the morning,
And there in the road he stood
Beyond the crimson daisies

And the bush of southernwood.
Then side by side together
Through the grey-walled place we went,
And O the fear departed,
And the rest and sweet content !

Son, sorrow and wisdom he taught me,
And sore I grieved and learned
As we twain grew into one ;
And the heart within me burned
With the very hopes of his heart.
Ah, son, it is piteous,
But never again in my life
Shall I dare to speak to thee thus ;
So may these lonely words
About thee creep and cling,
These words of the lonely night
In the days of our wayfaring.
Many a child of woman
To-night is born in the town,
The desert of folly and wrong ;
And of what and whence are they grown ?
Many and many an one
Of wont and use is born ;
For a husband is taken to bed
As a hat or ribbon is worn.
Prudence begets her thousands ;
' Good is a housekeeper's life,
So shall I sell my body
That I may be matron and wife.'
' And I shall endure foul wedlock
And bear the children of need.'
Some are there born of hate,
Many the children of greed.
' I, I too can be wedded,
Though thou my love hast got.'
' I am fair and hard of heart,
And riches shall be my lot.'
And all these are the good and the happy,
On whom the world dawns fair.
O son, when wilt thou learn
Of those that are born of despair,

As the fabled mud of the Nile
That quickens under the sun
With a growth of creeping things,
Half dead when just begun?
E'en such is the care of Nature
That man should never die,
Though she breed of the fools of the earth,
And the dregs of the city sty.
But thou, O son, O son,
Of very love wert born,
When our hope fulfilled bred hope,
And fear was a folly outworn.
On the eve of the toil and the battle
All sorrow and grief we weighed,
We hoped and we were not ashamed,
We knew and we were not afraid.

Now waneth the night and the moon;
Ah, son, it is piteous
That never again in my life
Shall I dare to speak to thee thus.
But sure from the wise and the simple
Shall the mighty come to birth;
And fair were my fate, beloved,
If I be yet on the earth
When the world is awaken at last,
And from mouth to mouth they tell
Of thy love and thy deeds and thy valour,
And thy hope that nought can quell.

W. Morris

CCCCXIX

AIRLY BEACON

Airly Beacon, Airly Beacon;
 Oh the pleasant sight to see
Shires and towns from Airly Beacon,
 While my love climbed up to me!

Airly Beacon, Airly Beacon;
 Oh the happy hours we lay
Deep in fern on Airly Beacon,
 Courting through the summer's day!

Airly Beacon, Airly Beacon;
    Oh the weary haunt for me,
All alone on Airly Beacon,
    With his baby on my knee !

C. Kingsley

CCCCXX

THE TOYS

My little son, who look'd from thoughtful eyes
And moved and spoke in quiet grown-up wise,
Having my law the seventh time disobey'd,
I struck him, and dismiss'd
With hard words and unkiss'd,
His Mother, who was patient, being dead.
Then, fearing lest his grief should hinder sleep,
I visited his bed,
But found him slumbering deep,
With darken'd eyelids, and their lashes yet
From his late sobbing wet.
And I, with moan,
Kissing away his tears, left others of my own;
For, on a table drawn beside his head,
He had put, within his reach,
A box of counters and a red-vein'd stone,
A piece of glass abraded by the beach
And six or seven shells,
A bottle with bluebells,
And two French copper coins, ranged there with
    careful art,
To comfort his sad heart.
So when that night I pray'd
To God, I wept, and said :
Ah, when at last we lie with trancèd breath,
Not vexing Thee in death,
And thou rememberest of what toys
We made our joys,
How weakly understood,
Thy great commanded good,

Then, fatherly not less
Than I whom thou hast moulded from the clay,
Thou'lt leave Thy wrath, and say,
' I will be sorry for their childishness.'

C. Patmore

CCCCXXI

THE BLESSED DAMOZEL

The blessed damozel leaned out
    From the gold bar of Heaven;
Her eyes were deeper than the depth
    Of waters stilled at even;
She had three lilies in her hand,
    And the stars in her hair were seven.

Her robe, ungirt from clasp to hem,
    No wrought flowers did adorn,
But a white rose of Mary's gift,
    For service meetly worn;
Her hair that lay along her back
    Was yellow like ripe corn.

Herseemed she scarce had been a day
    One of God's choristers;
The wonder was not yet quite gone
    From that still look of hers;
Albeit, to them she left, her day
    Had counted as ten years.

(To one, it is ten years of years.
    . . . . Yet now, and in this place,
Surely she leaned o'er me—her hair
    Fell all about my face. . . .
Nothing : the autumn-fall of leaves.
    The whole year sets apace.)

It was the rampart of God's house
    That she was standing on;
By God built over the sheer depth
    The which is Space begun;
So high, that looking downward thence
    She scarce could see the sun.

It lies in Heaven, across the flood
   Of ether, as a bridge.
Beneath, the tides of day and night
   With flame and darkness ridge
The void, as low as where this earth
   Spins like a fretful midge.

Around her, lovers, newly met
   'Mid deathless love's acclaims,
Spoke evermore among themselves
   Their heart-remembered names;
And the souls mounting up to God
   Went by her like thin flames.

And still she bowed herself and stooped
   Out of the circling charm;
Until her bosom must have made
   The bar she leaned on warm,
And the lilies lay as if asleep
   Along her bended arm.

From the fixed place of Heaven she saw
   Time like a pulse shake fierce
Through all the worlds.   Her gaze still strove
   Within the gulf to pierce
Its path; and now she spoke as when
   The stars sang in their spheres.

The sun was gone now; the curled moon
   Was like a little feather
Fluttering far down the gulf; and now
   She spoke through the still weather.
Her voice was like the voice the stars
   Had when they sang together.

(Ah sweet !   Even now, in that bird's song
   Strove not her accents there,
Fain to be hearkened ?   When those bells
   Possessed the midday air,
Strove not her steps to reach my side
   Down all the echoing stair ?)

'I wish that he were come to me,
  For he will come,' she said.
'Have I not prayed in Heaven?—on earth,
  Lord, Lord, has he not pray'd?
Are not two prayers a perfect strength?
  And shall I feel afraid?

'When round his head the aureole clings,
  And he is clothed in white,
I'll take his hand and go with him
  To the deep wells of light;
As unto a stream we will step down,
  And bathe there in God's sight.

'We two will stand beside that shrine,
  Occult, withheld, untrod,
Whose lamps are stirred continually
  With prayer sent up to God;
And see our old prayers, granted, melt
  Each like a little cloud.

'We two will lie i' the shadow of
  That living mystic tree
Within whose secret growth the Dove
  Is sometimes felt to be,
While every leaf that His plumes touch
  Saith His Name audibly.

'And I myself will teach to him,
  I myself, lying so,
The songs I sing here; which his voice
  Shall pause in, hushed and slow,
And find some knowledge at each pause,
  Or some new thing to know.'

(Alas! we two, we two, thou say'st!
  Yea, one wast thou with me,
That once of old. But shall God lift
  To endless unity
The soul whose likeness with thy soul
  Was but its love for thee?)

' We two,' she said, ' will seek the groves
    Where the lady Mary is,
With her five handmaidens, whose names
    Are five sweet symphonies,
Cecily, Gertrude, Magdalen.
    Margaret and Rosalys.

' Circlewise sit they, with bound locks
    And foreheads garlanded;
Into the fine cloth white like flame
    Weaving the golden thread,
To fashion the birth-robes for them
    Who are just born, being dead.

He shall fear, haply, and be dumb
    Then will I lay my cheek
To his, and tell about our love,
    Not once abashed or weak;
And the dear Mother will approve
    My pride, and let me speak.

' Herself shall bring us, hand in hand,
    To Him round whom all souls
Kneel, the clear-ranged unnumbered heads
    Bowed with their aureoles:
And angels meeting us shall sing
    To their citherns and citoles.

' There will I ask of Christ the Lord
    Thus much for him and me:—
Only to live as once on earth
    With Love,—only to be,
As then awhile, for ever now
    Together, I and he.'

She gazed and listened and then said,
    Less sad of speech than mild,—
' All this is when he comes.' She ceased.
    The light thrilled towards her, fill'd
With angels in strong level flight.
    Her eyes prayed, and she smil'd.

(I saw her smile.)　　But soon their path
　　Was vague in distant spheres :
And then she cast her arms along
　　The golden barriers,
And laid her face between her hands,
　　And wept.　(I heard her tears.)

D. G. Rossetti

CCCCXXII

When our two souls stand up erect and strong,
Face to face, silent, drawing nigh and nigher,
Until the lengthening wings break into fire
At either curvèd point,—what bitter wrong
Can the earth do to us, that we should not long
Be here contented ?　Think.　In mounting higher,
The angels would press on us, and aspire
To drop some golden orb of perfect song
Into our deep dear silence.　Let us stay
Rather on earth, Beloved, where the unfit
Contrarious moods of men recoil away
And isolate pure spirits, and permit
A place to stand and love in for a day,
With darkness and the death-hour rounding it.

E. B. Browning

CCCCXXIII

CORRELATED GREATNESS

O nothing, in this corporal earth of man,
That to the imminent heaven of his high soul
Responds with colour and with shadow, can
Lack correlated greatness.　If the scroll
Where thoughts lie fast in spell of hieroglyph
Be mighty through its mighty habitants ;
If God be in His Name ; grave potence if
The sounds unbind of hieratic chants ;
All's vast that vastness means.　Nay, I affirm
Nature is whole in her least things exprest,

Nor know we with what scope God builds the worm.
Our towns are copied fragments from our breast;
And all man's Babylons strive to impart
The grandeurs of his Babylonian heart.

F. Thompson

CCCCXXIV

OMAR'S LAMENT

Alas, that Spring should vanish with the Rose!
That Youth's sweet-scented Manuscript should close!
     The Nightingale that in the branches sang,
Ah, whence, and whither flown again, who knows!

Ah Love! could thou and I with Fate conspire
To grasp this sorry Scheme of Things entire,
     Would not we shatter it to bits—and then
Re-mould it nearer to the Heart's Desire?

E. FitzGerald

CCCCXXV

MIMNERMUS IN CHURCH

You promise heavens free from strife,
     Pure truth, and perfect change of will;
But sweet, sweet is this human life,
     So sweet, I fain would breathe it still;
Your chilly stars I can forgo,
This warm kind world is all I know.

You say there is no substance here,
     One great reality above:
Back from that void I shrink in fear,
     And child-like hide myself in love:
Show me what angels feel.   Till then,
I cling, a mere weak man, to men.

You bid me lift my mean desires
     From faltering lips and fitful veins
To sexless souls, ideal quires,
     Unwearied voices, wordless strains:

My mind with fonder welcome owns
One dear dead friend's remembered tones.

Forsooth the present we must give
  To that which cannot pass away;
All beauteous things for which we live
  By laws of time and space decay.
But oh, the very reason why
I clasp them, is because they die.

W. Cory

CCCCXXVI

LOVE AMONG THE RUINS

Where the quiet-coloured end of evening smiles,
    Miles and miles
On the solitary pastures where our sheep
    Half-asleep
Tinkle homeward thro' the twilight, stray or stop
    As they crop—
Was the site once of a city great and gay,
    (So they say)
Of our country's very capital, its prince
    Ages since
Held his court in, gathered councils, wielding far
    Peace or war.

Now,—the country does not even boast a tree,
    As you see,
To distinguish slopes of verdure, certain rills
    From the hills
Intersect and give a name to (else they run
    Into one)
Where the domed and daring palace shot its spires
    Up like fires
O'er the hundred-gated circuit of a wall
    Bounding all,
Made of marble, men might march on nor be pressed,
    Twelve abreast.

And such plenty and perfection, see, of grass
        Never was !
Such a carpet as, this summer-time, o'erspreads
        And embeds
Every vestige of the city, guessed alone,
        Stock or stone—
Where a multitude of men breathed joy and woe
        Long ago ;
Lust of glory pricked their hearts up, dread of
        shame
        Struck them tame ;
And that glory and that shame alike, the gold
        Bought and sold.

Now,—the single little turret that remains
        On the plains,
By the caper overrooted, by the gourd
        Overscored,
While the patching houseleek's head of blossom
        winks
        Through the chinks—
Marks the basement whence a tower in ancient time
        Sprang sublime,
And a burning ring, all round, the chariots traced
        As they raced,
And the monarch and his minions and his dames
        Viewed the games.

And I know, while thus the quiet-coloured eve
        Smiles to leave
To their folding, all our many-tinkling fleece
        In such peace,
And the slopes and rills in undistinguished grey
        Melt away—
That a girl with eager eyes and yellow hair
        Waits me there
In the turret whence the charioteers caught soul
        For the goal,
When the king looked, where she looks now,
        breathless, dumb
        Till I come.

But he looked upon the city, every side,
          Far and wide,
All the mountains topped with temples, all the
     glades'
          Colonnades,
All the causeys, bridges, aqueducts,—and then,
          All the men !
When I do come, she will speak not, she will stand,
          Either hand
On my shoulder, give her eyes the first embrace
          Of my face,
Ere we rush, ere we extinguish sight and speech
          Each on each.

In one year they sent a million fighters forth
          South and North,
And they built their gods a brazen pillar high
          As the sky,
Yet reserved a thousand chariots in full force—
          Gold, of course.
Oh heart ! oh blood that freezes, blood that burns !
          Earth's returns
For whole centuries of folly, noise and sin !
          Shut them in,
With their triumphs and their glories and the rest !
          Love is best.
                                        R. Browning

CCCCXXVII

THE PAGAN WORLD

In his cool hall, with haggard eyes
The Roman noble lay;
He drove abroad, in furious guise,
Along the Appian way.

He made a feast, drank fierce and fast
And crown'd his hair with flowers—
No easier nor no quicker pass'd
The impracticable hours.

The brooding East with awe beheld
Her impious younger world.
The Roman tempest swell'd and swell'd,
And on her head was hurl'd.

The East bow'd low before the blast
In patient, deep disdain;
She let the legions thunder past
And plunged in thought again.

So well she mused, a morning broke
Across her spirit grey;
A conquering, new-born joy awoke,
And fill'd her life with day.

' Poor world,' she cried, ' so deep accurst,
That runn'st from pole to pole
To seek a draught to slake thy thirst—
Go, seek it in thy soul ! '

She heard it, the victorious West,
In crown and sword array'd !
She felt the void which mined her breast,
She shiver'd and obey'd.

She veil'd her eagles, snapp'd her sword,
And laid her sceptre down;
Her stately purple she abhorr'd,
And her imperial crown.

She broke her flutes, she stopp'd her sports,
Her artists could not please;
She tore her books, she shut her courts,
She fled her palaces;

Lust of the eye and pride of life
She left it all behind,
And hurried, torn with inward strife,
The wilderness to find.

Tears wash'd the trouble from her face !
She changed into a child !
'Mid weeds and wrecks she stood—a place
Of ruin—but she smiled !

M. Arnold

CCCCXXVIII

THE SOUL SUPREME

' Yet between life and death are hours
To flush with love and hide in flowers;
　　What profit save in these?' men cry:
　　' Ah, see, between soft earth and sky,
What only good things here are ours!'
　They say, ' What better would'st thou try,
What sweeter sing of? or what powers
　　Serve, that will give thee ere thou die
More joy to sing and be less sad,
More heart to play and grow more glad?'

Play then and sing; we too have played,
We likewise, in that subtle shade.
　　We too have twisted through our hair
　　Such tendrils as the wild Loves wear,
And heard what mirth the Maenads made,
　　Till the wind blew our garlands bare
And left their roses disarrayed,
　　And smote the summer with strange air,
And disengirdled and discrowned
The limbs and locks that vine-wreaths bound.

We too have tracked by star-proof trees
The tempest of the Thyiades
　　Scare the loud night on hills that hid
　　The blood-feasts of the Bassarid,
Heard their song's iron cadences
　　Fright the wolf hungering from the kid,
Outroar the lion-throated seas,
　　Outchide the north-wind if it chid,
And hush the torrent-tongued ravines
With thunders of their tambourines.

But the fierce flute whose notes acclaim
Dim goddesses of fiery fame,
　　Cymbal and clamorous kettledrum,
　　Timbrels and tabrets, all are dumb

That turned the high chill air to flame;
  The singing tongues of fire are numb
That called on Cotys by her name
  Edonian, till they felt her come
And maddened, and her mystic face
Lightened along the streams of Thrace.

For Pleasure slumberless and pale,
And Passion with rejected veil,
  Pass, and the tempest-footed throng
Of hours that follow them with song
Till their feet flag and voices fail,
  And lips that were so loud so long
Learn silence, or a wearier wail;
  So keen is change, and time so strong,
To weave the robes of life and rend
And weave again till life have end.

But weak is change, but strengthless time
To take the light from heaven, or climb
  The hills of heaven with wasting feet.
  Songs they can stop that earth found meet,
But the stars keep their ageless rhyme;
  Flowers they can slay that spring thought sweet,
But the stars keep their spring sublime;
  Passions and pleasures can defeat,
Actions and agonies control,
And life and death; but not the soul.

                              A. C. Swinburne

CCCCXXIX

DOVER BEACH

The sea is calm to-night.
The tide is full, the moon lies fair
Upon the straits;—on the French coast the light
Gleams and is gone; the cliffs of England stand,
Glimmering and vast, out in the tranquil bay.
Come to the window, sweet is the night air!
Only, from the long line of spray
Where the sea meets the moon-blanch'd land,

Listen ! you hear the grating roar
Of pebbles which the waves draw back, and fling,
At their return, up the high strand,
Begin, and cease, and then again begin,
With tremulous cadence slow, and bring
The eternal note of sadness in.

Sophocles long ago
Heard it on the Aegean, and it brought
Into his mind the turbid ebb and flow
Of human misery; we
Find also in the sound a thought,
Hearing it by this distant northern sea.

The Sea of Faith
Was once, too, at the full, and round earth's shore
Lay like the folds of a bright girdle furl'd.
But now I only hear
Its melancholy, long, withdrawing roar,
Retreating, to the breath
Of the night wind, down the vast edges drear
And naked shingles of the world.

Ah, love, let us be true
To one another ! for the world, which seems
To lie before us like a land of dreams,
So various, so beautiful, so new,
Hath really neither joy, nor love, nor light,
Nor certitude, nor peace, nor help for pain;
And we are here as on a darkling plain
Swept with confused alarms of struggle and flight
Where ignorant armies clash by night.

M. Arnold

CCCCXXX

There rolls the deep where grew the tree.
    O earth, what changes hast thou seen !
    There where the long street roars, hath been
The stillness of the central sea.

The hills are shadows, and they flow
    From form to form, and nothing stands;
    They melt like mist, the solid lands,
Like clouds they shape themselves and go.

But in my spirit will I dwell,
    And dream my dream, and hold it true;
    For tho' my lips may breathe adieu
I cannot think the thing farewell.

                    Lord Tennyson

CCCCXXXI

CLOUDS

Down the blue night the unending columns press
In noiseless tumult, break and wave and flow,
Now tread the far South, or lift rounds of snow
Up to the white moon's hidden loveliness.
Some pause in their grave wandering comradeless,
And turn with profound gesture vague and slow,
As who would pray good for the world, but know
Their benediction empty as they bless.

They say that the Dead die not, but remain
Near to the rich heirs of their grief and mirth.
I think they ride the calm mid-heaven, as these,
In wise majestic melancholy train,
And watch the moon, and the still raging seas,
And men, coming and going on the earth.

                    R. Brooke

CCCCXXXII

A FAREWELL

Flow down, cold rivulet, to the sea,
    Thy tribute wave deliver:
No more by thee my steps shall be,
    For ever and for ever.

Flow, softly flow, by lawn and lea,
    A rivulet then a river:
No where by thee my steps shall be,
    For ever and for ever.

But here will sigh thine alder tree,
  And here thine aspen shiver;
And here by thee will hum the bee
  For ever and for ever.

A thousand suns will stream on thee,
  A thousand moons will quiver;
But not by thee my steps shall be,
  For ever and for ever.
                        Lord Tennyson

CCCCXXXIII

DREAM LAND

Where sunless rivers weep
Their waves into the deep,
She sleeps a charmèd sleep:
  Awake her not.
Led by a single star,
She came from very far
To seek where shadows are
  Her pleasant lot.

She left the rosy morn,
She left the fields of corn,
For twilight cold and lorn
  And water springs.
Through sleep, as through a veil
She sees the sky look pale,
And hears the nightingale
  That sadly sings.

Rest, rest, a perfect rest
Shed over brow and breast;
Her face is toward the west,
  The purple land.
She cannot see the grain
Ripening on hill and plain;
She cannot feel the rain
  Upon her hand.

Rest, rest, for evermore
Upon a mossy shore;
Rest, rest at the heart's core
   Till time shall cease :
Sleep that no pain shall wake;
Night that no morn shall break,
Till joy shall overtake
   Her perfect peace.

C. G. Rossetti

CCCCXXXIV

DEPARTURE

It was not like your great and gracious ways !
Do you, that have nought other to lament,
Never, my Love, repent
Of how, that July afternoon,
You went,
With sudden, unintelligible phrase,
And frighten'd eye,
Upon your journey of so many days,
Without a single kiss, or a good-bye?
I knew, indeed, that you were parting soon ;
And so we sate, within the low sun's rays,
You whispering to me, for your voice was weak,
Your harrowing praise.
Well, it was well,
To hear you such things speak,
And I could tell
What made your eyes a glowing gloom of love,
As a warm South-wind sombres a March grove.
And it was like your great and gracious ways
To turn your talk on daily things, my Dear,
Lifting the luminous, pathetic lash
To let the laughter flash,
Whilst I drew near,
Because you spoke so low that I could scarcely hear.
But all at once to leave me at the last,
More at the wonder than the loss aghast,

With huddled, unintelligible phrase,
And frighten'd eye,
And go your journey of all days
With not one kiss, or a good-bye,
And the only loveless look the look with which you
    pass'd :
'Twas all unlike your great and gracious ways.

C. Patmore

CCCCXXXV

REMEMBRANCE

Cold in the earth—and the deep snow piled above
    thee,
Far, far, removed, cold in the dreary grave !
Have I forgot, my only Love, to love thee,
Severed at last by Time's all-severing wave ?

Now, when alone, do my thoughts no longer hover
Over the mountains, on that northern shore,
Resting their wings where heath and fern-leaves
    cover
Thy noble heart for ever, ever more ?

Cold in the earth—and fifteen wild Decembers,
From those brown hills, have melted into spring :
Faithful, indeed, is the spirit that remembers
After such years of change and suffering !

Sweet Love of youth, forgive, if I forget thee,
While the world's tide is bearing me along;
Other desires and other hopes beset me,
Hopes which obscure, but cannot do thee wrong !

No later light has lightened up my heaven,
No second morn has ever shone for me;
All my life's bliss from thy dear life was given,
All my life's bliss is in the grave with thee.

But, when the days of golden dreams had perished,
And even Despair was powerless to destroy;
Then did I learn how existence could be cherished,
Strengthened and fed without the aid of joy.

Then did I check the tears of useless passion—
Weaned my young soul from yearning after thine;
Sternly denied its burning wish to hasten
Down to that tomb already more than mine.

And, even yet, I dare not let it languish,
Dare not indulge in memory's rapturous pain;
Once drinking deep of that divinest anguish,
How could I seek the empty world again?

E. Brontë

CCCCXXXVI

NOVEMBER

The feathers of the willow
Are half of them grown yellow
    Above the swelling stream;
And ragged are the bushes,
And rusty now the rushes,
    And wild the clouded gleam.

The thistle now is older,
His stalk begins to moulder,
    His head is white as snow;
The branches all are barer,
The linnet's song is rarer,
    The robin pipeth now.

R. W. Dixon

CCCCXXXVII

THE DYING YEAR

A spirit haunts the year's last hours
Dwelling amid these yellowing bowers:
    To himself he talks;
For at eventide, listening earnestly,
At his work you may hear him sob and sigh
    In the walks;
    Earthward he boweth the heavy stalks
Of the mouldering flowers:
    Heavily hangs the broad sunflower
      Over its grave i' the earth so chilly
    Heavily hangs the hollyhock,
      Heavily hangs the tiger-lily.

The air is damp, and hush'd, and close,
As a sick man's room when he taketh repose
    An hour before death;
My very heart faints and my whole soul grieves
At the moist rich smell of the rotting leaves,
    And the breath
    Of the fading edges of box beneath,
And the year's last rose.
    Heavily hangs the broad sunflower
      Over its grave i' the earth so chilly;
    Heavily hangs the hollyhock,
      Heavily hangs the tiger-lily.
               Lord Tennyson

CCCCXXXVIII

THE DARKLING THRUSH

I leant upon a coppice gate
    When Frost was spectre-gray,
And Winter's dregs made desolate
    The weakening eye of day.
The tangled bine-stems scored the sky
    Like strings of broken lyres,
And all mankind that haunted nigh
    Had sought their household fires.

The land's sharp features seemed to be
    The Century's corpse outleant,
His crypt the cloudy canopy,
    The wind his death-lament.
The ancient pulse of germ and birth
    Was shrunken hard and dry,
And every spirit upon earth
    Seemed fervourless as I.

At once a voice arose among
    The bleak twigs overhead
In a full-hearted evensong
    Of joy illimited;
An aged thrush, frail, gaunt, and small,
    In blast-beruffled plume,
Had chosen thus to fling his soul
    Upon the growing gloom.

So little cause for carollings
　　Of such ecstatic sound
Was written on terrestrial things
　　Afar or nigh around,
That I could think there trembled through
　　His happy good-night air
Some blessed Hope, whereof he knew
　　And I was unaware.

T. Hardy

CCCCXXXIX

CHILD'S SONG

What is gold worth, say,
Worth for work or play,
Worth to keep or pay,
Hide or throw away,
　　Hope about or fear?
What is love worth, pray?
　　Worth a tear?

Golden on the mould
Lie the dead leaves roll'd
Of the wet woods old,
Yellow leaves and cold,
　　Woods without a dove;
Gold is worth but gold;
　　Love's worth love.

A. C. Swinburne

CCCCXL

DIRGE IN WOODS

A wind sways the pines,
　　And below
Not a breath of wild air;
Still as the mosses that glow
On the flooring and over the lines
Of the roots here and there
The pine-tree drops its dead;
They are quiet, as under the sea.
Overhead, overhead

Rushes life in a race,
As the clouds the clouds chase ;
    And we go,
And we drop like the fruits of the tree,
      Even we,
      Even so.
          G. Meredith

CCCCXLI

REQUIEM

Under the wide and starry sky,
Dig the grave and let me lie.
Glad did I live and gladly die
    And I laid me down with a will.

This be the verse you grave for me :
Here he lies where he longed to be ;
Home is the sailor, home from sea,
    And the hunter home from the hill.
          R. L. Stevenson

CCCCXLII

I strove with none, for none was worth my strife,
  Nature I loved and, next to Nature, Art :
I warm'd both hands before the fire of life ;
  It sinks, and I am ready to depart.
          W. S. Landor

CCCCXLIII

A DEDICATION

My new-cut ashlar takes the light
  Where crimson-blank the windows flare :
By my own work, before the night,
  Great Overseer, I make my prayer.

If there be good in that I wrought,
  Thy hand compelled it, Master, Thine ;
Where I have failed to meet Thy thought
  I know, through Thee, the blame was mine.

One instant's toil to Thee denied
  Stands all Eternity's offence;
Of that I did with Thee to guide
  To Thee, through Thee, be excellence.

The depth and dream of my desire,
  The bitter paths wherein I stray,
Thou knowest Who hast made the Fire,
  Thou knowest who hast made the Clay.

Who, lest all thought of Eden fade,
  Bring'st Eden to the craftsman's brain,
Godlike to muse o'er his own Trade
  And manlike stand with God again!

One stone the more swings into place
  In that dread Temple of Thy worth—
It is enough that through Thy grace
  I saw naught common on Thy earth.

Take not that vision from my ken;
  O, whatsoe'er may spoil or speed,
Help me to need no aid from men,
  That I may help such men as need!

                              R. Kipling

CCCCXLIV

REQUIESCAT

Strew on her roses, roses,
  And never a spray of yew!
In quiet she reposes:
  Ah, would that I did too!

Her mirth the world required;
  She bathed it in smiles of glee.
But her heart was tired, tired,
  And now they let her be.

Her life was turning, turning,
  In mazes of heat and sound.
But for peace her soul was yearning,
  And now peace laps her round.

Her cabin'd, ample spirit,
    It flutter'd and fail'd for breath.
To-night it doth inherit
    The vasty hall of death.

                                M. Arnold

CCCCXLV

CROSSING THE BAR

Sunset and evening star,
    And one clear call for me!
And may there be no moaning of the bar,
    When I put out to sea.

But such a tide as moving seems asleep,
    Too full for sound and foam,
When that which drew from out the boundless
        deep
    Turns again home.

Twilight and evening bell,
    And after that the dark!
And may there be no sadness of farewell,
    When I embark;

For tho' from out our bourne of Time and Place
    The flood may bear me far,
I hope to see my Pilot face to face
    When I have crost the bar.

                                Lord Tennyson

CCCCXLVI

PROSPICE

Fear death?—to feel the fog in my throat,
    The mist in my face,
When the snows begin, and the blasts denote
    I am nearing the place,
The power of the night, the press of the storm,
    The post of the foe;
Where he stands, the Arch Fear in a visible form,
    Yet the strong man must go:

For the journey is done and the summit attained
    And the barriers fall,
Though a battle's to fight ere the guerdon be gained,
    The reward of it all.
I was ever a fighter, so—one fight more,
    The best and the last!
I would hate that death bandaged my eyes, and
    forbore,
    And bade me creep past.
No! let me taste the whole of it, fare like my
    peers,
    The heroes of old,
Bear the brunt, in a minute pay glad life's arrears
    Of pain, darkness, and cold.
For sudden the worst turns the best to the brave,
    The black minute's at end,
And the elements' rage, the fiend voices that rave,
    Shall dwindle, shall blend,
Shall change, shall become first a peace out of pain,
    Then a light, then thy breast,
O thou soul of my soul! I shall clasp thee again,
    And with God be the rest!

                R. Browning

CCCCXLVII

'*IN NO STRANGE LAND*'

O world invisible, we view thee,
O world intangible, we touch thee,
O world unknowable, we know thee,
Inapprehensible, we clutch thee!

Does the fish soar to find the ocean,
The eagle plunge to find the air—
That we ask of the stars in motion
If they have rumour of thee there?

Not where the wheeling systems darken,
And our benumbed conceiving soars!—
The drift of pinions, would we hearken,
Beats at our own clay-shuttered doors.

The angels keep their ancient places ;—
Turn but a stone, and start a wing !
'Tis ye, 'tis your estrangèd faces,
That miss the many-splendoured thing.

But (when so sad thou canst not sadder)
Cry ;—and upon thy so sore loss
Shall shine the traffic of Jacob's ladder
Pitched betwixt Heaven and Charing Cross.

Yea, in the night, my Soul, my daughter,
Cry,—clinging Heaven by the hems ;
And lo, Christ walking on the water
Not of Gennesareth, but Thames !

F. Thompson

CCCCXLVIII

No coward soul is mine,
No trembler in the world's storm-troubled sphere :
    I see Heaven's glories shine,
And faith shines equal, arming me from fear.

O God within my breast,
Almighty, ever-present Deity !
    Life—that in me has rest,
As I—undying Life—have power in Thee !

Vain are the thousand creeds
That move men's hearts : unutterably vain ;
    Worthless as withered weeds,
Or idlest froth amid the boundless main,

To waken doubt in one
Holding so fast by Thine infinity ;
    So surely anchored on
The steadfast rock of immortality.

With wide-embracing love
Thy Spirit animates eternal years,
    Pervades and broods above,
Changes, sustains, dissolves, creates, and rears.

Though earth and man were gone,
And suns and universes ceased to be,
  And Thou were left alone,
Every existence would exist in Thee.

  There is not room for Death,
Nor atom that his might could render void :
  Thou—THOU art Being and Breath,
And what THOU art may never be destroyed.

E. Brontë

CCCCXLIX

THE CHOICE

Think thou and act; to-morrow thou shalt die.
Outstretched in the sun's warmth upon the shore,
Thou say'st : ' Man's measured path is all gone
    o'er :
Up all his years, steeply, with strain and sigh,
Man clomb until he touched the truth; and I,
Even I, am he whom it was destined for.'
How should this be ? Art thou then so much more
Than they who sowed, that thou shouldst reap
    thereby ?

Nay, come up hither. From this wave-washed
    mound
Unto the furthest flood-brim look with me;
Then reach on with thy thought till it be drown'd.
Miles and miles distant though the last line be,
And though thy soul sail leagues and leagues
    beyond,—
Still, leagues beyond those leagues, there is more
    sea.

D. G. Rossetti

𝕰𝖓𝖉 𝖔𝖋 𝖙𝖍𝖊 𝕲𝖔𝖑𝖉𝖊𝖓 𝕿𝖗𝖊𝖆𝖘𝖚𝖗𝖞

NOTES

INDEX OF WRITERS

AND

INDEX OF FIRST LINES

NOTES

(1861—1891)

Summary of Book First

THE Elizabethan Poetry, as it is rather vaguely termed, forms the substance of this Book, which contains pieces from Wyat under Henry VIII to Shakespeare midway through the reign of James I, and Drummond who carried on the early manner to a still later period. There is here a wide range of style;—from simplicity expressed in a language hardly yet broken-in to verse,—through the pastoral fancies and Italian conceits of the strictly Elizabethan time,—to the passionate reality of Shakespeare : yet a general uniformity of tone prevails. Few readers can fail to observe the natural sweetness of the verse, the single-hearted straightforwardness of the thoughts :—nor less, the limitation of subject to the many phases of one passion, which then characterized our lyrical poetry —unless when, as in especial with Shakespeare, the 'purple light of Love' is tempered by a spirit of sterner reflection. For the didactic verse of the century, although lyrical in form, yet very rarely rises to the pervading emotion, the golden cadence, proper to the lyric.

It should be observed that this and the following Summaries apply in the main to the Collection here presented, in which (besides its restriction to Lyrical Poetry) a strictly representative or historical Anthology has not been aimed at. Great excellence, in human art as in human character, has from the beginning of things been even more uniform than mediocrity, by virtue of the closeness of its approach to Nature :—and so far as the standard of Excellence kept in view has been attained in this volume, a comparative absence of extreme or temporary phases in style, a similarity of tone and manner, will be found throughout :—something neither modern nor ancient, but true and speaking to the heart of man alike throughout all ages.

PAGE NO.

2   3   *whist :* hushed, quieted.

—   4   *Rouse Memnon's mother :* Awaken the Dawn from the dark Earth and the clouds where she is resting. This is one of that limited class of early mythes which may be reasonably interpreted as representations of natural phenomena. Aurora in the old mythology is mother of Memnon (the East), and wife of Tithonus (the appearances of Earth and Sky during the last hours of Night). She leaves him every morning in renewed youth, to prepare the way for Phoebus (the Sun), whilst Tithonus remains in perpetual old age and grayness.

3   —   l. 23 *by Peneus' stream :* Phoebus loved the Nymph Daphne whom he met by the river Peneus in the vale of Tempe. L. 27 *Amphion's lyre :* He was said to have built the walls of Thebes to the sound of his music. L. 35 *Night like a drunkard reels :* Compare Romeo and Juliet, Act II, Scene 3: 'The grey-eyed morn smiles,' &c.—It should be added that three lines, which appeared hopelessly misprinted, have been omitted in this Poem.

4   6   *Time's chest :* in which he is figuratively supposed to lay up past treasures. So in Troilus, Act III, Scene 3, 'Time hath a wallet at his back,' &c. In the *Arcadia, chest* is used to signify *tomb.*

5   7   A fine example of the highwrought and conventional Elizabethan Pastoralism, which it would be unreasonable to criticize on the ground of the unshepherdlike or unreal character of some images suggested. Stanza 6 was perhaps inserted by Izaak Walton.

6   8   This beautiful lyric is one of several recovered from the very rare Elizabethan Song-books, for the publication of which our thanks are due to Mr. A. H. Bullen (1887, 1888).

8   12   One stanza has been here omitted, in accordance with the principle noticed in the Preface. Similar omissions occur in a few other poems. The more serious abbreviation by which it has been attempted to bring Crashaw's 'Wishes' and Shelley's 'Euganean Hills,' with one or two more, within the scheme of this selection, is commended with much diffidence to the judgment of readers acquainted with the original pieces.

9   13   Sidney's poetry is singularly unequal; his short life, his frequent absorption in public employment, hindered doubtless the development of his genius. His great contemporary fame, second only, it appears, to Spenser's, has been hence obscured. At times he is heavy and even prosaic; his simplicity is rude and bare; his verse unmelodious. These, however, are the 'defects of his merits.' In

a certain depth and chivalry of feeling,—in the rare
and noble quality of disinterestedness (to put it in
one word),—he has no superior, hardly perhaps an
equal, amongst our Poets; and after or beside
Shakespeare's Sonnets, his *Astrophel and Stella*, in the
Editor's judgment, offers the most intense and powerful picture of the passion of love in the whole range
of our poetry.—*Hundreds of years :* ' The very
rapture of love,' says Mr. Ruskin; ' A lover like
this does not believe his mistress can grow old
or die.'

12 19 Readers who have visited Italy will be reminded of
more than one picture by this gorgeous Vision of
Beauty, equally sublime and pure in its Paradisaical
naturalness. Lodge wrote it on a voyage to ' the
Islands of Terceras and the Canaries;' and he
seems to have caught, in those southern seas, no
small portion of the qualities which marked the
almost contemporary Art of Venice,—the glory and
the glow of Veronese, Titian, or Tintoret.—From the
same romance is No. 71: a charming picture in the
purest style of the later Italian Renaissance.
The clear (l. 1) is the crystalline or outermost
heaven of the old cosmography. *For a fair there's
fairer none :* If you desire a Beauty, there is none
more beautiful than Rosaline.

14 22 Another gracious lyric from an Elizabethan Song-
book, first reprinted (it is believed) in Mr. W.
J. Linton's ' Rare Poems,' in 1883.

15 23 *that fair thou owest :* that beauty thou ownest.

16 25 From one of the three Song-books of T. Campion,
who appears to have been author of the words
which he set to music. His merit as a lyrical poet
(recognized in his own time, but since then forgotten) has been again brought to light by Mr.
Bullen's taste and research :—*swerving* (st. 2) is his
conjecture for *changing* in the text of 1601.

20 31 *the star Whose worth's unknown, although his height
be taken :* apparently, Whose stellar influence is
uncalculated, although his angular altitude from the
plane of the astrolabe or artificial horizon used by
astrologers has been determined.

20 32 This lovely song appears, as here given, in Puttenham's ' Arte of English Poesie,' 1589. A longer and
inferior form was published in the ' Arcadia ' of
1590: but Puttenham's prefatory words clearly assign
his version to Sidney's own authorship.

23 37 *keel :* keep cooler by stirring round.

24 39 *expense :* loss.

—   40 *prease :* press.

25 41 *Nativity, once in the main of light :* when a star has
risen and entered on the full stream of light;—
another of the astrological phrases no longer familiar.

Crooked eclipses: as coming athwart the Sun's apparent course.

Wordsworth, thinking probably of the 'Venus' and the 'Lucrece,' said finely of Shakespeare: 'Shakespeare *could* not have written an Epic; he would have died of plethora of thought.' This prodigality of nature is exemplified equally in his Sonnets. The copious selection here given (which from the wealth of the material, required greater consideration than any other portion of the Editor's task),—contains many that will not be fully felt and understood without some earnestness of thought on the reader's part. But he is not likely to regret the labour.

26 42 *upon misprision growing:* either, granted in error, or, on the growth of contempt.

—   43 With the tone of this Sonnet compare Hamlet's 'Give me that man That is not passion's slave,' &c. Shakespeare's writings show the deepest sensitiveness to passion :—hence the attraction he felt in the contrasting effects of apathy.

26 44 *grame:* sorrow. Renaissance influences long impeded the return of English poets to the charming realism of this and a few other poems by Wyat.

28 45 Pandion in the ancient fable was father to Philomela.

29 47 In the old legend it is now Philomela, now Procne (the swallow) who suffers violence from Tereus. This song has a fascination in its calm intensity of passion; that 'sad earnestness and vivid exactness' which Cardinal Newman ascribes to the master-pieces of ancient poetry.

31 50 *proved:* approved.

—   51 *censures:* judges.

—   52 Exquisite in its equably-balanced metrical flow.

32 53 Judging by its style, this beautiful example of old simplicity and feeling may, perhaps, be referred to the earlier years of Elizabeth. *Late* forgot: lately.

35 57 Printed in a little Anthology by Nicholas Breton, 1597. It is, however, a stronger and finer piece of work than any known to be his.—St. 1 *silly:* simple; *dole:* grief; *chief:* chiefly. St. 3 *If there be . . .:* obscure : Perhaps, if there be any who speak harshly of thee, thy pain may plead for pity from Fate.

This poem, with 60 and 143, are each graceful variations of a long popular theme.

36 58 *That busy archer:* Cupid. *Descries:* used actively; *points out.*—'The last line of this poem is a little obscured by transposition. He means, *Do they call ungratefulness there a virtue?*' (C. Lamb).

37 59 *White Iope:* suggested, Mr. Bullen notes, by a passage in Propertius (iii, 20), describing Spirits in the lower world :

Vobiscum est Iope, vobiscum candida Tyro.

PAGE NO.

38 62   *cypres* or *cyprus*,—used by the old writers for *crape :* whether from the French *crespe* or from the Island whence it was imported. Its accidental similarity in spelling to *cypress* has, here and in Milton's Penseroso, probably confused readers.

39 63   *ramage :* confused noise.

41 66   ' I never saw anything like this funeral dirge,' says Charles Lamb, ' except the ditty which reminds Ferdinand of his drowned father in the Tempest. As that is of the water, watery; so this is of the earth, earthy. Both have that intenseness of feeling, which seems to resolve itself into the element which it contemplates.'

43 70   Paraphrased from an Italian madrigal.

> . . . . . Non so conoscer poi
> Se voi le rose, o sian le rose in voi.

44 72   *crystal :* fairness.

45 73   *stare :* starling.

— 74   This ' Spousal Verse ' was written in honour of the Ladies Elizabeth and Katherine Somerset. Nowhere has Spenser more emphatically displayed himself as the very poet of Beauty : The Renaissance impulse in England is here seen at its highest and purest.
The genius of Spenser, like Chaucer's, does itself justice only in poems of some length. Hence it is impossible to represent it in this volume by other pieces of equal merit, but of impracticable dimensions. And the same applies to such poems as the *Lover's Lament* or the *Ancient Mariner*.

46 —   *entrailed :* twisted. *Feateously :* elegantly.

48 —   *shend :* shame.

49 —   *a noble peer :* Robert Devereux, second Lord Essex, then at the height of his brief triumph after taking Cadiz : hence the allusion following to the Pillars of Hercules, placed near Gades by ancient legend.

— —   *Elisa :* Elizabeth.

50 —   *twins of Jove :* the stars Castor and Pollux : *baldric,* belt; the zodiac.

52 79   This lyric may with very high probability be assigned to Campion, in whose first Book of Airs it appeared (1601). The evidence sometimes quoted ascribing it to Lord Bacon appears to be valueless.

Summary of Book Second

THIS division, embracing generally the latter eighty years of the Seventeenth century, contains the close of our Early poetical style and the commencement of the Modern. In Dryden we see the first master of the new : in Milton, whose genius dominates here as Shakespeare's in the former book,— the crown and consummation of the early period. Their splen-

did Odes are far in advance of any prior attempts, Spenser's
excepted : they exhibit that wider and grander range which
years and experience and the struggles of the time conferred
on Poetry. Our Muses now give expression to political feeling, to religious thought, to a high philosophic statesmanship
in writers such as Marvell, Herbert, and Wotton : whilst in
Marvell and Milton, again, we find noble attempts, hitherto
rare in our literature, at pure description of nature, destined
in our own age to be continued and equalled. Meanwhile the
poetry of simple passion, although before 1660 often deformed
by verbal fancies and conceits of thought, and afterwards by
levity and an artificial tone,—produced in Herrick and Waller
some charming pieces of more finished art than the Elizabethan :
until in the courtly compliments of Sedley it seems to exhaust
itself, and lie almost dormant for the hundred years between
the days of Wither and Suckling and the days of Burns and
Cowper.—That the change from our early style to the modern
brought with it at first a loss of nature and simplicity is un-
deniable : yet the bolder and wider scope which Poetry took
between 1620 and 1700, and the successful efforts then made to
gain greater clearness in expression, in their results have been
no slight compensation.

PAGE NO.
58 85   l. 8 *whist :* hushed.
—   —   l. 32 *than :* obsolete for *then : Pan :* used here for the
         Lord of all.
59 —   l. 38 *consort :* Milton's spelling of this word, here
         and elsewhere, has been followed, as it is uncertain
         whether he used it in the sense of *accompanying,* or
         simply for *concert.*
61 —   l. 21 *Lars and Lemures :* household gods and spirits
         of relations dead. *Flamens* (l. 24) Roman priests.
         That twice-batter'd god (l. 29) Dagon.
62 —   l. 6 *Osiris,* the Egyptian god of Agriculture (here,
         perhaps by confusion with Apis, figured as a Bull),
         was torn to pieces by Typho and embalmed after
         death in a sacred chest. This mythe, reproduced in
         Syria and Greece in the legends of Thammuz, Adonis,
         and perhaps Absyrtus, may have originally signified
         the annual death of the Sun or the Year under the in-
         fluences of the winter darkness. Horus, the son of
         Osiris, as the New Year, in his turn overcomes Typho.
         L. 8 *unshower'd* grass : as watered by the Nile only.
         L. 33 *youngest-teemed :* last-born. *Bright-harness'd*
         (l. 37) armoured.
64 87   *The Late Massacre :* the Vaudois persecution, carried
         on in 1655 by the Duke of Savoy. No more mighty
         Sonnet than this ' collect in verse,' as it has been
         justly named, probably can be found in any language.
         Readers should observe that it is constructed on the
         original Italian or Provençal model. This form, in a

PAGE NO.

language such as ours, not affluent in rhyme, presents great difficulties; the rhymes are apt to be forced, or the substance commonplace. But, when successfully handled, it has a unity and a beauty of effect which place the strict Sonnet above the less compact and less lyrical systems adopted by Shakespeare, Sidney, Spenser, and other Elizabethan poets.

65 88 Cromwell returned from Ireland in 1650, and Marvell probably wrote his lines soon after, whilst living at Nunappleton in the Fairfax household. It is hence not surprising that (st. 21-24) he should have been deceived by Cromwel 's professed submissiveness to the Parliament which, when it declined to register his decrees, he expelled by armed violence :—one despotism, by natural law, replacing another. The poet's insight has, however, truly prophesied that result in his last two lines.

This Ode, beyond doubt one of the finest in our language, and more in Milton's style than has been reached by any other poet, is occasionally obscure from imitation of the condensed Latin syntax. The meaning of st. 5 is 'rivalry or hostility are the same to a lofty spirit, and limitation more hateful than opposition.' The allusion in st. 11 is to the old physical doctrines of the non-existence of a vacuum and the impenetrability of matter :—in st. 17 to the omen traditionally connected with the foundation of the Capitol at Rome :—*forced*, fated. The ancient belief that certain years in life complete natural periods and are hence peculiarly exposed to death, is introduced in st. 26 by the word *climacteric*.

68 89 *Lycidas :* The person here lamented is Milton's college contemporary, Edward King, drowned in 1637 whilst crossing from Chester to Ireland.

Strict Pastoral Poetry was first written or perfected by the Dorian Greeks settled in Sicily : but the conventional use of it, exhibited more magnificently in *Lycidas* than in any other pastoral, is apparently of Roman origin. Milton, employing the noble freedom of a great artist, has here united ancient mythology, with what may be called the modern mythology of Camus and Saint Peter,—to direct Christian images. Yet the poem, if it gains in historical interest, suffers in poetry by the harsh intrusion of the writer's narrow and violent theological politics.— The metrical structure of this glorious elegy is partly derived from Italian models.

69 — l. 11 *Sisters of the sacred well :* the Muses, said to frequent the Pierian Spring at the foot of Mount Olympus.

70 — l. 10 *Mona :* Anglesea, called by the Welsh poets, the Dark Island, from its dense forests. *Deva* (l. 11) the Dee : a river which may have derived its magical

PAGE NO.

character from Celtic traditions : it was long the
boundary of Briton and English.—These places are
introduced, as being near the scene of the shipwreck.
Orpheus (l. 14) was torn to pieces by Thracian women.
Amaryllis and *Neaera* (l. 24, 25) names used here for
the love-idols of poets : as *Damoetas* previously for a
shepherd. L. 31 *the Blind Fury :* Atropos, fabled to
cut the thread of life.

71 89   *Arethuse* (l. 1) and *Mincius :* Sicilian and Italian
waters here alluded to as representing the pastoral
poetry of Theocritus and Vergil. L. 4 *oat :* pipe,
used here like Collins' *oaten stop* l. 1, No. 186, for
Song. L. 12 *Hippotades :* Aeolus, god of the Winds.
Panope (l. 15) a Nereid. Certain names of local deities
in the Hellenic mythology render some feature in the
natural landscape, which the Greeks studied and
analysed with their usual unequalled insight and
feeling. *Panope* seems to express the boundlessness
of the ocean-horizon when seen from a height, as
compared with the limited sky-line of the land in
hilly countries such as Greece or Asia Minor. *Camus*
(l. 19) the Cam : put for King's University. *The sanguine flower* (l. 22) the Hyacinth of the ancients :
probably our Iris. *The Pilot* (l. 25) Saint Peter,
figuratively introduced as the head of the Church on
earth, to foretell ' the ruin of our corrupted clergy,'
as Milton regarded them, ' then in their heighth '
under Laud's primacy.

72   —   l. 1 *scrannel :* screeching; apparently Milton's coin-
age (Masson). L. 5 *the wolf :* the Puritans of the
time were excited to alarm and persecution by a few
conversions to Roman Catholicism which had recently
occurred. *Alpheus* (l. 9) a stream in Southern Greece,
supposed to flow underseas to join the Arethuse.
Swart star (l. 15) the Dog-star, called swarthy because
its heliacal rising in ancient times occurred soon after
midsummer : l. 19 *rathe :* early. L. 36 *moist vows :*
either tearful prayers, or prayers for one at sea.
Bellerus (l. 37) a giant, apparently created here by
Milton to personify Belerium, the ancient title of the
Land's End. *The great Vision :*—the story was that
the Archangel Michael had appeared on the rock by
Marazion in Mount's Bay which bears his name.
Milton calls on him to turn his eyes from the south
homeward, and to pity Lycidas, if his body has
drifted into the troubled waters off the Land's End.
Finisterre being the land due south of Marazion, two
places in that district (then through our trade with
Corunna probably less unfamiliar to English ears),
are named,—*Namancos* now Mujio in Galicia, *Bayona*
north of the Minho, or perhaps a fortified rock (one
of the *Cies* Islands) not unlike Saint Michael's Mount,
at the entrance of Vigo Bay.

PAGE NO.

73 89   l. 6 *ore :* rays of golden light.   *Doric lay* (l. 25) Sicilian pastoral.

75 93   *The assault* was an attack on London expected in 1642, when the troops of Charles I reached Brentford.   ' Written on his door ' was in the original title of this sonnet. Milton was then living in Aldersgate Street.

     The Emathian Conqueror : When Thebes was destroyed (B.C. 335) and the citizens massacred by thousands, Alexander ordered the house of Pindar to be spared.

76 —   l. 2, *the repeated air Of sad Electra's poet :* Plutarch has a tale that when the Spartan confederacy in 404 B.C. took Athens, a proposal to demolish it was rejected through the effect produced on the commanders by hearing part of a chorus from the *Electra* of Euripides sung at a feast. There is however no apparent congruity between the lines quoted (167, 168 Ed. Dindorf) and the result ascribed to them.

— 95   A fine example of a peculiar class of Poetry ;—that written by thoughtful men who practised this Art but little. Jeremy Taylor, Bishop Berkeley, Dr. Johnson, Lord Macaulay, have left similar specimens.

78 98   These beautiful verses should be compared with Wordsworth's great Ode on *Immortality :* and a copy of Vaughan's very rare little volume appears in the list of Wordsworth's library.—In imaginative intensity, Vaughan stands beside his contemporary Marvell.

79 99   *Favonius :* the spring wind.

80 100   *Themis :* the goddess of justice. Skinner was grandson by his mother to Sir E. Coke :—hence, as pointed out by Mr. Keightley, Milton's allusion to the *bench.* L. 8 : Sweden was then at war with Poland, and France with the Spanish Netherlands.

82 103   l. 28 *Sidneian showers :* either in allusion to the conversations in the ' Arcadia,' or to Sidney himself as a model of ' gentleness ' in spirit and demeanour.

85 105   Delicate humour, delightfully united to thought, at once simple and subtle. It is full of conceit and paradox, but these are imaginative, not as with most of our Seventeenth Century poets, intellectual only.

88 110   *Elizabeth of Bohemia :* Daughter to James I, and ancestor of Sophia of Hanover. These lines are a fine specimen of gallant and courtly compliment.

89 111   Lady M. Ley was daughter to Sir J. Ley, afterwards Earl of Marlborough, who died March, 1629, coincidently with the dissolution of the third Parliament of Charles' reign. Hence Milton poetically compares his death to that of the Orator Isocrates of Athens, after Philip's victory in 328 B.C.

93 118   A masterpiece of humour, grace, and gentle feeling,

all, with Herrick's unfailing art, kept precisely within the peculiar key which he chose,—or Nature for him,—in his Pastorals. L. 2 *the god unshorn :* Imberbis Apollo. St. 2 *beads :* prayers.

96 123 With better taste, and less diffuseness, Quarles might (one would think) have retained more of that high place which he held in popular estimate among his contemporaries.

99 127 *From Prison :* to which his active support of Charles I twice brought the high-spirited writer. L. 7 *Gods :* thus in the original ; Lovelace, in his fanciful way, making here a mythological allusion. *Birds,* commonly substituted, is without authority. St. 3, l. 1 *committed :* to prison.

100 128 St. 2 l. 4 *blue-god :* Neptune.

104 133 *Waly waly :* an exclamation of sorrow, the root and the pronunciation of which are preserved in the word *caterwaul.* *Brae,* hillside : *burn,* brook : *busk,* adorn. *Saint Anton's Well :* below Arthur's Seat by Edinburgh. *Cramasie,* crimson.

105 134 This beautiful example of early simplicity is found in a Song-book of 1620.

106 135 *burd,* maiden.

107 136 *corbies,* crows : *fail,* turf : *hause,* neck : *theek,* thatch —If not in their origin, in their present form this, with the preceding poem and 133, appear due to the Seventeenth Century, and have therefore been placed in Book II.

108 137 The poetical and the prosaic, after Cowley's fashion, blend curiously in this deeply-felt elegy.

112 141 Perhaps no poem in this collection is more delicately fancied, more exquisitely finished. By placing his description of the Fawn in a young girl's mouth, Marvell has, as it were, legitimated that abundance of 'imaginative hyperbole' to which he is always partial : he makes us feel it natural that a maiden's favourite should be whiter than milk, sweeter than sugar—' lilies without, roses within.' The poet's imagination is justified in its seeming extravagance by the intensity and unity with which it invests his picture.

113 142 The remark quoted in the note to No. 65 applies equally to these truly wonderful verses. Marvell here throws himself into the very soul of the *Garden* with the imaginative intensity of Shelley in his *West Wind.*—This poem appears also as a translation in Marvell's works. The most striking verses in it, here quoted as the book is rare, answer more or less to stanzas 2 and 6 :—

Alma Quies, teneo te ! et te, germana Quietis,
Simplicitas ! vos ergo diu per templa, per urbes
Quaesivi, regum perque alta palatia, frustra :
Sed vos hortorum per opaca silentia, longe
Celarunt plantae virides, et concolor umbra.

PAGE NO.

115 143 St. 3 *tutties :* nosegays. St. 4 *silly :* simple.
L'Allégro and *Il Penseroso.* It is a striking proof of Milton's astonishing power, that these, the earliest great Lyrics of the Landscape in our language, should still remain supreme in their style for range, variety, and melodious beauty. The Bright and the Thoughtful aspects of Nature and of Life are their subjects : but each is preceded by a mythological introduction in a mixed Classical and Italian manner.—With that of *L'Allégro* may be compared a similar mythe in the first Section of the first Book of S. Marmion's graceful *Cupid and Psyche,* 1637.

116 144 *The mountain-nymph ;* compare Wordsworth's Sonnet, No. 254. L. 38 is in *apposition* to the preceding, by a syntactical license not uncommon with Milton.

118 — l. 14 *Cynosure ;* the Pole Star. *Corydon, Thyrsis,* &c. : Shepherd names from the old Idylls. *Rebeck* (l. 28) an elementary form of violin.

119 — l. 24 *Jonson's learned sock :* His comedies are deeply coloured by classical study. L. 28 *Lydian airs :* used here to express a light and festive style of ancient music. The ' Lydian Mode,' one of the seven original Greek Scales, is nearly identical with our ' Major.'

120 145 l. 3 *bestead :* avail. L. 19 *starr'd Ethiop queen :* Cassiopeia, the legendary Queen of Ethiopia, and thence translated amongst the constellations.

121 — *Cynthia :* the Moon : Milton seems here to have transferred to her chariot the dragons anciently assigned to Demeter and to Medea.

122 — *Hermes,* called Trismegistus, a mystical writer of the Neo-Platonist school. L. 27 *Thebes,* &c. : subjects of Athenian Tragedy. *Buskin'd* (l. 30) tragic, in opposition to *sock* above. L. 32 *Musaeus :* a poet in Mythology. L. 37 *him that left half-told :* Chaucer in his incomplete ' Squire's Tale.'

123 — *great bards :* Ariosto, Tasso, and Spenser, are here presumably intended. L. 9 *frounced :* curled. *The Attic Boy* (l. 10) Cephalus.

124 146 Emigrants supposed to be driven towards America by the government of Charles I.

125 — l. 9, 10. *But apples,* &c. A fine example of Marvell's imaginative hyperbole.

— 147 l. 6 *concent :* harmony.

128 149 A lyric of a strange, fanciful, yet solemn beauty :— Cowley's style intensified by the mysticism of Henry More.—St. 2 *monument :* the World.

129 151 Entitled ' A Song in Honour of St. Cecilia's Day : 1697.'

Summary of Book Third

It is more difficult to characterize the English Poetry of the Eighteenth century than that of any other. For it was an age not only of spontaneous transition, but of bold experiment: it includes not only such absolute contrasts as distinguish the 'Rape of the Lock' from the 'Parish Register,' but such vast contemporaneous differences as lie between Pope and Collins, Burns and Cowper. Yet we may clearly trace three leading moods or tendencies:—the aspects of courtly or educated life represented by Pope and carried to exhaustion by his followers; the poetry of Nature and of Man, viewed through a cultivated, and at the same time an impassioned frame of mind by Collins and Gray:—lastly, the study of vivid and simple narrative, including natural description, begun by Gay and Thomson, pursued by Burns and others in the north, and established in England by Goldsmith, Percy, Crabbe, and Cowper. Great varieties in style accompanied these diversities in aim: poets could not always distinguish the manner suitable for subjects so far apart: and the union of conventional and of common language, exhibited most conspicuously by Burns, has given a tone to the poetry of that century which is better explained by reference to its historical origin than by naming it artificial. There is, again a nobleness of thought, a courageous aim at high and, in a strict sense manly, excellence in many of the writers:—nor can that period be justly termed tame and wanting in originality, which produced poems such as Pope's Satires, Gray's Odes and Elegy, the ballads of Gay and Carey, the songs of Burns and Cowper. In truth Poetry at this, as at all times was a more or less unconscious mirror of the genius of the age: and the many complex causes which made the Eighteenth century the turning-time in modern European civilization are also more or less reflected in its verse. An intelligent reader will find the influence of Newton as markedly in the poems of Pope, as of Elizabeth in the plays of Shakespeare. On this great subject, however, these indications must here be sufficient.

PAGE NO.

194 153   We have no poet more marked by rapture, by the ecstasy which Plato held the note of genuine inspiration, than Collins. Yet but twice or thrice do his lyrics reach that simplicity, that *sinceram sermonis Attici gratiam* to which this ode testifies his enthusiastic devotion. His style, as his friend Dr. Johnson truly remarks, was obscure; his diction often harsh and unskilfully laboured; he struggles nobly against the narrow, artificial manner of his age, but his too scanty years did not allow him to reach perfect mastery.

PAGE NO.

St. 3 *Hybla :* near Syracuse. *Her whose . . . woe :* the nightingale, ' for which Sophocles seems to have entertained a peculiar fondness '; Collins here refers to the famous chorus in the *Oedipus at Colonus.* St. 4 *Cephisus :* the stream encircling Athens on the north and west, passing Colonus. St. 6 *stay'd to sing :* stayed her song when Imperial tyranny was established at Rome. St. 7 refers to the Italian amourist poetry of the Renaissance : In Collins' day, Dante was almost unknown in England. St. 8 *meeting soul :* which moves sympathetically towards Simplicity as she comes to inspire the poet. S. 9 *Of these :* Taste and Genius.

The Bard. In 1757, when this splendid ode was completed, so very little had been printed, whether in Wales or in England, in regard to Welsh poetry, that it is hard to discover whence Gray drew his Cymric allusions. The fabled massacre of the Bards (shown to be wholly groundless in Stephens' *Literature of the Kymry*) appears first in the family history of Sir John Wynn of Gwydir (cir. 1600), not published till 1773 ; but the story seems to have passed in MS. to Carte's History, whence it may have been taken by Gray. The references to *high-born Hoel* and *soft Llewellyn ;* to *Cadwallo* and *Urien ;* may, similarly, have been derived from the ' Specimens ' of early Welsh poetry, by the Rev. E. Evans :—as, although not published till 1764, the MS., we learn from a letter to Dr. Wharton, was in Gray's hands by July 1760, and may have reached him by 1757. It is, however, doubtful whether Gray (of whose acquaintance with Welsh we have no evidence) must not have been also aided by some Welsh scholar. He is one of the poets least likely to scatter epithets at random : ' soft ' or gentle is the epithet emphatically and specially given to Llewelyn in contemporary Welsh poetry, and is hence here used with particular propriety. Yet, without such assistance as we have suggested, Gray could hardly have selected the epithet, although applied to the King (p. 141-3) among a crowd of otners, in Llygad Gwr's Ode, printed by Evans.—After lamenting his comrades (st. 2, 3) the Bard prophesies the fate of Edward II, and the conquests of Edward III (4) : his death and that of the Black Prince (5) : of Richard II, with the wars of York and Lancaster, the murder of Henry VI (*the meek usurper*), and of Edward V and his brother (6). He turns to the glory and prosperity following the accession of the Tudors (7), through Elizabeth's reign (8) : and concludes with a vision of the poetry of Shakespeare and Milton.

140 159   l. 13 *Glo'ster :* Gilbert de Clare, son-in-law to Edward. *Mortimer,* one of the Lords Marchers of Wales.

PAGE NO.

141 159 *High-born Hoel, soft Llewellyn* (l. 15) ; the *Dissertatio de Bardis* of Evans names the first as son to the King Owain Gwynedd : Llewelyn, last King of North Wales, was murdered 1282. L. 16 *Cadwallo* : Cadwallon (died 631) and Urien Rheged (early kings of Gwynedd and Cumbria respectively) are mentioned by Evans (p. 78) as bards none of whose poetry is extant. L. 20 *Modred* : Evans supplies no *data* for this name, which Gray (it has been supposed) uses for Merlin (Myrddin Wyllt), held prophet as well as poet.—The Italicized lines mark where the Bard's song is joined by that of his predecessors departed. L. 22 *Arvon* : the shores of Carnarvonshire opposite Anglesey. Whether intentionally or through ignorance of the real dates, Gray here seems to represent the *Bard* as speaking of these poets, all of earlier days, Llewelyn excepted, as his own contemporaries at the close of the thirteenth century.

Gray, whose penetrating and powerful genius rendered him in many ways an initiator in advance of his age, is probably the first of our poets who made some acquaintance with the rich and admirable poetry in which Wales from the Sixth Century has been fertile,—before and since his time so barbarously neglected, not in England only. Hence it has been thought worth while here to enter into a little detail upon his Cymric allusions.

142 — l. 5 *She-wolf* : Isabel of France, adulterous Queen of Edward II.—L. 35 *Towers of Julius* : the Tower of London, built in part, according to tradition, by Julius Cæsar.

143 — l. 2 *bristled boar* : the badge of Richard III. L. 7 *Half of thy heart* : Queen Eleanor died soon after the conquest of Wales. L. 18 *Arthur* : Henry VII named his eldest son thus, in deference to native feeling and story.

144 161 The Highlanders called the battle of Culloden, Drumossie.

145 162 *lilting*, singing blithely : *loaning*, broad lane : *bughts*, pens : *scorning*, rallying : *dowie*, dreary : *daffin'* and *gabbin'*, joking and chatting : *leglin*, milkpail : *shearing*, reaping : *bandsters*, sheaf-binders : *lyart*, grizzled : *runkled*, wrinkled : *fleeching*, coaxing : *gloaming*, twilight : *bogle*, ghost : *dool*, sorrow.

147 164 The Editor has found no authoritative text of this poem, to his mind superior to any other of its class in melody and pathos. Part is probably not later than the seventeenth century : in other stanzas a more modern hand, much resembling Scott's, is traceable. Logan's poem (163) exhibits a knowledge rather of the old legend than of the old verses.— *Hecht*, promised ; the obsolete *hight* : *mavis*, thrush :

PAGE NO.

ilka, every : *lav'rock*, lark : *haughs*, valley-meadows : *twined*, parted from : *marrow*, mate : *syne*, then.

148 165 The Royal George, of 108 guns, whilst undergoing a partial careening at Spithead, was overset about 10 A.M. Aug. 29, 1782. The total loss was believed to be nearly 1000 souls.—This little poem might be called one of our trial-pieces, in regard to taste. The reader who feels the vigour of description and the force of pathos underlying Cowper's bare and truly Greek simplicity of phrase, may assure himself *se valde profecisse* in poetry.

151 167 A little masterpiece in a very difficult style : Catullus himself could hardly have bettered it. In grace, tenderness, simplicity, and humour, it is worthy of the Ancients : and even more so, from the complete-ness and unity of the picture presented.

155 172 Perhaps no writer who has given such strong proofs of the poetic nature has left less satisfactory poetry than Thomson. Yet this song, with ' Rule Britannia ' and a few others, must make us regret that he did not more seriously apply himself to lyrical writing.

156 174 With what insight and tenderness, yet in how few words, has this painter-poet here himself told *Love's Secret !*

157 177 l. 1 *Aeolian lyre :* the Greeks ascribed the origin of their Lyrical Poetry to the Colonies of Aeolis in Asia Minor.

158 — *Thracia's hills* (l. 9) supposed a favourite resort of Mars. *Feather'd king* (l. 13) the Eagle of Jupiter, admirably described by Pindar in a passage here imitated by Gray. *Idalia* (l. 19) in Cyprus, where *Cytherea* (Venus) was especially worshipped.

159 — l. 6 *Hyperion :* the Sun. St. 6—8 allude to the Poets of the Islands and Mainland of Greece, to those of Rome and of England.

160 — l. 27 *Theban Eagle :* Pindar.

163 178 l. 5 *chaste-eyed Queen :* Diana.

164 179 From that wild rhapsody of mingled grandeur, ten-derness, and obscurity, that ' medley between inspira-tion and possession,' which poor Smart is believed to have written whilst in confinement for madness.

165 181 *the dreadful light :* of life and experience.

166 182 *Attic warbler :* the nightingale.

168 184 *sleekit*, sleek : *bickering brattle*, flittering flight : *laith*, loth : *pattle*, ploughstaff : *whyles*, at times : *a daimen-icker*, a corn-ear now and then : *thrave*, shock : *lave*, rest : *foggage*, after-grass : *snell*, biting : *but hald*, without dwelling-place : *thole*, bear : *cranreuch*, hoar-frost : *thy lane*, alone : *a-gley*, off the right line, awry.

175 188 *stoure*, dust-storm : *braw*, smart.

176 189 *scaith*, hurt : *tent*, guard : *steer*, molest.

177 191 *drumlie*, muddy : *birk*, birch.

PAGE NO.

178 192 *greet*, cry : *daurna*, dare not.—There can hardly exist
a poem more truly tragic in the highest sense than
this : nor, perhaps, Sappho excepted, has any Poetess
equalled it.

180 193 *fou*, merry with drink : *coost*, carried : *unco skeigh*,
very proud : *gart*, forced : *a'eigh*, aside : *Ailsa craig*,
a rock in the Firth of Clyde : *grat his een bleert*,
cried till his eyes were bleared : *lowpin*, leaping :
linn, waterfall : *sair*, sore : *smoor'd*, smothered :
crouse and *canty*, blithe and gay.

181 194 Burns justly named this ' one of the most beautiful
songs in the Scots or any other language.' One stanza,
interpolated by Beattie, is here omitted :—it contains
two good lines, but is out of harmony with the
original poem.   *Bigonet*, little cap : probably altered
from *béguinette : thraw*, twist : *caller*, fresh.

182 195 Burns himself, despite two attempts, failed to im-
prove this little absolute masterpiece of music, tenderness, and simplicity : this ' Romance of a life ' in
eight lines.—*Eerie :* strictly, scared : uneasy.

183 196 *airts*, quarters : *row*, roll : *shaw*, small wood in a
hollow, spinney : *knowes*, knolls.   The last two
stanzas are not by Burns.

184 197 *jo*, sweetheart : *brent*, smooth : *pow*, head.

— 198 *leal*, faithful.   St. 3 *fain*, happy.

185 199 Henry VI founded Eton.

188 200 Written in 1773, towards the beginning of Cowper's
second attack of melancholy madness—a time when
he altogether gave up prayer, saying, ' For him to implore mercy would only anger God the more.' Yet
had he given it up when sane, it would have been
' major insania.'

191 203 The Editor would venture to class in the very first
rank this Sonnet, which, with 204, records Cowper's
gratitude to the Lady whose affectionate care for
many years gave what sweetness he could enjoy to a
life radically wretched.   Petrarch's sonnets have a
more ethereal grace and a more perfect finish ; Shakespeare's more passion ; Milton's stand supreme in
stateliness ; Wordsworth's in depth and delicacy.
But Cowper's unites with an exquisiteness in the
turn of thought which the ancients would have called
Irony, an intensity of pathetic tenderness peculiar to
his loving and ingenuous nature.—There is much man-
nerism, much that is unimportant or of now exhausted
interest in his poems : but where he is great, it is
with that elementary greatness which rests on the
most universal human feelings. Cowper is our highest
master in simple pathos.

193 205 Cowper's last original poem, founded upon a story
told in Anson's ' Voyages.'   It was written March
1799 ; he died in next year's April.

195 206 Very little except his name appears recoverable with

regard to the author of this truly noble poem, which
appeared in the 'Scripscrapologia, or Collins' Doggerel
Dish of All Sorts,' with three or four other pieces of
merit, Birmingham, 1804.—*Everlasting :* used with
side-allusion to a cloth so named, at the time when
Collins wrote.

Summary of Book Fourth

IT proves sufficiently the lavish wealth of our own age in
Poetry, that the pieces which, without conscious departure
from the standard of Excellence, render this Book by far the
longest, were with very few exceptions composed during the
first thirty years of the Nineteenth century.   Exhaustive
reasons can hardly be given for the strangely sudden appear-
ance of individual genius : that, however, which assigns the
splendid national achievements of our recent poetry to an impulse from the France of the first Republic and Empire is in-
adequate. The first French Revolution was rather one result,—
the most conspicuous, indeed, yet itself in great measure
essentially retrogressive,—of that wider and more potent spirit
which through enquiry and attempt, through strength and
weakness, sweeps mankind round the circles (not, as some
too confidently argue, of Advance, but) of gradual Trans-
formation : and it is to this that we must trace the literature
of Modern Europe.   But, without attempting discussion
on the motive causes of Scott, Wordsworth, Shelley, and
others, we may observe that these Poets carried to further
perfection the later tendencies of the Century preceding, in
simplicity of narrative, reverence for human Passion and
Character in every sphere, and love of Nature for herself :—
that, whilst maintaining on the whole the advances in art made
since the Restoration, they renewed the half-forgotten melody
and depth of tone which marked the best Elizabethan writers:
—that, lastly, to what was thus inherited they added a rich-
ness in language and a variety in metre, a force and fire in
narrative, a tenderness and bloom in feeling, an insight into
the finer passages of the Soul and the inner meanings of the
landscape, a larger sense of Humanity,—hitherto scarcely attained, and perhaps unattainable even by predecessors of not
inferior individual genius. In a word, the Nation which, after
the Greeks in their glory, may fairly claim that during six
centuries it has proved itself the most richly gifted of all
nations for Poetry, expressed in these men the highest strength
and prodigality of its nature.   They interpreted the age to
itself—hence the many phases of thought and style they present :—to sympathize with each, fervently and impartially,
without fear and without fancifulness, is no doubtful step in
the higher education of the soul. For purity in taste is abso-
lutely proportionate to strength—and when once the mind has
raised itself to grasp and to delight in excellence, those who
love most will be found to love most wisely.

494 *Notes*

But the gallery which this Book offers to the reader will aid him more than any preface. It is a royal Palace of Poetry which he is invited to enter:

> Adparet domus intus, et atria longa patescunt—

though it is, indeed, to the sympathetic eye only that its treasures will be visible.

PAGE NO.

197 208   This beautiful lyric, printed in 1783, seems to anticipate in its imaginative music that return to our great early age of song, which in Blake's own lifetime was to prove,—how gloriously! that the English Muses had resumed their 'ancient melody':—Keats, Shelley, Byron,—he overlived them all.

199 210   *stout Cortez*: History would here suggest *Balbóa*: (A.T.) It may be noticed, that to find in Chapman's Homer the ' pure serene ' of the original, the reader must bring with him the imagination of the youthful poet;—he must be ' a Greek himself,' as Shelley finely said of Keats.

202 212   The most tender and true of Byron's smaller poems.

203 213   This poem exemplifies the peculiar skill with which Scott employs proper names :—a rarely misleading sign of true poetical genius.

213 226   Simple as *Lucy Gray* seems, a mere narrative of what ' has been, and may be again,' yet every touch in the child's picture is marked by the deepest and purest ideal character. Hence, pathetic as the situation is, this is not strictly a pathetic poem, such as Wordsworth gives us in 221, Lamb in 264, and Scott in his *Maid of Neidpath*,—' almost more pathetic,' as Tennyson once remarked, ' than a man has the right to be.' And Lyte's lovely stanzas (224) suggest, perhaps, the same remark.

222 235   In this and in other instances the addition (or the change) of a Title has been risked, in hope that the aim of the piece following may be grasped more clearly and immediately.

228 242   This beautiful Sonnet was the last word of a youth, in whom, if the fulfilment may ever safely be prophesied from the promise, England lost one of the most rarely gifted in the long roll of her poets. Shakespeare and Milton, had their lives been closed at twenty-five, would (so far as we know) have left poems of less excellence and hope than the youth who, from the petty school and the London surgery, passed at once to a place with them of ' high collateral glory.'

230 245   It is impossible not to regret that Moore has written so little in this sweet and genuinely national style.

231 246   A masterly example of Byron's command of strong

PAGE NO.

thought and close reasoning in verse :—as the next is equally characteristic of Shelley's way ward intensity.

240 253 Bonnivard, a Genevese, was imprisoned by the Duke of Savoy in Chillon on the lake of Geneva for his courageous defence of his country against the tyranny with which Piedmont threatened it during the first half of the Seventeenth century,—This noble Sonnet is worthy to stand near Milton's on the Vaudois massacre.

241 254 Switzerland was usurped by the French under Napoleon in 1800 : Venice in 1797 (255).

243 259 This battle was fought Dec. 2, 1800, between the Austrians under Archduke John and the French under Moreau, in a forest near Munich. *Hohen Linden* means *High Limetrees*.

247 262 After the capture of Madrid by Napoleon, Sir J. Moore retreated before Soult and Ney to Corunna, and was killed whilst covering the embarkation of his troops.

257 272 The Mermaid was the club-house of Shakespeare, Ben Jonson, and other choice spirits of that age.

258 273 *Maisie :* Mary.—Scott has given us nothing more complete and lovely than this little song, which unites simplicity and dramatic power to a wild-wood music of the rarest quality. No moral is drawn, far less any conscious analysis of feeling attempted :— the pathetic meaning is left to be suggested by the mere presentment of the situation. A narrow criticism has often named this, which may be called the Homeric manner, superficial, from its apparent simple facility; but first-rate excellence in it is in truth one of the least common triumphs of Poetry.— This style should be compared with what is not less perfect in its way, the searching out of inner feeling, the expression of hidden meanings, the revelation of the heart of Nature and of the Soul within the Soul, —the analytical method, in short,—most completely represented by Wordsworth and by Shelley.

263 277 Wolfe resembled Keats, not only in his early death by consumption and the fluent freshness of his poetical style, but in beauty of character :—brave, tender, energetic, unselfish, modest. Is it fanciful to find some reflex of these qualities in the *Burial* and *Mary ?* Out of the abundance of the *heart* . . .

264 278 *correi :* covert on a hillside. *Cumber :* trouble.

265 280 This book has not a few poems of greater power and more perfect execution than *Agnes* and the extract which we have ventured to make from the deep-hearted author's *Sad Thoughts* (No. 224). But none are more emphatically marked by the note of exquisiteness.

266 281 st. 3 *inch :* island.

270 283 From *Poetry for Children* (1809), by Charles and Mary

PAGE NO.

	Lamb. This tender and original little piece seems clearly to reveal the work of that noble-minded and afflicted sister, who was at once the happiness, the misery, and the life-long blessing of her equally noble-minded brother.
278 289	This poem has an exaltation and a glory, joined with an exquisiteness of expression, which place it in the highest rank among the many masterpieces of its illustrious Author.
289 300	*interlunar swoon :* interval of the moon's invisibility.
294 304	*Calpe :* Gibraltar. *Lofoden :* the Maelstrom whirl-pool off the N.W. coast of Norway.
295 305	This lovely poem refers here and there to a ballad by Hamilton on the subject better treated in 163 and 164.
307 315	*Arcturi :* seemingly used for *northern stars. And wild roses, &c.* Our language has perhaps no line modulated with more subtle sweetness.
308 316	Coleridge describes this poem as the fragment of a dream-vision,—perhaps, an opium-dream?—which composed itself in his mind when fallen asleep after reading a few lines about 'the Khan Kubla' in Purchas' *Pilgrimage.*
312 318	*Ceres' daughter :* Proserpine. *God of Torment :* Pluto.
320 321	The leading idea of this beautiful description of a day's landscape in Italy appears to be—On the voyage of life are many moments of pleasure, given by the sight of Nature, who has power to heal even the worldliness and the uncharity of man.
321 —	l. 23 Amphitrite was daughter to Ocean.
325 322	l. 21 *Maenad :* a frenzied Nymph, attendant on Dionysos in the Greek mythology. May we not call this the most vivid, sustained, and impassioned amongst all Shelley's magical personifications of Nature?
326 —	l. 5 Plants under water sympathize with the seasons of the land, and hence with the winds which affect them.
327 323	Written soon after the death, by shipwreck, of Wordsworth's brother John. This poem may be pro-fitably compared with Shelley's following it. Each is the most complete expression of the innermost spirit of his art given by these great Poets :—of that Idea which, as in the case of the true Painter, (to quote the words of Reynolds,) ' subsists only in the mind : The sight never beheld it, nor has the hand expressed it : it is an idea residing in the breast of the artist, which he is always labouring to impart, and which he dies at last without imparting.'
328 —	*the Kind :* the human race.
331 327	*the Royal Saint :* Henry VI.

PAGE NO.

331 328 st. 4 *this* folk : *its* has been here plausibly but, perhaps, unnecessarily, conjectured.—Every one knows
the general story of the Italian Renaissance, of the
Revival of Letters.—From Petrarch's day to our
own, that ancient world has renewed its youth :
Poets and artists, students and thinkers, have
yielded themselves wholly to its fascination, and
deeply penetrated its spirit. Yet perhaps no one
more truly has vivified, whilst idealising, the picture
of Greek country life in the fancied Golden Age,
than Keats in these lovely (if somewhat unequally
executed) stanzas :—his quick imagination, by a kind
of ' natural magic,' more than supplying the scholar-
ship which his youth had no opportunity of gaining.

105 134 These stanzas are by Richard Verstegan (—c. 1635)
a poet and antiquarian, published in his rare *Odes*
(1601), under the title *Our Blessed Ladies Lullaby*,
and reprinted by Mr. Orby Shipley in his beautiful
Carmina Mariana (1893). The four stanzas here
given form the opening of a hymn of twenty-four.

Summary of Book Fifth

THIS division embraces the whole of the Victorian era and
a little more. The Victorian time was one of unparalleled
material prosperity for England, and was above all things
remarkable for the astonishing discoveries of science; yet
it was a time also of abundant poetry. If not equal in
splendour, or depth of inspiration, to the far briefer period
just preceding; if it can show no name quite equal to the
greatest names of the opening century; it is notable for the
relatively large number of poets who attained high distinction. It is especially rich in lyrical poetry, though an increased range and complexity of subject-matter, matched by
a great variety of metre, and a proneness in some poets to
inordinate length, tend to make the lyric overflow its natural
form. External circumstances fostered a certain com-
placency and conventional acquiescence; but prosperity
proved but a faint motive to song, and in the more enduring
expressions of the mind the note of inner disturbance and
dissatisfaction is far more clearly heard. The sudden out-
stripping of current thought by science agitated and be-
wildered many spirits; religious doubt, indignation with the
social results of the industrial revolution, a sense of dis-
located relation between the mind and the universe, tinged
and troubled the themes of verse. While some sought refuge
in the remoteness of romance, and explored the forgotten
riches of the Middle Ages, the primary human emotions—
complicated in Browning by a delight in the casuistry of
passion—continued, as ever, to provide the constant element

of song. Never before had the sights and sounds of the
English country so fondly permeated our poetry. The moods
of the age are most completely expressed in its representative
poet, Tennyson, who appears at his best in a selection limited
to lyric. A new clearness of colour and pictorial effect in
his early poems is developed more consciously by the mid-
Victorian group sometimes called pre-Raphaelite. Swinburne
added a splendour of swiftness to the movement of lyric
verse, though at a cost which left him the victim of his own
unexampled virtuosity. Finally we note the new eminence
of women in poetry, with the intellectual range of Mrs.
Browning, the passionate sincerity of Emily Brontë; to
name but these.

PAGE NO.

351 341   From *The Strayed Reveller :* a youth speaks to Circe
          and Ulysses in the portico of Circe's palace, at
          evening.

365 352   This is the latest version, published in *Poems by the
          Way,* of a poem which first appeared in *The Life and
          Death of Jason* as ' A sweet song sung not yet to any
          man.'

369 358   Quatrains 17–19 of *The Rubáiyát of Omar Khayyám.*
          Here, as in the quatrains printed on p. 454, the
          version of 1859 has been preferred to the later
          version. *Jamshyd, Bahram :* Kings in ancient
          Persia.

370 359   From *Nepenthe,* privately printed in or about 1839,
          and reprinted in 1897 by R. A. Streatfeild from the
          apparently unique copy in the British Museum.
          In the interval between the death of Byron and
          the rise of Tennyson Darley at one time seemed to
          promise high achievement. *Nepenthe* is inchoate and
          was never finished, but contains many splendours.

377 363   Though called ' a fragment,' this little poem is quite
          complete. If it was intended to ' moralize ' in some
          sort the description, we may be glad that Tennyson
          refrained from ' completing ' it.

378 364   Flecker was only thirty when he died of consump-
          tion in 1915. He had served in the Consular service at
          Smyrna and elsewhere in the Near East, and his
          best poems were inspired or coloured by his Oriental
          experiences. *Merou :* probably Merv; *Balghar :*
          the ancient capital of the Bulgarians. *Rum :* Con-
          stantinople.

379 365   The first chorus of *Atalanta in Calydon.*

380 366   Selected from *Love in the Valley,* a long lyric of
          loosely connected stanzas.

381 367   l. 10. *vair :* a kind of fur, but the word may be used
          in its heraldic sense of particoloured.

391 374   The prodigious length of so many of Swinburne's
          lyrics makes selection difficult. In this case the

PAGE NO.

first forty stanzas of the poem (*The Triumph of Time*) have been omitted.

l. 1. The singer is Rudel, the French troubadour who fell in love with the Countess of Tripoli from the report of her; sailed to Syria, fell sick on the voyage, and saw his lady at last, only to die in her arms.

399 383 Translated from a poem by Callimachus in the Greek Anthology.

399 384 l. 37. *Mantovano :* of Mantua. The poem was written ' at the request of the Mantuans.'

400 385 The story of *The Scholar Gipsy* is taken from Glanvil's *Vanity of Dogmatizing*, 1661.

409 389 Edward Thomas was killed in the War, 1917. He won distinction as an essayist, and only late in life turned from prose to verse, which he published under the name of Edward Eastaway.

410 391 The recent publication of many poems from MSS. never before printed has increased Clare's reputation. No one in our poetry has been so intimate in writing of the country, and of the country life as lived by the villager. Himself a peasant, he yet had a singular sensibility to beauty.—These pathetic lines were written in the asylum where his last years were spent.

416 398 l. 2. *The lave :* the rest.

417 399 Sorley, a poet of high promise and original power, was killed in action, 1915, at the age of twenty.

419 402 l. 6. *Twindles :* twirls. l. 9. *degged :* sprinkled. Hopkins, a Jesuit priest, who died in his early prime, was a learned experimenter in rhythm and metre. His truly poetic genius was original to the point of eccentricity.

420 403 l. 8. *Brow, bay, and tray :* the first, second and third antlers. l. 12. *Brocket :* a stag in his second year. l. 17. *Beamed :* having a horn of the fourth year. *Tined :* with tines or prongs.

422 404 l. 12. *Levuka,* one of the Fiji islands.

426 406 Founded on the account of Grenville's last fight in 1591 by Sir Walter Raleigh.

432 407 Admiral Robert Blake attacked and destroyed the Spanish Fleet at Santa Cruz in Teneriffe, April 20, 1657. Returning to England, ill and worn out, he died at the entrance to Plymouth Sound. The metre of this poem seems to have been suggested by the contrasted effect of alternate hexameter and iambic sometimes used by Horace in his Odes.

433 409 Wilfred Owen was killed in action, 1918, at the age of twenty-five. This sonnet powerfully expresses horror at the incalculable slaughter of youth in the Great War, as Rupert Brooke's *The Soldier* and other sonnets of 1914 express the exalted ardour with which youth entered on the conflict.

PAGE NO.

437 414   After the taking of Athlone in 1691, the Irish army was utterly defeated at Aughrim, and great numbers of the Irish were driven to take service abroad, especially with the French.

438 415   *Dark Rosaleen* : a personification of Ireland.

440 416   Dolben was only nineteen when he was drowned while bathing in the Welland. His poems were first published in 1911 by Robert Bridges, his school-friend at Eton.

441 417   The last stanza of this poem has been omitted.

457 427   This vision of the Roman and the Eastern world at the time of the coming of Christ is taken from *Obermann Once More.* Obermann is Arnold's name for E. F. de Sénancour (1770–1846), who wrote a book with that name for title.

459 428   These stanzas are from the Prelude to *Songs before Sunrise.*

462 431   Written at sea, in the Pacific.

467 438   Written on the last day of the nineteenth century.

472 447   This poem was found among Francis Thompson's papers when he died.

173 448   Emily Brontë's ' last lines.'

INDEX OF WRITERS

WITH DATES OF BIRTH AND DEATH

INDEX OF FIRST LINES